A COMMENTARY
ON THE
GREEK TEXT
OF THE
EPISTLE OF PAUL
TO
THE PHILIPPIANS

Based on the Greek Text

by

John Eadie, D.D., LL.D.

Foreword by Cyril J. Barber

1977 Reprint by
James and Klock Christian Publishing Co.
2527 Girard Avenue North   Minneapolis, Minnesota 55411

Originally published by:
T. and T. Clark, Edinburgh
1894

Printed by James & Klock in the U.S.A.
1977 Reprint

FOREWORD

The commentaries of Dr. John Eadie are their own best recommendation. In his day his name was a household word in Scotland. He contributed greatly to the elevating and enriching of the common life of the people by this own ministry and example. And through his teaching, he edified and enhanced the lives of those who, in time, would minister the Word of God to the congregations throughout the Bristish Isles.

John Eadie (1810-1876) was born in Alva, Stirlingshire, Scotland. His father, a widower, had married for the second time when nearly seventy. John was the only child of this union to survive infancy. He was encouraged in his studies by both his parents, and in due course enrolled in the University of Glasgow. In spite of severe financial restrictions he distinguished himself as a student and upon graduation was ordained into the ministry. He became the pastor of a large city congregation and there developed an awareness of the needs of people. He continued to serve as a pastor for forty-one years, and the ability to touch the heart of the man-in-the-street never left him.

By the time Eadie was twenty-eight, he was lecturing part-time in Hebrew at Anderson's College, Glasgow. Then, while still in his early thirties, he was installed as chairman of the Department of Biblical Literature in the Divinity Hall of the University of Glasgow. His duties as professor were now added to his pastoral ministry.

John Eadie's vast learning earned him the recognition of his colleagues, and in 1844 he was honored with the Doctor of Laws degree by the University of Glasgow. A few years later, in 1850, he received the Doctor of Divinity degree *honoris causa* from the University of St. Andrews.

In commenting on Dr. Eadie's many books one biographer wrote:
. . . [his] works were the result of much scholarly labour, the basis of the commentary being made on the grammatical structure of the Greek words, and the exegetical skill of the commentator applied to ascertain the precise meaning of the [biblical] writer.

In his exegetical commentary on Paul's Epistle to the Ephesians, Dr. Eadie sets out to "give a concise and full exposition . . . [and] exhibit the mind and meaning of the apostle, not only by a scientific analysis of his language but also by a careful delineation of the logical connection and sequence of his thoughts." Ephesians was first published in 1854. It was followed by commentaries on Colossians in 1856, Philippians in 1857 and Galatians in 1869. Thessalonians was published post-humously.

Of all the distinguished men of his age, John Eadie left to posterity one of the strongest and most vivid impressions of godly scholarship in the service of the church. We welcome the reprinting of this fine work.

Cyril J. Barber

TRUSTEES' NOTE.

———o———

THE Trustees on Dr. Eadie's Estate have resolved to issue a new edition of his Commentaries on the Epistles to the Galatians, Ephesians, Philippians, and Colossians, three of which are out of print. They believe the republication to be called for, as the distinctive place which these Commentaries hold has not yet been filled by other expository works. They also feel it to be due to the memory of the distinguished author, who, by his rare ability, extensive learning, and remarkable acquirements, all of which, through Divine grace, were consecrated to the study and interpretation of sacred Scripture, was enabled to bequeath a legacy so valuable to the Church of Christ. Few exegetical works will be found to equal these Commentaries in exact scholarship, while there are none, it may be truly said, that excel them in spiritual insight, in clear and masterly exhibition of the mind of the Divine Spirit, and in thorough sympathy with evangelical truth. The use of them will prove especially helpful in the study of the Divine word.

The Rev. William Young, M.A., of Parkhead Church, Glasgow, at the request of the Trustees, has kindly engaged to edit the volumes. In his qualifications for

this work, which requires both scholarship and ability,
they have the fullest confidence. While he has applied
a careful scrutiny to all the references, and suggested
such corrections and additions as he felt to be
necessary, he has made no alteration on the text,
which is wholly as it came from the hand of the
author.

The Trustees are gratified to add, that the republication of the Commentaries has been undertaken
by the Firm of Messrs. T. & T. Clark, Edinburgh,
to whose enterprise in the publication of valuable
theological works, the Christian Church is so much
indebted.

The issue commences with the Commentary on the
Epistle to the Ephesians, which was the first of the
author's exegetical works.

GEORGE JEFFREY.

DENNISTOUN, GLASGOW,
  October 1st, 1883.

PREFACE.

——o——

I HAVE little to add to the explanations made in the prefaces to my previous Commentaries on the Epistles to the Ephesians and Colossians. My object is still the same, however far I may fall short of realizing my own ideal—the development and illustration of the great apostle's thoughts, as they are expressed in his "weighty and powerful" letters. I humbly trust, that through a prolonged intimacy with his genius and style, my "profiting may appear to all." For one forms a gradual and happy acquaintance with the peculiarities of his mind and language through careful and continuous observation and study; just as, had we lived in those early times, we should have grown familiar, from being much in his company, with his gait, voice, features, and dress. While he writes after the same general pattern as do the other sacred penmen of the New Testament, he has an unmistakeable type of his own, has his own favourite turns and points, his own recurring modes of putting an argument or giving edge to an appeal, of rebutting an objection, or going off by some sudden suggestion into a digression or parenthesis. While these special features may be recognized in all his epistles, they occur naturally in a letter like that to the Philippians, which is thrown off without any steady or definite aim, and where neither designed exposition nor reproof forms the burden of the communication.

The first question then is—What is the precise meaning of
these sentences which the apostle wrote to the church in
Philippi ? or what is the sense which the church in that city
would most naturally ascribe to them ?   It is to be supposed
that they understood the document, and our effort is simply
to place ourselves in their intellectual or spiritual position.
We seek to comprehend the epistle by a careful analysis of
its clauses, an anxious survey of the context, and a cautious
comparison of similar idioms and usages ; while through a
profound sympathy with the writer, we seek to penetrate into
his mind, and be carried along with him in those mental
processes which, as they create the contents of the composition, impart to it its character and singularity.   Our knowledge of Greek is perfect only in so far as it enables us to
attach the same ideas to his words, which the apostle intended
to convey by them.   Every means must be employed to
secure this unity of intelligence—every means which the
progress of philological science places within our reach.   At
the same time, there is much which no grammatical law can
fix, for the meaning of a particle is often as much a matter of
æsthetics as of philology.   The citation of a grammatical
canon, in such cases, often proves only the possibility of
one meaning out of many, but does not decide on any one
with certainty ; while reliance on such isolated proof is
apt to degenerate into mere subtileness and refinement.   The
exegesis, or the ascertainment of the course of thought, must
determine many minute questions, not against grammar, but
in harmony with its spirit and laws.   Contextual scrutiny
and grammatical legislation have a happy reactionary influence, and any attempt to dissever them must tend to produce
one-sided and unsatisfactory interpretation.

But the meaning of the epistle to those who originally

received it being ascertained, the second question is—What
are the value and signification of the same writing for us?
What was simply personal between Paul and Philippi was
so far temporary, though it does suggest lessons of permanent
interest. But believing that the apostle was inspired, I
accept his dogmatic and ethical teaching as divine truth—
truth derived from God, and by God's own impulse and
revelation communicated to the churches. This unreserved
acceptance of scriptural truth is not at all hostile to the free
spirit of scientific investigation. But it is wholly contrary to
such a belief, and at variance with what I hold to be the
origin and purpose of the New Testament, to regard the
apostle's theology as made up of a series of Jewish theories,
not always clearly developed or skilfully combined and ad-
justed; or to treat it as the speculations of an earnest and
inquisitive mind, which occasionally lost itself among "deep
things," and mistook its modified and relative views for universal and absolute truth. What are called "St. Paul's
opinions," are conceived, worded, or presented by a conscious
mind, according to its own habits and structure; but they
are in themselves enunciations of divine truth, in and through
the Spirit of God, for all ages; while the private matters
mixed up with them show, that inspiration did not lift a man
above what is natural, that divine guidance did not repress
the instincts of a human temperament, check the genial outburst of emotion, or bar the record of mere impressions about
future and unrevealed events, such as the alternatives of the
apostle's own release or martyrdom.

With such convictions, and under this broad light, I have
endeavoured to examine this epistle; and "my heart's desire
and prayer to God is," that He who "gave the Word," and
"hath given us an understanding that we may know Him

that is true," may bless this honest and earnest effort to expound a portion of the "lively oracles." The love of the truth is homage to Him who shows Himself as the Spirit of Truth, while He is coming into His heritage as the Spirit of Love. On the reception and diffusion of the truth in no narrow spirit, and in no cold and crystallized formulas, but in all the breadth and living power with which Scripture contains and reveals it, depend what so many good men are now sighing for—the reunion of the churches and the conversion of the world.

JOHN EADIE.

13 Lansdowne Crescent, Glasgow,
November 1858.

THE LITERATURE OF THE EPISTLE.

—o—

How the course of the apostle was divinely shaped, so that it brought him to Philippi, is stated in Acts xvi. 6–12 :—" Now, when they had gone throughout Phrygia and the region of Galatia, and were forbidden of the Holy Ghost to preach the word in Asia, after they were come to Mysia, they assayed to go into Bithynia: but the Spirit suffered them not. And they, passing by Mysia, came down to Troas. And a vision appeared to Paul in the night: There stood a man of Macedonia, and prayed him, saying, Come over into Macedonia, and help us. And after he had seen the vision, immediately we endeavoured to go into Macedonia, assuredly gathering that the Lord had called us for to preach the gospel unto them. Therefore, loosing from Troas, we came with a straight course to Samothracia, and the next *day* to Neapolis; and from thence to Philippi, which is the chief city of that part of Macedonia, *and* a colony: and we were in that city abiding certain days." The apostle, during his second great missionary journey, had gone through a large portion of Asia Minor, and wished to extend his tour into proconsular Asia. But a curb, which he durst not resist, was laid upon him, though its precise object he might not be able at the moment to conjecture. The Holy Ghost, in forbidding him to preach in Asia, meant to turn his steps towards Europe. But he and his colleagues reached Mysia, and when they made an effort to pass into Bithynia, they were suddenly stopped on the frontier, for the " Spirit of Jesus " suffered them not to enter. This double check must have warned them of some ultimate purpose. Passing by Mysia, they came down to Troas, but not to labour, as they might have anticipated, in a city surrounded by the scenes of so many classical associations. The divine leading had so shut up their path as to bring them to the seaport from which they were to set sail for a new region, and for a novel enterprise. As Peter had been instructed and prepared by a vision to go to the house of a Roman soldier, so by a similar apparition Paul was beckoned across the Ægean sea to Europe. The low coasts of the Western world might be dimly seen by him under the setting sun; the spiritual wants of that country, still unvisited by any evangelist, must have pressed upon his mind; the anxious ponderings of the day prepared him for the vision of the night, when before him "there stood a man of Macedonia, and prayed him, saying, Come over into Macedonia and help us." He was now in a condition to respond to the prayer, for a narrow sea was the only barrier between him and the shores of northern Greece. The object of the vision could not be mistaken, and the supernatural limitations set to previous inland journeys would now be comprehended. The prediction had been verified in the apostle and his colleagues —"I will bring the blind by a way that they knew not, I will lead them in paths that they have not known;" and the promise, too, was now fulfilled—"I will make darkness light before thee, and crooked things straight," for the vision so impressed them that they were "assuredly gathering that the Lord had called us for to preach the gospel unto them." No time was lost—they loosed from Troas; the wind was fair— no weary tacking, no idle flapping of the sails in a calm; a steady southern breeze urged them through the current that rushes from the Dardanelles; they passed the island of Imbros, running "with a straight course to Samothracia," and cast anchor the same night, in the smooth water of its northern shore.[1] Half the voyage had been made, and next day, after skirting the isle of Thasos, they arrived at Neapolis, a harbour that seems to have stood in such a relation to Philippi as Ostia to Rome, Cenchrea to Corinth, Seleucia to Antioch, and Port-Glasgow, according to the original intentions of its founders, to Glasgow. When, at a subsequent period, Paul recrossed from Philippi to Troas, the voyage occupied five

[1] Conybeare and Howson, vol. i. p. 306.

days; but now, "the King's business required haste," and to speed it, "by His power He brought in the South Wind." The historian briefly adds, "and from thence to Philippi;" that is, along a path ten miles in length, ascending first a low ridge of hills, and then leading down to the city and the great plain between Haemus and Pangaeus, where their last battle was fought and lost by the republican leaders of Rome. After a sojourn of "certain days," the apostle and his companions went out to an oratory on the side of the river Gangites, and met with a few pious Jewish women and proselytes "which resorted thither." This humble spot was the scene of Paul's first preaching in Europe; but the divine blessing was vouchsafed, and the heart of Lydia was opened as she listened "unto the things which were spoken of Paul." It was "a man of Macedonia" that invited the apostle across into Europe; but his first convert was a woman of Thyatira, in Asia. The heart of a proselyte, who must have been an anxious inquirer before she relinquished Paganism, was in a more propitious state for such a change than either Jew or heathen, as it was neither fettered by the bigotry of the one, nor clouded by the ignorance of the other. The dispossession of a female slave, "who had a spirit of divination," happened soon after; her rapacious and disappointed masters, a co-partnery trading in fraud, misery, and souls, finding that the hope of their gain was gone, dragged Paul and Silas into the forum—εἰς τὴν ἀγοράν—before the magistrates, who, on hearing the charge, and without any judicial investigation, ordered the servants of God to be scourged, and then imprisoned. But their courage failed them not. On losing a battle in that neighbourhood, the vanquished warriors dared not to survive their defeat. The intriguing Cassius, "the last of the Romans," hid himself in his tent, and in his panic ordered his freedman to strike. Brutus fell upon his sword, and his sullen and desperate spirit released itself by this self-inflicted wound. But Paul and Silas, unjustly condemned at the bidding of a mob, "thrust into the inner prison, and their feet made fast in the stocks," fixed in that tormenting position, and their backs covered with "wounds and bruises and putre-fying sores which had not been closed, neither bound up, neither mollified with ointment"—these victims of wanton outrage did not bewail their fate, nor curse their oppressors, nor arraign a mysterious Providence, nor resolve to quit a service which brought them into such troubles, and desert a Master who had not thrown around them the shield of His protection, nor conclude that the vision at Troas had been a cunning and malignant lure to draw them on to Philippi, and to these indignities of stripes and a dungeon. No, " at mid-night Paul and Silas, rejoicing that they were counted worthy to suffer shame for His name," " prayed and sang praises unto God, and the prisoners heard them." The prison was shaken, and their " bands were loosed; " the jailor and all his house believed in God, and " he and all his were baptized." The prætors—οἱ στρατηγοί—in the morning sent an order to the lictors for the release of the prisoners; but Paul's assertion of his privilege as a Roman citizen, when reported to them, alarmed them ; and knowing what a penalty they had incurred by their infraction of the Valerian and Porcian laws, they came in person, and urged the departure of the evangelists from the city. " They went out of the prison, and entered into the house of Lydia ; and when they had seen the brethren, they comforted them and departed," passing through Amphipolis and Apollonia, and taking up their abode for a brief season in Thessalonica. Such were the apostle's experiences when he first trod the soil of Europe, and such the first conflict of Christianity with Hellenic heathenism and the savage caprice of Roman authority.

The apostle had not paused at Samothrace—an island renowned for its sanctity and its amulets, its gods and orgies, its Cybele and Cabiria—a scene where the mysteries of Eastern and Western superstition seem to have met and blended. Nor did he stop at Neapolis, the harbour of the Strymonic gulf, but he pressed on to Philippi ; and the ground of his preference seems to be given in the statement —" which is the chief city of that part of Macedonia, and a colony "—ἥτις ἐστὶν πρώτη τῆς μερίδος τῆς Μακεδονίας πόλις κολωνία. A reason is often assigned by the use of ἥτις— " inasmuch as it is." The adjective πρώτη may admit of a political or a geographical meaning. Some have regarded it as signifying " chief," much in the same way as it is rendered in our version. It cannot indeed mean the chief or capital

city of the province, for that was Thessalonica; and if there
existed at that period a minuter subdivision, the principal
town was Amphipolis.[1] Others look on the epithet as merely
designating the first city that lay on the apostle's route;
Neapolis being either regarded as only its seaport, or rather
as a town belonging to Thrace, and not to Macedonia.
Meyer, preceded by Grotius and followed by Baumgarten,[2]
advances another view, which joins πόλις and κολωνία—" the
first colony and city," and Philippi, in the Peutinger Tables,
stands before Amphipolis.   Without entering into any discussion of these opinions, we may only remark, that each of
them furnishes a sufficient reason for the apostle's selection of
Philippi as the spot of his first systematic labours in Europe.
If it was the first city of the province that lay on his journey,
then he naturally commenced to give it the help which the
man of Macedonia had prayed for.   If it was a chief city in
that part, there was every inducement to fix upon it as the
centre of farther operations ; and if it enjoyed special advantages as a city and colony, then, its importance in itself, and
in relation to other towns and districts, made it a fitting place
both for present work and subsequent enterprise.   You may
either say that Paul went to Philippi as the first city on his
path, for he had been summoned into Macedonia, and he
could never think of passing the first city which he came to ;
or that he formally selected Philippi because of its rank, and
because of its privileges as a Roman colony.   If the apostle
had taken this tour of his own accord, or as the result of plans
previously matured ; if he had traced out the itinerary of an
evangelistic campaign before he set out, then the latter hypothesis would appear the more plausible ; but if, as was the
case, his purpose was hastily formed, and the general idea of
traversing the province without any distinct regard to the
order or arrangements of the visits, was suggested by the
prayer of the representative man, then the first would appear
to be the more natural and simple hypothesis.

Philippi was anciently called Κρηνίδες or the " Springs," on

---

[1] Livy, xlv. 29. Wordsworth, in his *Commentary on Acts* (London, 1857),
supposes μερίς to mean a frontier or strip of borderland—viz. that by which
Macedonia is divided from Thrace, and of which *confinium* Philippi was the
chief city.

[2] *Apostolical History*, vol. ii. p. 114 ; Edinburgh (Clark).

account of its numerous fountains, in which the Gangites has
its sources.   Philip, about 358 B.C., enlarged the old town,
and fortified it, in order to protect the frontiers against
Thracian invaders, and named it after himself—Φίλιπποι [1]—
to commemorate the addition of a new province to his empire.
After the famous battle fought and won in its neighbourhood
by the Triumvirs, Augustus conferred special honours upon
the city, and made it a Roman colony.[2] A military settlement—*cohors prœtoria emerita*—had been made in it, chiefly
of the soldiers who had been ranged under the standard of
Antony, so that it was a protecting garrison on the confines
of Macedonia; such settlements being, as Cicero calls them,
propugnacula imperii.   A *colonia* was a reproduction, in
miniature, of the mother city Rome.   The Roman law ruled,
and the Roman insignia were everywhere seen.   The muni-
cipal affairs were managed by duumvirs or prætors.   Philippi
had also the *Jus Italicum*, or Quiritarian ownership of the
soil;[3] its lands enjoying the same freedom from taxation as
did the soil of Italy.   It thus possessed a rank far above that
of a *municipium* or a *civitas libera ;* but there is no proof that
Augustus gave it the title of πρώτη πόλις, or that it ever
assumed such an appellation like Pergamus, Smyrna, and
Ephesus.   The historian calls it κολωνία, the proper Roman
name, and does not use the Greek term ἀποικία, which had a
very different meaning—a settlement founded by a body of
adventurers or emigrants.   Its distinctive name seems here to
be given it on account of the events which so soon transpired
in connection with the apostle's labours.

    Highly favoured as Philippi had been, it was in need of
"help."   Political franchise and Roman rights, Grecian tastes
and studies, wide and varied commerce, could not give it the
requisite aid.   It was sunk in a spiritual gloom, which needed
a higher light than Italian jurisprudence or Hellenic culture
could bring it.   It was helpless within itself, and the "man"

---

[1] Strabo, οἱ νῦν Φίλιπποι πόλις Κρηνίδες ἐκαλοῦντο τὸ παλαιόν.   vii. 43 ; vol. ii.
p. 86.   Ed. Kramer, 1847.   Smith's *Dictionary of Greek and Roman Geography,*
vol. ii. *sub voce.*

[2] *Colonia Augusta Julia Philippensis.*   Akerman's *Numismatic Illustrations,*
p. 45.   London, 1846.

[3] Dion Cassius, li. 4.   *In provincia Macedonia Philippenses juris Italici sunt.*
Dig. Leg. xv. 68.

who represented it had appealed to the sympathies of a Jewish stranger, whose story of the cross could lift the darkness off its position and destiny. The spear and phalanx of Macedonia had been famous, and had carried conquest and civilization through a large portion of the Eastern world; the un of Greece had not wholly set, and Epicureans and Stoics yet mingled in speculation, and sought after "wisdom;" the sovereignty of Rome had secured peace in all her provinces, and her great roads not only served for the march of the soldier, but for the cortege of the trader; art and law, beauty and power, song and wealth, the statue and the drama, survived and were adored; but there was in many a heart a sense of want and of powerlessness, an indefinite longing after some higher good and portion, a painless and restless agitation, which only he of Tarsus could soothe and satisfy, with his preaching of the God-man—the life, hope, and centre of humanity. Probably about the year 53 Paul paid his first visit to Philippi. A second time does he seem to have visited it on his journey from Ephesus to Macedonia, 'Acts xx. 1, 2; and again when, to avoid the plots of his enemies, he returned to Asia through Macedonia, Acts xx. 6. Many remains of antiquity, such as are supposed to belong to the forum and the palace, are on the site of Philippi. The Turks now name it Felibedjik. Copies of its old coins may be seen in Eckhel, vol. ii. p. 75. The scenes and the ruins are described by Leake, *Northern Greece,* vol. iii., and Cousinéry, *Voyage dans Maced.* vol. ii. Mannert, *Geogr. der Griech. und Röm.* vol. vii. p. 217. Forbiger, *Alt. Geog.* vol. iii. p. 1070

II.—THE GENUINENESS OF THE EPISTLE.

The genuineness of the epistle had not been questioned till a very recent period. The early external testimonies in its favour are very abundant. Thus Polycarp, *ad Philip.* iii.[1]— οὔτε γὰρ ἐγὼ οὔτε ἄλλος ὅμοιος ἐμοὶ δύναται κατακολουθῆσαι τῇ σοφίᾳ τοῦ μακαρίου καὶ ἐνδόξου Παύλου, ὃς καὶ ἀπὼν ὑμῖν ἔγραψεν ἐπιστολάς. It is not necessary, as a matter of philology, to take the last noun as plural and as denoting more epistles than one, as Cotelerius, Hefele, and Jacobson have

---

[1] *Patres Apostol.* vol. ii. p. 470; ed. Jacobson.

shown in their notes on this quotation.   Rettig, *Quæst. Philip.*
p. 37.   The same father, in the eleventh chapter of this same
epistle to them,[1] says—*Ego autem nihil tale sensi in vobis vel
audivi, in quibus laboravit beatus Paulus qui estis (laudati) in
principio epistolæ ejus.*   Meyer, who holds that from the style
of the New Testament and the Apostolical Fathers, the word
ἐπιστολάς in the first quotation must be plural, supports
his view by the somewhat strange device of making *epistolæ*
here the nominative plural, as if the meaning were—"who
are in the beginning his epistles," or commendatory letters.
But in 2 Cor. iii. 2, 3, the place cited in proof by him, the
noun is in the singular—ἐπιστολὴ ἡμῶν, ἐπιστολὴ Χριστοῦ;
and the use of the plural *epistolæ*, according to Meyer's own
understanding of the clause, shows that the plural form may
have a singular reference even in Polycarp's style.   Irenæus,
Adversus Hæres., also writes, *Quemadmodum et Paulus Phi-
lippensibus ait,*[2] referring to the apostle's acknowledgment of
the subsidy sent to him by Epaphroditus ; and again, in
quoting this epistle, iv. 17, *Non inquiro datum, sed inquiro
fructum,* he prefaces by saying—*propter hoc et Paulus.*   There
are other allusions of the same kind, as *rursus ad Philippenses
ait,* quoting iii. 20 ; or *apostolus in ea quæ est ad Philippenses,*
quoting iii. 10 ; or *hoc est quod a Paulo dicitur,* quoting
ii. 15.[3]   Clement of Alexandria, in allusion to the apostle's
confession — "Not as though I had attained," etc. — says
αὐτοῦ ὁμολογοῦντος τοῦ Παύλου περὶ ἑαυτοῦ.   *Pædag.* i. 6.[4]
The epistle is quoted by Clement in various portions of his
writings :—thus i. 13, 29, ii. 1, 20, iv. 12, are quoted in the
fourth book of the *Stromata ;* i. 20 in the third book ; i. 9,
ii. 10 in the first book ; iii. 19 in *Pædag.* ii. ; ii. 15 in *Pædag.*
iii. ; ii. 6 in *Cohort. ad Gentes.*   These quotations are made
by Clement generally without any affirmation that they
belong to the epistle to the Philippians, though sometimes
they are ascribed to Paul.   Tertullian's evidence is as full :—
thus, *De Resurrectione Carnis,* cap. 23, quoting the declaration
—"If by any means I may attain to the resurrection of the
dead "—he prefaces by saying, *ipse (Paulus) cum Philippensibu*

---

[1] *Patres Apostol.* vol. ii. p. 486 ; ed. Jacobson.
[2] iv. 18, 4, vol. i. 616 ; *Opera,* ed. Stieren, 1853.
[3] *Ibid.* vol. i. pp. 583, 752, 753, 571.   [4] P. 107 ; *Opera, Coloniæ,* 1688.

scribit ;[1] then, in the twentieth chapter of his fifth book against *Marcion,*[2] he employs this epistle as an argument against the heretic ; again, in his *De Præscript.* cap. xxxvi., speaking of the places where the *authenticæ literæ* of the apostles are read, he says, *Si non longe es a Macedonia habes Philippos, habes Thessalonicenses.*[3] From Ephiphanius too, we learn that Marcion received this epistle ; for among the ten episties of Paul acknowledged by him he reckons δεκάτη πρὸς Φιλιππησίους. *Haer.* 42.[4] In the epistle of the churches of Vienne and Lyons, preserved in Eusebius' *Hist. Eccles.* lib. v. 2, ii. 6 is quoted. Cyprian, also, *Test.* iii. 39, quoting ii. 6, prefixes *item Paulus ad Philippenses.*[5] Eusebius placed this epistle among the universally acknowledged ones—ὁμολογουμένοις. It is found in the Syriac version, and in all the early synopses or catalogues of canonical books. Zeller, in the *Theol. Jahrb.* i. p. 61, objects that Clemens Romanus does not quote the Epistle to the Philippians, when he might have done so in the sixteenth chapter of his First Epistle to the Corinthians, where he inculcates the grace of humility. The argument is precarious. It cannot prove that Clement was unacquainted with our epistle, but only that he has omitted a citation directly to his purpose. Besides, as Brückner has remarked, we have the testimony of Polycarp, which belongs to this period.

Prof. Baur of Tübingen, in his *Die so-genannte Pastoralbriefe des Apost. Paulus,* published in 1835, suspected the genuineness of this epistle, because of the mention of bishops and deacons in it, as if these offices belonged to a later age. In the following year, in an article in the third part of the *Tübing. Zeitschrift,* p. 196, he intimated his doubts more decidedly. In 1841, in the Introduction to his *Die Christliche Lehre von der Dreieinigkeit und Menschwerdung Gottes,* where he treats of the doctrine of the pre-existence of Christ as taught in the New Testament, no citation is made of any passages from this epistle, not even of ii. 6. At length, in 1845, in his *Paulus der Apostel Jesu Christi,*[6] he formally attacked the epistle, and the next year his assault was followed up by his disciple Schwegler, whom Lünemann well

---

[1] Vol. ii. p. 497 ; *Opera,* ed. Oehler, 1854.   [2] *Ibid.* p. 333.
[3] *Ibid.* p. 34.   [4] *Opera,* p. 138 ; ed. Basil, 1544.
[5] P. 290 ; *Opera,* Parisiis, 1836.   [6] P. 458 ; Stuttgart, 1845.

names *impiger sententiarum Baurianarum interpres ac pro-
pugnator. Das nachapostol. Zeitalter, etc.*, vol. ii. p. 143;
Tübingen, 1846. The objections are trivial, and the wonder
is, that a mind so acute and accomplished as that of Baur
should ever have proposed them. They are arranged by
him under three separate heads; though we shall consider
them in a somewhat different order from that in which their
author has set them forth. Two excellent replies were made
to Baur :—*Pauli ad Philip. Epistola. Contra F. C. Baurium
defendit G. C. Amadeus Lünemann, e collegio Repetentum ac
Dr. Ph.*; Göttingen, 1847—*Epistola ad Philip. Paulo auctori
vindicata contra Baurium. Scripsit Brenno Bruno Brückner,
Cand. Theol.*; Lipsiæ, 1848.

I. Baur alleges some palpable anachronisms and contradictions.

1. The mention of Clement—iv. 3—is adduced to show
that the writer of the epistle must have lived in post-
apostolic times. Without any proof whatever, he identifies
this Clement with him whom tradition associates with Peter
at Rome, and him again with another of the same name, who
was a relative of the later imperial house. He refers to
Flavius Clement of Domitian's time, whom that emperor put
to death as an atheist, and who is referred to by Suetonius,[1]
Dion Cassius,[2] and Eusebius.[3] But it is contrary to all
evidence, to identify the Clement of Rome or the Clement
of the Homilies with the kinsman of this emperor. The
writers who refer to them never confound them—never confound a bishop of one age with a consul of another. The
author of the Epistle to the Corinthians stands out in his own
individuality to the men of his own and the following epoch.
Clemens Romanus is said to have been well-born—ἐξ εὐγενοῦς
ῥίζης—and was connected with the imperial family—πρὸς
γένους ὑπάρχων Καίσαρος—Τιβερίου. *Clementine Homilies*,
iv. 7, xiv. 10. But Flavius Clement was related to Domitian,
who put him to death—καίπερ ἀνεψιὸν ὄντα—and banished
his wife. As Suetonius says, he was charged *ex tenuissima*

[1] *Domitianus*, xv.
[2] *Hist.* lxvii. 14. His espousal of Jewish opinions—ἤθη τῶν Ἰουδαίων—giving
rise to a charge of atheism—ἔγκλημα ἀθιότητος—was evidently his becoming a
Christian convert.   [3] *Hist. Eccles.* iii. 14.

suspicione, there being alleged against him in his office—
contemptissima inertia. Nor, if the Clement of this epistle
were even Clemens Romanus, would the fact raise any
difficulty. There is, however, no proof that he was; at
least he was at Philippi when this epistle was written. See
Hefele, *Ap. Patr. Prolegomena*, p. 19; Ritschl, *Geschichte der
Entstehung der alt. kathol. Kirche*, p. 284. You may admit
an intermingling of traditions about the two Clements, and
yet maintain that the men were distinct. There is no proof
that the Roman Clement was a martyr; at least Irenæus,
Eusebius, and Jerome know nothing of such a death. The
questions as to whether he was a Jew or a Gentile; whether
he was a disciple of Peter or of Paul; whether he followed
Linus or Cletus, or preceded them; whether his first epistle
be interpolated, and his second be spurious altogether;—such
questions affect not the identity of the man, and the distinction
in position, office, and end, between him and the Clement the
husband of Domitilla, under Domitian. See the article "Clement
von Rom," in *Herzog's Real-Encyclopädie*, vol. ii. p. 720. The
trick of Baur is very manifest. It is a series of assumptions.
He assumes, first, that the Clement of this epistle, of whom
nothing is given but the name, and about whom nothing can
be conjectured but his present residence at Philippi, is Clemens
Romanus; next, that this Clemens Romanus is a myth, or that
he must be really Flavius Clemens, the martyred kinsman of
Domitian;[1] next, that the writer of our epistle refers to him,
and to this well-known imperial relationship, when he speaks
of his bonds being known in the prætorium, and sends a
salutation from them of Cæsar's household; and the inference
is, that as the Clemens of our epistle is no other than this
later Clemens, such a reference must show that the epistle
could not be written by Paul, but by some forger long after
his time. The ingenuity is too transparent. Would a forger
have placed such a Clement at Philippi? and would he not
have given him greater prominence? for certainly the apostle's
joy in his bonds, the publicity of these bonds in the prætorium,
his "strait between two," and his other expressed emotions,
can all be explained without reference to any such hypothesis.

---

[1] Baur says at p. 472—"*Diess ist die historische Grundlage der Sage vom
Römischen Clemens.*"

2. It is alleged by Baur, that the mention of "bishops and deacons" in the first verse, betrays also a post-apostolical origin. The proof, however, tends all the other way. The organization of the churches presupposes such office-bearers, as may be seen in Acts vi. 1–6, xx. 28 ; Rom. xvi. 1. The bishop and presbyter were then identical, and the names are sufficiently indicative of the character of the office.

3. Baur alleges that the author of the Epistle to the Philippians has totally misunderstood the apostle's pecuniary relations to the church at Philippi.[1] But he must have been a novice in fabrication, if with the other epistles before him he could allow himself to be so easily detected. The apostle writes thus in iv. 14, 15, 16—"Notwithstanding ye have well done that ye did communicate with my affliction. Now, ye Philippians, know also, that in the beginning of the gospel, when I departed from Macedonia, no church communicated with me, as concerning giving and receiving, but ye only. For even in Thessalonica ye sent once and again unto my necessity." Baur quotes, as opposed to this, 1 Cor. ix. 15—"But I have used none of these things ; neither have I written these things, that it should be so done unto me : for *it were* better for me to die, than that any man should make my glorying void." Baur's exegesis is, that this passage plainly teaches that Paul stood in no such relation to any church, as our epistle represents him as sustaining to the Philippian church, for he would not own himself indebted to any of them. But the apostle is not affirming that he refused all support from every church ; he only says, that he merely waived his right for good reasons with regard to the Corinthian church ; for when he was in the city of Corinth, he wrought as a tentmaker, and no doubt for the best of reasons. Besides, that he took support from other churches, while he would not take it from them, is plain from his own declaration, that they were an exception to his usual course—2 Cor. xi. 7, 8—"Have I committed an offence in

---

[1] Es lässt uns demnach auch das, was Phil. iv. 10 f., über eine speciellere Veranlassung des Briefs gesagt worden ist, nicht klar in die Verhältnisse hineinsehen, unter welchen er vom Apostel selbst geschrieben worden seyn soll, und es könnte somit schon diess die Vermuthung begründen, dass wir hier keine wirklichen Verhältnisse, sondern nur eine fingirte Situation vor uns haben, was, je näher wir die geschichtliche Motivirung des Briefs betrachten, nur um so wahrscheinlicher werden kann. P. 469.

abasing myself, that ye might be exalted, because I have preached to you the gospel of God freely? I robbed other churches, taking wages *of them*, to do you service." Nay more, in connection with this passage now quoted, the apostle affirms—verse 9—"And when I was present with you, and wanted, I was chargeable to no man: for that which was lacking to me the brethren which came from Macedonia supplied; and in all *things* I have kept myself from being burdensome unto you, and *so* will I keep *myself*." Now this is an assertion of the very same kind with that which Baur so strongly objects to as un-Pauline, in the epistle before us. The use of καί in the phrase ὅτι καὶ ἐν Θεσσαλονίκῃ—iv. 16 —cannot support his argument, as if the forger had 2 Cor. xi. 9 before his eyes, and took his cue from it, for the καί is used precisely in the same way in 1 Cor. i. 16—ἐβάπτισα δὲ καὶ τὸν Στεφανᾶ οἶκον. See comment on iv. 16. It is of no use to allege, as Baur does, that the apostle's stay in Thessalonica was brief—so brief, that two contributions could scarcely be necessary—for we know not all the circumstances; but we do know that in that city, and as a reproof probably to the sloth which he so earnestly reprimands in both his letters, he set an example of industry, working with his own hands, and might therefore be in need of the gift which was sent south to him from Philippi. Both Brückner and Lünemann slyly remark, that it is odd that Baur should, in proof of Paul's short stay in Thessalonica, cite the Acts of the Apostles—a book which he declares to be unworthy of all historical credit. *Paulus der Apostel*, pp. 146–150, 243. What more natural for the apostle than to refer to the earliness of their first pecuniary presents; or to say, that when he was leaving Macedonia, they supplied him; nay, to affirm, that prior to the period of his departure from the province, and when he was yet in Thessalonica, they sent once and a second time to his necessities? Baur seems to suppose that he who wrote these verses forgot that Thessalonica was in Macedonia. He renders—"when I was no more in Macedonia," no church communicated with me but you, for even in Thessalonica ye sent to me, as if Thessalonica had been a place reached after his departure from the Macedonian province. But this, again, is a complete misapprehension of the apostle's statement, which is of this kind—When I went out of Macedonia ye helped me; nay, at an earlier period still and before I left the province, ye helped me. So feeble are Baur's objections against the genuineness of the epistle, taken from supposed anachronisms or contradictions of fact alleged to be found in it.

II. Baur also raises objections from the style. Few forms of subjective reasoning and criticism are so deceptive as this. What belongs to æsthetics, and not to logic or history, can never form a wise or valid antagonism. For there are others as well qualified to judge as Baur can be, some of whom have on his and similar principles rejected others of the epistles but who yet declare unhesitatingly in favour of this one. De Wette, who will not admit Ephesians, has everything to say in favour of Philippians.

1. To object, with Baur, that subjectivity of feeling prevails in this epistle, is only to commend it,[1] for the writer had no definite polemical end in view, there being no special error or inconsistency in the Philippian church requiring rebuke or warning. Therefore he composes a letter to thank his beloved Philippians for a needed gift sent all the way to Rome, and remembers their repeated kindnesses to him from the very first. No wonder there is that he opens his heart and speaks in the fulness of his joy, follows no regular plan, but expresses his emotions as they rise within him; nay, in the fervour of his soul, occasionally repeats himself—his clauses being offhand and artless, and now and then complex because unstudied, the whole being the outpouring of a spirit that was gladdened alike by memory and hope and present relationship—blessing his distant converts for their past fidelity, and urging them to higher and yet higher spiritual attainment, cautioning them against errors into which they might be tempted, and portraying his own experience as an outline with which theirs might recognize a growing similarity, and find increasing blessedness, as the likeness filled and brightened into complete identity. This epistle is a convey-ance of thanks—a matter wholly personal, so that individuality

---

[1] *Im Uebrigen unterscheidet er sich von Ihnen* (Ephesians and Colossians) *hauptsächlich durch die in ihm vorherrschende Subjectivität des Gefühls.* P. 464.

and emotion must predominate. The apostle could not repress his feelings, like a man mechanically signing a receipt in a counting-room; but he utters his heart, or as one may say, he puts himself into his letter. An epistle of thanks for monies so received, could not but be a matter of feeling, and the gratitude of the apostle's loving and confiding heart would be no common emotion, and therefore his acknowledgment is no common composition.

2. To say, with Baur, that the epistle discovers no sufficient motive for the composition of it,[1] is to shut one's eyes; to affirm with him, that it is stale and flat,[2] is not only to be steeled against the exuberance of its sentiment, but also to turn a deaf ear to the very rhythm of many of its paragraphs; to object that it is marked by poverty of thought,[3] is to forget that it is not a treatise like the Epistle to the Romans, or an argumentative expostulation like the Epistles to the Corinthians; and to attack it, because it wants a certain formal unity, is tastelessly to overlook its naturalness, as it moves from one topic to another, referring now to one class of persons near the writer in Rome, and now to his own emotions in his imprisonment; then turning to his converts and bidding them be of good cheer in the midst of hostility; exhorting them to cultivate humility, love, and self-denying generosity, as seen in the example of Christ; next, telling them how he hopes to see them soon, and meanwhile sends Epaphroditus home to them; farther, improving the oppor-

---

[1] Hiemit hängt zusammen, was hauptsächlich ein weiteres Kriterium zur Beurtheilung des Briefs ist, dass man überhaupt eine motivirte Veranlassung zur Abfassung eines solchen Schreibens, einen bestimmter ausgesprochenen Zweck und Grundgedanken vermisst. Zwar wird gegen jüdische Gegner polemisirt, aber man kann sich des Eindrucks nicht erwehren, es geschehe diess nur desswegen, weil es einmal zum stehenden Character der paulinischen Briefe zu gehören schien. Es fehlt dieser Polemik durchaus an Frische und Natürlichkeit, an der Objectivität der gegebenen Verhältnisse. Pp. 464-5.

[2] Wie matt und interesselos das Ganze. P. 466.

[3] Man rühmt diess als einen eigenthümlichen Vorzug des Briefs, aber so zart und ansprechend auch die Empfindungen und Gesinnungen sind, die in ihm sich kund geben, so wenig ist dabei zu übersehen, dass monotone Wiederholung des zuvor schon Gesagten, Mangel an einem tiefer eingreifenden Zusammenhang, und eine gewisse Gedankenarmuth, deren Bewusstseyn den Verfasser selbst gedrückt zu haben scheint, wenn er zu seiner Entschuldigung sagt iii. 1—τὰ αὐτὰ γράφειν ὑμῖν, ἐμοὶ μὲν οὐκ ὀκνηρὸν, ὑμῖν δὲ ἀσφαλές—nicht minder hervorstechende Züge des Briefes sind. P. 464.

tunity, and bidding them beware of false teachers and of inconsistent professors; summoning them, as he proceeds, to rejoice, to be of one mind, and to seek for perfection in the exercise of virtue; and, lastly, sending his acknowledgment for the gift which they had so kindly and considerately sent him, and wafting to them salutations from the brethren, and from the saints of Cæsar's household.

Baur fixes upon iii. 1—"To write the same things to you, to me indeed is not grievous, but for you it is safe," as a proof of poverty of thought. See our interpretation of the passage. The phrase, so far from arguing scantiness of ideas, is only an index of earnestness; or rather a proof, that while a throng of new subjects might be pressing on the writer's mind, he could even forego the pleasure of introducing them, and for the safety of his readers, reiterate statements previously made to them. Baur also objects to the phrase δικαιοσύνην τὴν ἐν νόμῳ—iii. 6—but the apostle is there speaking from a previous standpoint—from a point of view which he had occupied in his unconverted state.

3. The record of the apostle's experience, iii. 4, is declared to be a feeble copy of 2 Cor. xi. 18.[1] There is similarity, but not great similarity. Both are references to his past life, and therefore we anticipate a necessary likeness of allusion. But the purposes are different. In the second epistle to the Corinthians the vindication is of his public or official life and its sufferings and successes; in this epistle the self-portraiture has reference to personal experience. In the former he speaks as an apostle, but in the latter as a saint. The first is terse and vehement—a lofty and disdainful chal-

---

[1] Wie lässt sich verkennen, dass der Verfasser des Briefs die Stelle im Corinthierbriefe vor Augen hatte, und an sie auf eine Weise sich hielt, wie vom Apostel selbst nicht geschehen seyn kann? Nur aus der starken heftigen Sprache, in welcher der Apostel—2 Cor. xi.—sich gegen seine Gegner ausspricht, lässt es sich auch erklären, wie der Verfasser in der steigernden Weise der Nachahmer sich sogar den Ausdruck κύνες erlauben konnte. Wie unmotivirt, wie mit Gewalt herbeigezogen ist aber hier dieses Reden des Apostels von sich, wenn wir es mit der Art und Weise vergleichen, wie er sich mit seinen Gegnern in der Originalstelle auseinandersetzt wo man sogleich sieht, welche Sache es gilt. Welches schwache leblose Nachbild haben wir dagegen hier! Wie Allbekanntes sagt der Apostel über seine frühern Lebensverhältnisse, wie kleinlich ist die Hervorhebung der achttägigen Beschneidung, wie unpaulinisch der Begriff einer δικαιοσύνη ἐν νόμῳ, wie matt und interesselos das Ganze. P. 466.

lenge to his antagonists, if ever they had done what he had
done, or endured what he had endured : the last is calm in
its fervour, and exhibits his soul in its perfect repose upon
Christ Jesus his Lord, and in its aspirations after complete
likeness to Him.   The idea of plagiarism is wholly out of the
question when the subjects are so different.   Detail in speaking of his Jewish descent is natural to him—Rom. xi. 1—for
the subject admitted of minute and climactic treatment.

4. Baur objects to peculiar words.   Granted that κατατομή,
the concision, is a hard expression ;[1] but fully harder is ἀπο-
κόψονται, Gal. v. 12, as very many explain it.   Granted that
the epithet κύνες is not fine ; but neither are ψευδαπόστολοι,
ἐργάται δόλιοι ; οἱ διάκονοι αὐτοῦ—Σατανᾶς, in 2 Cor. xi. 13
14, 15, and κύνες did not at least sound in the East so awkwardly as with us.   Baur mistakes the nature of the contrast
between περιτομή and κατατομή.   The apostle does not by
any means degrade the Abrahamic rite in itself, or call Jews
the false˛ circumcision; but he simply implies that the circumcision which the Judaists insisted on as essential to
salvation is useless and spurious.   Compare too, for similar
ideas, Rom. ii. 25–29—an epistle which Baur acknowledges
to be genuine.   Nor is it the case that the contrast is
distorted, as if the idea of quality in περιτομή were opposed
to that of quantity expressed by κατατομή.   The notion of
quality belongs to both nouns, and it alone could the apostle
mean to express.   See our comment on the place.

On the other hand, many terms and phrases in this epistle,
being such as we find in the other epistles, indicate identity
of authorship.   Lünemann has made a considerable collection
of them.   The following are Pauline phrases :—γινώσκειν
ὑμᾶς βούλομαι, i. 2—compare 1 Cor. x. 1, xi. 3 ; Rom. i. 13,
xi. 25 : δοκιμάζειν τὰ διαφέροντα, i. 10—found in Rom. ii.
18 : καυχᾶσθαι ἐν Χριστῷ, iii. 3—found in 1 Cor. i. 31 ;
2 Cor. x. 17 : μάρτυς γάρ μου ἐστὶν ὁ Θεός, i. 8—found in
Rom. i. 9 : πιστεύειν εἰς Χριστόν, i. 29, exceedingly common

---

[1] Wie unfein wird sie iii. 2, durch die harten Worte βλέπετε τοὺς κύνας, wie
gezwungen durch den gesuchten Gegensatz zwischen κατατομή und περιτομή,
Zerschnittene und Beschnittene, eingeleitet ! Die Christen sollen die wahre
περιτομή, die Juden die falsche oder die κατατομή seyn, aber wie schief ist der
qualitative Unterschied zwischen der wahren und falschen Beschneidung durch
die quantitative Steigerung der περιτομή zu einer κατατομή ausgedrückt. P. 465.

in the Gospel of John, but also found in Paul, as in Rom. x.
14; Gal. ii. 16; Acts xix. 4. The names Χριστός, Ἰησοῦς,
Κύριος, preceded by ἐν, to denote the sphere of spiritual
action, feeling, or enjoyment, as to "hope in the Lord,"
"rejoice in the Lord," etc.—allusions to ἡ ἡμέρα Χριστοῦ, as
the period of glory and perfection—characterize this epistle
and all the others ascribed to the apostle. We have ἔργον
Χριστοῦ in ii. 30, and ἔργον Κυρίου, in the same sense, in
1 Cor. xvi. 10; εἰς κενὸν ἔδαμον in ii. 16, and in the same
view εἰς κενὸν τρέχω ἢ ἔδραμον, Gal. ii. 2. It is true there
are some ἅπαξ λεγόμενα, but we have them in every epistle.
We have such as αἴσθησις, i. 9; συναθλέω, i. 27, iv. 3;
πτύρεσθαι, i. 28; σύμψυχοι, ii. 2; ἁρπαγμός, ii. 6; ὑπερυψοῦν,
ii. 9; καταχθόνιος, ii. 10; ἰσόψυχον, ii. 20; ἀδημονεῖν, ii.
26; παραπλήσιον, ii. 27; παραβολεύειν, ii. 30; σκύβαλον,
iii. 8; ἐξανάστασις, iii. 11; ἐπεκτείνεσθαι, iii. 14; προσφιλής,
iv. 8; ἀρετή, iv. 8; ἀναθάλλω, iv. 10; μεμύημαι, iv. 12.
But the occurrence of such terms can never be a proof of
spuriousness, for ἅπαξ λεγόμενα are found in the Epistles to
Rome, Corinth, and Galatia, which Baur himself receives as
genuine. At the same time, we have certain Pauline terms
—words all but peculiar to the apostle, and the use of which
betokens his authorship. Thus we have τί γάρ, i. 18; εἴπως,
iii. 11; οὐχ ὅτι, iii. 12; τὸ λοιπόν, iv. 8—turns of expression
common with the apostle. Again, such words as ἀπρόσκοποι,
i. 10; ἐπιχορηγία, i. 19; ἀποκαροδοκία, i. 20; ἀντικείμενοι,
i. 28; εἰλικρινεῖς, i. 10; κενοδοξία, ii. 3; δικαιοσύνη, iii. 9;
βραβεῖον, iii. 14; and πλοῦτος, iv. 19—are favourite and
characteristic terms. The adjective κενός, and the phrase εἰς
κενόν, are the Pauline phrases, in this and the other epistles,
for failure real or anticipated, and κοπιᾶν is the peculiar verb
employed to denote apostolical labour. Have we not, in a
word, the image and likeness of the apostle in this style, not
only in its separate and characteristic idioms and expressions,
but in its entire structure—in its sustained passages as well
as in its briefer clauses—in its longer arguments as well as in
its more abrupt transitions? Why, in a word, be entangled
among such minutiæ, when the whole letter is so Pauline in
what is peculiar to itself, and in what is common to it with
other epistles? in its order and in its loose connection; in its

unwonted expressions and in its mannerisms; in its doctrines
insisted on and in its errors warned against; in its illustration
of his teaching by the experience of the teacher; in his
spirit of disinterested zeal in spite of every drawback; in his
manly confession that he felt his privations while he was
contented under them; and in his constant recognition of
union to Christ as the sphere of joy, love, strength, hope,
stedfastness, confidence, peace, and universal spiritual fulness.

III. Baur adduces doctrinal objections. The only dogmatic
part of the epistle—ii. 6–11—is, according to him, Gnostic
in its ideas and language. Indeed, the whole epistle, as he
affirms, "moves in the circle of Gnostic ideas and expressions"
—not opposing them, but rather acquiescing in them.[1] The
phrases οὐχ ἁρπαγμὸν ἡγήσατο τὸ εἶναι ἴσα Θεῷ, ἐν ὁμοιώματι
ἀνθρώπων γενόμενος, σχήματι εὑρεθεὶς ὡς ἄνθρωπος, ἐπουρανίων
—καταχθονίων, are laid hold of as belonging to the Gnostic
vocabulary; and as proving that he who has so employed
them, must have lived after the apostle's time, and when the
Gnostic heresy had acquired wide range and influence. Now,
if a heresy shall arise which clings to Scripture for support,
what can you expect but it shall, in its speculations and
defences, employ the words of Scripture, and dexterously affix
its own meaning to them? What has heresy usually been
but such artful or innocent misinterpretation? In the daring
and dreamy descriptions of the divine nature and of the
celestial hierarchy, which characterize Gnosticism, such terms
as the apostle has used may be found; but the natural inference is, that the epistle gave rise to them, and not they to
the epistle. Some of the passages referred to by Baur are
found in Irenæus. In his book, *Contra Hæreses*, i. 1, he has
the words—ὅμοιόν τε καὶ ἴσον τῷ προβαλλόντι;[2] and the
mother of another Æon is described—πρόφασιν μὲν ἀγάπης,

---

[1] Wie die beiden zuvor erörterten Briefe (Eph. and Colos.) bewegt sich auch
der Philipperbrief im Kreise gnostischer Ideen und Ausdrücke, und zwar gleich-
falls so, dass er sie nicht sowohl bestreitet, sondern sich vielmehr an sie ansch-
liesst und mit der nöthigen Modification sich aneignet. Die in dogmatischer
Hinsicht stets für ebenso wichtig als schwierig gehaltene Stelle Phil. ii. 5, scheint
nur aus der Voraussetzung erklärt werden zu können, dass der Verfasser des
Briefs gewisse gnostische Zeitideen vor Augen hatte. P. 458.

[2] i. 1, 1, vol. i. p. 14; *Opera*, ed. Stieren, 1855.

τόλμης δέ.[1] We have such phrases as παραυτίκα δὲ κενωθεῖσαν,[2] or ἐν εἰκόνι τοῦ ἀοράτου πατρός.[3] But what do these expressions prove? They are not similar in meaning with those found in this epistle, and they belong to the domain of metaphysical mysticism. Our interpretation of the passage gives the sense we attach to it. See *in loc.*
The expression οὐχ ἁρπαγμὸν ἡγήσατο is in no way derogatory to Christ's claim and dignity. The alternatives were τὸ εἶναι ἴσα Θεῷ, and ἑαυτὸν κενοῦν, and Jesus voluntarily preferred the latter, and assumed humanity. For Christ's pre-existence is a Pauline doctrine, though Baur denies it. Rom. ix. 5, xi. 36 ; 1 Cor. viii. 6 ; 2 Cor. viii. 9. Does not μορφὴ Θεοῦ resemble εἰκὼν τοῦ Θεοῦ ? 2 Cor. iv. 4. What absurdity to find a parallel to this ἁρπαγμός and the origin of the term in the wild, daring, and restless attempt of the Valentinian Sophia to penetrate the essence of the All-father, and become one with Him—the Absolute ; or, as Baur says of this Æon—*er will das Absolute erfassen, begreifen, ihm gleich, mit ihm Eins werden?* To give the phrase ἐν ὁμοιώματι ἀνθρώπων a Docetic meaning, is ridiculous, and is affixing a technical sense to a popular term. Rom. viii. 3. The meaning is, he appeared as other men appeared ; notwithstanding his possession of a divine nature, his appearance was the ordinary appearance of humanity. He had the form of God, and he assumed as really the form of a man. Baur also frames a dilemma—" Were he already God, wherefore should he first desire to become what he already was ? and were he not yet like God, what an eccentric, unnatural, and self-contradictory thought [4]—' to be equal with God' ! " The true meaning is, not that He was originally less than God, and

---

[1] *Iren.* i. 2, 2, p. 18.   [2] *Ibid.* i. 4, 1, p. 46.
[3] *Ibid.* i. 5, 1, p. 58.
[4] Welche eigenthümliche Vorstellung ist es doch, von Christus zu sagen, er habe es, obgleich er in göttlicher Gestalt war, nicht für einen Raub gehalten, oder, wie die Worte grammatisch genauer zu nehmen sind, es nicht zum Gegenstand eines *actus rapiendi* machen zu müssen geglaubt, Gott gleich zu seyn. War er schon Gott, wozu wollte er erst werden, was er schon war, war er aber noch nicht Gott gleich welcher excentrische, unnatürliche, sich selbst widersprechende Gedanke wäre es gewesen, Gott gleich zu werden? Soll nicht eben dieses Undenkbare eines solchen Gedankens durch den eigenen Ausdruck οὐχ ἁρπαγμὸν ἡγήσατο bezeichnet werden ? Wie kommt denn aber der Verfasser dazu, etwas so Undenkbares auch nur verneinend von Christus zu sagen ? P. 458.

strove to be on equality with Him. Nor is being God, and
being like God, the same idea. It is not, as Baur would
seem to suppose—being God, He thought it no robbery to
be equal with God. For it is not of essence, but of form,
that the apostle speaks. Equality with God, in the possession
of this form, was no object of ambition to him; he laid it
aside, and assumed the form of a servant. Very different this
from the Gnostic and Valentinian image of Wisdom descending from the πλήρωμα into the κένωμα. The phrase ἐκένωσεν
ἑαυτόν is identical in spirit with ἐπτώχευσε, though different
in form—2 Cor. viii. 9—and has no sort of affinity with the
Gnostic γενέσθαι ἐν κενώματι, which seems to mean that
annihilation which happened to the Æon Sophia, or rather
to its cupidity—ἐνθύμησις. The Gnostic nomenclature has
much the same connection with the Pauline writings as the
book of Mormon has with the English Scriptures; and were
the Greek original lost, some critic might rise up a thousand
years after this, and affirm with some show of erudition, and
a parade of parallel terms, that the most of the epistles of the
English Testament did not originate under James VI., but
must have been fabricated by men who knew the system of
the Latter-day saints, and had studied its so-called Bible. It
is needless to enlarge. Neither ingenuity nor erudition characterizes the objector's argument against the epistle; so far
from borrowing Gnostic ideas and terms, it again and again,
as if by anticipation, condemns the heresy. It calls the
Saviour Lord or Κύριος, which, according to Epiphanius, the
Gnostics would not. It ascribes a body to the exalted Jesus
—which the Gnostics denied; and assigns a body also to
glorified believers, but the Gnostics held that it would be
burnt up and destroyed. Of the day of Christ, or the coming
of Christ, Gnosticism knew nothing, for its benighted disciples
did not hope, after death, " to be with Christ." [1]   But, indeed,
the entire argument of Baur against the genuineness of this
epistle, is what Alford calls " the very insanity of hypercriti-
cism. . . . According to him, all *usual* expressions prove its
spuriousness, as being taken from other epistles; all *unusual*
expressions prove the same, as being from another than St.
Paul. Poverty of thought, and want of point, are charged

[1] Brückner, p. 13.

against it in one page; in another, excess of point, and undue vigour of expression."

We need say nothing in conclusion of the attack of this epistle by the English Evanson, in his *Dissonance of the Four Gospels*, who, indeed, was earlier than Baur in cold and insipid negation. Nor need we do more than allude to Schrader,[1] who has thrown suspicion on the latter part of the epistle, and for reasons not a whit stronger than those of Baur. A Paley[2] says on this topic—"Considering the Philippians as his readers, a person might naturally write upon the subject as the author of the epistle has written, but there is no supposition of forgery with which it will suit."

III.—UNITY AND INTEGRITY.

Heinrichs in his *Prolegomena* started the idea that the epistle as we have it is made up of two distinct letters, the first reaching to the end of the first clause in iii. 1—"Finally, brethren, farewell in the Lord," along with iv. 21, 23, intended for the church; and the second, including the remaining portion of the epistle, and meant for the apostle's more intimate friends. Paulus, adopting the hypothesis, but reversing its order, imagines that the first letter was for the bishops and deacons. The theory is baseless, for the use of τὸ λοιπόν may be otherwise explained. See Commentary on the phrase. Though we should admit that the phrase τὰ αὐτὰ γράφειν may imply that the apostle had written other epistles to the Philippians, there is still no proof that we have a sample of any of them in our present canonical book. Heinrichs' arguments are not worth refutation; but they have been replied to, *seriatim*, by Krause, Hoelemann, and Matthies.[3] The first part of the epistle may be more general, and the second more special; but to divide any production on such a principle would be chimerical in the extreme. May not a man have a general and a special purpose in writing a single letter? Nay more, is not the latter half of the second chapter as special as

---

[1] *Der Apostel Paulus*, vol. v. pp. 231–233, 240. See, on the other hand, Hoelemann's *Prolegomena*, p. 59 ; Neudecker's *Einleit.* § 93.

[2] *Horæ Paulinæ*, chap. vii.

[3] See also Schott's *Isagoge*, § 70.

any paragraph in the third or fourth chapters; and are not the four last verses of the third chapter, and the fifth, sixth, seventh, and eighth verses of the fourth chapter, as general as any paragraph in the earlier half of the epistle? There is nothing of an exoteric or esoteric tone about its various sections, nor is any such distinction warranted by the use of τέλειοι, iii. 15. The transitions depend upon no logical train —as the thoughts occurred they were dictated. And we can never know what suggested to the apostle the order of his topics. We can conceive him about to finish his epistle at iii. 1, and with τὸ λοιπόν; but a conversation with Epaphroditus, or some train of thought in his own mind, directed and moulded by the Spirit of God, may have led him to launch out again after he seemed to be nearing the shore.

IV.—THE CIRCUMSTANCES OF THE PHILIPPIAN CHURCH,
AND THE OCCASION OF THE EPISTLE.

This Epistle was not written for any polemical or practical purpose. Its object is neither to combat error nor establish truth, nor expose personal or ecclesiastical inconsistencies, nor vindicate his apostolical prerogative and authority. A gift had been sent him to Rome, from a people that had distinguished themselves by similar kindnesses in former times. The churches in Macedonia were poor, but "their deep poverty abounded unto the riches of their liberality." They contributed the gift to the apostle when he needed it, and it was enhanced alike by their poverty and his want. As a prisoner he could not support himself by labour as at Thessalonica and Corinth, and he might not feel that he had a claim for maintenance upon the church in Rome. He had not founded the church there, and as he was not sowing "spiritual things" he did not expect to reap "carnal things." The gift from this small, poor, and distant people, whom he had not seen for some years, was therefore very opportune; and the receipt of it, combined with a knowledge of all their circumstances, was to him a source of great exhilaration. Epaphroditus, who had brought the contribution, was to convey the apostle's thanks to the donors, and he takes occasion, in returning these thanks, to address some counsels to

his beloved people, to tell them how he prayed for them and
hoped well of them, and what was his own condition at Rome,
as they would be anxious to hear of it from himself ; to inform
them what a spirit of tender considerateness ought to reign
among them ; how Timothy was soon coming to them ; how
they ought to be on their guard against false teachers and
immoral free-thinkers ; how they should rejoice in the Lord,
and pursue all that is spiritually elevated and excellent ; and
all this—before he formally acknowledges the receipt of the
subsidy. His thoughts turn to himself and them alternately.
They had not, like other churches, given him reason for regret
or censure. He was fond of them, and what he had suffered
among them had endeared them to him. He did not forget
that " we were shamefully entreated at Philippi ; " but the
recollection made them all the dearer to him, by what he had
endured for them. The majority of the church seem to
have been proselytes or converted heathens, and to the paucity
of Jews in the membership may be ascribed this continuous
attachment to their spiritual founder, and the absence of those
prejudices and misunderstandings that so soon sprang up in
some of the other churches.

That the Philippian church was in trial and exposed to
danger is evident from several allusions. At an earlier period
they had "a great trial of affliction," and the conclusion of
the first chapter indicates that the same perils still continued.
The apostle says, i. 28, 29, 30 :—" And in nothing terrified
by your adversaries : which is to them an evident token of
perdition, but to you of salvation, and that of God. For unto
you it is given in the behalf of Christ, not only to believe
on Him, but also to suffer for His sake ; having the same
conflict which ye saw in me, *and* now hear *to be* in me." We
cannot tell who their antagonists were. There is no ground
for supposing that they were Jews especially, for there were
apparently so few in the place that they do not seem to have
possessed a synagogue.[1] The probability is, that the popula-

---

[1] The place of worship, προσευχή, was by the river-side—and as the correct
reading is ἔξω τῆς πύλης—"without the gate." Thus Josephus, *Antiq.* xiv. 10,
23, says of the magistrates of an Eastern city, that they allowed to the Jews—
τὰς προσευχὰς ποιῖσθαι πρὸς τῇ θαλάσσῃ, κατὰ τὸ πάτριον ἔθος. Tertullian also says
of the Jews—*per omne litus quocunque in aperto aliquando jam preces ad cœlum
mittunt. De Jejun.* xvi. vol. i. p. 877 ; *Opera,* ed. Oehler. The same author

tion generally was hostile to them, and that the rancorous feeling manifested against Paul and Silas on their first visit, continued to show itself in a variety of forms against their converts. But persecution did not intimidate them. They did not become cowardly and regretful, or sullen and spiteful. They had "abundance of joy," feeling as James counsels his readers—"My brethren, count it all joy when ye fall into divers temptations." That joy the apostle bids them still cherish, and the soul of his letter is—"Rejoice in the Lord." Because the opposition which they encountered drove all worldly gladness from them, it forced them to a more vivid realization of their union to Christ, the source of all joy. Persecution only raked away the ashes, so that the spiritual flame was steady and brilliant.

But this very condition had a tendency to create spiritual pride. Men so upborne are apt to forget themselves. As Dr. Davidson remarks[1]—"The highest spirituality stands near the verge of pride, superciliousness, and vainglory." The earnest injunctions enforced by the example of Christ, in the beginning of the second chapter, plainly point to such a tendency. There were also two ladies who are entreated by the apostle to be of the same mind in the Lord, and others are asked to help them to this reconciliation. The Philippians are exhorted "to stand fast in one spirit and one mind." We dare not say that factions actually existed, but there were jealousies and alienations of feeling. Yet there is no proof that false teaching had created parties and produced schism;[2] so that the broad assertions and hypotheses of many on this subject cannot be received. The Philippians are warned against Judaizers, but there is no evidence that Judaizers had, as in Galatia, made havoc among them; and they are told of others who are enemies of the cross, not from dogmatic perversity, but from immoral lives.

speaks of the Jewish *orationes littorales*. *Ad Nationes*, xiii. *ibid.* p. 334. When the proseuchæ in Alexandria were destroyed, the Jews resorted to the neighbouring beaches—ἐπὶ τοὺς πλησίον αἰγιαλούς. Philo, *in Flac.* p. 982. Thus, too, *In qua te quæro proseucha?* Juvenal, iii. 295. Biscoe *on the Acts*, p. 181; ed. Oxford, 1840.

[1] Introduction, vol. ii. p. 381.

[2] Schinz, *Die Christliche Gemeinde zu Philippi. Ein exegetischer Versuch von W. H. Schinz;* Zürich, 1833. Cruse, *De statu Philip.*, etc.; Hafniæ, 1734; or Walch, *Acta Pauli Philippensia;* Jenæ, 1736.

Storr, Flatt, Eichhorn, Guericke, and Rheinwald are as much without evidence in supposing the existence of a Judaizing faction, as is Bertholdt in imagining that the apostle condemns certain false doctrines which sprang from Sadducean influence. As if they had still been safe and uncontaminated, they are commanded so to stand in the Lord as to form a contrast to those whose end is destruction, and their fellowship for the gospel had been uninterrupted. Against the errors and tendencies incidental to their situation, or which might be originated by their history, experience, and temperament, their sagacious monitor frankly warns them. For the stream, if it receive tributaries which have flowed through a muddy soil, is in danger of being discoloured.

V.—PLACE AND TIME AT WHICH THE EPISTLE WAS WRITTEN.

The general opinion has been, that the epistle was written at Rome. Œder[1] proposed Corinth; Paulus and Böttger[2] fix on Cæsarea; and Rilliet thinks this theory plausible. The probabilities are all against Cæsarea. The phrase οἰκία Καίσαρος could not surely be applied to Herod's family. The dwelling of Herod at Cæsarea is indeed called πραιτώριον, for the word had a secondary or general significance; and it is used of the dwelling of the Procurator in Jerusalem. See under i. 13. When he was in custody at Cæsarea, Paul, as a Roman citizen, could at any time appeal to Cæsar against any sentence passed upon him, and his condition could not therefore have that uncertainty about it which he speaks of in i. 23, 24, 25. There he could ward off martyrdom at least for a period. All the allusions are best explained by the supposition, that the apostle wrote the epistle in Rome—his bonds being made known in the barracks of the imperial life-guards—his enemies filled with spite, and his life in danger—and the gospel achieving such signal triumphs as warranted him to send salutations to Philippi from Cæsar's household.

The tone of the epistle in reference to himself, seems to

---

[1] *De tempore scriptæ prioris ad Timotheum atque ad Philippenses epistolæ Paulinæ Progr.;* Jenæ, 1799. See, on the other hand, Credner, *Einleitung,* p. 425; Wolf's *Prolegomena :* and Hemsen, *Der Ap. Paulus,* etc., p. 680.

[2] *Beiträge,* etc., i. 47.

place it later than those written by him to Ephesus and Colosse. Dangers were thickening around him, sorrows were pressing upon him, and the future was wrapt in dark uncertainty. The period must have been later than the two years with which the book of the Acts closes—the period when he was at liberty to preach and to teach, "with all confidence, no man forbidding him." Still more, Epaphroditus had brought him money, and tarried so long as allowed the Philippians time to hear that their messenger had been sick; nay, the apostle had heard that they had received such intelligence. Some considerable time therefore must have elapsed. He does not now ask their prayers for "utterance," as when he wrote to the Ephesians. Eph. vi. 19. Burrus, the prefect of the prætorian guards—the στρατοπεδάρχης—to whose care Paul as a prisoner was entrusted, was a man of a benignant spirit, and under him the two years of comparative freedom may have been enjoyed. But Burrus died or was poisoned [1] in 62; and the government of Nero rapidly degenerated. The power of Seneca over the emperor was destroyed by the death of Burrus, and he sank into undisguised infamy.[2] He married a Jewish proselytess, and she might listen to the apostle's Jewish antagonists. These changes wrought a correspondent alteration in the apostle's circumstances. His liberty was abridged; he was lodged in the prætorium, and a violent death seemed to be at hand. Such was his condition, when in the summer or autumn of 63, or in the beginning of 64, he composed the Epistle to the Philippians. Wieseler places it in 62 (*Chronologie des Apost. Zeitalters*, p. 458); and Davidson agrees with him. Lardner had adopted the same chronology. *Works*, vol. vi. p. 74; ed. London, 1834.

VI.—CONTENTS OF THE EPISTLE.

Address and Salutation.

Paul and Timothy, servants of Christ Jesus, to all the saints in Christ Jesus who are in Philippi, with the bishops

---

[1] *Incertum valetudine an veneno.* Tacitus, *Annal.* xiv. 51.

[2] Tacitus, *Annal.* xiv. 52. *Mors Burri infregit Senecæ potentiam, quia nec bonis artibus idem virium erat, altero velut duce amoto, et Nero ad deteriores inclinabat.*

and deacons, Grace to you and peace from God our Father and the Lord Jesus Christ.

Proof of his Attachment.

I thank my God on my whole remembrance of you, always in every supplication of mine, making, with joy, supplication for you all, on account of your fellowship for (in favour of) the gospel from the first day until now, being confident of this very thing, that He who has begun in you a good work, will perform it until the day of Christ Jesus, even as it is right in me to think this on behalf of you all, because I have you in my heart, both in my bonds, and in the defence and confirmation of the gospel—you, all of you, as being fellow-partakers with me of grace.   For God is my witness, how I do long for you all in the bowels of Christ Jesus; and this I pray, that your love yet more and more may abound in full knowledge, and in all judgment, so that ye may distinguish things that differ, in order that ye may be pure and offenceless anent the day of Christ—being filled with the fruit of righteousness, which is by Jesus Christ, to the glory and praise of God.

History of the Writer's own Condition, and its Results.

But I wish you to know, brethren, that things with me have resulted to the furtherance of the gospel, so that my bonds have become known in Christ in the whole prætorium, and to all the rest ; and the greater part of the brethren putting in the Lord confidence in my bonds are more abundantly bold to speak the word without fear.   Some indeed, even for envy and contention, but some also for goodwill, preach Christ,— the one party indeed, of love, knowing that I am set for the defence of the gospel ; but the other party proclaim Christ out of faction, not purely, thinking to stir up affliction to my bonds. What then ?   Notwithstanding, in every way, whether in pretence or in sincerity Christ is proclaimed, even in this I do rejoice, yea and I shall rejoice.   For I know that this shall fall out for salvation to me, through your supplication and the supply of the Spirit of Jesus Christ; according to my firm expectation and hope that in nothing I shall be ashamed, but

with all boldness, as always, so also now Christ shall be magnified in my body, whether by life or by death : for to me to
live is Christ, and to die is gain.　But if to live in the flesh,
if this to me be fruit of labour, then what I shall choose I wot
not ; yea, I am put into a strait on account of the two, inasmuch
as I have the desire for departing to be with Christ, for it is
much by far better, but to abide in the flesh is more necessary
on your account.　And being persuaded of this I know that
I shall abide and remain with you all for the advancement
and joy of your faith, that your boasting may abound in
Jesus Christ in me, on account of my coming again to you.

General Admonition in the Circumstances.

Only let your conversation be worthy of the gospel of
Christ, in order that whether having come and seen you, or
whether being absent I may hear of your affairs, that ye are
standing in one spirit, with one soul striving together for the
faith of the gospel, and in nothing terrified by the adversaries—
the which is to them a token of perdition, but to you of salvation, and that from God.　For to you was it granted, on behalf
of Christ, not only to believe on Him, but also on behalf of
Him to suffer ; as you have the same conflict which you saw
in me, and now hear of in me.

Special Injunctions.

If, then, there be any exhortation in Christ, if any comfort [1]
of love, if any fellowship of the Spirit, if any bowels and mercies, fulfil ye my joy, to the end that ye mind the same thing,
having the same love, with union of soul minding the one
thing—minding nothing in the spirit of faction nor in the
spirit of vainglory, but in humility, counting others better
than themselves—looking each of you not to your own things,
but each of you also to the things of others.

This last Injunction illustrated and enforced by the Example of Christ.

For let this mind be in you which was also in Christ Jesus ;

[1] Ellicott in his version omits to translate παραμύθιον. [Correct in Second
Edition.]

who, being in the form of God, reckoned not the being on a parity with God a prize to be snatched at, but emptied Himself, having taken the form of a servant, having been made in the likeness of men, and having been found in fashion as a man, He humbled Himself, having become obedient unto death—yea, unto the death of the cross. Wherefore God also did highly exalt Him, and gave Him the name which is above every name, that in the name of Jesus every knee should bow—of them in heaven, of them on earth, and of them under the earth—and that every tongue should confess that Jesus Christ is Lord, to the glory of God the Father.

Inferential Counsels to guide them, and secure the Apostle's own Reward.

Wherefore, my beloved, as ye always obeyed, not as in my presence only, but now much more in my absence, carry out your own salvation with fear and trembling, for God it is who worketh in you both to will and to work, of His own good pleasure. All things do without murmurings and doubts, that ye may be blameless and pure; children of God beyond reach of blame, in the midst of a crooked and perverse generation, among whom ye appear as luminaries in the world; holding forth the word of life for rejoicing to me against the day of Christ, that I did not run in vain nor yet labour in vain. But, if I am even being poured out on the sacrifice and service of your faith, I rejoice and give joy to you all; yea, for the very same reason do ye also joy and give joy to me.

Personal Matters.

But I hope in the Lord Jesus shortly to send Timothy to you, that I also may be of good spirit when I have known your affairs; for I have no one like-minded who will really care for your affairs, for the whole of them seek their own things, not the things of Jesus Christ. But his tried character ye know, that as a child a father, he served with me for the gospel. Him, then, I hope to send immediately, whenever I shall have seen how it will go with me; but I trust in the Lord that I myself also shall shortly come. Yet I judged it necessary to send Epaphroditus on to you, my brother

and fellow-labourer, and fellow-soldier, but your deputy and
minister to my need, forasmuch as he was longing after you
all, and was in heaviness, because ye heard that he was
sick; for he really was sick, nigh unto death, but God had
mercy on him, and not on him alone, but on me also, that I
should not have sorrov upon sorrow. The more speedily,
therefore, have I sent him, in order that having seen him ye
may rejoice again, and that I too may be the less sorrowful.
On that account receive him in the Lord with all joy, and hold
such in honour, because for the work of Christ he came
near even to death, having hazarded his life that he might
supply your deficiency in your service towards me.   Finally,
my brethren, rejoice in the Lord.

Warning against Judaists.

To write to you the same things to me indeed is not
grievous, but for you it is safe.   Look to the dogs, look to the
evil-workers, look to the concision.   For we are the circumcision, who by the Spirit of God do serve and make our boast
in Christ Jesus, and have no trust in the flesh—though I am
in possession too of trust in the flesh.

The Apostle's Spiritual History and Experience.

If any other man thinketh that he has confidence in the
flesh, I more: circumcised on the eighth day, of the race of
Israel, of the tribe of Benjamin, a Hebrew of the Hebrews, as
to the law a Pharisee, as to zeal persecuting the church, as to
the righteousness which is in the law being blameless.   But
whatever things were gain to me, these for Christ's sake I
have reckoned loss; yea, indeed, for that reason I also
(still) reckon them all to be loss, on account of the excellency
of the knowledge of Christ Jesus my Lord, for whose sake
I suffered the loss of them all, and do account them to be
but refuse, that I may gain Christ and be found in Him, not
having mine own righteousness, which is of the law, but that
which is through the faith of Christ—the righteousness which
is of God upon faith; so that I may know Him, and the power
of His resurrection, and the fellowship of His sufferings, while
I am being made conformable to His death, if anyhow I may

arrive at the resurrection from the dead. Not that I have already obtained, either have already been perfected ; but I am pressing on, if indeed I may seize that for which also I was seized by Christ. Brethren, I do not reckon myself to have seized ; but one thing I do—forgetting indeed the things behind, but stretching forth to the things before, towards the mark I am pressing on for the prize of the high calling of God in Christ Jesus. Let as many of us then as be perfect think this, and if in any respect ye think otherwise,[1] yea this shall God reveal to you. Howbeit whereto we have reached,[2] by the same do ye walk on.

Other Warnings.

Be together followers of me, brethren, and observe them who are walking in such a way as ye have us for an example : for many walk, of whom many times I told you, but now tell you even weeping, that they are those who are the enemies of the cross of Christ ; whose end is destruction, whose God is their belly, and whose glory is in their shame—persons they, who are minding earthly things. For our country is in heaven, out of which we await a Saviour, the Lord Jesus Christ, who shall transform the body of our humiliation, so that it be conformed to the body of His glory, according to the working of His power even to subdue all things to Himself. Wherefore, my brethren, beloved and longed for, my joy and crown, so stand in the Lord, beloved.

Minuter Counsels to Members of the Church.

Euodia I exhort, and Syntyche I exhort, to be of one mind in the Lord ; yea, I ask thee too, true yoke-fellow, assist these women, for they laboured hard with me in the gospel, along with Clement, too, and my other fellow-labourers, whose names are in the book of life. Rejoice in the Lord always ; again

---

[1] Bishop Horsley, in his twenty-seventh sermon, renders the clause thus— "And if in any thing you be variously minded, God shall reveal even this to you—that is, the thing concerning which you have various minds."

[2] The three verbs—καταντήσω, ἔλαβον, ἐφθάσαμεν, are rendered by the one English verb "attain"—"attained," both in the Authorized Version and in that of Ellicott. The Greek words present the same idea under different images, but the difference might be marked in the translation.

will I say, rejoice. Let your forbearance be known to all men. The Lord is at hand. Be careful for nothing; but in everything by prayer and supplication with thanksgiving, let your requests be made known before God; and so the peace of God, which passeth all understanding, shall guard your hearts and your thoughts in Christ Jesus. Finally, brethren, whatsoever things are true; whatsoever things are seemly; whatsoever things are right; whatsoever things are pure; whatsoever things are lovely; whatsoever things are of good report; whatever virtue there is, and whatever praise there is, these things think upon; the things which also ye learned and received, and heard and saw in me, these things do. And the God of peace shall be with you.

Business.

But I rejoiced in the Lord greatly, that now at length ye flourished again in mindfulness for my interest, for which indeed ye were mindful, but ye lacked opportunity. Not that I speak on account of want, for I have learned, in the circumstances in which I am, to be content. I know also to be abased, I know also to abound; in everything and in all things, I have been instructed both to be full and to be hungry, both to abound and to be in want. I can do all things in Him strengthening me. Howbeit ye did well in that ye had fellowship with my affliction. But you, Philippians, are yourselves also aware, that in the introduction of the gospel, when I departed from Macedonia, no church communicated with me to account of gift and receipt but you only; for even in Thessalonica, both once and a second time, ye sent to me for my necessity. Not that I seek for the gift, but I seek for the fruit which does abound to your account. But I have all things and I abound; I have been filled, having received from Epaphroditus the things sent from you—an odour of a sweet smell—a sacrifice acceptable, well-pleasing to God. But my God shall supply all your need according to His riches in glory in Christ Jesus. Now to God and our Father be the glory for ever and ever. Amen.

Conclusion.

Salute every saint in Christ Jesus. There salute you the

brethren who are with me: there salute you all the saints, chiefly they who are of Cæsar's household. 𝕿𝖍𝖊 𝖌𝖗𝖆𝖈𝖊 𝖔𝖋 𝖙𝖍𝖊 𝕷𝖔𝖗𝖉 𝕵𝖊𝖘𝖚𝖘 𝖇𝖊 𝖜𝖎𝖙𝖍 𝖞𝖔𝖚𝖗 𝕾𝖕𝖎𝖗𝖎𝖙.

VII.—COMMENTATORS ON THE EPISTLE.

We need scarcely mention the commentaries of the Greek Fathers—Chrysostom, Theophylact, Theodoret, Oecumenius, with others found in the *Catena*, or those of the Latin Pelagius and Ambrosiaster, or those of Erasmus, Calvin, Zuingli, Bucer, Beza, Hunnius, Grotius, Schmidius, Crocius, Zanchius, Piscator, Aretius, etc. There are the Romish Estius, a-Lapide, and Justiniani; and there are also the Protestant Clericus, Calovius, Calixtus, Vorstius, Schotanus, Balduin, Tarnovius, Musculus, Hyperius, Wolf, van Til, Jaspis, Küttner, Heumann, Bengel, Storr, Flatt, Hammond, Michaelis, Rosenmüller, Whitby, Pierce, Macknight, Heinrichs, and Schrader. Every one knows the New Testaments of Bloomfield and Alford, and the quartos of Conybeare and Howson. Of more special expositions on the epistle, we have Velasquez—*In Epistolam Pauli ad Philippenses, Commentarii*; Antverpiæ, 2 vols. folio, 1637. Breithaupt—*Animadversiones exeget. et dogmat. pract. in Epistolam ad Philippenses*; Halæ, 1703. Am Ende—*Pauli Ap. ad Philipp., Epistola ex recensione Griesbach.—nova versione Latina et annotatione perpetua illustrata*; Wittebergæ, 1798. J. F. Krause—*Observat. crit. exeget. in Pauli Epistolam ad Philippenses*, cap. i. ii.; Regiomont. 1810. F. A. W. Krause—*Die Briefe an die Philipper und Thessalonicher*; Frankfurt am Main, 1790. Rheinwald—*Commentar über den Brief Pauli an die Philipper*; Berlin, 1827. Matthies — *Erklärung des Briefes Pauli an die Philipper*; Greifswald, 1835. Van Hengel—*Commentarius Perpetuus in Epistolam Pauli ad Philippenses*; Lugduni Batavorum et Amstelodami, 1838. Hoelemann—*Commentarius in Epistolam divi Pauli ad Philippenses*; Lipsiæ, 1839. Rilliet — *Commentaire sur l'Épître de l'Apôtre Paul aux Philippiens*; Genève, 1841. Müller—*Commentatio de locis quibusdam Epistolæ Pauli ad Philippenses*; Hamburgi, 1843. De Wette—*Kurze Erklärung der Briefe an die Colosser, an Philemon, an die Epheser und Philipper*; Leipzig, 1843.

Meyer—*Kritisch exegetisches Handbuch über den Brief an die Philipper;* Göttingen, 1847. Baumgarten-Crusius—*Commentar über die Briefe Pauli an die Philipper und Thessalonicher;* Jena, 1848. Peile—*Annotations on the Apostolical Epistles,* vol. ii.; London, 1849. Wiesinger—*Die Briefe des Apostels Paulus an die Philipper, an Titus, Timotheus, und Philemon;* Königsberg, 1850. Beelen, *Commentarius in Epistolam S. Pauli ad Philippenses;* ed. secunda, Lovanii, 1852. Bisping — *Erklärung der Briefes an die Epheser, Philipper, Kolosser, und des ersten Briefes an die Thessalonicher;* Münster, 1855. Ellicott—*A Critical and Grammatical Commentary on St. Paul's Epistles to the Philippians, Colossians, and to Philemon, with a Revised Translation;* London, 1857. Ewald—*Die Sendschreiben des Apostels Paulus übersetzt und erklärt;* Göttingen, 1857. We need scarcely allude to more popular treatises, such as Daillé—*Sermons sur l'Épître aux Philippiens;* 1644-47. De Launay—*Paraph. et Expos. sur les Épîtres de St. Paul;* Charenton, 1650. Passavant—*Versuch einer praktischen Auslegung des Briefes Pauli an die Philipper;* Basel, 1834. Kähler—*Auslegung der Epistel Pauli an die Philipper in 25 Predigten;* Kiel, 1855. Florey—*Bibelstunden über den Brief St. Pauli an die Philipper;* Leipzig, 1857. There are similar works in English, of very unequal merit, such as Airay, 1618; Acaster, 1827; Baynes, 1834; Neat, 1841; Hall, 1843; Toller, 1855.

NOTE.

In the following pages, when Buttmann, Matthiæ, Kühner, Winer, Stuart, Green, Jelf, Madvig, Scheuerlein, and Krüger are simply quoted, the reference is to their respective Greek grammars; and when Suidas, Suicer, Passow, Robinson, Pape, Wilke, Wahl, Bretschneider, and Liddell and Scott are named, the reference is to their respective lexicons. If Hartung be found without any addition, we mean his *Lehre von den Partikeln der griechischen Sprache*, 2 vols., Erlangen, 1832; and the mention of Bernhardy without any supplement, represents his *Wissenschaftliche Syntax der griechischen Sprache;* Berlin, 1829. The majority of the other names are those of the commentators or philologists enumerated in the previous chapter. The references to Tischendorf's New Testament are to the second edition.

COMMENTARY ON THE PHILIPPIANS.

CHAPTER I.

AFFER the usual address and salutation, the apostle, turning at once to the close and confidential relations subsisting between him and the Philippian church, tells them that his entire reminiscence of them gave him unmixed satisfaction, and led him to thank God for them; that in this cheerful state of mind he prayed always in all his prayers for all of them; that his special ground of thanksgiving was their FELLOWSHIP FOR THE GOSPEL, which had existed among them from the period of their conversion to the present moment, and which, he was persuaded, God would perpetuate and mature among them. Then he intimates that this favourable opinion of them was no notion loosely taken up by him, but one well warranted, since he loved them dearly as joint partakers of grace with himself. That Christian affection was no idle emotion, for it found expression in constant and joyous prayer. And that prayer which he had mentioned in the fourth verse as his uniform practice, had this for its theme, that their love might grow, and be furnished with a fuller knowledge and a truer spiritual discrimination, so that a higher state of moral excellence might be attained by them, along with a life of ampler fruits—to the glory and praise of God.

(Ver. 1.) Παῦλος καὶ Τιμόθεος, δοῦλοι Χριστοῦ Ἰησοῦ— "Paul and Timothy, servants of Christ Jesus." The received text reads Ἰησοῦ Χριστοῦ, but B, D, E, etc., declare for the reverse order of the names. For some remarks on Timothy and the association of his name with that of the apostle, see under Col. i. 1. There, indeed, Paul calls himself an apostle, but here both are simply and equally designated δοῦλοι—the

following genitive being that of possession, and the epithet
itself being one of close relationship as well as labour.   1 Cor.
vii. 22.   There is no sure ground for the conjecture of Rilliet,
that Timothy is mentioned because probably he wrote the
letter from Paul's dictation.   As little foundation is there for
the opinion of Müller, taken from Huther, that the addition
by Paul of another name to his own was intended to show
that the letter was written *per muneris officium et publice*, for
the epistle is without any traces of such a purpose; and there
is no great likelihood in the notion of Van Hengel, that the
apostle placed Timothy on a level with himself, because as he
was so soon to despatch him to Philippi, he wished him to
appear invested with all his own great authority.   Timothy
is associated with Paul as one who was well known to this
church, who had been with him on his first visit, who afterwards was sent by him to labour in Macedonia, and who
cherished a fervent regard for the welfare of the Philippian
saints.   Acts xvi. 1, 10, xix. 22 ; Phil. ii. 19, 20.

Paul does not here style himself an apostle as is his wont,
either because his apostolical prerogative had not been called
in question among them, or because their intimacy with him
was so close, that he felt that his office was ever in their
thoughts of him and their care for him, associated with his
person.   That it is rash to make decided inferences from the
style of the apostle's address, is evident from the fact, that
five different forms are employed by him.   1. He names
himself alone and formally as an apostle—Rom. i. 1 ; 1 Cor.
i. 1 ; Gal. i. 1 ; Eph. i. 1 ; and, as might be expected, in the
pastoral epistles.   2. He associates another name with his
own, but still marks out his own apostleship, as " Paul
an apostle, and Timothy our brother "—2 Cor. i. 1 ; Col. i. 1.
3. He joins others to himself without giving any distinctive
epithet either to himself or them ; as, " Paul, Silvanus, and
Timothy," in both Epistles to the Thessalonians.   4. In the
letter to Philemon he calls himself a prisoner, and subjoins
Timothy as a brother.   5. In this epistle he adds Timothy,
but unites both under the simple and comprehensive term
δοῦλοι.   The corresponding epithet in Hebrew had already
been consecrated, Num. xii. 7 ; Josh. i. 2, ix. 24 ; 1 Chron.
vi. 49 ; and δοῦλος occurs in the Septuagint, Neh. x. 29.

In its Oriental form it passed away from its more distinctive meaning, and was incorporated into proper names, as in Abdallah, Abednego, etc.

πᾶσιν τοῖς ἁγίοις ἐν Χριστῷ Ἰησοῦ, τοῖς οὖσιν ἐν Φιλίπποις, σὺν ἐπισκόποις καὶ διακόνοις—"to all the saints in Christ Jesus who are in Philippi, with the bishops and deacons." Consult our note on ἅγιος, Eph. i. 1. The preposition ἐν points out the source and sustentation of this ἁγιότης—union with Christ Jesus. As Theophylact says, those who are in Christ Jesus are ἅγιοι ὄντως. In the fulness of his heart, the apostle writes to ALL the saints, not, as van Hengel supposes, that he wished to show that he made no distinction in his regard between those who had, and those who had not, sent him a pecuniary gift. There would be probability in the notion of De Wette, that the apostle formally embraced them all, to intimate his elevation above their parties and conflicts, if the term did not occur again and again in the epistle, as the expression of the writer's earnest and universal affection—i. 4, 7, 8, 25, ii. 17, 26, iv. 23. The city of Philippi, and the entrance of the gospel to it, have been spoken of in the Introduction.

The apostle adds, σὺν ἐπισκόποις καὶ διακόνοις. The preposition σύν intimates close connection—*Cohaerenz*, as Krüger calls it, and so far differs from μετά, which indicates mere co-existence, Krüger, § 68, 13. The reading συνεπισκόποις, followed by Chrysostom, and found in B², D³, and C, must be at once rejected. Following it, the Greek Father understands the epistle to be addressed to the clergy—τῷ κλήρῳ, the compound noun being taken as if in apposition with ἁγίοις. But why should bishops and deacons be so unwontedly singled out? Chrysostom answers, Because they had sent the pecuniary gift through Epaphroditus to the apostle. Others more generally, as Meyer, that they had been instrumental in collecting the sums for which he thanks them in the conclusion of the epistle. Heinrichs opines that the mention of office-bearers was only *mero casu ;* Müller and Rilliet, that the phrase merely describes or represents a properly organized church. The opinion of Wiesinger is at least as probable, that the real reason is to be found in the circumstances of the church, and that there was a tendency to undue

assumption on the part of some individuals, which needed
such an effective check as was implied in the special acknowledgment of those who bore office in it. Tl.; official term
ἐπίσκοπος, of Greek origin, is in the diction of the New
Testament the same as πρεσβύτερος, of Jewish usage—the
name expressive of gravity and honour; διάκονος being the
correlate found in connection with the former, and νεώτερος
or νεανίσκος standing in a similar relation to the latter—
Acts xx. 17, 28 ; 1 Pet. v. 1, 5 ; Tit. i. 5, 7. The Syriac
renders the term here by ܩܫܝܫܐ — elders. The origin
of the special office of deacon is given in Acts vi.—the
end of the institution being διακονεῖν τραπέζαις, or to
exercise a supervision, ἐπὶ τῆς χρείας ταύτης. The epithet
διάκονος is not, as Chrysostom seems to suppose, a second
name for the bishop ; for he says καὶ διάκονος ὁ ἐπίσκοπος
ἐλέγετο. A bishop might indeed be a "server," as Paul was
a servant; but the word, as is plain from other portions of
the New Testament, describes a distinct class of office-bearers.
The mention of ἐπίσκοποι in the plural, and the naming of
both classes of office-bearers after the general body of
members, indicate a state of things which did not exist in the
second century.—See Canon Stanley's *Sermons and Essays on
the Apostolic Age*, p. 67, and compare Neander, Vitringa,
Bingham, Rothe, Baur, and other authors on the general
subject. Hammond, in order to vindicate the form of modern
Episcopacy, maintains that the bishops were those of a district of which Philippi was a metropolitan centre, but the
language warrants no such inference. Chrysostom has asked,
"Were there several bishops in one city? Certainly not ;
but he thus called the presbyters,"—ἀλλὰ τοὺς πρεσβυτέρους
οὕτως ἐκάλεσε. The placing of the office-bearers after the
church seems to have scandalized Thomas Aquinas, but he
saves his hierarchical convictions by suggesting—*apostolum
servasse ordinem naturæ, quo grex solet præcedere suum pastorem;
hinc in processionibus, populus præcedit, clerus et prælati
sequuntur.*

(Ver. 2.) Χάρις ὑμῖν καὶ εἰρήνη ἀπὸ Θεοῦ Πατρὸς ἡμῶν,
καὶ Κυρίου Ἰησοῦ Χριστοῦ — "Grace to you, and peace
from God our Father, and from the Lord Jesus Christ."

See at length on the terms of the salutation under Eph. i. 2.

(Ver. 3.) Εὐχαριστῶ τῷ Θεῷ μου ἐπὶ πάσῃ τῇ μνείᾳ ὑμῶν —" I thank my God on the whole remembrance of you." How different this εὐχαριστῶ τῷ Θεῷ μου from the abrupt θαυμάζω ὅτι of Gal. i. 6!—satisfaction expressed in the one, and surprise and sorrow in the other. The noun μνεία is rendered " mention " in the margin of the English Bible, and the rendering is adopted by van Hengel. The idea of mention is indeed based on that of remembrance ; for it is that kind of mention which memory so naturally prompts and fashions, and may therefore be expressed by ποιεῖσθαι μνείαν, as in Rom. i. 9 ; Eph. i. 16. But such a verb is not employed here, and " remembrance " is the better rendering. The preposition ἐπί marks the ground, or occasion, of the apostle's gratitude. Winer, however, gives it a temporal signification, § 48. The phrase, ἐπὶ πάσῃ τῇ μνείᾳ, is not to be translated " on every remembrance," though such an interpretation be as old as Chrysostom—ὁσάκις ὑμῶν ἀναμνησθῶ. Beelen and Conybeare follow this rendering of the Authorized Version ; but the article forbids it. Winer, § 18, 4.[1] The meaning is not, " as often as I remember you, I thank my God," but " on my whole remembrance of you, I thank my God." There was no disturbing element, no sharp or sudden recollection, which suggested any other exercise than thanksgiving. His entrance to the city, the oratory by the river-side, Lydia's baptism, and the jailor's conversion — his entire connection with them filled his memory with delight. The incidents of his second visit are not recorded ; but his whole association with the Philippian church prompted him to devout acknowledgment. He has changed at once in this verse to the first person, ror, though Timothy's name occurs in the salutation, the epistle is in no sense a joint production. Few will agree with Pierce, Homberg, and others, that ὑμῶν is subjective, and that the meaning is, " I thank my God for your whole remembrance of me." For the grounds

---

[1] This inexact rendering is also adopted by Ellicott in his version [*upon all my remembrance* in Second Edition], but the older English versions are correct. Thus Wycliffe—" I do thankingis to my God in al mynde of you ; " and Tyndale —" I thank my God with all remembrance of you."

of his thanksgiving, as subsequently stated, determine the reference.

(Ver. 4.) Πάντοτε ἐν πάσῃ δεήσει μου ὑπὲρ πάντων ὑμῶν μετὰ χαρᾶς τὴν δέησιν ποιούμενος—" Always in every supplication of mine making supplication for you all with joy." It does not affect the sense whether ὑπὲρ πάντων ὑμῶν, standing in the middle of the verse, be joined to the words before it—δεήσει μου, as in the English Version, or to those after it, τὴν δέησιν ποιούμενος. The latter construction cannot be pleaded for from the absence of the article before ὑπὲρ πάντων. Winer, § 20, 2. The second δέησις with its article, refers to the previous δέησις, but the first term needs not be limited or defined by ὑπὲρ πάντων. The participial connection with the previous verse is common in the apostle's style. Many, such as Theophylact, Bengel, and Rilliet, join a portion of this verse to the preceding—" I thank my God on the whole remembrance of you always in every prayer of mine for you all." The verse so understood details the periods, or scenes, when the memory of the apostle excited him to thanks ; but such a connection is not necessary. Hoelemann connects εὐχαριστῶ with ὑπὲρ πάντων ὑμῶν. " I thank my God on account of you all ; " but such a connection is unnatural, destroys the point, and encumbers the order of the thought. The apostle says, in the third verse, that his whole remembrance of them prompted him to thanksgiving ; and in the verse before us, he tells them that he prayed—δέησιν ποιούμενος ; that they were included in every prayer of his—ἐν πάσῃ δεήσει ; that he prayed not for a fraction of them, but for the whole of them—πάντων ; that he did this, not periodically, but always—πάντοτε ; that this supplication had the companionship of a gladdened heart—μετὰ χαρᾶς ; and that this gladness of heart in prayer based itself—ἐπὶ πάσῃ τῇ μνείᾳ ὑμῶν. The recurrence of the terms πάσῃ, πάντοτε, πάσῃ, πάντων in these two verses, shows the exuberant feeling of the writer. " To make request with joy," is not, as Baumgarten-Crusius says, a mere circumlocution for thanksgiving ; but it implies that the suppliant thanks while he asks, and blesses as he petitions. The apostle might pray for others in anguish or doubt ; but he knew so much of the Philippian church, of its faith, its consistency, and its attachment to the truth and to himself, that when he prayed for it so uniformly, no suspicions clouded his soul. What higher rapture could an apostle feel than that occasioned by the memory of his successes, and their gracious and permanent results? No heart was more susceptible of this joy than the apostle's, and none felt more keenly the pang of disappointment and sorrow, when either truth was forsaken or adulterated, or love was supplanted by envying and strife.

(Ver. 5.) Ἐπὶ τῇ κοινωνίᾳ ὑμῶν εἰς τὸ εὐαγγέλιον ἀπὸ πρώτης ἡμέρας ἄχρι τοῦ νῦν—"On account of your fellowship in favour of the gospel, from the first day even until now." The apostle in these words expresses the grounds of his εὐχαριστῶ. Calvin, Grotius, De Wette, van Hengel, and Ewald connect the verse with the preceding one, as if it gave the ground of the μετὰ χαρᾶς. The statement is true so far, for the joy which accompanied the apostle's prayer sprang from the very same source as his thanksgiving. The thanksgiving was based on memory, and the joy on present knowledge ; but still both alike pointed especially to this κοινωνία. The recollection prompted thanksgiving, for the fellowship had commenced at an early period ; and when he made supplication, he pleaded with gladness, for that fellowship had remained unbroken from its origin to the present time so that ἐπὶ τῇ κοινωνίᾳ is primarily connected with εὐχαριστῶ, and has, at the same time, a subordinate relation to μετὰ χαρᾶς. It is true that εὐχαριστῶ is followed twice by ἐπί ; but it does not result, as De Wette maintains, that the preposition has two different significations. The connection in both cases is nearly the same. I thank my God on account of, ἐπί, " my whole remembrance of you," and then a parallel and explanatory clause intervening—the special element in that remembrance which excited thanksgiving, is brought out by the same particle, ἐπὶ τῇ κοινωνίᾳ ὑμῶν. We cannot agree with Ellicott's remarks on the alleged double sense of ἐπί, that verse 4 marks the object on which the thanksgiving rests, verse 5 when it takes place, and verse 6 why it takes place ;[1] for it is the third verse which, looking to the past, points out the ground or occasion of the thanksgiving—his whole remembrance ; while verse 4 shows how it expressed

---

[1] [These numbers seem to be misprints in Ellicott for 3, 4, 5.]

itself in prayer, verse 5 gives more fully its solid foundation, as Mr. Ellicott had already said, and verse 6, glancing into the future, shows how the feeling was intensified by the apostle's persuasion about them. But what is the meaning of the unusual phrase—κοινωνία εἰς τὸ εὐαγγέλιον ?

1. It is plain that whatever κοινωνία means, the phrase εἰς τὸ εὐαγγέλιον cannot be taken as a genitive, as if the meaning were "on account of your participation of the gospel." This is one view of Calvin, and the opinion of Estius, Flatt, and Heinrichs, following the interpretation of Theodoret, κοινωνίαν δὲ τοῦ εὐαγγέλιον τὴν πίστιν ἐκάλεσε.

2. Some would restrict the fellowship to intercourse or community of interest with the apostle, and that in either of two aspects. The lower view is that of Bisping and others, who take the term as referring principally to giving and receiving—the pecuniary symbols of affection. The higher view is that of Chrysostom and Theophylact, who understand the word as including sympathy with the apostle in his labours and sufferings; the latter thus explaining it—ὅτι κοινωνοί μου γίνεσθε καὶ συμμερισταὶ τῶν ἐπὶ τῷ εὐαγγελίῳ πόνων. Both these views may be implied; but still they are only two indications or fruits of fellowship.

3. Nor can we wholly coincide in the opinion of Meyer, Müller, and Alford, that κοινωνία means "entire accord, unanimous action;" or as Rilliet has it, "bon accord." First, it is plain that there was a tendency in the Philippian church to faction, disunion, and jealousy. The prayer, in verse 9, that their love might abound yet more and more, is referred to by Meyer as a proof that love existed; but still such a prayer is a token that love was deficient. The pointed exhortation in i. 27, "to stand fast in one spirit, with one mind striving together;" the injunction in ii. 2, to "be like-minded, of one accord, of one mind;" the call to lowliness, and the caution against vainglory in ii. 3, 4, 5, 6, 7; the command to "do all things without murmuring," in ii. 14; the similar lesson in iii. 16, 17; and the personal request to two women to be "of the same mind," iv. 2;—all betoken that the apostle more than suspected tendencies to alienation and feud; and his joy must have been modified by the

lamented imperfection of that very grace which Meyer supposes him to select and eulogize as its principal source.

4. The noun κοινωνία, with its cognate verb and adjective, which have been variously rendered by our translators, has, for its generic idea, that of common participation. That participation may be a palpable copartnery, Luke v. 10 ; 1 Cor. x. 18 ; 2 Cor. viii. 23 ; 1 Tim. v. 22 ; Heb. ii. 14, x. 33. Or it may be participation in pecuniary generosity, Rom. xii. 13, xv. 26 ; 2 Cor. viii. 4, ix. 13 ; Gal. vi. 6 ; Phil. iv. 15 ; 1 Tim. vi. 18 ; Heb. xiii. 16. In five of these passages, Rom. xii. 13, xv. 26, 2 Cor. viii. 4, ix. 13, Heb. xiii. 16, the reference is to eleemosynary contribution, and some of them may bear an active sense. But there is also a special evangelical fellowship, which is often named, as in Rom. xv. 27, 1 Cor. i. 9, 1 John i. 3 ; and that fellowship is characterized as being of the spirit, 2 Cor. xiii. 14, Phil. ii. 1, or as being with the Son of God generally, 1 Cor. i. 9, 1 John i. 3, 6, and with His sufferings especially, Phil. iii. 10, 1 Pet. iv. 13. The noun is followed by the genitive of the thing participated in, or with εἰς, denoting its object. Winer, § 49, a. We therefore take κοινωνία in a general sense, and the following clause so closely connected with it, through the non-repetition of the article, as assigning its end or purpose. Winer, § 20, 2. Thus understood, it denotes participation, or community of interest, in whatever had the gospel for its object. All that belonged to the defence and propagation of the gospel was a matter of common concern to them—of sympathy and co-operation. The pecuniary contributions sent to the apostle and acknowledged in this epistle, are, of necessity, included. Such generally is the view of Wiesinger, Schinz, van Hengel, Hoelemann, and Ellicott, and in it on the whole we concur. For in the seventh verse the apostle seems more fully to explain his meaning, when he calls the Philippians συγκοινωνούς μου, as if in reference to the κοινωνία of the verse before us. Now the relation of that fellowship for the gospel is there described as being "in its defence and confirmation." Viewed as a Christian community, they had exhibited a fellowship in reference to the gospel—κοινωνία εἰς τὸ εὐαγγέλιον—and the apostle thanked God for it. Immediately, as he dwells on the same idea, that fellowship takes a more personal aspect,

inasmuch as it included himself in its circle—συγκοινωνούς μου—and its purpose, as he refers to his own work, assumes a more definite form, ἐν τῇ ἀπολογίᾳ καὶ βεβαιώσει τοῦ εὐαγγελίου.[1] This fellowship had continued without interruption— ἀπὸ πρώτης ἡμέρας ἄχρι τοῦ νῦν, "from the first day until now." It had not been like an intermittent spring, but like a fountain of perpetual outflow. The clause is thus connected with κοινωνία, and marks its unbroken duration. Some, like Beza and Bengel, connect it with εὐχαριστῶ—a connection which would be tautological, for the idea is expressed already; and others, as Meyer, Rilliet, and Lachmann join it to the following participle, πεποιθώς. This is also erroneous. It needs not that τῇ be repeated before ἀπὸ πρώτης any more than before εἰς τὸ εὐαγγέλιον. The apostle's purpose is to point out the ground of his thanksgiving, and to give it prominence. Remembrance excited his gratitude, but the past merged into the present, and memory and consciousness coalesced, because the fellowship was not simply a thing of days gone by, for it had lasted from its first manifestation to that very moment ; nay, its existence was proved and illustrated by the delegation of Epaphroditus to Rome. The development of the apostle's thought necessitates the connection of this clause with κοινωνία, as a " subordinate temporal definition ; " and it also starts the idea which is followed out in the subsequent verse.

(Ver. 6.) Πεποιθὼς αὐτὸ τοῦτο, ὅτι ὁ ἐναρξάμενος ἐν ὑμῖν ἔργον ἀγαθὸν, ἐπιτελέσει ἄχρις ἡμέρας Ἰησοῦ Χριστοῦ—" Being confident of this very thing, that He who has begun in you a good work, will perform it until the day of Christ Jesus." The apostle usually places πεποιθώς at the beginning of the sentence, i. 25, ii. 24, Philem. 21, 2 Cor. ii. 3, and uses other parts of the verb in a similar way. Gal. v. 10 ; Rom. ii. 19 ; 2 Thess. iii. 4 ; Heb. xiii. 18. The participle is parallel to ποιούμενος, and like it dependent on εὐχαριστῶ. He thanked and he prayed in this confidence, a confidence which at once deepened his gratitude, and gave wings of joy to his supplications. The participle may have a faint causal

---

[1] Pierce and the Improved Version render the clause, "as being joint-contributors to the gift which I have received ! "

force as Ellicott says, "seeing I am confident;" but the idea
is only auxiliary to the main one expressed in the preceding
verse. The emphatic phrase αὐτὸ τοῦτο, "this very thing,"
refers to what follows, which is the real accusative, and is
introduced by ἵνα in Eph. vi. 22, Col. iv. 8; by ὅπως in
Rom. ix. 17; and here by ὅτι. Winer, § 23, 5. The use of
the demonstrative pronouns is not, as Madvig says, § 27, a,
"to mark the contents and compass (der Inhalt und Umfang)
of the action," which is done by the clause beginning with ὅτι
—but rather to emphasize it—and show that in the writer's
mind it has a peculiar unity and prominence. The reference
in ὁ ἐναρξάμενος is to God, and is all the more impressive that
He is not formally named. The participle, though it often
takes the genitive, here governs the accusative. Kühner,
§ 512, 5. We cannot lay any stress on the preposition ἐν, in
composition with it, as may be shown by its use both in
the classics and in the Septuagint. The words ἐν ὑμῖν are
"in you," not among you, for in the following verse the
apostle records an individual judgment of them. By ἔργον
ἀγαθόν is not meant vaguely and generally a work of faith
and love, as a-Lapide and Matthies suppose; but that special
good work, that κοινωνία, which the apostle has just particu-
larized. The article is not prefixed, but the reference is
plain. That fellowship is a work divine in its source, and
bears the stamp of its originator. He who began it will
carry it on—ἐπιτελέσει, and that—ἄχρις ἡμέρας Χριστοῦ
Ἰησοῦ. The position of these proper names is reversed in
some codices. The expression is not to be frittered down into
a mere perpetuo, as Am Ende does, nor can we agree with
Theophylact and Œcumenius, in supposing the apostle to
include in the phrase, successive generations of those whom
he addressed. The period of consummation specified by the
apostle has been much disputed. The opinion is very common
that the second and personal advent of the Saviour is meant,
the apostle believing that it was to happen soon, and in his
own day. Without passing a definite and dogmatic opinion
on the subject, we may only say, that we cannot well comprehend how an inspired man should have been permitted to
teach a falsehood, not simply to give it as his own private
judgment or belief, but to place it on record, authoritatively,

among the true sayings of God. The day of Christ is His
return; but may it not be such a return as He promised to
the Eleven at the Last Supper, "I will come again and receive
you unto myself"? The apostle's confidence that their united
public spirit would continue, rested on his knowledge of God's
character and methods of operation. The good work originated
by Him is not suffered to lapse, but is fostered and blessed
till His end be accomplished. His own connection with the
work, and its inherent goodness, pledge Him to the continuation of it. So wayward and feeble is the human heart, even
when it binds itself by a stipulation, or fortifies itself by a
vow, that had this fellowship depended on themselves, the
apostle would have had no confidence in its duration. His
sad experience had shown him that men might repeat follies
even while they were weeping over them, and engage anew
in sins, while they were in the act of abjuring them. On
the other hand, and to his deep vexation, had he seen graces
languish amidst professed anxiety for their revival, and good
works all but disappear under the admitted necessity of their
continuance and enlargement.

Those who maintain the doctrine of the perseverance of the
saints, take proof from this verse, though certainly without un-
disputed warrant, and it must be in the form of development;
for it refers to a particular action, and is not in itself a general
statement of a principle; and those who oppose this tenet are
as anxious to escape from the alleged inference. The Fathers
of the Council of Trent qualify the statement by the addition,
nisi ipsi homines illius gratiæ defuerint. Beelen, professor of
the Oriental Languages in the Catholic University of Louvain,
gives the verse this turn or twist, *confido fore ut Deus perficiat,
hoc est, confido fore ut vos per Dei gratiam perficiatis opus bonum
quod cœpistis.* Such a perversion is not much better than
Wakefield's, who translates, "he among you who has begun a
good work, will continue to do well till death." Nor, in fine,
can we say with Œcumenius, that the apostle ascribes the
work to God, ἵνα μὴ φρονῶσι μέγα, "lest they should be
filled with too much pride." He had a higher motive in
giving utterance to the precious truth, that what is good in
the church, has its root and life in God, that therefore He
is to be thanked for it, as is most due, and that prayer is to

be offered joyously about it, in the assurance that He who
began it will not capriciously desert it, but will carry it
forward to maturity. It is εὐχαριστῶ—δέησιν ποιούμενος—
πεποιθώς. The apostle now proceeds to vindicate the assertion
which he had made.

(Ver. 7.) Καθώς ἐστι δίκαιον ἐμοὶ τοῦτο φρονεῖν ὑπὲρ πάντων ὑμῶν—"Even as it is right for me to think this on
behalf of you all." The form καθώς, from καθά, καθό, belongs
to the later Greek (Phrynichus, Lobeck, p. 426), and is
probably of Alexandrian origin. Matt. xxi. 6; Eph. i. 4;
1 Cor. i. 6. The verb is not "to care for," as Wolf contends,
nor, as van Hengel thinks, is it to be confined to the prayer—
"sine scrupulo interpretamur sicuti me decet hoc vobis omnibus
appetere; scilicet, omni cura et precibus." In the interpretation
of Storr, followed by Hoelemann, the accusative τοῦτο simply
expresses manner—"I give thanks to God, and offer prayer
for all of you with joy, as indeed it becomes me thus to think
concerning you." But it refers to the good opinion already
expressed in the previous verse—αὐτὸ τοῦτο. By the use of
ὑπέρ the apostle indicates that his opinion was favourable to
them, and by δίκαιον he characterizes that opinion as one
which it behoved him in the circumstances to entertain. Col.
iv. i; Eph. vi. 1. The mode of expression in classic Greek
would be different—δίκαιός ἐγώ εἰμι, Herodotus, i. 32; and
δίκαιόν ἐστιν ἐμέ, Herodotus, i. 39; Jelf, § 669, 677.

διὰ τὸ ἔχειν με ἐν τῇ καρδίᾳ ὑμᾶς—"because I have you
in my heart"—the heart being the seat or organ of affection.
2 Cor. vii. 3. Am Ende, Oeder, Storr, and Rosenmüller,
reverse this interpretation—"Because you have me in your
heart." The position of the pronouns may warrant such a
translation; but the apostle is writing of himself and of his
relation to the church in Philippi. The expression denotes
strong affection—as in Latin, in sinu gestare, Terent. Adelph.
iv. 5, 75; or, as in Ovid's Trist. v. 2, 24, Te tamen in toto
pectore semper habet. The apostle vindicates the favourable
opinion he had formed of them from his love to them, as
standing in a special relation towards him. Though this
opinion sprang from his affection, it was still a right one—
δίκαιον—and not one formed merely secundum legem caritatis,
as van Hengel and Ellicott suppose.

The connection of the next clause is matter of dispute:—

ἔν τε τοῖς δεσμοῖς μου, καὶ ἐν τῇ ἀπολογίᾳ καὶ βεβαιώσει τοῦ εὐαγγελίου, συγκοινωνούς μου τῆς χάριτος πάντας ὑμᾶς ὄντας—" both in my bonds and in the defence and confirmation of the gospel, you all as being partakers with me of grace." Chrysostom, Meyer, De Wette, and Alford join the first clause to the preceding one:—" Because I have you in my heart both in my bonds and in the defence and confirmation of the gospel." The sense is tolerable; but it does not harmonize with the course of thought. To say that he loves them in his bonds, and when he pleaded the cause of the gospel, is not assigning a reason why he thought so highly of them—πεποιθώς—but to say that they were partakers of his grace both in his bonds and in his evangelical labours, and as such beloved by him, is a proof that he was justified in forming and expressing such a good opinion and anticipation of them. He had thanked God for the κοινωνία εἰς τὸ εὐαγγέλιον; and being assured that such a good work was divine in its origin, and would be carried on till the day of Christ, it became him to give utterance to this thought, on account of the affection he bore to them as participants with him of grace.

The apostle calls them συγκοινωνούς μου τῆς χάριτος πάντας ὑμᾶς ὄντας—" all of you as being fellow-partakers with me of grace." The reading *gaudii* in the Vulgate, and some Latin fathers, comes from the reading χαρᾶς. The repetition of ὑμᾶς, though such a form is not used by the most correct writers (Bernhardy, 275), is only pleonastic in appearance, but really emphatic in nature, and made necessary by the length of the intervening sentence and the use of πάντας. Matthiae, § 465, 4. The pronoun μου is most probably connected with the adjective συγκοινωνούς, and not as by Rilliet with χάριτος; so that the rendering will not be as Alford gives it—" partakers of my grace," but rather " partakers with me of grace." Matthiae, § 325; § 405, 1. The construction of two genitives of different relations with a noun does not often happen. Winer, § 30, 3. The χάρις is certainly not, as Rilliet makes it, *reconnaissance*, " acknowledgments "—and as certainly not the apostolic office, as Am Ende and Flatt take it—both explanations quite foreign to the order of thought. Nor can we understand the term simply and broadly of the grace of the gospel, as is done by Robinson, Hoelemann, Heinrichs, De Wette, and Alford. The previous clause limits the grace, or decides it to be that form of grace which is appropriate to imprisonment and evangelical labour. But we cannot, with Chrysostom, Calvin, Grotius, Estius, Rheinwald, and Meyer, restrict it to suffering, as we hold that the χάρις refers equally to ἀπολογία with δεσμοῖς, for the fellowship, which is the leading idea, was not confined to suffering, but had existed from the first day to the present, and that entire period was not one of unbroken tribulation to the apostle. It is true that at that moment the apostle was in bonds, and in those bonds did defend and confirm the truth. But the idea seems to be that they had been co-partakers of his grace in evangelical labour, and that such participation with him did not cease, even though he was a prisoner in Rome. For he says :—

ἔν τε τοῖς δεσμοῖς μου—" both in my bonds ;" and he adds—

καὶ ἐν τῇ ἀπολογίᾳ καὶ βεβαιώσει τοῦ εὐαγγελίου, " and in the defence and confirmation of the gospel." The use of τε—καί, indicates that the two clauses contain separate ideas, and that the one preceded by καί has the stress laid on it. Hartung, i. 98 ; Klotz, Devarius, ii. 740 ; Winer, § 53, 4. The genitive belongs to both substantives, which are not synonymous as Rheinwald supposes, and do not form a hendiadys as Am Ende and Heinrichs regard them — ἀπολογίᾳ εἰς βεβαίωσιν. The words are distinct in sense ; the first meaning a pleading or defence as before a tribunal, Acts xxii. 1, xxv. 16 ; or in a less authoritative mode, 1 Cor. ix. 3, 1 Pet. iii. 15. It is needless to restrict the meaning to such a formal defence as is recorded in 2 Tim. iv. 16. It was the apostle's uniform work, on all times and occasions, to answer for the gospel against its adversaries, whether they impugned its doctrines or suspected its tendencies, libelled its preachers or called in question the facts and evidences on which it rested. But, as the non-repetition of the article shows, the defence and confirmation were closely connected, were but different aspects of one course of action. The first was more elementary, and the last more positive and advanced—the first warded off objections, and the second might consist of proofs. The confirmation resulted from the defence. The gospel stood out in power and demonstration, when its opponents were silenced, and the objections brought against it, no matter from what quarter, found to be groundless. That grace which had enabled the apostle to bear his chain, and to defend and confirm the gospel, was common to the Philippians with himself; therefore did he cherish them in his heart, and thank God for such fellowship. And he appends a further vindication of his sentiment.

(Ver. 8.) Μάρτυς γάρ μου ὁ Θεός—" For God is my witness." The Stephanic text adds ἐστίν, on the authority of A, D, E, J, K, and many mss. and versions, and we are inclined to receive it, though it be wanting in B, F, G. True, its insertion by a transcriber appears like a natural completion of the common formula, but the balance of evidence is in its favour. The apostle appeals to the Searcher of hearts for the truth of his statements. It was not the language of courteous exaggeration, nor that intensity of phrase in which common friendship so often clothes itself, never dreaming that its words are to be literally interpreted. But the apostle wrote only the truth—his words were the coinage of his heart. Rom. i. 9 ; 1 Thess. ii. 5. " God is my witness "—

ὡς ἐπιποθῶ πάντας ὑμᾶς ἐν σπλάγχνοις Χριστοῦ Ἰησοῦ— "how I long for you all in the bowels of Christ Jesus." The order of the proper names is inverted in the received text. The particle ὡς may either introduce the fact of the apostle's longing, or may indicate its intensity. It may be either " that," or " how much." The strong language of the verse may decide for the latter, against Rilliet and Müller. The apostle wishes them to know not so much the fact as the earnestness of his longings. Chrysostom says beautifully— οὐ τοίνυν δυνατὸν εἰπεῖν πῶς ἐπιποθῶ· οὐ γὰρ δύναμαι παραστῆσαι τῷ λόγῳ τὸν πόθον. The verb is sometimes followed by an infinitive, as in Rom. i. 11, 2 Cor. v. 2 ; occasionally by πρός ; but here by the accusative of person, as in 2 Cor. ix. 14, Phil. ii. 26. He does not indicate any special blessing he craved for them ; he longed after themselves. They were the objects of his warmest affection, and though he was absent from them, he yearned toward them—a proof surely that he had them in his heart. The simple form of the verb is not found in the New Testament, and this compound form represents more than one Hebrew word in the Septuagint. Ἐπί, as in some other compound verbs, does not intensify the meaning, but rather indicates direction—πόθον ἔχειν ἐπί τινα. Fritzsche, *ad Rom.* vol. i. p. 30, 31 ;[1] Winer, § 30, 10, (*b*). The verb is diluted in meaning, if it be regarded as signifying only to love ; though in Ps. cxix. 131 it represents the Hebrew אֵב.

And the mode is described by the following clause :— ἐν σπλάγχνοις Χ. Ἰ., " in the bowels of Christ Jesus." For the usage of σπλάγχνα, see under Col. iii. 12. The strange peculiarity of this phrase has led not a few to weaken its force. We wonder that Storr should have taken up the opinion that σπλάγχνα may mean objects of love, and ἐν be equivalent to *tanquam*—" I love you as being the objects of the love of Christ Jesus." Such a rendering has not a shadow of support. At the other extreme is the view of Hoelemann, that the words mean, " as the Lord loves His own." Nor is Χ. Ἰ. the genitive of object—" I love you with a heart glowing with love to Christ ; " nor yet that of origin—" I love you with an affection originated by Christ." Nor can we assent to Rilliet, who gives ἐν the sense of " after the manner of,"— I love you after the model of Christ—*tel étant ;* or, as van Hengel paraphrases, *in animo penitus affecto, ut animus fuit Christi Jesu ;* or, as Beza has it, *teneri et materni affectûs.* We agree with Meyer, that ἐν retains its local sense, and that the apostle identifies himself with Christ, as in Gal. ii. 20, " Christ liveth in me." The Christian nature of that longing he felt for them is expressed by this striking clause ; for he had the heart of Christ within him, and under its impulses he fondly yearned over his Philippian converts. As Beelen, abridging Bengel, says, *in pectore Pauli non tam ipsius quam*

---

[1] Fritzsche says that in the fourth dialogue of Lucian, the simple and compound verbs are used indiscriminately—*promiscue ponuntur.* We are inclined to demur to this statement. Ganymede says of his father—ποθῶ γὰρ ἤδη αὐτόν—and Jupiter afterwards tells him, that if he tasted nectar, he would never desire milk again—οὐκ ἔτι ποθήσεις τὸ γάλα. But when Jupiter bids him be of good courage and be merry, and long no more for earth, he says—καὶ μηδὲν ἐπιπόθει τῶν κάτω. That is to say, the use of ἐπί to denote direction, gives a slight force to the meaning—this pointing of the verb by means of the preposition towards its object, indicates additional emotion.

Christi cor palpitabat. Krause, Grotius, Hoog, and Heinrichs approach this sense, but lose its point when they give as the general meaning, *amorem vere Christianum.*

(Ver. 9.) The apostle had shown them what kind desires he felt towards them, and what joyous anticipations he cherished for them. He had also intimated that he uniformly prayed for them, and he now proceeds to tell them the substance of his prayer.

Καὶ τοῦτο προσεύχομαι ἵνα—" And this I pray that." The καί may look back to verse 4, or it may be regarded simply as connecting the two statements—his opinion about them, and his prayer for them. There is no ground for Rilliet's and Müller's idea that προσεύχομαι depends on ὡς, as does ἐπι-ποθῶ. Quite a new sentiment is started, and the preceding verse winds up and corroborates the ardent expressions which go before it. The accusative τοῦτο gives emphasis to the theme of petition in itself, and that petition, viewed in its purpose, is preceded by ἵνα, as often occurs. There is little doubt that the contents of the prayer are also so far indicated by the conjunction. To pray for this end is not very different from to pray for this thing.

His prayer was on this wise—

ἵνα ἡ ἀγάπη ὑμῶν ἔτι μᾶλλον καὶ μᾶλλον περισσεύῃ ἐν ἐπι-γνώσει καὶ πάσῃ αἰσθήσει—"that your love may abound yet more and more in knowledge and in all judgment." Love existed among them, but yet it was deficient, if not in itself, yet in some endowments. The precise nature of this love has been variously understood. Strange is the freak of Bullinger and others, that ἡ ἀγάπη ὑμῶν is, as in old ecclesiastical language, the abstract used for a concrete, and simply a form of address—"I pray, beloved, that ye may grow yet more and more." Suicer, *sub voce.*

1. Some take it for love to the apostle himself, as do the Greek fathers, with Grotius and van Hengel. But the epithets which follow could not apply to a mere personal attachment.

2. Nor can we, with Calovius and others, take it as love to God and Christ, as that is not specially the grace in question.

3. Neither can we, with others, regard it as love to God and men—Christian love in its high and comprehensive essence and form, for we think that the context specifies its province

and mode of operation. Alford and Meyer are right in referring it to κοινωνία ; but as they restrict the meaning of this word to mutual accord, so they regard ἀγάπη as only signifying love to one another. We give κοινωνία a more extensive meaning, and consider ἀγάπη as its root and sustaining power. It is love for Christ's image and Christ's work—for all that represents Him on earth—His people and His cause ; that holy affection which, while it unites all in whom it dwells, impels them to sympathize with all suffering, and co-operate with all effort, in connection with the defence and confirmation of the gospel. Such is general'y also the view of Ellicott and Wiesinger. The apostle prayed that their love might grow— ἐν ἐπιγνώσει καὶ πάσῃ αἰσθήσει. The two substantives are not synonymous, as Rheinwald and Matthies hold. There is no ground for Bisping's distinction of them, that the first signifies more theoretical, and the other more practical knowledge. The first substantive denotes accurate knowledge. See under Eph. i. 17. The second, which occurs only here, means power of perception. Physically, it denotes perception by the senses, especially that of touch ; and in the plural, it signifies the organs of such perception—the senses themselves. The transition to a spiritual meaning such as that of apprehension is obvious. See under Col. i. 9. It might be rendered ethical tact, that faculty of moral discernment which is quick and unerring in its judgment, and by a peculiar insight arrives easily and surely at its conclusions. It is not experimental or practical knowledge, as some have thought; but that faculty of discernment which works as if from an inner sense. A similar allusion is made by the apostle in Heb. v. 14, where he describes such as have their senses exercised to discern both good and evil—τὰ αἰσθητήρια. The apostle adds πάσῃ, all discernment. We regard πάσῃ as intensive, and cannot agree with those who seem to deny that it rarely, if ever, has such a meaning. In these two elements, the apostle prayed that their love should grow yet more and more —ἔτι μᾶλλον καὶ μᾶλλον. Pindar, *Pyth.* 10, 88 ; Raphel. *in loc.* The ἐν does not signify "through," as Heinrichs and Schinz take it, nor does it mean "along with," as Rheinwald and Hoelemann suppose. Winer, § 50, 5. For ἐν following περισσεύω usually points out that in which the increase

consists. 1 Cor. xv. 58; 2 Cor. iii. 9, viii. 7; Col. ii. 7.
Their love was to increase in these qualities, knowledge and
insight. De Wette takes ἐν as denoting manner and way.
But in only one of the instances adduced by him does this
verb occur (Eph. i. 8), and there the connection is doubtful.
The apostle's desire was that the love of the Philippians
might acquire a profounder knowledge, and not be tempted
to misplace itself, and that it might attain a sharper and
clearer discernment, and so be prevented from being squandered
on unworthy subjects, or directed to courses of conduct which
had the semblance but not the reality of Christian rectitude
and utility. If love grew in mere capacity, and without
the increase of these safeguards, it was in hazard of forming
unworthy and profitless attachments. Passion, without such
guides or feelers, is but blind predilection. "Fellowship for
the gospel" is still the thought in the apostle's mind, and that
love which had led them to it, needed for its stability a deeper
knowledge of the truths which characterized the gospel, and
required for its development a clearer faculty of apprehending
the character of the men best qualified, and the measures best
adapted to its "defence and confirmation." One purpose was—
(Ver. 10.) Εἰς τὸ δοκιμάζειν ὑμᾶς τὰ διαφέροντα—ἵνα—"So
that ye may distinguish things that differ." Two purposes are
specified in this verse, the nearer expressed by εἰς τό, and the
ultimate by ἵνα. Commentators differ as to the meaning of
the clause, and philologically the words will bear either interpretation. They have been supposed to mean, as in our
version, to "approve the things that are excellent," as in the
Vulgate—ut probetis potiora. This view has been espoused
by Chrysostom, Erasmus, Estius, Piscator, Bengel, Flatt, Storr,
Am Ende, Rosenmüller, Rheinwald, Rilliet, Meyer, Bisping,
Beelen, and Ellicott. On the other hand, the translation we
have first given, is adopted by Theodoret, Beza, Wolf, Pierce,
Heinrichs, Matthiae, van Hengel, Hoelemann, Hoog, Müller,
De Wette, Wiesinger, Alford, Robinson, Bretschneider, and
Wahl. In itself the difference is not material; for this discrimination is made among things that differ, just that things
which are excellent may be approved. But as discrimination
is the immediate function of αἴσθησις, we prefer giving such
a signification to the clause. The verb δοκιμάζειν denotes to

try or test, as metal by fire—1 Cor. iii. 13—and then generally to distinguish as the result of such trial, and thence to approve. Rom. xiv. 22 ; 1 Cor. xvi. 3 ; 1 Thess. ii. 4. In the phrase τὰ διαφέροντα, difference is the prime idea, but as such difference is based on comparison or contrast, the secondary notion of betterness, value, or excellence, is naturally developed. Matt. x. 31, xii. 12 ; Luke xii. 7, 24. In these three passages the comparison is distinctly brought out, and the difference idiomatically marked. Some even render the word by συμφέροντα—things which are useful or convenient, *utilia*. We prefer, then, the ordinary meaning of the terms. See Bretschneider, *sub voce* διαφέρω, and Theophylact on Rom. ii. 18, where he thus explains the word—κρίνειν τὶ δεῖ πρᾶξαι καὶ τὶ μὴ δεῖ πρᾶξαι.

The final purpose is thus announced by ἵνα—

ἵνα ἦτε εἰλικρινεῖς καὶ ἀπρόσκοποι—" that ye may be pure and offenceless." The composition of the first term is disputed, whether it be εἴλη κρίνω, to prove by the sunlight, or εἶλος [εἴλη] κρίνω, to test by rapid shaking, *volubili agitatione*. The former opinion is usually adopted, though Stallbaum[1] contends for the latter. Hesychius renders the term by τὸ καθαρόν, ἄδολον, and sometimes it is defined by τὸ ἀμιγές. Whatever be its derivation, its meaning is apparent. It refers to internal disposition, to the absence of sinister motive and divided allegiance, or it describes the purity and sincerity of that heart which is guided by the spiritual tact and discriminative power which the apostle prays for.

The epithet ἀπρόσκοποι is taken sometimes in an active sense, not causing others to stumble, as in 1 Cor. x. 32. Meyer adopts this view, and Alford's objection to it cannot be sustained, viz., " that in the text *other men* are not in question." For the leading term ἀγάπη necessarily implies other men as its objects, and that κοινωνία in which it embodies itself, has other men as its allies and auxiliaries. While the intransitive meaning gives a good sense, we are inclined to Meyer's view, inasmuch as the possession of love, and the growth of it in knowledge and discernment, would prevent them from rudely jostling others not of their own opinion, or doing anything which, with a good intention, might mislead

[1] Plato, *Phaedo*, 77, A.

E

or throw a stumbling-block in the path of those round about them.

It is needless, with Ewald and others, to give a wholly doctrinal sense to τὰ διαφέροντα, though it would be wrong to exclude it altogether. Love without that guidance which has been referred to, might form unworthy attachments, might wound itself in its blindness, and retard the very interests for the promotion of which it had eagerly set itself. It must understand the gospel in its purity, and learn to detect unwarranted additions and supplements. It must have tact to distinguish between the real and the seeming, between the claims of an evangelist, and the specious pretensions of a Judaizer. And, thus, if that love which had shown itself in fellowship for the gospel, grew in knowledge and power of perception, they would be pure; their affection ruled by intelligence would have but one desire, to defend and confirm the gospel, in participation of the apostle's own grace; and they would give no offence, either by a zeal which in its excess forgot the means in the end, or cherished suspicions of such as did not come up to its own warmth, or could not sympathize with its favourite modes of operation or expression.

εἰς ἡμέραν Χριστοῦ—" for the day of Christ." More than time is implied. Verse 6, ἄχρις. The day of Christ is kept in view, and this sincerity and offencelessness prepare for it, and lead to acceptance in it.

(Ver. 11.) Πεπληρωμένοι καρπὸν δικαιοσύνης τὸν διὰ ᾽Ιησοῦ Χριστοῦ, εἰς δόξαν καὶ ἔπαινον Θεοῦ. The singular form καρπὸν τόν, is preferred to the plural of the Received Text on preponderant authority. " Being filled with the fruit of righteousness, which is by Jesus Christ to the glory and praise of God." The passive participle has καρπόν in the accusative, Winer, § 32, 5, though the genitive is also found, as in Rom. xv. 14. The difference of aspect seems to be that the genitive marks that out of which the fulness is made up, while the accusative points out that on which the action of the verb takes effect in making up the fulness, and not simply that, as Ellicott says, toward which the action tends. On κάρπος, see Eph. v. 9; Col. i. 9. The meaning of δικαιοσύνη is not so clear. Some, like Rilliet and Bisping, refer it to justification. That idea is involved in it; but the term, without any adjunct, and as applied to character, seems to signify moral rectitude, and is noted by its obedience to the divine law. Rom. v. 7, vi. 13. See under Eph. v. 9. The fruit which springs from this righteousness is to be possessed not sparingly, but richly; and for such fulness does the apostle present his prayer. His pleading for them is, that their life might not be marked merely by the absence of insincerity and offence, but that they might be adorned with all such Christian graces as result from the new nature—the deeds which characterize the "new man created in righteousness." And this was the last subject or purpose of the petition; for love increasing in knowledge and spiritual discernment, knowing what genuine obedience is, and what is but the semblance of it, appreciating the gospel and cherishing communion with those who oftentimes in suffering extend and uphold it, keeping the day of Christ in view and preparing for it—moves and enables the whole nature to "bring forth fruit unto holiness."

And such fruit is not self-produced, but is—

διὰ ᾽Ιησοῦ Χριστοῦ—"by Jesus Christ," in and through His gracious operations upon the heart by His Spirit. Righteousness is of His creation, and all the fruits of it are through Him, not by His doctrine or by faith in Him, but through Himself. The apostle emphasizes this element τὸν—διὰ ᾽I. X.

The phrase εἰς δόξαν καὶ ἔπαινον Θεοῦ—"to the glory and praise of God," does not seem to belong to the previous words merely, but to the entire clause. The being filled with such fruits of righteousness—fruits grown only through Christ, redounds to the glory and praise of God—the ultimate end of all His works. Glory is the manifestation of His nature and character, and praise is that grateful homage which salutes it on the part of His people. Eph. i. 6; Phil. ii. 11. We can scarcely suppose with the Greek fathers, that the apostle, with such thoughts and emotions in his soul, tacitly forms in this clause a contrast between any merit that might be imagined to belong to him as founder and teacher of the Philippian church, and the glory which is due to God alone.

After this affectionate greeting, commendation, and prayer, the apostle turns to his present condition. As the Philippians were aware of his imprisonment, he strives at once to console them by the assurance that his bonds had rather favoured than retarded the progress of the gospel—for the cause and nature of his incarceration had not only become widely known, but the greater part of the brethren had derived fresh courage from his captivity for the more abundant proclamation of the word. There was, indeed, a party hostile to him, who preached Christ to give him new annoyance; but these others did it from affection to him, and in co-operation with his great work. So far, however, from being chafed or grieved that his antagonists preached from so bad a motive, he rejoiced that Christ was preached in any way; and he would still continue to rejoice, since it would contribute to his salvation through their prayers, and the supply of the Divine Spirit. For he had the expectation and hope, that he would have no reason to take shame to himself; but that, on the other hand, Christ should be magnified in his body, whether he should survive or die—magnified, in the one case, because for him to live was Christ; and magnified, in the other case, for death was gain: his life, if prolonged, being service for Christ, and his death the enjoyment of Christ's presence and reward. So that he did not know which to choose—death on the one hand being in itself preferable, for it is being with Christ; but life on the other hand being needful for the spiritual benefit of the Philippian church. Finally, the apostle intimates his persuasion that he shall remain, in order to aid their Christian graces, so that they might have ground of spiritual exultation by his return to them.

(Ver. 12.) Γινώσκειν δὲ ὑμᾶς βούλομαι, ἀδελφοί—" But I wish you to know, brethren." By the use of δέ, the apostle passes on to new and individual matter—to his own present condition and its results. No doubt the members of the Philippian church sympathized with him, bewailed his thraldom, and earnestly prayed for his liberation. Perhaps they had expressed a wish for definite information from himself. Therefore, as far as possible, he relieves their anxieties, takes an elevated and cheering view of his circumstances, and assures them that his incarceration had rather forwarded the great cause to which his life had been directed. He is solicitous that they should be acquainted with a few striking facts —γινώσκειν—placing the term in the first and emphatic position. The more usual forms of similar expression are found in Rom. i. 13 ; 1 Cor. xii. 1 ; 2 Cor. i. 8 ; 1 Thess. iv. 13. What he proceeds to tell must have been both novel and gratifying to those saluted by the endearing appellation— " brethren." For he announces—

ὅτι τὰ κατ᾽ ἐμὲ μᾶλλον εἰς προκοπὴν τοῦ εὐαγγελίου ἐλή-λυθεν—" that things with me have resulted rather to the furtherance of the gospel." The phrase κατ᾽ ἐμέ, as in Eph. vi. 21, Col. iv. 7, signifies " what belongs to me "—my present condition. It does not signify " things against me," as Erasmus and others suppose. For a somewhat similar use of the verb, see Rom. iii. 8. The phrase seems to intimate an overruling providence, for it was by no accident that the event was so, and his enemies did not intend it. In the use of μᾶλλον, the idea of comparison is not wholly dropt. Winer, § 35, 4. His imprisonment must have been considered in itself as adverse to the propagation of the gospel ; and the comparison in μᾶλλον is—more than might have been anticipated. Imprisonment had defeated its purpose, and, so far from suppressing, had promoted Christianity. It was not meant to do this, nor yet was it expected ; but he says ἐλήλυθεν, " it has so turned out." Wisd. xv. 5. " Surely the wrath of man shall praise Thee." The term προκοπή belongs to the later Greek, though the verb προκόπτειν was of classical usage. Lobeck, ad Phryn. 85 ; 1 Tim. iv. 15. Hesychius defines it by αὔξησις. The word occurs often in Plutarch, Polybius, Diodorus, Josephus, and Philo. Compare Elsner, Loesner, especially Wetstein, in loc. When the Philippians were made aware of this fact, their sorrow at his captivity would be somewhat modified, and though they might grieve at the confinement of the man, they would be comforted that the cause with which he was identified had not been arrested in its progress. In the last chapter of the epistle, he tells them that, personally, he was content ; and here he assures them that the word of the Lord was not bound along with its preacher. Nowhere does he commiserate his condition, dwell on the weight of his chain, or deal out invectives against his foes. He omits the purely personal, and hastens to set before his readers the features of alleviation. What happened then at Rome has often occurred in the history of the church ;

hostile influences ultimately contributing to the advancement of the church. Man proposes, but God disposes. The cloud, while it obscures the sun, sends down the fertilizing shower. The first effect of his imprisonment is next given—

(Ver. 13.) Ὥστε τοὺς δεσμούς μου φανεροὺς ἐν Χριστῷ γενέσθαι ἐν ὅλῳ τῷ πραιτωρίῳ καὶ τοῖς λοιποῖς πᾶσιν—" So that my bonds have become known in Christ in the whole prætorium, and to all the rest." The conjunction ὥστε is followed by the infinitive denoting result, and, as often happens, no demonstrative precedes. On the difference of ὥστε with the infinitive, and with the indicative, see Klotz, Devarius, ii. p. 772. The apostle gives a first result of his present condition, which tended to forward the gospel. The cause of his imprisonment had come to be known widely, and such knowledge could not be without its fruits. We agree with Meyer and Wiesinger that the words φανεροὺς ἐν X. must be connected—" made manifest in Christ." The position of the terms seems to demand this connection—and not such an arrangement as τοὺς δεσμούς μου ἐν X., as De Wette construes it. "In Christ" is, in connection with Christ, Eph. iv. 1. His incarceration had come to be understood in its connection with Christ; not surely the fact of it, but the cause and character of it. Waiting under an appeal to the emperor, he had been discovered to be no common prisoner. It had transpired that his official connection with Christ, and his fearless prosecution of the work of Christ, had led to his apprehension and previous trial in Palestine, and not sedition, turbulence, or suspected loyalty—the usual political crimes of his nation. It was widely known that he suffered as a Christian and as an apostle, especially as the preacher of a free and unconditioned gospel to the Gentiles. And his bonds were naturally made manifest in Christ, first in the edifice where he dwelt—

ἐν ὅλῳ τῷ πραιτωρίῳ. Our translators adopted a common idea in rendering πραιτώριον by palace. In this they followed the Greek commentators—one of whom says, "For up to that time they so called the palace." Erasmus, Beza, Estius, a-Lapide, Bengel, and Rheinwald hold, with some variation, the same opinion. The word does sometimes, in a general way, signify the palace of a king, as in Juvenal x. 161—

sedet ad prœtoria regis. Also in Act. Thom. § 3, we have the
phrase πραιτώρια βασιλικά. Others, from its name, have
supposed it to be the judgment-hall of the prætor. So Luther
renders it, "Richthaus," and he is followed by the early
English translators, as by Wycliffe, who gives "in eche moot
halle." The word is so used in the Gospels, in connection
with the scene of our Lord's trial, Matt. xxvii. 27; Mark xv.
16, etc. Cicero refers to Verres as dwelling *in domo prœtorio,
quœ regis Hieronis fuit.* Thus Huber, Calvin, Grotius, Rheinwald, and Mynster, regard it as a part of the royal edifice—
urbanum juri dicendo auditorium. The noun thus denoted
sometimes the dwelling of a provincial governor—nay, it
came to signify a magnificent private building (*alternas servant
prœtoria ripas,* Statius, S. 1, 3, 25), much in the same way
that a Glasgow merchant, building a turreted summer residence
on some rock or eminence on the western coast, dignifies it
by the name of a "castle." But the palace of the Roman
emperor was never called prætorium. The noun signifies
here, the *castra prœtoriana*—the barracks of the imperial life-
guards. The tent of the commander-in-chief was originally
called the *prœtorium*—head-quarters; and a council of war,
from being held there, received the same designation—(*prœtorio
dimisso,* Livy, xxx. 5). The name was ultimately given to
the imperial body-guards, and was naturally transferred to
the edifice in Rome which contained them. It was built by
Sejanus, not far from the *Porta Viminalis.* The cohorts were
stationed there, who did duty in turn at the imperial residence.
The emperor himself was regarded as prætor, the immediate
commanding-officer being called *prœfectus prœtorio,*[1] and in
Greek στρατοπεδάρχης. Thus we read, that when Paul was
brought to Rome, ὁ ἑκατόνταρχος παρέδωκε τοὺς δεσμίους τῷ
στρατοπεδάρχῃ, Acts xxviii. 16. Such an office was at this
time held by Burrus, and the apostle was probably committed
to his charge. A portion of this military mansion was close
upon the palace, or *domus palatina*—παλάτιον—of which it
is said, that in it ὁ Καῖσαρ ᾤκει καὶ ἐκεῖ τὸ στρατήγιον εἶχε,

---

[1] This meaning was first vindicated by Perizonius in an academic tract on the
subject, Franeker, 1687. Huber produced a reply in the following year, and
Mynster attempts to vindicate a similar view in his *Kleine Theol. Schriften,*
p. 178, Copenhagen, 1825.

Dio Cassius, liii. 16. Suetonius, *Octav.* 49. Drusus, we are
told by the last author, when imprisoned in the prætorium,
was located *in ima parte palatii.* A large camp of the prætorian guards was also established outside the walls—(*castra
prætorianorum,* Tacitus, *Hist.* i. 31); but those on immediate
duty had their residence near the royal dwelling. It may be
added, that Josephus carefully distinguishes between the
palace and the prætorium, between the Βασίλειον and that
στρατόπεδον in which Agrippa was imprisoned under a
military guard. Thus, the soldiers who relieved one another
in keeping the apostle, came to learn that he was no vulgar
malefactor, but that he had been the expounder of a new
faith—a man of pure and irreproachable life—no fanatic or
leveller, or selfish demagogue. And there is no doubt that
many of them must have been impressed with his serene
heroism, and the visible peace of his untroubled conscience,
as he waited for a trial which might send him to the block.
And the cause of his imprisonment was not only known in
the whole prætorium, but beyond it—

καὶ τοῖς λοιποῖς πᾶσιν—" and to all the rest;" not simply
to others of the body-guards, more than those which came into
contact with him, or to those of the cohort beyond the city, as
Wieseler and Conybeare narrow the allusion, but to persons
beyond the prætorium. Nor does the language refer to places,
as some of the Greek fathers suppose, when they supply ἐν.
Neither can τοῖς λοιποῖς have any conventional signification,
such as that which van Hengel assigns it—*hominibus exteris
quibuscunque.* The texts referred to by him cannot for a
moment sustain his strange exegesis. The expression is a
popular and broad one, meaning that his bonds were made
known in Christ, far beyond the imperial barracks; that in a
large circle in the city itself, the reason of his incarceration
was fully comprehended and appreciated. How, indeed, could
it be otherwise? Immediately on his arrival, he assembled
the chiefs of the Jews, and addressed them in a style which
led to no little disputation among themselves; and we are
told, also, that for the space of two years, the apostle
" received all that came in unto him, preaching the kingdom
of God, and teaching those things which concern the Lord
Jesus Christ with all confidence, no man forbidding him."

Acts xxviii. 30, 31. The second result of his imprisonment follows.

(Ver. 14.) Καὶ τοὺς πλείονας τῶν ἀδελφῶν ἐν Κυρίῳ πεποιθότας τοῖς δεσμοῖς μου, περισσοτέρως τολμᾶν ἀφόβως τὸν λόγον λαλεῖν—" And the greater part of the brethren putting in the Lord confidence in my bonds, are more abundantly bold to speak the word without fear." This verse represents another result of the apostle's imprisonment, and shows how it rather tended to the progress of the gospel. He is happy in the majority; his imprisonment had an inspiriting effect on them. The words ἐν Κυρίῳ may be joined to ἀδελφῶν, as they are by Luther, van Hengel, De Wette, and Alford; but, more probably, as Winer—§ 20, 2—suggests, they qualify the participle πεποιθότας, Gal. v. 10; Phil. ii. 24; 2 Thess. iii. 4; and so Rilliet, Meyer, and Bisping take them. The words denote having, or taking confidence in the Lord. The phrase ἐν Κυρίῳ does not mean the ground of confidence, but defines its nature or sphere. Meyer and others rightly take τοῖς δεσμοῖς as the ground or occasion of confidence—vertrauend meinen Banden—inasmuch as these bonds were a testimony to the entire truth, power, and glory of the gospel. They were the proofs of his inflexible integrity, of his honest and sincere convictions as to the freedom and simplicity of the gospel. The majority gathered confidence from them. They were charmed and convinced by his manly integrity, his undaunted endurance, his open and candid avowal of his past career, and his willingness to seal his testimony with his blood. What might have been supposed to damp and discourage them, had the opposite effect; it cheered and stimulated them. The result was natural; past timidity vanished, and they " ventured more abundantly to speak the word without fear." The adverb περισσοτέρως is not, with Grotius, to be taken as qualifying ἀφόβως, or as forming with it a comparative ἀφοβοτέρως. Its position connects it with τολμᾶν—" more abundantly ventured;" the comparison being —more than when he had not been imprisoned. The adverb ἀφόβως is not pleonastic—those brethren had ventured to preach before, but perhaps with some caution; now they dared more frequently, and with perfect composure. The sight of the apostle inspired them with his own heroism. It

might have been feared that his bonds would have made his
friends more wary, lest they should incur a similar fate; but
so far from such an ignoble result, there was a positive revival
of courage and zeal among them; their labours multiplied in
number, and increased in boldness, and thus the apostle's
circumstances had resulted rather to the furtherance of the
gospel. Some codices have, after λόγον, τοῦ Θεοῦ, and others
τοῦ Κυρίου. On the authority of A and B, Lachmann adopts
the former, as do many of the versions. But the reading
seems to be a gloss, adopted from the familiar expression—
" word of God," as in Acts iv. 31.

(Ver. 15.) But while the apostle in this statement includes
the majority, there were some exceptions. There was a party
actuated by a very different spirit—

Τινὲς μὲν καὶ διὰ φθόνον καὶ ἔριν—τὸν Χριστὸν κηρύσσουσιν.
" Some indeed, also, for envy and contention, preach Christ."
By τινές, the apostle does not refer to a section of the previous
πλείονες. The καί indicates that another and distinct party is
noticed; not, as Rilliet writes, parmi les Chrétiens qui ont
repris courage, and as Rheinwald and Hoelemann suppose.
Had he merely meant to characterize the πλείονες into two
parties, there was no occasion to say τινές. There is, as
Ellicott says, an implied contrast in καί, while it points out
an additional party. Hartung, 1, 136, etc. The preposition
διά refers to the motive, not the purpose of preaching—envy
and contention. Winer, § 49, c ; Matt. xxvii. 18 ; Mark xv. 10.
This class of men were jealous of the apostle's influence, and
strove to defy him, to undermine his reputation and authority,
and gall and gainsay him by their modes of speech and action.
What this party was, will be immediately discussed. It was
an Anti-Pauline faction, but we cannot regard it as simply a
Judaizing one. The apostle adds—

τινὲς δὲ καὶ δι' εὐδοκίαν τὸν Χριστὸν κηρύσσουσι—" but some
also preach Christ for goodwill." The persons indicated by
τινές are probably those contained in πλείονες, and so named,
or spoken of as a party here, from being placed in contrast
with the first τινές. The preposition διά points out, again,
the motive, and that motive is goodwill to the apostle himself,
and not, as many suppose, either goodwill to the cause, or to
men's salvation. The φθόνος and ἔρις on the one hand, and

this εὐδοκία on the other hand, are purely personal to the apostle, as indeed he proceeds at once to explain.

The 16th and 17th verses are transposed in the Received Text. The idea of preserving conformity to the division of parties in the preceding verse, seems to have suggested the change, as if, when the apostle had referred to the envious and contentious preachers first, he must, in the same order, give his explanation of them. Heinrichs, without any authority, reckons both explanatory verses as spurious. Müller vindicates the arrangement of the Textus Receptus for very frivolous reasons. The best MSS. place them in the reverse order of the Received Text, and by putting the verse last which describes the factious preachers, the force of τί γάρ, in the 18th verse, is more vividly brought out.

(Ver. 16.) Οἱ μὲν ἐξ ἀγάπης, εἰδότες ὅτι εἰς ἀπολογίαν τοῦ εὐαγγελίου κεῖμαι—"The one party indeed (preach Christ) of love, knowing that I am set for the defence of the gospel." The first clause is a nominative, and the supplement is "preach Christ." For we agree with Alford, against Meyer, van Hengel, De Wette, and Ellicott, that οἱ ἐξ ἀγάπης and οἱ ἐξ ἐριθείας, are not simply generic descriptions, as in Rom. ii. 8; Gal. iii. 7. Ellicott objects that in this verse ἐξ ἀγάπης would only be a repetition of διὰ εὐδοκίαν. And so it is, but with an explanatory purpose—and so with the other pair of opposite terms. And the apostle does not "reiterate" simply the nature of the difference of feeling in the two parties, but he adds the cause of it, for the participles εἰδότης and οἰόμενοι preserve their true causal signification. Under the hypothesis which we are opposing, the words τὸν Χριστὸν καταγγέλλουσιν come in awkwardly, and would hardly be expressed in verse 17; but they occur in our construction as the expected complement. Still the meaning is not very different, whether the party is characterized by love, or whether love be assigned as the motive of their preaching. Yet, as preaching is specially regarded in the paragraph as the development or result of feeling, we take the clause as describing that feeling; not as simply designating a party, but as specifying a motive in active operation. They preached Christ out of love; and their affection was intelligently based—

εἰδότες ὅτι εἰς ἀπολογίαν τοῦ εὐαγγελίου κεῖμαι—"knowing

that I am appointed for the defence of the gospel." The noun
ἀπολογία is "vindication"—the defence of the truth, freeness,
adaptation, and divine origin of the gospel. Luther, Estius,
Am Ende, Matthies, and van Hengel, take κεῖμαι in a literal
sense—"I lie in prison, or in misery." The idea is far-
fetched and unnecessary. The verb means as often, "to be
set aside for," or "to be appointed to." Luke ii. 34 ; 1 Thess.
iii. 3. What then is the reference ?

1. Some, as Estius, a-Lapide, and Pierce, understand by
ἀπολογία, the apostle's formal vindication of himself and his
cause before Nero. But this is too restricted a view, though
such a defence is not to be excluded.

2. Chrysostom's idea of ἀπολογία is peculiar. He refers us
to Paul's answer at the judgment-seat of God. "I am
appointed to preach, they help with me, and they are diminish-
ing the weight of that account which I must give to God."
The apostle, however, is not speaking of his account to God,
but of his special work in defending the gospel, which those
who loved him knew how to appreciate (verse 7); nor is
ἀπολογία ever used of the solemn and final reckoning.

3. Others bring out this thought,—These friends see me
imprisoned, and they supply my forced abstinence from labour
by their preaching. Such is the view of Estius, Hoelemann,
and van Hengel. But this lays the emphasis more on the
apostle's imprisonment than on his high function ; and the
latter is more expressly in the writer's view.

4. Meyer, Wiesinger, and De Wette, place the emphasis
properly on the words—"for the defence of the gospel." His
friends recognized the apostle's position and task, and laboured
in sympathy to assist him in it. It was not because he could
not defend the gospel that they took the work upon them,
for they had been engaged in similar effort before ; only his
incarceration gave them new spirit and intrepidity. They
had recognized the apostle's special function ; it struck a
tender chord in their hearts, and so far as in them lay they
carried out his labours. As they well knew that he had been
set for the defence of the gospel, they felt that they could
not better probe their love to him than by appreciating his
vocation, acting in his spirit, and seeking, above all things, to
realize the noble end to which he had devoted his life.

(Ver. 17.) Οἱ δὲ ἐξ ἐριθείας τὸν Χριστὸν καταγγέλλουσιν οὐχ ἁγνῶς—" But the others preach Christ of faction, not purely." There is no specific difference between κηρύσσουσι and καταγγέλλουσι, Acts xvii. 3, 23 ; Col. i. 28. The first verb is already applied to both parties. Hesychius defines the one term by the other ; but the former verb is of most frequent occurrence ; the latter being confined to the book of Acts and Paul's epistles. The noun ἐριθεία is not from ἔρις, and signifying " contention," as Theodoret has it—τὸ τῆς ἔριδος πάθος ; for the apostle formally distinguishes ἔρις and ἐριθεία in 2 Cor. xii. 20 and in Gal. v. 20, in both which cases the two nouns occur in the same verse. It is from ἔριθος, a day-labourer, Hom. Il. xviii. 550 ; the resemblance to ἔριον being perhaps accidental—Passow, *sub voce ;* Benfey, i.56—Fritzsche, in his *Excursus* appended to the second chapter of Romans. The idea of " mercenary " soon followed that of labour for hire, out of which sprang that of emulation and worthless self-seeking—*malitiosa fraudum machinatio.* The term ἐριθεία, as Fritzsche remarks, includes both the φθόνος and ἔρις of the fifteenth verse. Liddell and Scott fall away from the true meaning of the word, and do not distinguish it from ἔρις, when in their Lexicon they give " contention " as its meaning in the New Testament. The φιλονεικία of Suidas and Theophylact comes nearer the true idea. This party, therefore, in proclaiming Christ, did not do it ἁγνῶς—preach with pure intent. Ἁγνῶς καὶ καθαρῶς, Hesiod, *Opera et Dies,* 339. Thus the adjective is used, 2 Cor. vii. 11. The adverb characterizes not the contents, but the motive or spirit of their preaching. Bengel's idea is baseless, when he says they preached—*non sine fermento Judaico ;* or, as Am Ende says in the same spirit, that in their preaching—*multa igitur addunt, multa silent.* And the motive of their preaching is truly nefarious—

οἰόμενοι θλίψιν ἐγείρειν τοῖς δεσμοῖς μου—" thinking to stir up affliction to my bonds," meaning it, but not effecting it.[1] Ἐγείρειν, on the conclusive authority of A, B, D¹, F, G, is preferred to the ἐπιφέρειν of the Received Text, which was probably in its origin an explanatory term, like the

---

[1] *Nisi quod mihi nocere se crediderunt,* is Cicero's translation (*Tusc.* i. 41) of the Greek—ἀλλ' οἰόμενοι βλάπτειν, Plato, *Apologia Soc.* § 33.

προσφέρειν of Theophylact. The participle οἰόμενοι is parallel
to εἰδότες, and with the same causal force, though it is at the
same time explanatory of οὐχ ἀγνῶς. Their purpose was to
aggravate the apostle's imprisonment. They did God's work
in the devil's spirit. No wonder Chrysostom exclaims—Ὦ
τῆς ὠμότητος, ὢ τῆς διαβολικῆς ἐνεργείας—"O, the cruelty!
O, the devilish energy!" In what way they thought to
accomplish their object, it is difficult now to tell. Chrysostom simply calls them unbelievers. We cannot agree with
Grotius, Le Clerc, Balduin, and those who imagine that this
party were Jews, who went about calumniating the gospel
and its preachers, with the view of bringing more hardships
upon the apostle ; the result being that they only excited
curiosity, and led many to inquire about the real nature of
the new sect. Nor do we think that they were Judaizers of
the ordinary class, who represented the apostle as an enemy
to the law, and excited the Jews against him. That they
belonged to this class, has been held by many, and, among
others, by Neander, Meyer, De Wette, and Ellicott. It is
difficult to suppose that these preachers were Judaizers.
For—

1. The apostle usually condemns the Judaizers—calls
them by many bitter epithets, and represents them as subverting the gospel to such an extent, that upon their theory
Christ had died in vain, Gal. ii. 21. And the apostle, as
Wiesinger says, would in this case have appeared "double-
tongued" to the Philippians ; for in this very epistle, referring
to such errorists, he inveighs with special antipathy against
them—" Beware of dogs ; beware of evil workers ; beware of
the concision." In this passage, however, the apostle says
nothing of erroneous teaching, but only of a bad spirit. He
does not reject their doctrines as mutilated or adulterated :
he only reprobates their motives.

2. They are represented as preaching Christ. It is true
the article is used, ὁ Χριστός, which some suppose to have a
special reference to the Messiahship and their proclamation
of it in a Jewish or secular sense. But then the well-affected
party are said also to preach the Christ—τὸν Χριστόν. The
preaching in its substance was the same with both. Nor can
any difference be inferred from the employment of two verbs

—κηρύσσω and καταγγέλλω; the one denoting the work of a
herald, and the other that of a messenger; for the first verb
in verse 15 characterizes the preaching of both parties; and
in the preaching described by the second verb in verse 18,
the apostle expresses his hearty concurrence. Can it be supposed for a moment that the apostle could call any form of
Judaistic teaching the preaching of Christ; or use the same
emphatic phrase as descriptive both of sound and of pernicious
instruction ? His friends " preach Christ," and no one doubts
that by this language he approved of their doctrine; those
disaffected toward him " preach Christ " too, the difference
being in their respective spirit and motives.

3. The apostle virtually sanctions such preaching. For, no
matter in what spirit Christ is preached, whether in pretence
or in truth—provided He is preached at all, the prisoner is
contented and happy. Surely he could never have employed
such language, if false views of Christ had been propounded,
such views as the Judaizers were in the habit of insisting
upon—the necessity of circumcision, and the perpetual obligation of the Mosaic law. Was it possible for Paul to rejoice
in a style of preaching at Rome, which he so strongly denounced
in Galatia ? Or could he regard the promulgation of such
views as in any sense the " furtherance of the gospel " ? The
conclusion then is, that a form of preaching called, without
reserve or modification, the preaching of Christ, and one in
which the apostle rejoices, in spite of the malicious and
perverse motives of those who engaged in it, cannot be the
common and carnal Judaistic error which plagued and injured
so many of the early churches. Neander [1] is obliged to make
the supposition, that Paul thinks of the Judaizing gospel in
its effects upon the heathen, when he thus speaks of it. But
there is no ground for such an assumption, and such a preaching would profit them nothing. Had the Judaizers given the
mere facts of Christ's life, it might have been well ; but such
a simple narrative would not have suited their purpose, for
they could not detail those facts without connecting with
them certain dogmas on the obligation and character of the
Mosaic ritual. Nor can Meyer be listened to, when he says
that Judaizing preaching was less displeasing to the apostle

[1] *On Philippians*, p. 26 ; Edin., Clark.

in Rome, than in Greece or Asia, as the church there had not been founded by him, and was not specially under his apostolical jurisdiction. What this preaching was not, one may thus safely decide.

But it is not so easy to determine what this preaching of Christ was, or how it could be intended to add affliction to the apostle's bonds. Chrysostom and his followers hold that the intention of such preaching was to stir up the hostility of Nero, and other enemies of the gospel, so that the apostle's situation might be embittered; the preaching of Jesus as the Christ being most offensive to the Romans, and the unbelieving Jews making use of it to enrage the heathen rulers. But the apostle does not say that the Jews charged the Christians with preaching the Messiahship; the Christians did it themselves. And if they preached the Messiahship in any such form as made it a rival to the imperial sovereignty, would not such a course have equally endangered themselves, and led to their own apprehension and trial? Nor can we suppose the meaning to be, that by their busy publication of Judaizing doctrine, his antagonists thought to annoy the apostle by preaching what they knew he had so resolutely condemned, and to endanger him by holding him up as an enemy to the Mosaic institute, and the venerated "customs" of his country. For we have endeavoured to show in the preceding paragraphs that such preaching could not be called, as the apostle calls it—preaching Christ; nor could he have tolerated it, far less have given it his seeming approval and countenance. Others, again, as Storr, van Hengel, and Rilliet, suppose that by "affliction" the apostle means mental suffering, produced by such factious disposition and conduct. It is possible that this view may be the most correct. The noun θλίψις will bear such a meaning, and it is the intended result of that ἐριθεία—unprincipled emulation and intrigue. The apostle speaks of affliction in addition to his bonds—not a closer imprisonment, or a heavier chain, or an attempt to infuriate the emperor and prejudge his appeal, but something over and above his bonds—perhaps chagrin and sorrow at the misrepresentation of his position and character. May we not therefore regard the phrase — " I rejoice, and will rejoice," as the opposite of those emotions which they strove to produce within him? They laboured to surround him with circumstances which should cause him "affliction," but they failed. He could not but blame their motives, while he rejoiced in the result. They must have set themselves in rivalry with him, must have hoped to ruin his reputation, and damage his apostolical commission, in the way in which they did his work. By their detraction of his character in and through an imitation of his labours, they trusted to chafe and vex him. But as they deserved, they were egregiously disappointed. They thought that he would be afflicted, but he was rejoiced.

If this hypothesis be correct, as we think it is, then we may come to a more satisfactory conclusion as to the nature of the faction referred to. That it consisted of Jews is almost certain. But these Jews might not be Judaizers. In the Corinthian church there was a party that said, "I am of Cephas"— followers of the apostle of the circumcision, and hostile to those who named themselves from Paul. It is very probable that this Petrine party held high views about the law; but there is no hint in the epistle to the Corinthian church that they either held or taught such mischievous errors as were propagated in Galatia. Minor matters of ceremonial seem rather to have occupied them. Chap. viii. and x. But there is no question that the apostle's authority was impugned in Corinth, and in all likelihood by the Petrine party, because he had not been personally called by Jesus, as Simon had been; and by the same party, his right to pecuniary support from the churches seems to have been denied or disputed. While, therefore, there was comparative purity in the section that took Peter for its head and watchword, there was also keen and resolute opposition to the person and prerogative of the apostle of the Gentiles. To meet all the requirements of the case before us, we have only to suppose that such a party was found at Rome, and the fourteenth chapter of the epistle to that church seems to indicate their existence. If there was a company of believing Jews, who held the essential doctrines of the gospel, but was combative on points of inferior value, and in connection with the social institutions of their people, and who, at the same time, were bitter and unscrupulous antagonists of the apostle from such an impression

F

of his opinions as is indicated by James in Acts xxi. 20, 21 —then such a party might preach Christ, and yet cherish toward Paul all those feelings of envy and ill-will which he ascribes to them. Chrysostom touches the truth when he represents them as being jealous of the apostle—φθονοῦντες τῇ δόξῃ. Calvin writes feelingly—"Paul assuredly says nothing here, which I myself have not experienced. For there are men living now who have preached the gospel with no other design, than to gratify the rage of the wicked by persecuting pious pastors."

(Ver. 18.) Τί γάρ; πλὴν παντὶ τρόπῳ εἴτε προφάσει εἴτε ἀληθείᾳ, Χριστὸς καταγγέλλεται, καὶ ἐν τούτῳ χαίρω, ἀλλὰ καὶ χαρήσομαι—"What then? but yet, in every way, that Christ is preached—whether in pretence, whether in truth— even in this I do rejoice, yea, and I shall rejoice." The elliptical phrase τί γάρ expresses an interrogative inference, and is much the same as the *quid enim*, or *quid ergo*, of the Latin authors.[1] Rom. iii. 3. There is no use in attempting to fill out the idiom with διαφέρει, or ἄλλο or μοι μέλει, as is done by the Greek expositors ; nor is the *refert* of Bengel, or the *sequitur* of Grotius, at all necessary. Kühner, § 8332, i. ; Klotz, ad Devar. ii. p. 247, etc. ; Hartung, i. p. 479 ; Hoogeveen, *Doctrina Part.* p. 539. The adverb πλήν [2] has also in such idiom a peculiar meaning, *nur dass*, as Passow gives it—" only that." As if the paraphrase might be—" What then? shall I fret because some men preach Christ of strife and intrigue, and think to embitter my imprisonment ? No, for all that ; in spite of all this opposition to myself, only let Christ be preached from any motive, false or genuine, yes, in the fact of such preaching I rejoice." The first answer to τί γάρ is only implied, and not written—shall I feel affliction added to my bonds ? shall I be chafed or grieved ? while the second in contrast to it is expressed—the antagonism being noted by πλήν. Though in the phrase παντὶ τρόπῳ the apostle says —" every form," yet the following words show that he had two forms especially in his eye, for he adds :—

εἴτε προφάσει εἴτε ἀληθείᾳ—" whether in pretence or in

---

[1] Cicero, *de Fin.* ii. 22, 72 ; Horace, *Sat.* i. 1, 7.
[2] After πλήν, A, F, G insert ὅτι ; while B has simply ὅτι, without πλήν. Probably both are results of an ancient gloss, as Meyer conjectures.

sincerity." These two nouns are often opposed by Philo and
the classical writers, as is shown in the collected examples of
Loesner, Raphelius, and Wetstein. The dative in both cases
is that of manner, or is a modal case. Winer, § 31, 6.[1] The
first noun, πρόφασις, is employed to express a prominent element of the old Pharisaical character, its want of genuineness ;
or that its professed motive was not its real one, that its
exceeding devotion was but a show, Matt. xxiii. 13 ; Mark
xii. 40 ; Luke xx. 47. When the sailors, during Paul's
voyage to Rome, wished to escape from the ship, and for this
purpose lowered a boat under the pretext of preparing to let
go an anchor, their manœuvre is described by the same term,
Acts xxvii. 30. The word denotes that state of mind in which
the avowed is not the true motive ; in which there is made
to *appear* (as the etymology indicates) what does not exist.
Hos. x. 4 ; John xv. 22. The contrasted noun, ἀλήθεια,
signifies here genuineness or integrity, John iv. 23, 24 ; 1
John iii. 18. The Hebrew אֱמֶת has occasionally a similar
meaning, Ex. xviii. 21 ; Neh. vii. 2 ; and especially 1 Sam.
xii. 24 ; 1 Kings ii. 4, iii. 6, where it is represented by the
Greek term before us. Χριστὸς καταγγέλλεται ; see Col. i. 28.
A different meaning is assigned to the first noun by the
Vulgate, which renders *per occasionem ;* followed by Luther,
who translates *zufallens ;* and vindicated by Grotius, and by
Hammond who brings out this idea—"by all means, whether
by occasion only, that is, accidentally, and not by a designed
causality ; or whether by truth, that is, by a direct real way
of efficiency." But though the term has sometimes such a
meaning, the antithesis in the clause itself, the common usage
of the two confronted nouns, and the entire context dis-
countenance the supposition. In fact, πρόφασις is simply
the οὐχ ἁγνῶς of the 17th verse ; while ἀλήθεια embodies the
δι᾽ εὐδοκίαν of the 15th, and the ἐξ ἀγάπης of the 16th verses.
The two nouns so placed in opposition represent, not difference
in the substance, but in the purpose of preaching. They have
an ethical reference. For if Christ was preached in either
way, the apostle must allude not to contents, but design. In
the one case, Christ was really preached, but the motive was

[1] Both nouns in a similar idiom are often found in the accusative, among
the classical writers. Krüger, § 46, 3, 5 ; Matthiae, § 425.

hollow and fallacious. It was neither from homage to Him, or love to souls, or an earnest desire to advance the gospel. In the other case, preaching was a sincere service—"out of a true heart, and with faith unfeigned." The apostle, looking at the fact, and for a moment overlooking the motive, exclaims :—

καὶ ἐν τούτῳ χαίρω ἀλλὰ καὶ χαρήσομαι—"and in this I rejoice ; yea, and I will rejoice." For χαίρω ἐν, see Col. i. 24. The pronoun τούτῳ does not refer specially to Christ ; nor yet, vaguely, to the entire crisis, as Meyer takes it; but directly to the preaching. To render it, with Ellicott, "in this state of things," is too broad, and would not be wholly true : for the apostle must have grieved over the wicked motives of those preachers, though he rejoiced in their preaching. We must subtract from "this state of things," what must have caused him sorrow ; there being left the fact that Christ was proclaimed, and in that he rejoiced. "In this preaching, be the motive what it may, I rejoice." The ἀλλά is still slightly adversative, as it stands between the present χαίρω and the future χαρήσομαι—not only now, or at present, *but* I will also rejoice. See an explanation of the idiom under Eph. v. 24. As happens with many barytone verbs, in Attic the future of χαίρω is χαιρήσω—but in the other dialects, and in the New Testament, the middle form is employed. Matthiae, § 255 ; Winer, § 15. The apostle felt that impurity of motive might modify, but not prevent all good result; and that, as long as its true character was concealed, such preaching might not be without fruit. He knew the preaching of Christ to be a noble instrument, and though it was not a clean hand which set in motion, still it might effect incalculable good. For truth is mighty, no matter in what spirit it is published ; its might being in itself, and not in the breath of him who proclaims it. Disposition and purpose belong to the preacher and his individual responsibility ; but the preaching of Christ has an innate power to win and save. The virtue lies in the gospel, not in the gospeller; in the exposition, and not in the expounder.

Not that the apostle was or could be indifferent to the motive which ought to govern a preacher of the gospel. Not as if he for a moment encouraged neutrality or lukewarmness, or thought that unconverted men might be safely entrusted with the precious function. But he simply regards the work and its fruits, and he leaves the motive with Him who could fully try it—the Judge of all. Vindictive and jealous feeling toward himself, he could pity and pardon, provided the work be done. He could well bear that good be achieved by others, even out of envy to himself. The mere eclat of apostleship was nothing to him, and he could not forbid others, because they did not follow himself. Those men who so preached Christ, were therefore neither heretics nor gross Judaizers,[1] subverting the faith. Their preaching is supposed to be the means of saving souls. The Greek expositors notice the abuse which some heretics—τινὲς ἀνόητοι —made of the apostle's statement, and they answer, that he does not warrant such a style of preaching—does not say καταγγελλέσθω, but καταγγέλλεται—merely relating a fact, not issuing a sanction. Chrysostom calls attention to the apostle's calmness—that he does not inveigh against his enemies, but simply narrates what has occurred.

This verse was the subject of long and acrimonious dispute during the Pietist controversy in Germany. The question was generally, Whether unconverted men are warranted or qualified to preach the gospel; or specially, Whether the religious knowledge acquired by a wicked man can be termed theology, or how far the office and ministry of an impious man can be pronounced efficacious, or whether a licentious and godless man be capable of divine illumination? It is obvious that such questions are not determined by the apostle, and that there is no solution of them in this passage. His language is too vague, and the whole circumstances are too obscure, to form a foundation for judgment. The party referred to here preached Christ from a very unworthy personal motive, and the apostle rejoiced in the preaching, though he might compassionate and forgive the preachers. We cannot argue a general rule from such an exceptional case. But apart from any casuistry, and any fanaticism which the Pietists might exhibit, their general principle was correct, and it was in opposition to their tenets, and as a rebound from them, that men were admitted into pulpits to preach

[1] Chrysostom admits that they preached sound doctrine—ὑγιῶς μὲν ἐκήρυττον.

the gospel without any evidence that they believed in it, and that it was not required of them to be religious themselves, ere they taught religion to others. In the same way scholars were installed into chairs, from which they taught the language of Abraham, as the readiest means of scoffing at Abraham's faith, and descanted on the writings of the apostles, as the most effectual method of reviling and undermining that religion which they had founded. We hold it to be the right principle—that the best preparation for preaching the Crucified One, is to have His spirit; that to be His, is the sure qualification for obeying His commission, and that an unchristian man has no call to take part in the vindication or enforcement of the religion of Christ.

(Ver. 19.) Οἶδα γὰρ ὅτι τοῦτό μοι ἀποβήσεται εἰς σωτηρίαν —"For I know that this shall fall out unto my salvation." Lachmann, by his punctuation, connects this clause immediately with the preceding one, and he is right. The apostle's avowal of future joy bases itself on an anticipated result. He felt a joy which others might not suppose, and it was no evanescent emotion, for it was connected with the most momentous of all blessings—his salvation. The γάρ introduces a confirmatory explanation or reason. That this salvation—σωτηρία—is not, as many from the Greek fathers downwards suppose, temporal deliverance, is evident from the instrumentality referred to—" your intercession, and the supply of Christ's spirit." These were not indispensable to his liberation, but to his soul's health. A change in Nero's heart, a mere whim of the moment, might have secured his freedom. The prior question, however, is the reference in τοῦτο.

1. Many, with Theodoret, refer it to the afflictive circumstances in which the apostle was placed, or to the dangers which lowered around him, in consequence of the envious and vindictive preachers—οἱ ἐντεῦθεν φυόμενοι κίνδυνοι. But the apostle thought too lightly of this danger, if it really existed, to give it such prominence. What was merely personal, had no interest for him ; what concerned the cause, at once concentrated his attention, and begat emotion within him.

2. Theophylact, Calvin, Rheinwald, van Hengel, De Wette, and Beelen, refer τοῦτο to the 17th verse—the preaching of Christ out of envy and strife, and for the

purpose of adding to the apostle's troubles. " Such preaching, instead of adding to my affliction, shall contribute to my
salvation." But this connection carries back the reference
too far, and breaks the continuity.

3. Others suppose the allusion to be to the preaching of the
gospel; to its greater spread, as Rilliet, Matthies, and Alford;
or to the general character of it, as Hoelemann—*si vel interdum
de causis subdolis factum.* These opinions appear to be somewhat away from the context:

4. For we apprehend that it is simply to the sentiment of the
preceding verse that the apostle refers. In that verse he tells
them that, in spite of the opposite conclusion some might come
to, he rejoiced in the fact that Christ was preached, whatever
might be the motive of the preacher. And now he assigns
the reason of that joy. He does not mean either that the
gospel so proclaimed would achieve the salvation of others,
as Grotius imagined, or with Heinrichs, that it would produce his own, for it had already been secured. The preaching of the gospel to others, and the spread of it in Rome, or
in Italy, could not in itself exercise any saving power upon
him; nor could he have any doubt that the gospel which
himself had believed and preached, should issue in his eternal
happiness. We therefore understand the τοῦτο to refer to
the state of mind described in the former verse—his joy in
the preaching of Christ, from whatever motive. For this
state of mind indicated his supreme regard for Christ—that
he preferred Him above everything—that he could bear to
be an object of malevolence and jealousy, if so his Master was
exalted—and that, provided Christ was preached, he cared
not for tarnished fame or heavier affliction. This mental
condition was an index to him of a healthy spiritual state.
Salvation must be the issue, when Christ was so magnified in
the process. On the contrary, if he had felt chagrin and disappointment—if he had grudged that any should preach but
himself, or any name should obtain prominence in the churches
but his own—if actual or apprehended addition to his sufferings
had either made him repent his own preaching, or infuriated
him at the preaching of others—then a temperament so unlike
Him whom he professed to serve, might justly have made him
doubt his salvation, or the certainty of its future possession.

But his present Christ-like frame of spirit was salvational, if
the expression may be coined—it was an index of present
attainment, and the sure instrument of subsequent glory. It
was the " ear," which is seen not only to follow the blade, but
which also betokens the " full corn." There is no good ground
for Alford's confining the meaning of σωτηρία to salvation, " in
degree of blessedness, not in reference to the absolute fact."
The verb ἀποβήσεται rather forbids it. Salvation will turn
out to be the result—salvation, first as a fact, and also in every
element which the apostle expected. Luke xxi. 13. The
clause occurs in the Septuagint. Job xiii. 16. And in this
spirit the apostle adds—

διὰ τῆς ὑμῶν δεήσεως—" through your supplication." He
knew that they prayed for him—such was their vivid interest
in him, and such a conviction the use of the article τῆς seems
to imply. And he believed in the efficacy of their prayers—
that their entreaty would bring down blessing upon him. His
high function as an apostle did not elevate him above the need
of their intercession. 2 Thess. iii. 1, 2 ; Philem. 22. He
virtually claims it, for he professes to enjoy their sympathy.
And, as the general result of their prayers, he subjoins—

καὶ ἐπιχορηγίας τοῦ πνεύματος Ἰησοῦ Χριστοῦ—" and the
supply of the spirit of Jesus Christ." Ἐπιχορηγία, see Eph.
iv. 16. Conybeare says, " ἡ ἐπιχορηγία τοῦ χορηγοῦ would
mean the supplying of all needs of the chorus by the choregus ;
and that therefore the phrase before us signifies the supplying
of all needs by the spirit." Theophylact and Œcumenius,
Zanchius, Grotius, Rilliet, Alford, and Wiesinger take the
genitive as that of object, viz. that the Holy Spirit Himself
forms the supply. Theophylact explains by saying, ἐπιχο-
ρηγηθῇ πλεῖον τὸ πνεῦμα. With Theodoret, Calvin, Rheinwald, van Hengel, and Ellicott, we prefer taking the genitive
as that of subject—πνεύματος χορηγοῦντος τὴν χάριν. The
apostle refers to that necessary supply which the Holy Spirit
furnishes, that universal and well-timed assistance which He
imparts. This seems to be on the whole the better and more
natural interpretation. The use of the participle ἐπιχορηγῶν
with τὸ πνεῦμα in Gal. iii. 5, affords no ground of decision
as to the genitive of the noun here ; nor can the use of the
genitive in Eph. iv. 16 determine the matter. Neither can

we assent to Alford's argument, taken from the position of
the words, as such an argument is often doubtful, and no
author has always followed tamely the same order. The
connection of the two clauses has been disputed; that is,
whether ὑμῶν belongs to ἐπιχορηγίας as well as δεήσεως.
Meyer, Alford, and Baumgarten-Crusius hold that the connection is of this nature—"through your prayer and your
supply of the Spirit of Christ." But such an exegesis cannot
be defended on the ground that διά, or διὰ τῆς, or the simple
article, is not repeated; for such a repetition is unnecessary,
and according to a well-known law, the article is omitted
before a second noun, when both nouns have a defining
genitive. Winer, § 19, 5. Still the apostle's thought seems
to be, that the supply of the Spirit to him would be the result
of their prayers for him. For the Spirit is not to be explained
away as merely meaning divine power, *vis divina*, as Am Ende
renders. It is the Holy Spirit—who is here called the Spirit
of Jesus Christ. The reason of such an appellation, it is not
difficult to discover; for it does not rest on any dogmatic
grounds, or any metaphysical views of the distinctions and
relations of the persons in the Trinity. The genitive is that
of possession or origin, the spirit which Jesus has or dispenses.
The exaltation of the Redeemer secured the gift of the Holy
Ghost, which it is His exalted prerogative to bestow. The
Spirit represents Christ, for He comes in Christ's name, as
another Paraclete, enlightens with Christ's truths, purifies with
Christ's blood, comforts with Christ's promises, and seals with
Christ's image.

(Ver. 20.) Κατὰ τὴν ἀποκαραδοκίαν καὶ ἐλπίδα μου, ὅτι ἐν
οὐδενὶ αἰσχυνθήσομαι—"According to my firm expectation
and hope, that in nothing I shall be ashamed." The preposition κατά is in connection with οἶδα γάρ of the preceding
verse. My knowledge that it shall issue in my salvation, is
based upon, or rather is "in accordance with," my expectation
and hope. The two nouns, ἀποκαραδοκία and ἐλπίς, have
much the same signification, only the latter has a meaning in
advance of the former—hope being surer than expectation—
and having in it a deeper conviction of certainty, or resting
itself on a surer foundation. The view of Bretschneider, *sub
voce*, is the reverse, but wrong. Hope is expectation combined

with assurance. The noun ἀποκαραδοκία is found in Rom. viii. 19. Its composition has been variously resolved; most probably it is κάρα, "the head," and δοκεύειν, "to observe." It is, according to the *Etymologicum Magnum*, τῇ κεφαλῇ προβλέπειν, or as Œcumenius describes it here, as ἐλπίδα ἥν τις καὶ αὐτὴν ἐπικινῶν τὴν κεφαλὴν δοκεύει καὶ περισκοπεῖ. The preposition ἀπό is not, as some say, meaningless or quiescent; but it is not properly intensive; rather, as Ellicott says, it is local. It marks the point from which one looks out, or the place whence the thing expected is to come; and the additional idea is to look out, or continue to look out, till the thing looked for comes out of its place. The notion is, therefore, more that of continuance than earnestness, though certainly a persistent look will deepen into an earnest one. The word is well discussed in that family production, *Fritzschi-orum Opuscula*, p. 150. The apostle did not speak at random, or from any vague and dreamy anticipations. He felt that he was warranted so to write. And what he had referred to was not something in which he had little interest, something which might happen in the course of events, but towards which he was indifferent. He was tremblingly alive to the result, and his soul was set upon it.

The next clause tells the personal object of his hope— "that in nothing I shall be ashamed." It is wrong on the part of Estius and Matthies to render ὅτι, "for," or "because," as if the clause were confirmative. The ὅτι introduces the object of hope; but with the other view the expectation and hope would refer vaguely to the preceding verse. The verb represents the Heb. בּוֹשׁ in the Septuagint. Ps. xxxiv. 4, lxix. 3; 2 Cor. x. 8; 1 John ii. 28. The apostle does not mean to say, that in nothing should he be put out, as the common phrase is, or made to appear abashed and terrified. This is the view of Matthies and van Hengel, the latter of whom gives it as, *ut in nulla re ab officio deflectam*. A different view is held by Chrysostom, who has these words, "Whatever happens, I shall not be ashamed, *i.e.* they will not obtain the mastery over me." "They, forsooth, expected to catch Paul in this snare, and to quench the freedom of the gospel." This view is too restricted, for the apostle says, ἐν οὐδενί, "in nothing," not simply in living and preaching. The idea is not that shame would fall upon him principally if he died, or ceased to speak with boldness. The pronoun οὐδενί is neuter, and does not refer either to the Philippians, as if he were saying, "in none of you I shall be ashamed," or to those preaching Christ at Rome, as if he meant to affirm, "in none of them shall I be ashamed." "In nothing," says the apostle, "shall I feel ashamed." He should preserve his trust and confidence; no feeling of disgrace or disappointment should creep over him. He should maintain his erectness of spirit, and not hang his head like one who had come short of his end, or had been the victim of vain expectations. The verb αἰσχυνθήσομαι is in virtual contrast with ἀποβήσεται εἰς σωτηρίαν. He felt assured that neither in this hope nor any other should he be ashamed. His state of mind was such, that no emotion of shame could come near him. Christ's work was doing in the meantime, and in that he rejoiced, no matter what the motive that led to it; and though he was a fettered prisoner, and his enemies might be traducing him, yet he was assured that now, as heretofore, he should not be brought into shame, as if his life had been a failure; for, should he live, Christ should be glorified; and should he die, the same result would equally happen. And he speaks now in a more positive tone—

ἀλλ' ἐν πάσῃ παρρησίᾳ ὡς πάντοτε καὶ νῦν μεγαλυνθήσεται Χριστὸς ἐν τῷ σώματί μου—" but with all boldness, as always and now, Christ shall be magnified in my body." Shame is the contrast of boldness, for he who feels ashamed is a coward. Ἐν πάσῃ is in antithesis to ἐν οὐδενί. He had been bold in days gone by, in crises which had passed away; and as it had been always, so it would be now—καὶ νῦν. What the apostle expected and hoped was, that Christ should be magnified in his body. The verb μεγαλύνω is to make or declare great, and often in the sense of praise; for praise is the laudatory expression of the divine greatness. It tells how great He is, or how great He has disclosed Himself to be. The meaning here is, that Christ should be evinced in His greatness—disclosed in His majesty. Rilliet takes the verb in the sense of grandir—se developper; the development of Christ within himself, in allusion to Gal. ii. 20, iv. 19. But, as has been well remarked by Wiesinger, "the added words, ἐν τῷ σώματί μου, are fatal to this supposition." Nor is there any instance of the use of the term in such a personal sense. In Luke i. 58, it is said that the Lord made great His mercy—exhibited extraordinary kindness.

The next words are peculiar. The apostle does not say "in me," but "in my body"—ἐν τῷ σώματί μου. The two forms of expression are not to be confounded. The following clause explains why terms so precise have been employed. Life and death are both predicated of the body; therefore he says, in my body—

εἴτε διὰ ζωῆς εἴτε διὰ θανάτου—"whether by life or by death." It is all one—whether he live or die, the magnifying of Christ is secured on either alternative. If he lived, he should yet labour for Christ; and if his life were cut short, Christ should be glorified in the courage of his martyrdom, and the entrance of the martyr to heaven. Come what may—the glorification of Christ—the highest aim of his heart is secured.

The apostle rejoiced that Christ was preached, no matter what might be the motive; and this prevailing emotion, he was assured, would result in salvation. He was confident that he should not be left in shame: for the glorification of Christ, the prime object of his existence, would be brought about in his body, whether he lived or whether he died. While one party preached Christ of love, in alliance with him, and in acknowledgment of his high position; and the other preached Christ of envy and self-seeking—supposing to add affliction to his bonds; in the midst of this turmoil, he was happy and contented. His trial was pending, and he felt that Christ would be glorified, whether he should be liberated from prison to preach again, or whether he should leave his cell only to be conducted to the block. If, in either case, Christ should be glorified, his salvation was a secure result. And he proceeds to prove what he has said of the magnification of Christ, whether by life or by death. For in either way it may happen—there may be two forms, but there is only one result.

(Ver. 21.) Ἐμοὶ γὰρ τὸ ζῆν Χριστὸς, καὶ τὸ ἀποθανεῖν κέρδος—"For me to live is Christ, and to die is gain." [1]

---

[1] We need scarcely allude to the reading—χρηστόν—suggested by the Arabic version of Walton's Polyglott, advocated by Michaelis and Verschuir, and placed even by Griesbach among readings not to be wholly slighted.

The particle γάρ introduces the confirmatory statement. Christ shall be magnified in my body, whether by life or by death—by life, for to me to live is Christ; by death, for death to me is gain.

A considerable number of expositors take the verse as one connected sentence, with κέρδος as the one predicate—" for to me in life and in death Christ is gain "—*mihi enim in vivendo Christus est et moriendo lucrum.* Such is the view of Calvin, Beza, Musculus, E. Schmid, Raphelius, Knatchbull, a-Lapide, Vorstius, Gataker, Airay,[1] Suicer, etc. But it cannot be supported. It requires such adjustment and assistance as to give it a very unnatural appearance. Though κατά should be supplied to both infinitives, the sentence has a very clumsy and un-Pauline shape. Besides, the infinitives are not of the kind that form such an absolute accusative as is usually but erroneously resolved by κατά. Jelf, § 581 ; Krüger, § 46, 4, 1. Such an accusative has what this last grammarian calls *Erstrecken,* or extended reference ; but such a construction, while it might apply to the first infinitive, could not to the last. The natural division is to take Χριστός with the first clause as predicate, and κέρδος with the last. In such an exegesis as that we have referred to, Χριστός would be most anomalously placed. Nor would the verse so understood be in close connection with the preceding statement as either illustrative or confirmatory of it. The sentiment, To me living or dying, Christ is gain, is in itself no proof of the assertion that Christ would be magnified in his body, whether by life or by death. Personal gain to himself in either case is not surely identical with the glorification of Christ—at least there is nothing in the language to justify or explain such a conclusion. Besides, as the alternatives are strongly marked—" by life or by death ; " and as they are in direct antagonism, we expect to find that the mode of glorification will also differ, and that such a difference will be implied in the clause added for explanation and proof. But there is no such distinction if this unwarranted exegesis be admitted.

Luther again reverses the order of subject and predicate,

[1] Gataker, in his edition of M. Antoninus, p. 350, says of Airay—*solus interretum reverendus D. Airœus noster apostoli mentem assecutus videtur.*

and renders "*Christus ist mein Leben, und Sterben ist mein Gewinn*"—Christ is my life, and death is my gain. This exposition is adopted by Storr and Flatt, the former of whom attaches the first clause to the preceding verse. Œcumenius had also paraphrased αὐτὸν ἔχω τὴν ζωήν. But the translation is forbidden by the use of the infinitive with the article as the subject, and by the position of the terms. Rilliet looks upon ζῆν as referring to the higher spiritual life—*la vie par excellence*—*la vie seule digne de ce nom*, and as in contrast with τὸ ζῆν ἐν σαρκί in verse 22. But this last phrase, so far from being in contrast with τὸ ζῆν in this verse, is only exegetical of it. The life which the apostle refers to is life on earth, opposed to death, or the cessation of his present being—the ζωή of the preceding verse. And the contrast implied in ἀποθανεῖν would be all but destroyed. He speaks of continuance on earth, and of departure from it, and shows how, in each case, Christ should be magnified in his body.

Christ, says the apostle, shall be magnified in my body by life, " for to me to live is Christ." The position of ἐμοί shows the special stress which the writer lays upon it. He speaks solely of himself and his personal relation. The force of the ethical dative is—" in so far as I am personally concerned." [1] It does not mean " in my judgment," as Beelen gives it both in his commentary and his recently-published grammar,[2] § 31, B. The phrase τὸ ζῆν is similarly found in some authors, as quoted by Wetstein. If I live, he affirms, my life shall be Christ, an expressive avowal indeed. The use of such terms shows the completeness of Paul's identification with Christ. Christ and life were one and the same thing to him, or, as Bengel puts it—*quicquid vivo, Christum vivo*. Might not the sentiment be thus expanded ? For me to live is Christ—the preaching of Christ the business of my life ; the presence of Christ the cheer of my life ; the image of Christ the crown of my life ; the spirit of Christ the life of my life ; the love of Christ the power of my life ; the will of Christ the law of my life ; and the glory of Christ the end of my life. Christ was the absorbing element of his life. If he travelled, it was on Christ's errand ; if he suffered, it was in Christ's service.

---

[1] Michelsen, *Casuslehre der Lat. Sprach.* p. 212.

[2] *Grammatica Græcitatis Novi Testamenti*, etc.; Lovanii, 1857.

When he spoke, his theme was Christ; and when he wrote, Christ filled his letters. There is little doubt that the apostle refers in his utmost soul to the glorification of Christ by the diffusion of the gospel. It had been so, and the spirit of his declaration is, that it would be so still. Nay, it was his pride or his effort to preach where the name of Jesus had never been proclaimed. He liked to lay the foundation, leaving the erection of the structure to others. He chose the distant parts of labour and danger—the "regions beyond "— and he would not "boast in another man's line of things made ready to his hand."

And when did the apostle utter this sentiment? It was not as he rose from the earth, dazzled into blindness by the Redeemer's glory, and the words of the first commission were ringing in his ears. It was not in Damascus, while, as the scales fell from his sight, he recognized the Lord's goodness and power, and his baptism proclaimed his formal admission to the church. Nor was it in Arabia, where supernatural wisdom so fully unfolded to him the facts and truths which he was uniformly to proclaim. It sprang not from any momentary elation as at Cyprus, where he confounded the sorcerer, and converted the Roman proconsul. No, the resolution was written at Rome in bonds, and after years of unparalleled toil and suffering. His past career had been signalized by stripes, imprisonment, deaths, shipwreck, and unnumbered perils, but he did not regret them. He had been "in weariness and painfulness, in watchings often, in hunger and thirst, in fastings often, in cold and nakedness," but his ardour was unchilled; and let him only be freed, and his life prolonged, and his motto still would be—" For me to live is Christ." It did not repent the venerable confessor now, when he was old, infirm, and a prisoner, with a terrible doom suspended over him, that he had done so much, travelled so much, spoken so much, and suffered so much for Christ. Nor was the statement like a suspicious vow in a scene of danger, which is too often wrung from cowardice, and held up as a bribe to the Great Preserver, but forgotten when the crisis passes, and he who made it laughs at his own timidity. No. It was no new course the apostle proposed—it was only a continuation of those previous habits which his bondage

had for a season interrupted. Could there be increase to a
zeal that had never flagged, or could those labours be multiplied which had filled every moment and called out every
energy ? In fine, the saying was no idle boast, like that of
Peter at the Last Supper—the flash of a sudden enthusiasm
so soon to be drowned in tears. For the apostle had the
warrant of a long career to justify his assertion, and who can
doubt that he would have verified it, and nobly shown that
still, as hitherto, for him to live was Christ ? He sighed not
under the burden, as if age needed repose ; or sank into self-
complacency, as if he had done enough, for the Lord's commission was still upon him, and the wants of the world were
so numerous and pressing, as to claim his last word, and urge
his last step. It was " such an one as Paul the aged, and
now also a prisoner of Jesus Christ," who placed on record
the memorable clause, inscribed also on his heart—" for me
to live is Christ."

καὶ τὸ ἀποθανεῖν κέρδος—"and to die is gain." The tense
of the verb is changed in this clause from the present to the
past. In the first clause, the presence or duration of life—
τὸ ζῆν—is Christ ; but in the second clause it is not the act
of dying, but the result of it, or that which supposes it to be
past and over—τὸ ἀποθανεῖν—which is gain. Wiesinger
expresses the real difficulty of this clause, when he says—
" from its close relation to μεγαλυνθήσεται, we expect an
explanation of how Christ is to be magnified by the apostle's
death ; but κέρδος really expresses nothing upon it." To
surmount this difficulty, some apply the κέρδος to Christ.
Müller says—*quod autem alteram versus partem attinet, et
mori est lucrum, i.e., sors etiam exoptatior, scriptor haud dubie
in animo habebat, quod oppositum flagitat ; et si mihi mori-
undum est morior Christo, itaque etiam morte mea Christus
celebratur ; sed fervidiore animi commotione abrepto, alia cogitatio obversatur quæ eum id quod dicturus erat plene proloqui
non sinit.* This explanation necessitates a filling up of the
sentence, which its simplicity neither needs nor warrants. The
emphatic ἐμοί confines the κέρδος personally to the apostle.
Nor is there any ground on the same account for the exegesis
of Grotius—*morte mea aliquos Christo lucrabor ;* or that of
Heinrichs—*sin subeundum supplicium, vel inde lucrum enas-*

cetur, et lætitiores faciet res Christiana profectus. Nor does Wiesinger himself meet the difficulty which himself describes. He looks back especially to the 19th verse, and to the phrase —" it shall turn out for salvation to him, according to the firmly-cherished hope, that Christ will be magnified in him, whether by life or by death, *since to him individually it is all one* whether he should live or die, whether Christ should be magnified by his life or by his death." This is true so far, for the apostle speaks personally—ἐμοί. But still, if he say —Christ shall be magnified in my death—you expect him to say how, since he has explained the parallel clause—Christ shall be magnified in my life. Wiesinger inserts the thought —" it is all the same to me whether He be magnified by the one way or the other;" an assertion which may be true in itself, and warranted by what follows, but something more than can be borne out by the simple γάρ. And even with this explanation, κέρδος does seem to involve some element of glorification to Christ, as Wiesinger admits, but does not explain. There is no doubt that ἐμοί means—as far as regards myself individually; and there is no doubt that the clause—for me to live is Christ, explains how Christ should be magnified in his life. And we therefore take it for granted, that the next clause explains how Christ should be glorified in his death. And how? Because that death would be gain, and the fact of its being gain to him was a magnification of Christ. "For me to live is Christ, and I shall magnify Him; and to die is gain, and therefore He is magnified in it." There are thus two questions—why death was gain, and how in that gain Christ was magnified?

Death, it cannot be doubted, was gain to the apostle in a personal sense. It removed him from suffering and disquietude, lifted him up out of a prison, and translated him into the presence of Christ. It gave him heaven for earth, enjoyment for labour, and spiritual perfection for incomplete holiness. It brought him into the presence of his exalted Lord, to bear His image, live in His splendour, and hold pure and uninterrupted fellowship with Him. That gain is not to be counted—it surmounts calculation. It was to leave the imperfect society of earth for the nobler fellowship of the skies; to pass from service involving self-denial, tears, and

G

suffering, to the crown which cannot fade ; to rise above the process of discipline involving constant watchfulness and prayer, to a perfe t assimilation to his Divine Master. There is also a comparison implied in κέρδος. While life would be Christ, death would be Christ too, but in a far higher sense. Still there would be the glorification of Christ, but in another form, and the superiority of the last to the first is indicated by κέρδος. To live is " Christ ; " but, as he himself says, death is " to be with Christ," and therefore, in comparison with life, it is gain. For it would be Christ to him more fully than life could be—Christ to be praised for ever, without the clog of an animal frame to exhaust the worshipper, or the warring of the law in his members to distract or suspend his adoration and joy. And in his possession of such a gain, Christ would be magnified, for His love had prepared it, His death had brought it within his reach, and His grace and spirit had prepared him for it. And if he should be called to suffer as a martyr, and such a prospect could not but rise before the mind of a prisoner in the prætorium, pending an appeal to the frantic and ungovernable Nero, then his courage and constancy in sealing his testimony with his blood, and in being made conformable to his Lord's death, would of itself glorify Christ in the exhibition of that meek and majestic demeanour, which the consciousness of Christ's presence alone could inspire and sustain. The expression about the gain of death seems to have been of proverbial currency. Socrates (Plato, *Apolog.* 32) declares under certain suppositions—κέρδος ἔγωγε λέγω ; but Lucian pronounces as might be expected—οὐδενὶ τὸ θανεῖν κέρδος. Many examples in which death is called loss, ζημία, may be found in Wetstein. Libanius, *Or.* xxvi., says, with a feeling very different from the apostle's—οἷς βαρὺ τὸ ζῆν, κέρδος ὁ θάνατος. So in Sophocles, *Antig.* 474. Bos, *Exercit.* p. 193.

(Ver. 22.) Εἰ δὲ τὸ ζῆν ἐν σαρκὶ, τοῦτό μοι καρπὸς ἔργου, καὶ τί αἱρήσομαι, οὐ γνωρίζω—" But if to live in the flesh, if this to me be fruit of labour, and what I shall choose, I know not." The general purport of this verse with its connection is pretty apparent, but from its compactness it is not easy to furnish a strict analysis. The apostle felt that both in life and death, Christ should be magnified, and in the preceding

verse he assigns the reason; nay, it would seem that he
prefers that Christ should be glorified in his death, as death
to him would be gain. But in a moment he feels that really
he ought to have no preference. By the use of κέρδος he has
given a preference to death; but the commands of Christ, the
claim of the churches, and the wants of the world, rush upon
him, and he so far retracts his preference as to allow, that if
prolonged life be necessary to the full harvest of his ministry,
he will not make a choice. He had virtually made a choice
in saying "death is GAIN;" but still, if there was more work
for him on earth, he would at least hesitate in coming to a
decision. And then he depicts his state of mind; there is
in it the strong desire to depart and be with Christ, which
nobody can doubt is far better; but there is also the obligation, if the Lord so will it, to abide on earth, and be of service
in the gospel.

The particle εἰ is syllogistic, or puts a case, and may be
almost rendered by "since," as it presents a fact in the form
of a premiss. Δέ is continuative, but introduces a contrast.
It is plain that τὸ ζῆν ἐν σαρκί describes his natural life or its
prolongation, as if there had been present to his mind an
ideal contrast between the higher and future life unclothed,
which is involved in κέρδος, and the present and lower form
of embodied existence on earth. It does not seem necessary,
with Beza, van Hengel, and others, to attach any collateral
idea to σάρξ, such as that of frailty—*afflicta et misera.* Gal.
ii. 20; 1 Cor. xv. 50; Heb. ii. 14. There are different
ways of pointing and reading the verse, most of them abounding more or less in supplement. Hoelemann thus disguises
and reads it—εἰ δὲ τὸ ζῆν καρπὸς ἐν σαρκὶ τοῦτό (*i.e.,* τὸ
ἀποθανεῖν), μοι καρπὸς ἔργου—"but if to live be fruit in the
flesh, or mere earthly fruit, then this (that is, death) is to me
fruit in reality." But the contrasts here supposed are not
tenable—that of τό with τοῦτο, and of σαρκί with ἔργου.
Granting that debility and fragility are often associated with
σάρξ, yet we can scarcely take ἐν σαρκί as an adverbial
phrase qualifying καρπὸς understood; nor can ἔργου, even with
such a contrast, signify "in reality." We should have
expected ἐν ἔργῳ at the least; but ἔργον never has such a
meaning, even in the phrase which Hoelemann adduces—

ἐν λόγῳ ἢ ἐν ἔργῳ (Col. iii. 17), where it signifies in act, and not in reality. It may be remarked that καρπός has been apparently suggested by κέρδος—the last is gain ultimate and positive; the other is the fruit of apostolic service in the present life. The apostle is ready to resign for a season the κέρδος, that he may reap a little longer this intermediate καρπός.

Another interpretation which takes καρπὸς ἔργου in an unwarranted sense, is that of Beza, followed by Cocceius and several other critics, who give the words the Latin sense of operæ pretium, thus—An vero vivere in carne mihi operæ pretium sit, et quid eligam, ignoro—" Whether to live in the flesh be worth my while, and what I shall choose, I know not." In sentiment, this exegesis is opposed to the distinct assertions of the following verses. The apostle could not be ignorant whether it were of advantage to remain on earth— nay, he takes it for granted that it was worth his while to stay, as his life was needful to the churches, and would result in the furtherance and joy of their faith. Nor can καρπὸς ἔργου be well rendered into operæ pretium. Besides, if in dependence on οὐ γνωρίζω, the clause εἰ τὸ ζῆν and the clause καὶ τί αἱρήσομαι do not correspond in structure. The exegesis we have just considered is virtually that of Conybeare, who renders—" but whether this life in the flesh be my labour's fruit, and what I shall choose, I know not." The place given to τοῦτο in the translation cannot be defended, and it is liable generally to the last objection stated.

A third form of exegesis supplies ἐστί μοι, and makes a complete sentence of the words down to καὶ τί—" And if to live in the flesh, this is the fruit of my labour," as in the Authorized Version. If I am to live, then I shall have the more fruit of my labour, as Bengel says—hunc fructum inde habeo, ut plus operis facere possim. He takes the words καρπὸς ἔργου as if in apposition—Paulus ipsum opus pro fructu habet. A similar exposition was held by Pelagius, and is also adopted by Storr, Flatt, and Matthies, who renders—wenn aber das Leben im Fleische so 'st mir dieses ein—καρπὸς ἔργου—" if there is life in the flesh, it is to me fruit of labour." This exegesis, which makes the second clause form the apodosis, seems, besides introducing a supplement, to render *καί* superfluous in the next clause, and introduces a grating ellipse.

A fourth mode of explanation supposes an aposiopesis, and therefore endeavours to express the latent thought of the apostle. Thus Zegerus—"and if to live in the flesh is the fruit of my labour, *and if to die is gain,* then what to choose I wot not." That is to say, the apostle is supposed not to express the second member of the sentence—*alterum jam mente per-tractans.* Rilliet's paraphrase is—"I ought not to desire death;" and it is to this mental thought that the apostle adds —"and I know not which I should choose." Müller holds a similar supposition. Nobody doubts the existence of such a figure of speech, though critics have unduly multiplied instances of it. But it is found principally in sentences uttered under excitement, where well-known idioms occur, or where words are supplied by tone and gesture. There, in fact, appears no necessity for reverting to it here, though the meaning brought out is generally correct.

The Greek fathers generally, Luther, Calvin, Heinrichs, Schrader, van Hengel, De Wette, Meyer, Wiesinger, Bisping, Peile, Ellicott, and Alford, connect the verb γνωρίζω with the clause before it, and regard the words down to *καί* as forming one sentence. De Wette's version is—"If life in the flesh, this be my labour's fruit, what I shall choose, I know not." Meyer's paraphrase is—"but if remaining in fleshly life, this, and none other, is to me fruitful for my official work, so am I in uncertainty as to the choice which I should make between both." Among such as hold this view, which we regard as the right one, there are minor differences, and also errors.

The pronoun τοῦτο represents and sums up the entire phrase —τὸ ζῆν ἐν σαρκί. See under Eph. ii. 8. There is no Hebraism in the usage, as Glassius supposes, *Phil. Sac.* i. 177. The use of ἐκεῖνα in Mark vii. 15, referred to by Winer, § 23, 4, is somewhat similar. Bernhardy, § 283. If to live in the flesh, "*this*," Meyer says—"this, and not death." Perhaps he makes the contrast rather strong. It may be "*this*" on which I have laid so little stress, as to call death in comparison with it gain. We cannot agree with Meyer in rendering καρπός— *emolumentum,* nor does Rom. i. 13 sustain such a sense. It means product or result, the context showing of what nature it is.

The genitive ἔργου refers to his special work. Acts xiii. 2 ; 1 Thess. v. 13. It is not the genitive of object, as if the meaning were " fruitful for the work," but the genitive of subject, and is simply—" fruit from my work," or in connection with it. The apostle then affirms virtually that his continuance in life would be tantamount to reaping additional fruit in his work. If he lived, he should work, and that work by God's blessing would not be in vain. The train of thought is this : he had said—" for me death is gain ; " but in an instant he pauses, not to retract the thought, but to subordinate it to present duty, for abode on earth would yet add to the spiritual harvest which his labours had produced. As if he meant to say—but since to live in the flesh, since this will be fruit to me from my labour, then I know not what choice to make.

And so the Syriac reads : ܘܐܢ ܐܠ ܚܝܐ ܒܣܪ.

The apostle thus shows, that it was not weariness of life, chagrin, or present evil, that prompted the expression—" death is gain." Very different was his motive from that expressed by the pagan—θανεῖν ἄριστόν ἐστι ἢ ζῆν ἀθλίως—" better die than live miserably." *Phil. apud Stobæum.* His was a calm and settled conviction ; and had there been no more work for him on earth, he would have longed to enjoy the gain. So that he did not know what election to make—on which alternative to place the preference :—

καὶ τί αἱρήσομαι οὐ γνωρίζω—" and what I shall choose, I know not." The τί stands for the more precise πότερον—as *quis* for *uter* in Latin. Matt. ix. 5, xxi. 31, etc. The verb γνωρίζω usually signifies to make known or declare, and many, as Rheinwald and van Hengel, give it such a meaning here— *non dico.* Bengel has—*non explico mihi.* Probably the meaning is—" I do not apprehend," and thus it is different from οἶδα and γινώσκω. Ast, *Lex. Plat. sub voce.* It seems to intimate, that with a desire or effort to know, such knowledge could not be attained. " And what I shall choose, I cannot make out." The future αἱρήσομαι is used for the subjunctive. Winer, § 41, 4, *b.* The two forms have very much the connection which the forms " will " and " would " originally had in English. The verb is in the middle voice—" what I shall take for myself." The principal difficulty, however, is in relation to καί, at the beginning of the sentence.   Peile takes it as the apostle's substitute for the Hebrew *vau*, and quotes, as strictly analogous, a line of the *Agamemnon*—καὶ τίς τόδ' ἐξίκοιτ' ἂν ἀγγέλων τάχος—"and what messenger could come with such speed?"   But there is not a full analogy, for the question occurs in a dialogue.   Clytemnestra had asserted that Troy was taken just last night; the Chorus cannot credit the intelligence, but knowing the great distance of the city, cry—"And what messenger could come with such fleetness?"   In Scottish dialogue, it is very common to put "and" at the commencement of a question which implies either doubt or wonder—"And how did it happen?" etc.   Crocius and Heinsius take καί in a somewhat similar way, and give, as an illustration, Mark x. 26—καὶ τίς δύναται σωθῆναι; but the passages are by no means analogous.   It is also out of the question to render καί, *ideo* or *sane*, or by any other explanatory particle.   The καί is to be taken as signifying *and* or *also*, and as placed at the commencement of the apodosis.   Of this there are many examples in the New Testament, and among the classical writers.   Hartung, I. 130.   It carries this sense, that what follows καί is described as the result of what precedes, or as in close connection with it.   This granted, "and" that will follow.   The meaning then is—if to remain in the flesh, if this be to me labour's fruit, I am flung back on the other alternative, and what I shall choose, I wot not.   If I look simply at result, "to die is gain," I have no hesitation; but there is the other idea, that "to live is Christ;" I therefore find myself in a dilemma, and know not which to select.   In the following verse, the apostle states the alternatives more distinctly.

(Ver. 23.) Συνέχομαι δὲ ἐκ τῶν δύο—"But I am pressed on account of the two."   There is no doubt that δέ is preferable to γάρ, as it has the great majority of MSS., versions, and quotations in its favour.   The verb συνέχομαι denotes—to be held together, distressed, or perplexed, as in Luke xii. 50; Acts xviii. 5; 2 Cor. v. 14.   In using ἐκ, the apostle points out the sources of his strait; and, by δύο with the article, he marks the alternatives stated in the preceding, and not in the succeeding context, as Rheinwald and Müller suppose.   He has just said—"what to choose I wot not," and the choice lay between two things, life and death; and now he adds—

between these two I am held in suspense. Müller seems to imagine that a retrospective reference would have required ἐξ ἐκείνων δύο. The following clauses, however, though not grammatically referred to in δύο, are yet contained in it, and are now more fully explained in the text.

The apostle describes his dilemma, and it is an extraordinary one. Though he had a strong desire for heaven, and, indeed, had been in it (2 Cor. xii. 1-4) and knew it, yet was he willing to forego the pleasure for the sake of Christ's church on earth. For he thus describes himself—

τὴν ἐπιθυμίαν ἔχων εἰς τὸ ἀναλῦσαι καὶ σὺν Χριστῷ εἶναι —"having," or "inasmuch as I have the desire for departing and to be with Christ." The verb ἀναλύω signifies to unloose, to depart, and then emphatically to depart from life. 2 Tim. iv. 6. It is needless to inquire on what the image is based; whether, as Jaspis and Elsner maintain, on the departure of guests from a feast; or whether, as Perizonius supposes, from equestrian custom; or, as others conjecture, from the weighing of the anchor prior to the sailing of the vessel; or, as Müller preceded by Gataker imagines, from the nomad custom of striking the tent before the march. Departure, as the name or image of death, is so natural and so universal, that one needs not to give it any special or local origin. It is wrongly translated in the Vulgate by dissolvi, derived perhaps from the classical use of solvo. Drusius absurdly conjectured that the active stood for a passive. Compare also Schoettgen, Horæ Heb. i. 796. The construction with εἰς is rather unusual— 1 Thess. iii. 12, 13—for ἐπιθυμία is usually construed with the genitive, and sometimes with the infinitive preceded by the article. There is no reason to take it for the genitive, τοῦ ἀναλῦσαι; and we agree with Meyer that εἰς τὸ ἀναλῦσαι stands in relation to the entire clause—τὴν ἐπιθυμίαν ἔχων; the language having a certain strength and emphasis. That desire pointed steadily and uniformly εἰς, "in the direction of" decease. Winer, § 49, a, δ. The result of departure is to be "with Christ," and therefore death was gain. The apostle was in no ignorance as to his future state.[1] His death was not to him simply a departure from earth, or as Socrates (Plato, Apolog. 32) vaguely and cheerlessly calls it, a removal

[1] Lechler, Das Apostolische und das nachapost. Zeitalter; Stuttgart, 1857.

—εἰς ἄλλον τόπον. He knew what awaited him; and his
fondest view of heaven is expressed by the term—σὺν Χριστῷ.
And so in 1 Thess. iv. 17, v. 10, preceded by John xii. 26,
xvii. 24. He rejoices to look on heaven in its positive
aspect. It is to him the presence of Christ, and not merely
deliverance from the evils of life; not merely—

> " To leave all disappointment, care, and sorrow ;
> To leave all falsehood, treachery, and unkindness ;
> All ignominy, suffering, and despair,
> And be at rest for ever."

Of death, as an escape from such miseries, he does not speak,
though few had felt them so severely, for he had been weak in
every man's weakness, and burned with every man's offence.
2 Cor. xi. 29. To him life is Christ, and death is being with
Christ—the same blessedness in two aspects and stages, with
no time or region of dreary unconsciousness between. He
knew where Christ was, and where he should be with Him—
" at the right hand of God;" and he defers his "gain" to no
remote period, which supposes the resurrection to be passed,
but contemplates the being with Christ as the sure and immediate result of that departure which he desired. Though
his body should have fallen into the tomb, he speaks of *himself*
as being with Christ, himself though unembodied—assured of
his identity, and preserving his conscious personality, and so
being with Christ, as to derive from such fellowship enjoyments so pure and ample, that the thought of it impels him
to ecstasy :—

πολλῷ γὰρ μᾶλλον κρεῖσσον—" for it is much by far better."
The language is exuberant, the simple comparative being increased by another, μᾶλλον, and both intensified by πολλῷ.
Mark vii. 36 ; Winer, § 35, 1. The authorities as to γάρ are
divided. It has in its favour, A, B, and C, but it is omitted
in D, E, F, G, J, K. Some of them have πόσῳ for πολλῷ.
Tischendorf and Lachmann prefer γάρ, and perhaps rightly.
The preference of death over life was a personal matter. It
was better for him ; far better for him to be with Christ, than
to be away from Christ; far better to enjoy Christ than to
preach Christ; far better to praise Him than to suffer for
Him ; far better to be in His presence in glory, than to be
bound in a prison for Him at Rome. The contrast in the

apostle's mind, and as is evident from verse 21, is not between
heaven and earth generally, or between a world of sin and trial
and death, and a region of spiritual felicity and beauty, but
specially between the service of Christ here, and fellowship
with Him in glory. Even on the lowest view of the matter,
his avowal indicates the superior knowledge which the gospel
had furnished to the world. How melancholy the last words
of Socrates in the famed *Apology*—ὁπότεροι δὲ ἡμῶν ἔρχονται
ἐπὶ ἄμεινον πρᾶγμα, ἄδηλον παντὶ πλὴν ἢ τῷ θεῷ. Plat. *Op.*
ii. p. 366, ed. Bek. Individually, the servant of Christ
would not for a moment hesitate in making his choice; as a
saint, he could not have the slightest doubt; but as an apostle,
he felt that if earth was to be the scene of further successes
for Christ, he would yet consent to stay upon it, would, with
all his longing to depart, and with all his predilection for
being with Christ, still remain away from Him, for the benefit
of the churches. For he adds—

(Ver. 24.) Τὸ δὲ ἐπιμένειν ἐν τῇ σαρκὶ ἀναγκαιότερον δι'
ὑμᾶς—" But to abide in the flesh is more necessary on account
of you." To remain in the flesh, or to continue in my present
life—τῇ σαρκί—is placed in contrast to his departure. And
he calls this survival " more necessary," not more beneficial, as
Loesner, Am Ende, and others change it. The phrase δι' ὑμᾶς
is—" for your sakes, on your account "—placing his readers
in strong antithesis to himself and his own personal likings.
The force of the comparative ἀναγκαιότερον has been variously
resolved. Meyer understands it—as if the remaining were
more needful than the departure; van Hengel—that it is too
necessary to allow of his longing being realized. Nor is there
any need of saying, with Alford, " that the comparison contains
in itself a mixed construction between ἀναγκαῖον and αἱρετώ-
τερον, or the like." And it is refinement in Ellicott to suggest
a personal ἀναγκαῖον opposed to the comparative—departure a
thing felt needful, but remaining a thing more needful. There
is undue pressure in each of these forms of exegesis. The
apostle says, departure is better, stay more necessary; the one
better for himself, and the other more necessary for the churches.
The form of thought is changed. The κρεῖσσον, already expressed in reference to himself, is not repeated in reference to
his converts—better for me to decease, better for you that

I stay; but the idea of "better" is deepened into "more necessary," and is thus the more palpably bodied out, so as to give foundation to the avowal of the following verses.

(Ver. 25.) Καὶ τοῦτο πεποιθὼς οἶδα ὅτι μενῶ καὶ παραμενῶ πᾶσιν ὑμῖν—"And being persuaded of this, I know that I shall remain, and remain with you all." The τοῦτο is governed by πεποιθώς, not by οἶδα, and refers to the sentiment of the last clause—"Being assured of this, that abiding in the flesh is more needful for you." In expressing the idea of his stay, the apostle, in the fulness of his heart, uses two verbs, first μενῶ and then παραμενῶ. Tischendorf prefers the unusual compound συμπαραμενῶ, found in E, J, K, and some of the Greek fathers, whereas παραμενῶ has the primary authority of A, B, C, D¹, F, G. The second verb becomes personal in its reference, "I shall remain, and remain with." Not only should he survive, but survive in their company—the datives πᾶσιν ὑμῖν being governed by παρά in composition. Another compound of the same verb, ἐπιμένειν, had been already employed in ver. 24. The verb οἶδα retains its ordinary meaning, though the object known may be something with a future existence. And the effect of his remaining with them is next stated—

εἰς τὴν ὑμῶν προκοπὴν καὶ χαρὰν τῆς πίστεως—"for the advancement and joy of your faith." The genitive πίστεως is not, as by van Hengel and Baumgarten-Crusius, to be separated from προκοπήν, and attached solely to χαράν, as if the meaning were "for your advancement, and for the joy of your faith;" nor can this hypothesis be reversed, as by Beausobre—*pour votre avancement dans la foi et pour votre joie,* "for your progress in faith and for your joy." Nor yet is Macknight correct in rendering, "for the advancement of the joy of your faith." Nor is the phrase a hendiadys, as Am Ende and Flatt resolve it—that there may be a joyful increase of your faith. It refers equally to both nouns. Winer, § 19, 4; Middleton, p. 368. One end was—the advancement of their faith. It would be greatly increased by the apostle's presence and teaching, might grow into deeper vigour, and widen in the circuit of its objects. And his stay would be also for the joy of their faith. The genitive is in both cases that of possession. Their faith possessed a susceptibility of progress, and it would be excited and urged on; that faith, too, possessed or had in

it an element of joy, which would be quickened and developed.
There is no good reason for Ellicott's view in relation to the
two nouns, that the genitive has a difference of aspect, in the
last case being that of origin. Joy does spring out of faith—
the genitive of origin; but faith may be equally well regarded
as possessed of the joy which it originates. Alford makes the
genitive that of subject, but this in the case of the second
noun appears awkward; their faith was to increase, that is,
to be the subject of increase; and also to rejoice: but joy has
more of a personal character. Progress and joy are therefore
predicated as equally belonging to their faith, or as equally
possessed by it.

(Ver. 26.) *"Ἵνα τὸ καύχημα ὑμῶν περισσεύῃ ἐν Χριστῷ
Ἰησοῦ ἐν ἐμοί*—" That your matter of boasting may abound
in Jesus Christ in me." The *ἵνα* introduces a further purpose,
and *καύχημα* is matter of boasting. Rom. iv. 2; 1 Cor. v. 6,
ix. 15. We cannot, with Ellicott, regard this clause as
merely a definite and concrete form of the previous abstract
statement—" for the furtherance and joy of your faith." It
contains a concrete representation, but it also describes an
ulterior purpose. It supposes the increase of their joy and
faith, and expresses what this should effect. And the matter
of boasting is not vaguely their Christian state, or their possession of the gospel, but the conscious result brought out in
the last clause of the previous verse. That matter of boasting
was to abound in Christ Jesus—He being the inner sphere of
its abundance. The connection adopted by Rilliet is wrong,
for he joins *ἐν Χ. Ἰ.* to *καύχημα*, as if the meaning were, that
their boasting was occasioned—*par leur union avec Christ*.
The phrase *ἐν ἐμοί*, on the other hand, marks the outer element
or sphere of this matter of boasting. We cannot agree with
Alford in giving *ἐν* two senses in these two clauses, as if it
described the field of increase, on its first occurrence, and were
to be rendered " by means of," on its second occurrence. We
think that it bears the same signification in both instances—
that in both it describes the sphere of abounding joy—first,
higher and spiritual—in Christ; and secondly, lower and
mediate—in the apostle. And in him for the following
reason—

διὰ τῆς ἐμῆς παρουσίας πάλιν πρὸς ὑμᾶς—" on account of

my coming again to you." While ἐν has marked one relation
of this abounding joy to the apostle, διά points out another
of a public or instrumental nature. In the occurrence of
παρουσία—πρός, the primary force of the preposition is not
lost. The return of the released prisoner to Philippi would
be of incalculable benefit. It would furnish occasion for
deeper and more extended lessons on Christianity, so as that
their faith might make progress, and its joy might be resusci-
tated, and this possession of a faith conscious of progress and
buoyant with gladness, would furnish matter of abundant
boasting in Christ Jesus, through the apostle's visit.

In the previous paragraph, the apostle makes no allusion
to the Second Advent. Some, indeed, have held that originally
he imagined that he was to survive till that period, but that
afterwards he gradually and completely changed his mind ;
his belief being once, that Christ was coming to take him, but
ultimately, that he must depart, in order to be with Christ.
Now, it will not do to apply the dictum of Professor Jowett,
that " Providence does not teach men what they can teach
themselves," [1] for in Paul's case he received the gospel " by
the revelation of Jesus Christ," and surely a doctrine so important must have been among the lessons supernaturally
communicated, for it formed an essential portion of the truth.
Nor will it suffice to say, with Alford,[2] that as Jesus did not
know the day himself, higher knowledge cannot be expected
of His servant. Mark xiii. 32. Granting that this interpretation of Christ's words is correct, yet surely the same ignorance
could not be predicated of the exalted Saviour, whose Spirit
dwelt in the apostle, for the delegation of all power to Him
must ensure the possession of all knowledge. Besides, to say
that the apostle did not know the period, is not a sufficient
argument, for he does not admit his ignorance ; nay, on the
contrary, as these scholars hold, he taught that the Second
Coming was an imminent event. He who says, in the First
Epistle to the Thessalonians—" then," that is, after the dead
in Christ are raised, " we which are alive and remain shall be
caught up," if he meant to affirm that he and those to whom
he wrote would survive till the Lord's descent, must have
very soon altered his belief, for in a letter written to the same

[1] On 1 Thessalonians, p. 96.   [2] On 1 Thessalonians v. 13.

church shortly afterwards, he bids them on no account, and
under no teaching, whatever its pretensions, to entertain the
notion that the day of Christ was at hand.   Then he sketches
a portentous form of spiritual tyranny and impiety, which
must be developed and destroyed prior to the Second Coming,
and yet, in the very same document, he prays God to direct
the hearts of his readers "into patient waiting for Christ."
Could the apostle, after what he had written, still believe that
Christ was coming in his own day, or did he suppose that
himself was to witness the growth, maturity, and overthrow
of the Man of Sin ?   In the Epistle to the Romans also, he
describes the inbringing of the Jewish race, but at that time,
this inbringing could be regarded as no event very soon to
happen, for they were enemies so malignant, that he prays
and asks the Roman Christians to pray with him, that he
" may be delivered from them."   We cannot therefore believe,
with such indications of his earliest sentiments before us, that
the apostle, after waiting in vain for his Lord's coming, changed
or modified his view.   Nor in the discourses recorded in the
Acts do we find any tokens of such fluctuation.   In his address
at Athens, he refers to a day in which God will " judge the
world by that man whom he hath ordained," and as the
resurrection precedes the judgment, that Man Himself calls
this period of His wondrous power " the last day."   John vi.
39, 40.   Nor can we for a moment admit to Jowett, that
Jesus Himself shifts His ground in His various answers to
questions as to the time of His coming, for the different
replies indicate that the " coming " was by the questioners
differently understood.   Could the same Speaker understand
His " coming" in the very same sense, when He speaks of
Jerusalem compassed with armies, as one token of it, and yet
affirms that the gospel must be preached to all nations before
the " end " shall come ?   Can the words—" I will come again
and receive you unto myself"—have the same fulfilment as
these other words—" When the Son of man shall come in His
glory, and all the holy angels with Him, then shall He sit
upon the throne of His glory, and before Him shall be gathered
all nations " ?

    The declaration—" I have a desire to depart "—is by no
means at variance with that other avowal—" not for that we

would be unclothed." 2 Cor. v. 4. In the chapter where this last statement occurs, the apostle still says—" Willing rather to be absent from the body, and present with the Lord " —verse 8. The reluctance to be unclothed is natural, the spirit does not will to be unfleshed, but it submits to the intermediate process of divestment, only as a step toward ultimate and spiritual investiture — toward being finally " clothed upon." Or the meaning may be—we would prefer to be at once " clothed upon," without dying at all, that our mortal part may be " swallowed up," absorbed and assimilated by life, as in the translation of Enoch and Elijah, and in the sudden transmutation which shall pass over living believers when the Saviour comes. But in this paragraph of Second Corinthians there is no allusion to such coming, as forming any part of the argument ; the course of illustration being suggested and conditioned by the initial statement as to the dissolution of the earthly tabernacle.

The apostle has expressed himself very confidently as to his survival, liberation, and proposed visit to the Philippian church. He could scarcely have made a stronger asseveration—" Having this confidence, I know that I shall abide and continue with you all; that your rejoicing may be more abundant, by my coming to you again." Was the apostle's confidence warranted ? Or was his anticipation verified ? According to the chronology adopted by some, only a brief period elapsed between the writing of this letter and the decapitation of the apostle, the epistle being written in 62 or 63 A.D., and the martyrdom taking place in 64. Others affirm that the apostle was released as he expected, and that he made another and a last missionary tour into Asia Minor, passing over to Macedonia, and being " filled with the company " of the church at Philippi. The question of a second imprisonment at Rome has been long and keenly agitated, but this is not the place to enter into any analysis of the conflicting evidence derived either from traditionary hints, or certain exegetical inferences in the pastoral epistles. Suffice it to say, that difficulties are great on either hypothesis, and that such men as Baronius, Tille- mont, Usher, Pearson, Mosheim, Hug, Gieseler, Neander Olshausen, and Alford are on one side ; while Petavius Lardner, Hemsen, De Wette, Winer, Wieseler, Davidson, Schaff

and Meyer are on the other, holding that there was only one
imprisonment. The apostle's assertion in the preceding
paragraph is firm and decided; but we dare not argue upon
it, because it comes into direct collision with an assertion as
firm and decided, in Acts xx. 25—"And now I know that
ye all among whom I have gone preaching the kingdom of
God, shall see my face no more." If the apostle were imprisoned but once, the declaration written to the Philippians
is not in accordance with fact; and if he were released, and
allowed again to travel, then the previous declaration spoken
to the Ephesian elders at Miletus was not in accordance with
fact. So that in the discussion, no stress can be laid on the
apostle's own language—the οἶδα of Phil. i. 25, which would
favour a release and a second imprisonment, being balanced
by the οἶδα of Acts xx. 25, which would as certainly dis-
countenance it. The announcement of verse 25 sprang from
deep longing and affection, and is rather the outburst of
emotion than the utterance of prophetic insight. For by
the time the apostle comes to the middle of the second chapter, the impulse of the moment had passed away, his confidence
had drooped, the shadow had fallen upon him, and he writes
under a different forecasting—"Yea, and if I be offered upon
the sacrifice and service of your faith, I joy and rejoice with
you all. I trust in the Lord that I also myself shall come
shortly." Still different is his sentiment when he thus addresses Philemon—"Withal prepare me also a lodging, for I
trust that through your prayers I shall be given unto you."
Amidst these alternations, perhaps this last saying expresses
the real or prevailing state of the apostle's mind—his hope
that the prayers of the church might be heard for him, and
that God, in gracious answer to them, might prolong his life
and his usefulness. It seems therefore to be taught us, that
the apostle had no revelations ordinarily as to his own personal future; and that, though he possessed the Holy Spirit
when he expounded the gospel, and therefore expounded it
without error or the possibility of it, he was unable to divine
what was to befall himself in time to come, save in so far
as it was formally communicated to him. Such revelations
were not essential to the discharge of his duty, and were no
portion of that truth which he was inspired to make known.

Nay more, as if to show us that himself recognized such a distinction as we have been making, he says—" And now, behold, I go bound in the Spirit unto Jerusalem, not knowing the things that shall befall me there;" but he adds, that this ignorance was dissipated, though only in a general way— " save that the Holy Ghost witnesseth in every city, saying that bonds and afflictions abide me." Acts xx. 22, 23. Inspiration for official labour was necessarily bestowed, and did not descend to the minor sphere of personal contingencies. It did not keep Paul from errors of opinion as to the course of his travels—" We were forbidden of the Holy Ghost to preach the word in Asia "—" They assayed to go into Bithynia, but the Spirit suffered them not." Acts xvi. 6, 7. Nor did it preserve in him a perfect recollection of the past, for he could not tell at the moment how many persons he had baptized at Corinth. 1 Cor. i. 16. We have thus endeavoured to meet the difficulty suggested by the text, and such a solution is surely better than with many to dilute the plain meaning of οἶδα into *probabiliter sperare,* or to adopt the adventurous paraphrase of Peile—" Of this I feel quite sure, that *in the event of my continuing* in the flesh, it will be for your further-ance and joy in the faith."

The apostle now passes from these more personal matters. As the hope of revisiting his Philippian converts, and gladden-ing them with his presence, rose up before him, he naturally, as if in anticipation of this result, and in preparation for it, asks them to live and act in the meantime in harmony with their profession, especially to cherish a true unity in defence of the gospel, and to exhibit a fearless courage in front of their antagonists. For their self-possession would be a token of perdition to such adversaries, but to themselves one of salvation. And this divine augury they were to accept and trust in, inasmuch as it was given them to suffer for Christ, as well as to believe in Him; faith being the means of salvation, and suffering its index. Then, and to inspirit them under such tribulation, the apostle likens their conflict to his own—such as they had seen it at Philippi, and now heard of it as still raging at Rome. The idea of unity recurs to his mind while he speaks of the conflict, for unity was indispens-able to success, and he reverts to it in the beginning of next

H

chapter. The joy which he anticipated on his visit depended on their cultivation of it, and it was essential also to that " fellowship for the gospel " by which they had been so eminently characterized, and for which he gave unceasing thanks to God.

(Ver. 27.) Μόνον ἀξίως τοῦ εὐαγγελίου τοῦ Χριστοῦ πολιτεύεσθε—" Only let your conversation be worthy of the gospel of Christ." The adverb μόνον gives oneness to the advice, places it by itself, as if in solitary prominence—" my impressions being as I have described them, this one or sole thing would I enjoin upon you in the meanwhile." In Gal. ii. 10, v. 13, the adverb is used with similar specialty. Here it is placed emphatically before the verb, as in Matt. viii. 8, ix. 21, xiv. 36. Gersdorf, *Beiträge*, etc., p. 488. The verb πολιτεύεσθε occurs only here in the Epistles, but is used by the apostle of himself. Acts xxiii. 1. It denotes to be a citizen in a state, or to live as such a citizen, and then generally to live, to conduct oneself. Passow, *sub voce*. In Thucydides vi. 92, Alcibiades says, in self-vindication, " I kept my patriotism only while I enjoyed my civil rights"—ἐπολιτεύθην; but the verb came at length to be used quite vaguely. Here, however, it defines life in its public aspect, and is often so employed. Thus, in 2 Macc. vi. 1, and xi. 25, it occurs with νόμοις in the first instance, and ἔθη in the second, denoting that according to which life is or should be regulated. It is found often in Josephus, and is a favourite term with the Church Fathers. See Wetstein, Suicer, Krebs, and Loesner for examples. The apostle, in similar exhortations, uses περιπατεῖν, as in Eph. iv. 1 ; Col. i. 10 ; 1 Thess. ii. 12. In each of these cases, as here, that verb is construed with ἀξίως, followed respectively by τῆς κλήσεως ; τοῦ κυρίου, and τοῦ θεοῦ. For a somewhat similar purpose the apostle employs ἀναστρέφεσθαι. 1 Tim. iii. 15 ; Heb. xiii. 18 ; Eph. ii. 3. A πολίτευμα is implied, and all who form it, or are its citizens, are to demean themselves in harmony with the gospel. For the nature of the Christian πολίτευμα, which may have suggested this πολιτεύεσθε, see under iii. 20. The apostle, in his choice of this peculiar verb in preference to his more favourite one, looks at them as members of a community, bound closely by reciprocal connections, and under obligations to various correspondent duties, and therefore " the gospel of

Christ" should be the norm or standard by which they ought
to be guided. The genitive τοῦ X. is that of origin—the
gospel which Jesus has communicated. Winer, however,
prefers to take it as the genitive of object, § 30, 1. But the
phrase quoted by him and Ellicott does not sustain their
view—"the gospel of God concerning His Son." The genitive
Θεοῦ is there that of origin, and the object is introduced by
περί. Why should εὐαγγέλιον X. differ from εὐαγγέλιον
Θεοῦ? The meaning then is—this sole request do I make,
live as the gospel prescribes; and as the genitive τοῦ X. and
the last clause of the verse would seem to suggest, let your
church-life be in harmony with its spirit and precepts—that
rectitude, courage, and love, which Christ illustrated in His
teaching, and exemplified in His life. And one purpose of
the injunction was—

ἵνα εἴτε ἐλθὼν καὶ ἰδὼν ὑμᾶς εἴτε ἀπὼν ἀκούσω τὰ περὶ
ὑμῶν—"in order that, whether having come and seen you, or
whether being absent, I may hear of your affairs." The construction is idiomatic; the verb ἀκούσω belongs properly and
formally to εἴτε ἀπών—"or whether being absent, I may
hear;" but it belongs really also to the first clause—εἴτε
ἐλθών, and stands in antithesis to ἰδών. The construction is
therefore not full or perfect, and various supplements have
been proposed. Meyer suggests that the course of thought is
—that "whether having come and seen you, I may hear from
your own mouths how your affairs are, or else being absent, I
may hear of them from others." But the contrast is too
specially marked to be thus eked out; for the idea of being
present with them and seeing them, carries in it the thought
that all information would be at once obtained. Others
supply a verb—"in order that, whether having seen you, or
whether being absent I hear of your affairs, *I may know* that
ye stand fast." De Wette and Alford espouse this view.
Van Hengel repeats the verb—"in order that, whether
having come and seen you, or whether being absent, I hear of
your affairs, *I may hear* that ye stand fast." Rilliet supposes
a zeugma—the verb ἀκούσω referring specially to ἀπών, and
generally, but less correctly, expressing the result of ἰδών.
The verse is informal from its hurried thought—the ἀκούσω
being emphatic, and the sense of the first clause remaining

incomplete. The supposition of his absence is last expressed, and that dwelling on his mind moulds or appropriates the construction; the verb that would have been used on the hypothesis of seeing them is dropped, and that which implies his absence is alone expressed. The construction is easily understood, and it needs not a formal supplement. As a question of psychology, it is interesting to note that the apostle's mind, though under the guidance of the Holy Spirit, moved with perfect ease and freedom, and fell into those colloquial idioms and loose disturbed constructions, which so naturally happen when a warm-hearted man is rapidly and confidentially throwing his thoughts into a letter. By the phrase τὰ περὶ ὑμῶν is meant generally " your affairs or condition "—not absolutely, as Rheinwald and Matthies suppose, for the general phrase τὰ περὶ ὑμῶν is explained and specialized by the clause ὅτι στήκετε. Hoelemann's resolution of the idiom as an anakolouthon is very clumsy, supposing that ὅτι may be omitted, and στήκετε (στήκητε) connected with ἵνα; or supposing that the article may be dropt before περὶ ὑμῶν, as in the versions of the Vulgate and Syriac. The precise element of their condition, which the apostle wished to hear about, is next told—

ὅτι στήκετε ἐν ἑνὶ πνεύματι—" that ye are standing in one spirit." For the attraction involved in the construction of ἀκούσω with ὅτι, see Winer, § 66, 5. The verb στήκω, formed from ἕστηκα, and wholly unknown to classic usage, is often used of Christian condition—iv. 1; 1 Thess. iii. 8— and often expresses the adjoined idea of permanence or that of resolve and promptitude to maintain what is already possessed or enjoyed. 1 Cor. xvi. 13; Gal. v. 1; 2 Thess. ii. 15. The image here is that of spiritual conflict, to which unity of action on their part was indispensable. The πνεῦμα is not the Holy Spirit, as is maintained by Erasmus, Beza, Matthies, and van Hengel. For the following phrase, μιᾷ ψυχῇ, shows that the apostle describes the Christian spirit. He hoped to hear that they stood in one spirit—pervaded with one genuine spiritual emotion—and not arrayed into separate parties with divided sentiments. And he further explains what this unity should engage in—

μιᾷ ψυχῇ συναθλοῦντες τῇ πίστει τοῦ εὐαγγελίου—" with

one soul striving together for the faith of the gospel." It is wrong on the part of Chrysostom and others to join μιᾷ ψυχῇ to στήκετε. Some of the ancient versions, such as the Syriac and Vulgate, follow the same syntax. The participle συναθ-λοῦντες, while it points to antagonism, also implies co-opera-tion among themselves. The συν refers to themselves, and not to any co-operation with the apostle, as Luther, Beza, Bengel, van Hengel, and Meyer suppose. The reference in ver. 30, to the apostle's own conflict, is to something which they had seen in the past, and could imagine in the present—something to which their conflict was similar, but yet separate in reality. The object for which or on behalf of which they were to contend, is the faith of the gospel, πίστει being the *dativus commodi*, or as Theodoret gives it, ὑπὲρ ἀληθείας. Jude 3. This is better than, with Calvin, Beza, and Rhein-wald, to understand πίστει as the dative of instrument—the weapon with which the conflict is to be maintained. The view of Erasmus, adopted by Mynster, is still worse, for it personifies faith, and paraphrases thus—*adjuvantes decertantem adversus impios evangelii fidem.* By πίστει εὐαγγελίου is not meant God's calling of the Gentiles without subjecting them to the ceremonial law, as Pierce supposes, for Judaizing opponents are not in question. Nor can πίστις signify objectively the system of truth contained in the gospel—a sense which it never undisputedly has in the New Testament, though such a usage is very frequent among Christian writers of later times. In the passages adduced by Robinson as bearing this sense, there will be found the distinctive idea of belief—not truth in the aspect of something presented for belief, but of something forming the matter of belief. The apostle uses both πνεῦμα and ψυχή, and therefore recognized a distinction between them. In their separate use they are apparently interchange-able; for though they really represent different portions or aspects of our inner nature, it may be loosely designated by either of them. But the adjectives πνευματικός and ψυχικός are contrasted in reference to the body—1 Cor. xv. 44; and there is a similar contrast of character in Jude 19. Πνεῦμα is the higher principle of our spiritual nature, that which betokens its divine origin, and which adapts it to receive the Holy Spirit, and in which He works and dwells. Ψυχή, on the other hand, is the lower principle—the seat of instinct, emotions, and other powers connected with the animal life. It is allied to καρδία, but πνεῦμα to νοῦς. Πνεῦμα is the term applied generally to Christ in the Gospels; but in the account of the agony ψυχή occurs—ψυχή and σῶμα make up living humanity. Olshausen's *Opuscula,* p. 145; Usteri, *Paulin. Lehrbeg.* p. 404. The Philippians were to stand in one spirit, united in their inmost conviction, and they were to strive with one soul—those convictions not allowed to be latent, but stirring up volition, sympathy, and earnest co-operation. Such concord was essential to success, and on their possession of it the apostle's joy on his proposed visit to Philippi greatly depended. Chap. ii. 2. Wiesinger says, " even the caricature of true unity of mind and soul, a self-formed *esprit de corps,* what a power it has! What ought our church to be, what might it be, were it but to attest this uniting power of the divine Spirit?" If there be oneness of conviction and belief, should there not be " one spirit"? and if there be oneness of feeling, interest, and purpose, should there not be " one soul"? and as concert is indispensable to victory, should there not be mutual co-operation—" striving *together*"? But not only are unity and mutual support necessary to this conflict on behalf of the faith—there must also be a calm and stedfast courage.

(Ver. 28.) Καὶ μὴ πτυρόμενοι ἐν μηδενὶ ὑπὸ τῶν ἀντικειμένων —" And in nothing terrified by the adversaries." Luke xiii. 17, xxi. 15; 1 Cor. xvi. 9. The participle πτυρόμενοι, a word originally applied to a sacred animal,[1] is parallel to the previous συναθλοῦντες. They were to feel a panic in no respect, or in nothing were they to manifest trepidation or alarm. As those " adversaries" were known to themselves, the apostle does not specify them, and whatever their number, stratagem, or ferocity, the Philippian athletes were not to waver for a moment, far less to retreat. Their enemies were either the malignant Jewish or Pagan population which surrounded them, and made them " suffer," and before whose machinations some might be tempted to a compromise, or even to a relapse. The awful explanation is subjoined—

---

[1] It is applied to sacred horses—Diodorus Sic. ii. 19; and it may be followed either by the dative or the accusative.

ἥτις ἐστὶν αὐτοῖς ἔνδειξις ἀπωλείας ὑμῶν δὲ σωτηρίας—
"which is to them a token of perdition, but to you of your
salvation." The reading is disputed. The words ἥτις ἐστὶν
αὐτοῖς have weighty authority. Some MSS., such as A, B,
C², have ὑμῶν, but some, not of equal value, have ὑμῖν, and
others ἡμῖν. Meyer, Lachmann, and Alford prefer ὑμῶν, as if
ὑμῖν had been corrected and adapted to αὐτοῖς. The relative
ἥτις is feminine by attraction with ἔνδειξις, and has for its
antecedent the preceding clause. Winer, § 24, 3 ; Kühner, §
786, 3. The peculiar form of this pronoun is also explicative,
or expresses an opinion. Eph. iii. 13. "And in nothing
intimidated by your adversaries : inasmuch as this non-alarm
on your part is a token to them of perdition, but to you of
salvation." The noun ἔνδειξις is "evidence" marked and
manifest. Rom. iii. 25 ; 2 Cor. viii. 24. The *Vetus Itala*
renders it by *ostensio*, and the Vulgate by *causa*, a rendering
which Erasmus and a-Lapide attempted to shield, and which,
though Beelen does not receive it, seems to have suggested to
him the following strange statement—*Obiter nota, perspicue
hic doceri dogma de merito bonorum operum.* Ἀπώλεια, in
contrast with σωτηρία, is spiritual ruin, and αὐτοῖς is governed
by ἔνδειξις. The courage of the sufferer is proof to the
persecutor of his sin, whether he will take it or not, and is
also a witness to himself of his final bliss and safety. Very
strange is the turn which Pierce gives to the clause—"which
conduct of yours they will esteem a certain evidence of your
destruction." This is against the plain meaning. Pierce
wrongly supposes the adversaries to be Judaizers, and with
such men it is no new thing to make those things conditions
of salvation which God has not, and "then unmercifully to
damn those who do not submit to them." The token to the
adversary of his perdition must be, that in the unshaken
stedfastness of the Christian sufferer, he may infer the truth
of the belief which sustains him so to do and dare, and learn
what must be his own doom, if he continue to oppose
it, and persecute its adherents. On the other hand,
were the adversary to terrify the convert, or induce
him to hesitate or recant, then such cowardice or vacilla-
tion would naturally lead him to despise a religion which
could be so easily renounced, or was valued less than

life, and he would be confirmed in his blindness and cruelty:—

καὶ τοῦτο ἀπὸ Θεοῦ—" and this from God." The reference in τοῦτο is to the sentiment of the whole verse, and not, as Matthies and Hoelemann hold, to the perdition and salvation; nor simply to the salvation, as Calvin, Piscator, and Flatt argue; nor yet, as Wolf and Alford take it, merely to ἔνδειξις. Neither can τοῦτο refer to the following verse, as Clement of Alexandria[1] and Theodoret understand it, followed by Am Ende and Rilliet. In Eph. ii. 8, 1 Cor. vi. 6, the reference in a similar τοῦτο is to a previous sentiment, and in the verse before us the construction, on any other hypothesis, would be awkward and tautological. It is not the token itself which is from God, but the token with what it points to, and what gives it significancy. The courageous constancy of the sufferer is a sign to the adversary of his perdition, and to its own possessor of salvation, and the whole is of God. Not simply salvation, but the token of salvation; not simply perdition, but the token of it—this unique and singular phenomenon is of God. Rom. viii. 17; 2 Tim. ii. 12; 2 Thess. i. 5. The apostle, in the next place, proves and illustrates the statement.

(Ver. 29.) "Ὅτι ὑμῖν ἐχαρίσθη τὸ ὑπὲρ Χριστοῦ οὐ μόνον τὸ εἰς αὐτὸν πιστεύειν, ἀλλὰ καὶ τὸ ὑπὲρ αὐτοῦ πάσχειν— 'For to you was it granted, on behalf of Christ not only to believe on Him, but also on behalf of Him to suffer." The pronoun ὑμῖν has an emphatic prominence. The aorist is used, as the apostle refers indefinitely to an early period of their past Christian history; but that the suffering continued, also, to the moment of his writing, is evident from the following ἔχοντες. As Wiesinger remarks, Meyer wrongly confines ὅτι to the confirmation of the clause καὶ τοῦτο ἀπὸ Θεοῦ. We understand the reference to be broader, to cover, in fact, the statement of the entire preceding verse. It is not simply —the token to you is of God, for on you He has conferred the double grace of faith and suffering; but it is—you have a token of salvation which others have not; for, while others have faith, you have more. You are called to suffer, and your courage in suffering is an augury of salvation. Had

---

[1] *Strom.* iv. p. 510 ; *Opera,* Coloniæ, 1688.

you not been privileged to suffer as well as to believe, this peculiar token had not been enjoyed. Or, why have you this token of salvation in your own Christian fortitude? Because God has given you to suffer, as well as to believe. Faith in Christ is the means of salvation; but suffering is the evident token of salvation. The one secures it, the other foreshows it. The martyr is not saved, indeed, because he suffers; but his undaunted suffering betokens a present Saviour and a near salvation.

The construction of the next clause is reduplicated. After saying τὸ ὑπὲρ Χ., the apostle seems to have intended to add πάσχειν; but he interjects a new thought—οὐ μόνον—for the sake of an illustrative emphasis, and then resumes by repeating ὑπὲρ αὐτοῦ. There is no occasion to suppose a pleonasm. The construction indicates a natural and full-minded writer, who sometimes interrupts the regular flow of his thoughts by the sudden insertion of a modifying or explanatory clause, and then at once resumes, by a formal or a virtual repetition of the connecting words. Rom. iii. 25, 26; Eph. i. 13. The English version is therefore wrong in taking τὸ ὑπὲρ Χ. absolutely—"to you it is given in the behalf of Christ." It is a weak dilution of the phrase ὑπὲρ Χριστοῦ, to render it "in Christ's cause," as is done by Matthies and Rilliet, after Beza and Zanchius. The suffering has a reference as personal as the faith—εἰς αὐτόν—ὑπὲρ αὐτοῦ. The apostle felt that Christ's cause and Himself were one; nay more, so personal was the love of the early Christians, so much did the Redeemer Himself stand out in close relation to themselves, that the mere abstract idea of his cause never occurred to them. It was Himself on whom they believed, and not the testimony given by the apostles concerning Him. It was Himself for whom they suffered, and not for their own convictions and belief about Him. It had been given them, not only to believe on Christ, but also to suffer for Him—a double gift; and though the apostle does not say which is the higher, yet certainly that which shows the path may be inferior only to that which has opened it. Matt. v. 11, 12; Rom. v. 3; 2 Cor. xii. 10. Such suffering in believers, who, nevertheless, are in nothing terrified by their adversaries, is a divine gift, as well as faith, and indeed presupposes it; for no one can suffer for Christ till he has believed on Him. While then τὸ εἰς αὐτὸν πιστεύειν is ὄργανον σωτηρίας, this τὸ ὑπὲρ Χριστοῦ πάσχειν becomes ἔνδειξις σωτηρίας. The older expositors strain the apostle's language, when they employ it as a polemical weapon against different forms of Pelagianism: for he simply regards their condition generally and in both its features as a divine gift, or as the result of God's kindness. While their own adherence to Christianity exposed them to suffering, and the malice of unbelief wantonly wreaked itself upon them, yet this suffering is viewed as of a higher origin. The apostle is not teaching dogmatically that faith is of God's inworking; but he is telling historically that faith and suffering had been theirs, and that the coexistence of the two being a privilege of divine bestowment, warranted them to regard their undaunted belief as a token of salvation. The reasons adduced by Chrysostom and his followers for the apostle's sentiment cannot be all sustained. The object of the apostle is to encourage the Philippian church, and not, as Chrysostom supposes, to warn it against pride, by ascribing its faith and its suffering alike to God. The Greek father dwells on the value of the gift, and uses this striking comparison—this divine gift is higher than raising the dead; "for, in this case, I am only a debtor;" but, "in the other" ("if I suffer for Christ"), "I have Christ as a debtor to me." The language is bold, indeed, and rhetorical, and not without an element of truth. But deductions like these are rather far-fetched; nor do the apostle's words warrant them. His one object is to inspirit the Christians at Philippi, by showing that undauntedness in the midst of their tribulation would be an evidence of salvation granted by God; for the twofold gift of faith and suffering is from Him, the one as securing, and the other as foretokening salvation. The apostle now associates himself with his suffering brethren—

(Ver. 30.) Τὸν αὐτὸν ἀγῶνα ἔχοντες οἷον εἴδετε ἐν ἐμοὶ καὶ νῦν ἀκούετε ἐν ἐμοί—" As you have the same conflict which you saw in me, and now hear of in me." The construction is changed to the nominative—ὑμεῖς being directly before the writer's mind—you the sufferers; the clause with ὑμῖν being so far subsidiary, but not making a formal parenthesis

Winer, § 63, I, 2 ; Kühner, § 677. The apostle describes their struggle by asserting its similarity to his own, as if to show them that such suffering might have been anticipated, and that it ought, by them as by him, to be borne in hope and patience.

The form εἴδετε is the true reading, and is now generally adopted. The last phrase—ἐν ἐμοί—is not, as the Vulgate renders it—*de me*. It supposes the ideal presence of those to whom he wrote, and points out the scene of conflict. They had seen his conflict with enemies on his first visit to them—Acts xvi. 16, etc.; 1 Thess. ii. 2—and they now heard in this epistle of his being engaged at Rome in a similar warfare. The apostle seems to allude to what he had been stating as to his condition at Rome, and to the personal antagonism which he encountered. Meyer refers us back to verse 7, overlooking what the apostle had just been writing about himself. It is both on the part of the Philippians and himself a conflict with personal enemies or non-believers—not precisely with teachers of false doctrine. The apostle, while some preached of envy and strife against him, was imprisoned, and these rival preachers thought to stir up affliction to his bonds, but failed, while his enemies and accusers strove, no doubt, to bring him to trial and death. There may have been a party from Palestine waiting to charge him before the emperor's tribunal ; and with them, and all whom they instigated to seek his life, he was in conflict. It is evident that he spoke from experience when he tells the Philippians of the double grace of faith and suffering—verses 7 and 29.

The entire paragraph, though it do not take the form of admonition after the first clause of verse 27, is still to the same effect ; and the apostle, by so earnestly describing the condition of which he wished to hear as belonging to them, virtually exhorts them to seek and maintain it. If he hoped to hear certain things about them, such as their struggle in concert for the faith of the gospel, and their unscared courage before their enemies, it is implied that they should possess those features of social state and character. And what is this when divested of these immediate peculiarities, but that "fellowship for the gospel," on account of which he thanked God on his whole remembrance of them, and which had distinguished them "from the first day until now"? In the 5th verse, he mentions generally "fellowship for the gospel" as the prime distinction of the Philippian church; and in this last section he only throws it into bold relief, by describing the united struggle it necessitated, the opposition it encountered, and the calm intrepidity which it ought ever to maintain.

CHAPTER II.

THE apostle's mind has been carried away for a moment by a reference to the hostility which was frowning upon the Philippian church. But he immediately reverts to the admonition which he had started in verse 27. His theme is unity, the cultivation of the feelings which maintain it, and the repression of that selfishness and pride which always retard and so often destroy it. He had joy in their spiritual welfare, but he would have fulness of joy in their harmony and love. Therefore he solemnly calls upon them by four distinct appeals, to fill up the measure of his gladness. His earnestness makes it evident that he apprehended the existence among them of a spirit of jealousy, selfishness, and faction. This suspicion haunted and grieved him, or at least it moderated that delight which he would otherwise have felt in them, and which he so ardently longed to possess. His happiness would be at its height, provided that the one soul and the one mind reigned in the church. What a motive to conciliation and peace lay in the thought that his joy was so far dependent on the absence of feuds and schisms among them! Could they be so unthinking as to grieve their apostle by any report of their differences? And they were to beware of strife and vainglory as elements of disunion, and to cherish a spirit of humility and kind regard for one another's welfare. For Christ is then held up as the great model of self-denying condescension—He whom as Master, they had engaged to obey; and whom as Example, they were pledged to imitate.

(Ver. 1.) *Eἴ τις οὖν.* The illative particle *οὖν* carries us back in thought to verse 27, and not to the clauses immediately before it. The "exhortation" and "comfort" are not spoken of, as Barnes supposes, in reference to the afflictions and persecutions just referred to. They had been exhorted to "stand fast in one spirit, with one mind striving together;" and now they are solemnly adjured to study unanimity of opinion and

action. The simple verb ἐστί is to be supplied to the clauses.
The structure of the appeal is peculiar. In using εἰ, the apostle
does not doubt the existence of these graces or feelings either
absolutely, or as existing among the Philippians; but he says,
If these do exist among you, put them into action, or manifest
them, so as to fill up my joy. The admonition amounts in fact
to an adjuration. Hoogeveen, *Doctr. Part.* ed. Schütz, p. 151.[1]
By the existence of such graces among you—by the exhortation which is in Christ, by the comfort of love, by the fellowship of the Spirit, and by the attachments and sympathies of
the gospel, I adjure you to fulfil my joy by being like-minded.
That is to say, the four clauses are really so many arguments
why the Philippian church should perfect the apostle's happiness by their constant and cordial oneness of judgment and
pursuit. And these four clauses, beginning each with the
same formula εἴ τις, mark the intensity of the apostle's desire;
the arguments so expressed possessing a distinct individual
power, and having also a united energy arising from their
rapid accumulation. For the apostle writes, as Chrysostom
describes his style—λιπαρῶς, σφοδρῶς, μετὰ συμπαθείας
πολλῆς.

Εἴ τις οὖν παράκλησις ἐν Χριστῷ—"If there be any
exhortation in Christ." In the modal phrase ἐν Χριστῷ, the
preposition ἐν means neither *per* nor *propter*, means neither
"by" Christ, nor "on account of" Christ, as Storr and Heinrichs are disposed to render it. The words are taken by some
to denote the sphere of this παράκλησις; by others to point
out its source. In the one case, the meaning is, "if in Christ
there be any exhortation;" in the other, if "there be any
consolation felt," or "if ye have any consolation through union
with Christ"—*in communione Christi*, as van Hengel dilutes
it. We prefer the former, viewing παράκλησις as objective.
Remote from the right exegesis is the idea of Erasmus and
Am Ende, that ἐν X. is for τοῖς ἐν X.—"among those who
are Christians." Our exegesis does not, as van Hengel affirms,
require ἡ ἐν X. Winer, § 20, 2.

The noun παράκλησις, and its verb, have two distinct
meanings in the New Testament—that of exhortation, but
different from διδάσκειν; and that of comfort or encourage-

[1] As in *Iliad*, i. 40; *Æneid*, iii. 443.

ment. Examples of both are so numerous that they need
not be quoted. The meanings are allied in this way, that
the exhortation is often intended to impart comfort, or results
in it. Thus, Rom. xv. 4—διὰ τῆς παρακλήσεως τῶν γραφῶν,
is not simply through the consolation contained in Scripture,
but the body of consolatory truth which Scripture exhibits;
or, again, Matt. ii. 18—'Ραχὴλ—οὐκ ἤθελε παρακληθῆναι—
"Rachel would not be comforted," would not feel the effect
of words of condolence and solace presented to her. See
1 Cor. i. 10, and many other places. We do not thus take
it here in its specifically Hellenistic sense of comfort, as is
done by the Vulgate, Chrysostom, Theodoret, Calvin, Grotius,
and Heinrichs, but rather in that of exhortation or hortatory
power. 1 Cor. xiv. 3; 2 Cor. viii. 4; 1 Thess. ii. 3, 11.
Such is the view of Luther, Bos, De Wette, van Hengel,
Rheinwald, and Meyer. Those who give the noun the meaning
of comfort, add the idea of affording comfort to the apostle.
Thus Theodoret — εἴ τινα ἐμοὶ παράκλησιν προσενεγκεῖν
βούλεσθε—"if ye wish to afford me any comfort." Such
also is the view of Calvin. The supposition of Peter Lombard is as baseless—viz., that the apostle means personal
consolation found in the possession of spiritual blessing. But
it is not warranted by the words, nor the strain of address;
nor yet is the notion of Storr and others, who, giving a
peculiar emphasis to τις, render—"if exhortation tendered in
Christ's name is of any value among you." We therefore
take παράκλησις as meaning that kind of exhortation which
moves or induces, and which has its sphere of action in Christ.

The nature of this hortative address is to be gathered from
the context. It is not simply exhortation to good, derived
from the pardon which Christ bestows, the Spirit which He
sends down, the power which He communicates, or the example
which He has bequeathed. But it is implied that it is
exhortation to unity and concord—exhortation which has its
element, and by consequence finds its power in Christ. The
apostle exhorts, but, in doing so, he leads them at the same
time to a Higher than himself:—

εἴ τι παραμύθιον ἀγάπης—"if any comfort of love." As
in the former case, very many render this term vaguely by
"comfort;" but Matthies, De Wette, van Hengel, and Hoele-

mann, assign it rather the sense of encouragement—*blandum colloquium*. With the latter we are disposed to agree, for we think that this sense prevails uniformly in the New Testament. John xi. 19—Many of the Jews came to Martha and Mary— ἵνα παραμυθήσωνται αὐτάς—"that they might speak kind words to them." So 1 Thess. ii. 11, and 1 Thess. v. 14— where the phrase occurs—παραμυθεῖσθε τοὺς ὀλιγοψύχους— "encourage the weak-minded." The noun therefore means verbal encouragement, kind conversation, or that tender address which cheers or excites. The neuter form of the word only occurs here, but another and earlier form[1] is found—1 Cor. xiv. 3—λαλεῖ οἰκοδομὴν καὶ παράκλησιν καὶ παραμυθίαν— "uttereth edification, and exhortation, and comfort." The following noun ἀγάπης is the genitive of source. The apostle does not mean his own love to them, as van Hengel and Bretschneider suppose ; nor yet does he specially allude, as Heinrichs, Schrader, and Storr imagine, to consolation or love specially on the part of the Philippians towards himself. The expression is general. If there exist the "comfort of love," and that it does exist the apostle does not doubt, then he calls upon them to fulfil his joy. For if such παραμύθιον springs from love, should it not exercise itself in disarming prejudice, in hushing strife, in smoothing asperities, in removing misunderstandings, in preventing aberrations, and generally, by "its still small voice," knitting together the members of the church, and charming away those evils which so seriously endanger its peace ? The apostle thus appeals to another basis of harmony—love, and its winning tongue :—

εἴ τις κοινωνία πνεύματος—"if any fellowship of the Spirit," the genitive being that of object, as in 1 Cor. i. 9. That this striking expression denotes only community of feeling among themselves, or between them and the apostle, is the view of many expositors, though some of them, as De Wette, Usteri,[2] Rilliet, van Hengel, and Wiesinger, speak of such common feeling as produced by the Holy Ghost. We feel that such a meaning does not come up to the Pauline phrase, and that it is to the Holy Spirit that the apostle refers. For instances

---

[1] As to the comparative age, etc., of nouns in ια and ιον, see Lobeck, *ad Phryn.* p. 517.

[2] *Paulin. Lehrbeg.* p. 295.

of πνεῦμα, etc., with and without the article, see under Eph.
i. 17. Wiesinger admits, that in the apostolic benediction,
2 Cor. xiii. 14, the phrase *may* have such a signification;
but, indeed, what other could it have there? Nay, he adds,
" How remote would the connection be, between the existence
of such a fellowship with the Spirit of God, and the exhortation which follows—'fulfil ye my joy'!" This appears to us
to be a total and unaccountable misapprehension. For the
fellowship of the Divine Spirit is the very basis of that like-
mindedness, the existence and development of which the
apostle covets among them. That correct apprehension of the
same truths which leads to like-mindedness, the felt reception
of common blessings which creates one-heartedness, position
in the church as an organic unity which guards against schism
—all is effected by the Spirit of God, of whom they partake.
If there be the joint participation of the Spirit, as indeed there
is, then it becomes a mighty inducement and power in securing
the concord which would fulfil the apostle's joy, and give them
the elements of character which he immediately depicts. For,
then, participation of the Spirit would produce similarity of
tastes, pursuits, and predilections; nay, this κοινωνία πνεύματος
was the real basis of that κοινωνία εἰς τὸ εὐαγγέλιον to which
he had already adverted :—

εἴ τις σπλάγχνα καὶ οἰκτιρμοί—" if any bowels and mercies."
The singular form—τις—has the preponderant authority of
A, B, C, D, E, F, G, J; and of the Greek fathers, Chrysostom,
Œcumenius, and Theophylact, and has therefore been received
by Griesbach, Scholz, and Lachmann. But Winer rejects it,
§ 59, 5,[1] b, etc. Tischendorf also, in spite of all this evidence,
has τινα in his text, and he is followed by Alford and Ellicott.
Meyer says that τινα is necessary; De Wette, that τις is
grammatically impossible. These critics look upon τις as a
copyist's blunder; but how could such an ungrammatical
blunder be so widely circulated? There was some temptation to change τις into τινα, but none to write τις, which
would have the appearance of a grievous solecism. It is
needless to imagine, with van Hengel, that the apostle wrote
εἰ σπλάγχνα, and that the pronoun, from a pedantic desire of
uniformity, was inserted by some transcriber. Nor will it

[1] See Moulton's edition of Winer, p. 661, note 3.

I

do, as some propose, to supply ἔχει for οἰκτιρμοί, for that would be a yet greater difficulty. We are disposed to think that the anomaly is only formal. The two nouns σπλάγχνα and οἰκτιρμοί are technically plural, though singular in meaning, and having only the plural form in the New Testament, came, like similar words, to be treated as singulars in sense. Both as representing one Hebrew plural contain only one idea, so that the last of them is sometimes put in the genitive —"bowels of mercy." Standing out to the apostle's mind as one generic idea, he prefixed the singular τις, just as we say, in common English—"if there is any news." In the same way the phrase—"bowels of mercy"—is taken as one Christian characteristic. The substantive σπλάγχνα represents the Hebrew רַחֲמִים, and denotes the thoracic viscera, or as we say—"heart." Οἰκτιρμοί represents the same Hebrew term without a figure. See under Col. iii. 12 ; Tittmann, *Synon.* i. p. 69 ; Fritzsche, *ad Rom.* ii. 315. The bearing of this on the unity of the church is very apparent—that union which is described in the following verse by various connected epithets. For where tender feeling, as expressed by σπλάγχνα, does not exist, such union is impossible. Universal callousness would be universal antipathy. And then, as offences must come—and do often come—as one member may hurt his neighbour by love of pre-eminence, stiff adherence to his own opinion, or depreciation of such as differ from him, there is need for the exercise of these "mercies" in forgiving a brother's trespass up to "seventy times seven." By the existence of such kind and compassionating temper, the apostle pleads that they should fulfil his joy.

The relation of these four clauses has been variously understood. Calovius takes the "love" of the second clause as the love of God, and imagines that in the three clauses there is a reference to the Trinity, Son, Father, and Spirit. This dogmatic notion does not harmonize with the tenor of the context. Meyer again takes the first and third as objective, and the second and fourth as subjective. This is true so far, and he supposes all the four things described as existing on the part of the readers of the epistle, as if it were said, "If there be *among you* exhortation in Christ," etc. But we rather regard each as absolute, and this is the strongest way of

putting the case.   The apostle does not say "among you,"
but speaks in general terms.   It is implied, indeed, that such
qualifications or arguments for unity were among them; but
the apostle specifies them in themselves, without asserting
them to be embodied in the Philippian community.   Wiesinger
again takes the two first clauses as representing what proceeds from the apostle; and the third and fourth, what is to
exist on the part of his readers.   He supposes the παράκλησις
and παραμύθιον to be tendered by the apostle, and the
" fellowship of the Spirit," and " bowels and mercies," to exist
among the Philippians.   But his argument against Meyer
may be turned against himself—" Why should not the apostle
have expressed this, if such was his meaning ?"   There being
in short no indication of any change of reference, all the four
clauses must be similar.   There seems to be no warrant for
adding any formal reference, either to himself or his readers,
to any of them.   It is as if he had said, If there be such an
impulsive power as exhortation in Christ; if there be such a
preventive of strife as the kind speech of love; if there be
such a basis of unity as the fellowship of the Spirit; if there
be such a guard and balance as loving and compassionating
temper,—then I adjure you by these to fulfil my joy by your
visible and growing harmony.

(Ver. 2.) Πληρώσατέ μου τὴν χαράν—" Fulfil ye my joy ; "
that is, make my joy full or perfect.   The pronoun is, as
often, placed before its governing substantive.   Winer, § 22,
7, 1 ; Gersdorf, *Beitr.* 456.   He rejoiced over them, and in
their spiritual welfare ; but he enjoins them by all these
considerations to give him perfect gladness in them.   If a
spirit of unity reigned among them, it would be the fulness
of his joy :—

ἵνα τὸ αὐτὸ φρονῆτε—" that you think the same thing."
The conjunction ἵνα indicates purpose.   The object of his
obtestation was, that they might possess unanimity, and that
is represented to his own mind by ἵνα.   But in such a form
of expression, and after the imperative, that purpose assumes
the aspect of result.   He besought them, by all the arguments
of the previous verse, to fulfil his joy, but that is only personal and incidental ; for above and beyond it, and yet
connected with it as its cause, the ultimate end he sought

was their concord and union. It is clumsy in van Hengel to make ἵνα dependent on a ταύτην understood before χαράν. Bengel regards the clauses as four in number, and as corresponding in order to the four arguments of the previous verse. This is more ingenious than sound. Only three clauses are employed by the apostle to depict that condition of the church in which he should so heartily rejoice. Nor is there very material difference among them. The first clause is the more general, or it describes the result which the apostle proposed to himself in so solemnly counselling them—"that ye think the same thought." The last clause brings back the same idea strengthened—" with united soul thinking the one thing ; " while the intermediate clause may be taken to specify the means by which the double result is obtained—"having the same love." Hoelemann refers τὸ αὐτό to the sentiments of the previous verse, but this connection is unwarranted in itself, and by the ordinary use of τὸ αὐτό, as in Rom. xii. 16, xv. 5, 2 Cor. xiii. 11, and in the same epistle, iv. 2 ; nor can it mean, *idem atque ego.* Some, as Meyer and Wiesinger, look on the first clause as more fully defined by those which succeed it. Beza takes the first as the theme, and the others as the expansion of it. Calvin divides the idea, giving one clause a reference to doctrine, and one to the exercise of mutual charity. Musculus, Crocius, Am Ende, and Matthies hold a similar view. As we have indicated, we take the first phrase as denoting that result which the apostle coveted, and held up to himself as his chief design in this earnest and tender injunction. This " thinking of the same thing " is not to be confined to any sphere of opinion, but to all that might occupy their minds, or to all that pertained to the church. Not in trade, politics, or the common concerns of life, indeed, but in all things on which, as members of the church, they might be expected to form a judgment, they were to think the same thing, or to come to a unanimous decision. And this would not be a difficult achievement if they followed the next counsel :—

Τὴν αὐτὴν ἀγάπην ἔχοντες—" having the same love." We regard this as the great or only source and accompaniment of unanimity, though Chrysostom takes it as synonymous with the preceding clause. Equal love would develop equal opinions. The head would be ruled by the heart. The effect of mutual affection in creating oneness of sentiment is of daily experience. Seeming diversities are cemented, like as lumps of various metals, cast into the crucible, come out in refined and perfect amalgamation. Offensive individualism disappears in brotherly love :—

σύμψυχοι τὸ ἓν φρονοῦντες—" with union of soul minding the one thing." The use of this compound adjective, which occurs only here in the New Testament, intensifies the clause, as the third expression of a somewhat similar sentiment, and therefore it is most naturally taken along with the participle. It is not only—" that ye mind the same thing," but—" fellow-souled," or " in deep sympathy minding the one thing." We want English terms for those expressive Greek compounds. Van Hengel looks on this epithet, σύμψυχοι, as pointing out the source of the "same love." We regard it rather as a special result, as expressing that state of heart which this sameness of love produces, which, binding each to each, makes them to be like-souled—ὁμοίως καὶ φιλεῖν καὶ φιλεῖσθαι (Chrysos.). This last clause brings up the sentiment of the first in a more earnest and distinct form. To avoid a supposed tautology, Wells long ago proposed to give τὸ ἓν the sense of "the one thing needful;" while Grotius, followed by Bishop Middleton, assigns it a reference to the following verse—minding this one thing, viz. doing nothing in a factious spirit. The distinction made by Tittmann, and the reference suggested by him to the fourth verse, are both artificial (De Synon. p. 68). The apostle's ordinary phrase is τὸ αὐτό, and this peculiar form occurs only here. It is probable that τὸ ἓν differed very little from τὸ αὐτό, or only as being the stronger expression. This accumulation of clauses as the result of mental excitement and anxiety, imparts intensity to the counsel, without making any formal climax. His soul glowed as it dwelt on its theme; and recurrent phrases, not frigid repetitions, are the natural expressions of its warmth. The same earnestness accounts for the connection of the verb with its own participle, φρονῆτε—φρονοῦντες; Jelf, § 705, 3; Lobeck, Paralip. p. 532. The two idioms are sometimes used in the same sentence, as in Xenophon, Cyropœd. p. 58, ed. Hutch.; or in Polybius, i. 4—πρὸς ἕνα καὶ τὸν αὐτὸν σκοπόν; or in

Latin, *idemque et unum*, Sueton. *Nero*, 4, 3 ; *unum atque idem*, Cicero, *Cat.* 4, 7. Ἕν, without the article, would, as Green says (*Greek Gram.* p. 201), "signify numerical unity, as opposed to plurality, but the abstract implies uniformity, as contrasted with diversity." The reference does not seem to be to any apprehended differences on matters of faith, but simply to such differences as might arise in ecclesiastical relationship. Toward one another they were to feel, speak, and act in this spirit, so that inviolable unity should characterize them.

It is true that the apostle repeats virtually the same idea. Βαβαὶ, says Chrysostom, ποσάκις τὸ αὐτὸ λέγει ἀπὸ διαθέσεως πολλῆς. Yet, as we have said, we think it is not mere repetition, the first clause with ἵνα describing the purpose or the coveted result; the second pointing out in what spirit it is to be obtained; the third expressing a closer intimacy which ends in thinking the same thing, or being actually and visibly one-minded. The apostle then warns them :—

(Ver. 3.) Μηδὲν κατὰ ἐριθείαν μηδὲ κατὰ κενοδοξίαν— "Minding nothing in the spirit of faction and vainglory." The reading is doubtful. Instead of μηδέ, the Received Text has ἤ, which, however, has not the same amount of external authority as μηδὲ κατά.

The apostle here rebukes the passions which are so fatal to union. The best supplement is φρονοῦντες—not ποιοῦντες, as so many suppose ; the former being more in unison with the train of thought. The common and modal sense of κατά glides sometimes into that of occasion and motive (Winer, § 49, d) ; but here it retains its first signification. It tells how, or after what way, the action of the supplied participle is done. With the first of the nouns, ἐκ is used—i. 17—and presents a different aspect of relation. On the meaning of the first noun, see under i. 17. In its connection with κενοδοξία, one peculiar aspect of its meaning is brought out, and that is, that it does not signify contention for the love of it, troubling the waters to enjoy the confusion, but such contention as tends and is designed to secure pre-eminence. It is self-seeking—the restless battle to be first, no matter what opposition be encountered, or whose feelings or interests may suffer. Κενοδοξία occurs only here in the New Testament. Wisdom xiv. 14.

This self-conceit is silly, indeed, but prejudicial to peace. Inordinate self-display absorbs brother-love. What I think is soundest, what I propose is best, my reasons are irrefragable, and my schemes cannot be impugned; to differ from me is evidence of want of judgment; and to oppose me must be ascribed to consummate folly or unpardonable obstinacy. I must lead; why should not I? all must follow; and why should not they?

ἀλλὰ τῇ ταπεινοφροσύνῃ ἀλλήλους ἡγούμενοι ὑπερέχοντας ἑαυτῶν—" but in humility regarding others as better than themselves." The words τῇ ταπεινοφροσύνῃ are not to be joined to the participle, as *dativus excellentiæ*, or as forming *norma judicii*, as if the meaning were, Let each regard the other on account of his humility, better than himself. Baumgarten-Crusius thus gives it, and then eulogizes it as *ein sinnreicher Spruch*. But the position of the words plainly joins them to the participle ἡγούμενοι, and they are a modal dative, not, however, exchangeable with κατά and an accusative, or they may be a dynamical and influential dative, meaning " in " or " under the influence of " humility. The article is prefixed to the noun as an abstract term—the virtue of humility. Kühner, § 485; Middleton, on *Greek Article*, p. 91. This humility is one of the distinctive features of Christianity, for it rests in absolute dependence upon God for everything. Some of the heathen sages might arrive at its meaning, so far as creaturely relations could teach it. But that meaning is immeasurably deepened by the aspect of a sinner's relation to a Redeemer, who died for him in his state of utter unworthiness, bestows upon him blessings to which he has no claims, and notwithstanding all his demerits, maintains the spiritual life within him. Ever unworthy, and yet ever receiving, yea, having nothing that he has not received, how lowly the opinion one should ever form of himself![1] See under Eph. iv. 2; Col. iii. 12. This humility, placed here as the contrast to self-seeking and vainglory, was to be the spirit in which they should regard one another. It is the true way of forming an estimate. Humility dispels the self-importance which is continually taking and asserting the measure of its own claims, when it comes into contact with others. The

---

[1] Neander, *Geschichte der Pflanz.* p. 759; Trench *on Synon.* p. 71.

one bids its possessor undervalue all about him; the other bids him prefer them. The motto of the former is—first, either first or nothing; the sentiment of the latter is—"less than the least of all saints." The older casuists, and many commentators, refer to the difficulty of forming such an estimate of others. Is it possible to regard all others as superior to ourselves? But the answer is not difficult. Every man that knows his own heart finds, and must find, much in it to give him a low estimate of himself, and he cannot tell what graces may be cherished in the bosoms of those around him; they may be superior to his own. Nor has he any cause to be vain of any gifts conferred on him—"What maketh thee to differ?" The original gift, and the impulse to cultivate it, are alike from above. Not that any man is to underrate himself, or in any way to conceal his gifts or graces, for he would by such a spurious modesty be contravening the design of the great Benefactor. *Non tam stultæ humilitatis*, said Luther, *ut dissimulare velim dona Dei in me collata*. Humility is not undue self-depreciation, but may coexist with fervent gratitude for gifts enjoyed, a thorough consciousness of their number and value, and the utmost desire to lay out "the ten talents" to the utmost possible advantage. But where there is self-assertion or rivalry to secure the "chief seat" and win applause, then the impulses of such vanity necessarily create alienation and disorder. There is no warrant to make the distinction of Storr, referring "strife" to the Jew; or of Rheinwald, referring "vainglory" to the philosophic Gentile.

(Ver. 4.) Μὴ τὰ ἑαυτῶν ἕκαστοι σκοποῦντες ἀλλὰ καὶ τὰ ἑτέρων ἕκαστοι—"Looking each of you not to your own things, but each of you also to the things of others." The plural ἕκαστοι is preferred on good authority, such as A, B, F, G, etc., though in other cases it occurs only in the singular, and the participle σκοποῦντες is preferred to σκοπεῖτε, as the reading of A, B, C, D, E, F, G. This counsel is still in unison with the preceding advices. Some understand it as explanatory of the third verse—Regard not every man his own virtues and excellencies, but regard also the virtues and excellencies of others. Calvin, Musculus, Raphelius, Kiel,[1] Hoelemann,

[1] *Opuscula*, p. 172; Lipsiæ, 1821.

Müller, and Baumgarten-Crusius are of this opinion ; but it
is not so agreeable to the common idiom as the prevalent
one, and it does not harmonize with the example of Christ
which is immediately set forth. The verse brings out one
special phasis of the duty—let each regard others better than
himself. The verb σκοπεῖν, connected with such a phrase as
τὰ ἑαυτῶν, is to regard one's affairs, or seek his own individual
benefit, and is not, as Meyer remarks, materially different
from ζητεῖν, similarly used in 1 Cor. x. 24, 33, xiii. 5 ; Phil.
ii. 21. Examples abound in the classics, as may be seen in
the collection of them by Wetstein. Ζητεῖν is, however,
the stronger form, for it is the modal or instrumental idea of
σκοπεῖν embodied in active search. In the phrase ἀλλὰ καί,
the contrast is softened. Winer, § 55, 8 ; Fritzsche, ad Marc.
788. The first clause, if taken in an absolute sense, would
forbid all regard, and in every form, to one's own interests ;
but the introduction of καί so far modifies it, that it is
supposed to be allowed to a certain extent. The καί is therefore far from being superfluous, as Beelen loosely affirms.
The apostle condemns exclusive selfishness—l'égoïsme, as Rilliet
calls it, and he inculcates Christian sympathy and generosity.
One's "own things" are not worldly, but spiritual things.
This verse is, in fact, the theme which is illustrated down to
the 17th verse. The Philippians were not to consult each
his own interests, but to cherish mutual sympathy, and engage in mutual co-operation. They were not to disregard
their own things on pretence of caring for each other's—for
unless they had first cared for their own things, they were
not qualified to care for the things of others. Undue curiosity
and impertinent meddlings are far from the apostle's thought,
but he requires a holy solicitude and warm fellow-feeling—not
absolute self-abnegation, but a vivid substantial interest in the
spiritual welfare of others. It is not myself alone or in isola-
tion, as if others did not exist, but myself with them and they
with me, in earnest brotherhood and love. My object must not
be simply to outstrip them in religious attainment, but to bring
them and myself to a higher stage of Christian excellence.
Though charity seeketh not her own, still she has her own.

(Ver. 5.) Τοῦτο γὰρ φρονεῖτε ἐν ὑμῖν, ὃ καὶ ἐν Χριστῷ Ἰησοῦ
—"For let this mind be in you which was also in Christ

Jesus." Codices A, B, C¹, D, E, F, G, have φρονεῖτε, and
the Vulgate and Syriac support the reading. The reading
φρονείσθω is found in C³, J, K, and many other codices,
and is adopted by Alford. But φρονεῖτε has high uncial
authority, and cannot well be overthrown by any internal
argument derived from the structure of the sentence. The
probability is that the syntactic difficulty suggested φρονείσθω
as an emendation. The particle γάρ is not found in A, B,
C¹, and is omitted by Lachmann and Tischendorf. Meyer
suggests that the omission was caused by regarding the ἕκαστοι
of the last verse as the beginning of this one. If it be genuine,
its meaning is more than explicative, or as Ellicott renders,
"verily." It enforces, or gives a reason for the previous
injunction. We should expect the sentence to run thus—
Have ye this mind in you which Christ had also in Him;
whereas the clause reads—"which also was in Christ Jesus."
The passive aorist ἐφρονήθη must be supplied, and not ἦν, as
is done by Hoelemann. Καί, after the relative, indicates a
comparison between the two parts of the clause. Klotz,
Devarius, vol. ii. p. 636. The phrase ἐν ὑμῖν is not—"among
you," nor is it in any sense superfluous. It points out the
inner region of thought which this feeling is to occupy. "This
mind" is not a superficial deduction, nor a facile and supine
conviction, but a feeling which cannot be dislodged, and which
manifests its vitality and power in its incessant imitation of
Christ's example. The pronoun τοῦτο, placed emphatically,
refers, in our opinion, to the duty inculcated in the preceding
verse. The meaning is not, that every feature in Christ's
character should have a counterpart in theirs, as if the apostle
had generally said, Let the same mind be in you as was in
Christ Jesus—*ita animati estote, ut Christus Jesus erat ani-
matus*. Nor is the reference directly, as Keil and others suppose,
to the lowliness of mind already inculcated in v. 3 ; it is rather
to the self-denying generosity and condescension enjoined in
the previous verse, though these certainly can have no place
where self-seeking and vainglory occupy a ruling position.
Thus Victorinus—*imitantes Dominum, nos de aliis potius
cogitemus, quam de nobis ipsis.*

Now, the example of Christ is living legislation—law embodied and pictured in a perfect humanity. Not only does it

exhibit every virtue, but it also enjoins it. In showing what is, it enacts what ought to be. When it tells us how to live, it commands us so to live.

What the apostle means by the mind which was in Christ Jesus, he proceeds to explain. His object, in the following paragraph, is neither to prove Christ's Divinity, so as to confirm their faith, nor to argue the perfection of His atonement, so as to brighten their hopes. It is not his intention to dwell on His manhood, with a demonstration of its reality; or to adduce His death with evidence of its expiatory worth; or to dilate on His royal glories, with a summons that every one should look up and worship. His purpose is in no sense polemical. His appeal is not to the merits of His abasement, but to the depth and spirit of it; not to the saving results of His service, but to the form and motives of it. In short, he developes that "mind" which was in Christ, and which was manifested in His self-denying incarnation and death. The apostle's text is—"Look not every man at his own things, but every man also at the things of others;" and his argument is, Not only is this your duty, because there is precept for it; but it is your duty, because there is the noblest of all models for it. It was truly exemplified by Him —"Who being in the form of God, thought it not robbery to be equal with God, but made Himself of no reputation, and took upon Him the form of a servant."

The "form of God" on the one hand, and obedience to the death on the other, are the two termini; or the extent of our Lord's self-denying grace is measured by the distance between equality with God, and a public execution on a gibbet. The question depends to a great extent on the reference in the clause—"Who being in the form of God." Is it after He was born that the apostle so describes Him? Is it of the man Jesus, as He was among men, that this is predicated, or does the apostle take a backward step, and point to the previous impulse which had brought Him down to earth to be one of ourselves? Is the "form of God" descriptive of His incarnate dignity—λόγος ἔνσαρκος—or of His simple Divinity prior to His assumption of humanity—λόγος ἄσαρκος? Many maintain the former view, that it is solely of Jesus in His earthly state that the apostle speaks. But as the incarnation is not referred to till the next verse, and in the words—" He emptied Himself, and took on Him the form of a servant;" may it not be fairly inferred, that what is said of Him in the preceding clauses, describes Him as He was before this period of self-divestment, this assumption of a bondman's aspect, and His subsequent humiliation? De Wette argues from the use of the historic name Christ Jesus, the antecedent to ὅς. But by what other name could the apostle designate Him? For it is to the Mediator that he refers; so that while he gives Him His official designation and human name, may he not under these concrete terms include His pre-existent state? Though first applied to Him infleshed, these names designated a person who combined in His mysterious constitution divinity and humanity. What violation of propriety is there in saying that Christ Jesus was a possessor of the glory of the Godhead anterior to His incarnation? The application of these epithets does not, therefore, necessarily limit the apostle's allusion to one aspect of our Lord's nature and career. The names are given to the ascended Saviour in verses 10th and 11th, for He still wears humanity, though He is now seen to be " equal with God." Nor can it be objected, as on the part of Philippi,[1] that because the historical Jesus alone is our model, there can be on that account no descriptive allusion to His higher nature. For what made Him become the historical Jesus—what induced Him to discharge the functions of the Christ, and take the name of Jesus? The very application to Him of the names of Jesus Christ, presupposed a " mind" in Him which prompted Him to leave the glories and felicities of His Father's bosom—a mind which, in our place and circumstances, we are summoned to imitate, though at an infinite distance. For the apostle does not propose a literal imitation of our Lord's example in all its various steps down to crucifixion. That would be an impossibility. It is true that no man can imitate Christ's incarnation; but it is equally true that no one can, in its nature and purpose, imitate His death. But it is not the action, so much as the spirit of it, that the apostle delineates, and Christians may be summoned to possess in their own spheres and limits, as well

[1] *Die Thätige Gehorsam Christi*, p. 3 ; Berlin, 1841.

the condescension that brought Him down to the manger, as
the self-abasing generosity which led Him to the Cross. It
is another extraordinary statement of Philippi, that as the
humiliation here spoken of was put an end to by the ascension,
then, if that humiliation is held to consist of His assumption
of our nature, it must follow that when He ascended, He left
our nature behind Him. But we do not hold that it lay
solely in the incarnation, and every one sees that the glorification of the incarnate nature was as really the termination
of its inferior state, as would have been its abandonment.
The historical title, Christ Jesus, suggested the lesson which
the apostle wished to impress, for it belonged to the Saviour
in His state of condescension and suffering; and it still identifies the "Man of sorrows" with Him who was in the "form
of God," and with the exalted "Lord," to whom has been
given the name above every name.

As this passage has long been a chosen field of challenge in
polemical warfare, we need not wonder that so many names
can be quoted on both sides of the view which we have been
considering. For the opinion which we have defended are
Chrysostom and the Greek expositors; of the Reformation
period and subsequently, Beza, Vatablus, Zanchius, Clarius,
Calixtus, Cocceius, Crocius, Aretius; among the Catholics
Estius and a-Lapide; and among others of later date, Semler
Storr, Keil, Usteri, Kraussold, Hufnagel, Seiler, Lünemann
Müller, Hoelemann, Rilliet, Pye Smith, Neander, Meyer
Ellicott, Alford, Lechler, Beelen, and Bisping. Among those
who hold the opposite doctrine are to be found Novatian and
Ambrose among the Latin Fathers; Erasmus, Luther, Calvin
Piscator, Hunnius, Cameron, Musculus, Calovius, Le Clerc
Grotius, Bengel, Vorstius, Zachariae, Kesler, Heinrichs, var
Hengel, Am Ende, Rheinwald, Matthies, Baumgarten-Crusius
De Wette, Philippi, and Conybeare.

(Ver. 6.) Ὅς ἐν μορφῇ Θεοῦ ὑπάρχων—"Who being (o
existing) in the form of God." The meaning assigned to
μορφή is of primary importance. It denotes shape or figure
and we believe with Pott, that it has no connection by meta
thesis with the Latin *forma*. Hesychius defines it by ἰδέα
εἶδος; Suidas adds to these πρόσωψις; and the Syriac render
by ܕܡܘܬܐ "in likeness." If this be its meaning, it is no

to be confounded with φύσις or οὐσία. It may imply the possession of nature or essence, but it does not mean either of them. The Greek Fathers, and after them Calvin, Beza, Müller, Robinson, and others, have fallen into this blunder. Thus Chrysostom says—οὐκοῦν καὶ ἡ μορφὴ τοῦ Θεοῦ Θεοῦ φύσις. Gregory of Nyssa maintains the same definition— ἡ μορφὴ τοῦ Θεοῦ ταυτὸν τῇ οὐσίᾳ πάντως ἐστίν. Orat. contra Eunomium, ii. p. 566 ; ed. Paris, 1638. Cyril of Alexandria has the same notion of the identity of form and essence. Athanasius explains μορφή by πλήρωμα, and Augustine by naturalis plenitudo. Suicer, sub voce. Petavius, too, says (De Incarnatione, iii. 6)—formam hic pro natura sumi perspicuum est. Phavorinus, professing exactness of definition, gives—ἡ μορφὴ κυρίως, ἡ οὐσία. The Greek commentators, as may be seen in Chrysostom, were polemically necessitated to give the term such a meaning, and the pressure of the same feeling has shown itself in almost every century.

Wherever the word occurs in the New Testament, it refers to visible form, as in the next verse, and in Mark xvi. 12. And so, too, with μόρφωσις, 2 Tim. iii. 5. The verb μεταμορφόω, as applied to the transfiguration in Matt. xvii. 2, Mark ix. 2, has the same signification, referring simply to change of external aspect, and neither of essence nor person. In the Septuagint, μορφή represents the Chaldee זיו, denoting external appearance, and is applied to Nebuchadnezzar, in reference to his lunacy; to Belshazzar, when he saw the handwriting, and was appalled, and his " form was changed ; " and to Daniel himself (vii. 28), " my form returned to me." In the reference to Belshazzar and the prophet, the verb ἀλλοιόω is employed, and the change is principally one of countenance. It represents תַּבְנִית in Isa. xliv. 13—ὡς μορφὴν ἀνδρός, an idol in shape of a man ; and also תְּמוּנָה, Job iv. 16—καὶ οὐκ ἦν μορφὴ πρὸ ὀφθαλμῶν μου. The instances sometimes adduced to show that μορφή may mean nature, will not sustain the assertion. Robinson, after Schleusner, quotes Euripides, Bacch. 54—μορφήν τ᾽ ἐμὴν μετέβαλον εἰς ἀνδρὸς φύσιν. Besides that this is the somewhat loose language of poetry, it may be remarked that the quotation rather shows that φύσις may signify form, and not μορφή signify nature. Bacchus means not to say that he had abandoned Divinity,

but only that he had concealed its form in an assumed
humanity. He declares, in the previous clause, that he had
changed his form into a mortal one ; but he does not aver that
he had ceased to be immortal in essence. Toward the commencement of the drama, similar language is employed—
Μορφὴν δ' ἀμείψας ἐκ θεοῦ βροτησίαν πάρειμι—" And having
taken a mortal form in exchange for that of a God, I am
here." Another passage is adduced from Plato, where he says
of God the Best—μένει ἀεὶ ἁπλῶς ἐν τῇ αὑτοῦ μορφῇ. It is
hard to say how much Plato's idea of the Divinity was anthropo-
morphic ; but the sense is, not simply that He remaineth
always simply in the same essence, but that He unchangeably
manifests the same characteristics. Other and similar passages
have been adduced, in which μορφή is supposed to signify not
form, but that which form represents. But even granting
an occasional metonymy, we find the word used with precise
discrimination. Thus Josephus (*Contra Apion*, ii. 22) speaks
of God as being beginning, middle, and end of all things, and
adds, that by His works and blessings He is manifest, and
more glorious, too, than any being ; while, as to His form and
magnitude, He is to us most obscure—μορφήν τε καὶ μέγεθος
ἡμῖν ἀφανέστατος. The meaning, as the context shows, is,
that while so much may be learned from His works and ways,
there is no visible shape of Him—nothing to warrant any
idolatrous image. In the 34th chapter of the same treatise,
the author, in reprobating the lewdness and follies of the
mythology of the Greeks, says that they had deified madness
and fraud, and others of the vilest passions; or, as he expresses
it, εἰς θεοῦ φύσιν καὶ μορφὴν ἀνέπλασαν. The two nouns are
here distinguished ; those vile passions are supposed, first, to
receive the nature of God, and then to get His form. They
are conceived of as divine, and then their divinity is represented by a visible shape or idol. The examples selected by
Wetstein from the classics are scarcely to our point—since
every god had his special form, though μορφή and *forma* are
always used of shape or likeness, and not of mere essence,
and have very much the meaning of person.[1] We hold, therefore, that μορφή is form, and neither nature nor condition,

---

[1] Thus μορφὰς τῶν θεῶν, Xenophon, *Mem.* iv. ; *forma deorum*, Cicero, *De
Natura Deorum*, ii. 2 ; *formæque deorum*, Ovid, *Metam.* i. 73, etc.

though it may represent them.   Now form is that by which
we know or distinguish anything—that by means of which
objects are recognized.   One person is known from another
by his form.   True, God has no form, being pure spirit—"Ye
saw no manner of similitude in the day that the Lord spake
to you in Horeb."   The form of God must therefore signify—
the mode of divine manifestation—that by which His appearance is understood and characterized.   It was the bright
cloud for a long period in the history of ancient Israel.   The
insignia of Godhead were oft revealed in the olden time; and
we have what we take to be several descriptions of the form
of God, in Deut. xxxiii. 2 ; Ps. xviii. 6–15 ; Dan. vii. 9, 10 ;
Hab. iii. 3–11.   Such passages, describing the sublime tokens
of a Theophany, afford a glimpse into the meaning of the
phrase—form of God.   It is not the divine nature, but the
visible display of it—that which enables men to apprehend
it, and prompts them to adore it.

Now Jesus was in this form of God—$\dot{v}\pi\acute{a}\rho\chi\omega\nu$.   The
participle has a fuller meaning than $\check{\omega}\nu$.   It represents something on which stress is laid, something which is to be borne
in mind as essential to the argument.   Gal. ii. 14 ; Acts xvii.
27–29, xxi. 20.   Suidas makes it equivalent to $\pi\rho\sigma\epsilon\hat{\iota}\nu\alpha\iota$.
Pye Smith[1] speaks of it as, " in many cases, denoting a mode
already established, conspicuous, and dating from a prior
point of time."   Still it would not be warrantable to render
it " pre-existing in the form of God."   There is no use in
resolving the participial reference by *dum*, or by the concessive
"although," with Ellicott.   The simple statement is the most
emphatic.

This meaning, which we give to $\mu\rho\rho\phi\acute{\eta}$, is in harmony with
the spirit of the whole passage, and it is not materially different
from $\epsilon\hat{\iota}\delta\sigmaς$, John v. 37.   See under Col. i. 15.   It stands
here in contrast with the phrase $\mu\rho\rho\phi\grave{\eta}\nu$ $\delta\sigma\acute{\nu}\lambda\sigma\nu$ $\lambda\alpha\beta\acute{\omega}\nu$.   He
exchanged the form of God for that of a servant—came from
the highest point of dignity to the lowest in the social scale.
And we are the more confirmed in our view, because of the
following verb $\dot{\epsilon}\kappa\acute{\epsilon}\nu\omega\sigma\epsilon$, as this self-divestment plainly refers
to the previous $\mu\rho\rho\phi\acute{\eta}$.   It cannot mean divinity itself, for
surely Jesus never cast it off.   But He laid aside the form of

[1] *Scripture Testimony*, vol. ii. p. 405.

God, the splendour of divinity, and not the nature of it—the glory of the Godhead, and not the essence of it. Those who hold that the passage refers to Christ in His incarnate state, regard "the form of God" in various ways—some, like De Wette, referring it to the glory of the Godhead potentially (*potentiâ*) in Himself; others, like Grotius, finding it in His miracles; or, like Wetstein, in His transfiguration; or as many others, generally in His sayings and doings. At the same time, while we think that the apostle selects with special care the term μορφή, as signifying something different from nature, we must hold that no one can be in the form of God without being of the nature of God, the exhibition of the form implying the possession of the essence. Of Him who was in the form of God, it is now predicated—

οὐχ ἁρπαγμὸν ἡγήσατο τὸ εἶναι ἴσα Θεῷ. The phrase τὸ εἶναι ἴσα Θεῷ is peculiar, and as τό indicates, it expresses a united idea. Instead of the adverb ἴσως, the neuter singular and plural are frequently used. Passow, *sub voce.* Winer, § 27, 3. Many instances occur in the Septuagint. The case is common with other words, as πάντα, πολλά. Matthiae, § 443, e. It is therefore too rigid in Matthies to take ἴσα as denoting equal in the manifoldness of essence. It needs not κατά to be supplied, as some grammatical pedants contended, for adverbs of measure and degree have, with the verb of existence, the sense of predicates—Bernhardy, p. 337; John v. 18; Homer, *Odyssey,* x. 303—ἴσα θεοῖς. The idea expressed by the adverb is not resemblance, but sameness of quantity or measure; and so Pye Smith renders the clause— "the being on a parity with God." Tertullian employs the phrase *pariari Deo.*[1] What this parity is, and what its relation is to the μορφὴ Θεοῦ, we shall afterwards consider. The phrase τὸ εἶναι ἴσα Θεῷ is the object to the verb ἡγήσατο, while ἁρπαγμόν, as predicate, is emphatic from its position.

The meaning of this clause has excited no little inquiry, and principally with regard to ἁρπαγμός. The term is of rare occurrence, and therefore its meaning cannot be determined beyond dispute. To theorize upon its formation does not fully satisfy; for the meanings, abstract and concrete,

---

[1] *Adver. Marc.* v. 20, etc.; *Opera,* vol. ii. p. 334, ed. Oehler, Lipsiae, 1854.

K

respectively attached to nouns ending in μος and μα, pass into
one another—(Buttmann, § 119, 2, 11)—the first, according
to Kühner, § 370, embodying the intransitive notion of the
verb—the act of seizure ; and the second expressing the result
of its transitive notion—the thing seized. Such variations
are seen in διωγμός, δίωγμα ; φωτισμός, φώτισμα ; βαπτισμός,
βάπτισμα ; βδελυγμός, βδέλυγμα ; ὀνειδισμός, ὀνείδισμα, while
θεσμός, λαχμός, χρησμός, and other terms, have the meaning
of a word ending in μα.[1] So that from the mere form of the
uncommon substantive little definite can be gleaned. Nor
can we gather much from its use. It occurs nowhere else in
the New Testament, and, so far as known, only in two other
places among Greek authors, where it is not professedly a
quotation from this verse. The first is an ugly quotation
from a tract ascribed to Plutarch, where the word might be
rendered "rape."[2] The other is from Cyril of Alexandria,
in a passage where he says, "The angels declined Lot's invitation ; and had the patriarch been a churl, he would not have
pressed them further, but would have thought it fortunate
that they declined." But the good and generous host urged
them the more, and "did not out of a listless and imbecile
soul make their declinature a catch, or thing to be caught at
—ἁρπαγμόν."[3] The word has not the same meaning in these
two places. In the first quotation it signifies an action,
which Strabo explains by ἁρπαγή ; and, like the English
translation we have already given of it, and which is in fact
derived from it, it denotes a crime named from the force or
violence employed in connection with it. In the second instance it points out ideally something which an inhospitable
and niggardly soul would lay hold of ; viz., that if one declines
an invitation, you reckon his denial something you gladly
seize on as a pretext for dropping the subject. Therefore the
train of thought, connection, and logical dependence, must
chiefly guide us to the meaning of the term. The sense

---

[1] Eustathius on Homer says—Ὡς δὲ ξεσμὸς, ξέσμα, οὕτω δεσμὸς, δέσμα. Ῥωχμὸς
δὲ καὶ ῥῆγμα ταῦτα ἐστιν, ὡς καὶ βρεχμὸς καὶ βρέχμα, καὶ πλεχμὸς καὶ πλέχμα.—
Wakefield, *Sylva Crit.* Pars iii. p. 112.

[2] Καὶ τοὺς μὲν Θήβησι καὶ τοὺς Ἠλίδι φευκτίον ἔρωτας καὶ τὸν ἐκ Κρήτης καλούμενον
ἁρπαγμόν.—*De Lib. Educat., Opera Mor.* vol. i. p. 41, ed. Wyttenbach.

[3] Ὁ δὴ καὶ συνιεὶς ὁ δίκαιος μειζόνος κατεβιάζετο, καὶ οὐχ ἁρπαγμὸν τὴν παραίτησιν ὡς
ἐκ ἀδρανοῦς καὶ ὑδαριστέρας ἐποιεῖτο φρενός.—*Opera,* vol. i. pp. 2, 25.

hinges very much, as Pye Smith technically puts it, on the
solution of the question, where the protasis is supposed to
end, and the apodosis to begin.

I. Many join the two clauses closely, as if the one explained
or strengthened the other, or were a species of deduction
from it. The noun is then taken in an active sense—" and
did not think it robbery or a seizure to be equal with God."
But those who hold this general view, hold it with many
subordinate differences.

1. Some take the word in the plain and easy sense—of a
thing not one's own—He did not regard equality with God
as a possession not His by right, did not look upon it in any
sense as a usurpation. This has been a common exegesis, as
may be seen in Chrysostom, Theophylact, Œcumenius, Augustine, Pelagius, Beza, Calvin, Mynster, Estius, and many others.
There are shades of distinction, again, among such as hold
this view, but the general meaning with them all is, that
Jesus, in personating God, in assuming His name or receiving
His worship, deemed Himself guilty of no usurpation, or did
not in any sense take what was not His own, for He was
really and properly God.[1] Some forms of this exposition are
tinged more or less with inferential admixtures. Thus—

2. If one obtain booty, he glories in it, boasts of it, or
makes a show of it. So some present this idea—He did not
make a show of His equality with God.

Such generally is the notion of Luther, Grotius, Meric,
Casaubon, Osiander, Piscator, Wolf, Cameron, Calovius, Krebs,

---

[1] Thus Augustine—*Natura quippe illi fuerat Dei æqualitas, non rapina* . . .
*quia non alienum arbitratus est esse quod natus est, sed tamen quamvis æquali-
tatem Dei non fuerit arbitratus alienam, sed suam, semetipsum exinanivit.*
Contra Max. Lib. i. 4, p. 1050, vol. viii.; *Opera,* Parisiis, 1837. Or, again,
in his *De Symbolo*—*Non rapuit, quia naturaliter habuit.* P. 935, vol. vi.;
Opera, do. So also Beza—*Non ignoravit, se in ea re nullam injuriam cuiquam
facere, sed suo jure uti, nihilominus tamen quasi suo jure cessit ;* similarly Calvin
—*Sciebat sibi jus et fas esse non in carne humili apparere, nihilominus jure suo
cessit.* Estius, too—*Non existimavit æqualitatem Dei sibi esse rapinam, hoc est,
rem alienam et ex rapto usurpatam, ut propter hoc tantopere semet humiliaverit
. . . quasi dicat, Non hæc est causa humilitatis Christi, quippe qui non usur-
pative, sed vere Deus esset.* Calvin, however, gives ἡγήσατο a subjunctive
meaning, ἄν being understood ; as if the sense were—*non fuisset injuria, si
æqualis Deo apparuisset.* This is not much better than the suggestion of
Michaelis, that ὑπάρχων is or may be the genitive plural of ὕπαρχος.

Rosenmüller, Heinrichs, Flatt, and Rheinwald.[1] Their main idea is—that Jesus on earth did not revel in His divinity, but vailed it, did not make an ostentatious display of His Godhead, but concealed it. But in the opinion of many, not all who hold it, this exegesis is often bound up with a meaning given to μορφὴ Θεοῦ which we have already considered, and assigned reasons for rejecting—to wit that the phrase, "form of God," describes the incarnate Jesus, and it is so far consistent with itself in giving ἁρπαγμός the sense we have alluded to.

3. Again, if a person have usurped a thing, he grasps it very closely, the secret consciousness of his want of right not allowing him to abandon it for a moment. This signification therefore is assigned—He would not retain equality with God, as a robber does his prey. Ambrosiaster, Castalio, Vatablus, Matthies, Kesler, Hoelemann, and Usteri hold this notion. The views of these critics differ, indeed, in colouring, though we need not for our present purpose distinguish them.[2]

But none of these opinions commend themselves, for though they give ἁρπαγμός the usual meaning of nouns ending in μος, still the philology is no firm ground of explanation. It is vain to refer to the uses of ἁρπάζω, as in the words ascribed

---

[1] Thus Cameron, in his *Myrothecium*, p. 214—*Optime sic Gallice vertas, Il ne fit point de triomphe, de ce qu'il était égal à Dieu ; hoc est, non jactavit, non visus est gloriari et insolescere.* Thus, too, Pelagius—*Quod erat, humilitate celavit, dans nobis exemplum, ne in his gloriemur, quæ forsitan non habemus.*

[2] Chrysostom's illustration is—"Whatever a man robs and seizes contrary to his right, he dares not lay aside. He who possesses a dignity which is natural to him, fears not to descend from that dignity ; " and then he adds—"What do we say then ? That the Son of God feared not to descend from His right, for He did not regard His Deity as a matter of robbery. He was not afraid that any one should strip Him of that nature or that right, when He laid it aside, being assured that He should resume it. . . . He hid it, judging that He was not degraded by so doing, wherefore the apostle says not, ' He seized not,' but He did not reckon it a seizure, because He possessed not that estate by robbery, but by nature—as something not given Him, but permanent and safe." "Ὅταν ἁρπάσῃ τις καὶ παρὰ τὸ προσῆκον λάβῃ, τοῦτο ἀποθέσθαι οὐ τολμᾷ, δεδοικὼς μὴ ἀπόληται, μὴ ἐκπέσῃ· ἀλλὰ διὰ παντὸς αὐτὸ κατέχει. ὁ μέντοι φυσικόν τι ἔχων ἀξίωμα, οὐ δέδοικε καταβῆναι ἀπ' ἐκείνου τοῦ ἀξιώματος. Τί οὖν φαμεν ὅτι ὁ τοῦ Θεοῦ Υἱὸς οὐκ ἐφοβήθη καταβῆναι ἀπὸ τοῦ ἀξιώματος· οὐ γὰρ ἁρπαγμὸν ἡγήσατο τὴν θεότητα, οὐδὲ ἐδεδοίκει μή τις αὐτὸν ἀφέληται τὴν φύσιν ἢ τὸ ἀξίωμα· διὸ καὶ ἔκρυψεν, οὐδὲν ἡγούμενος ἐλαττοῦσθαι ἀπὸ τούτου. διὰ τοῦτο, οὐκ εἶπεν, οὐχ ἥρπασεν, ἀλλ' οὐχ ἁρπαγμὸν ἡγήσατο. οὐχ ἁρπάσας εἶχεν τὴν ἀρχήν, ἀλλὰ φυσικήν, οὐ διδομένην ἀλλὰ μόνιμον καὶ ἐν ἀσφαλείᾳ.

by Chrysostom to Arius—οὐχ ἥρπασε, and to the instances
of ἅρπαγμα in later writers. Heliodorus often uses it in the
sense of a thing to be caught at, and once connects it with
the verb ἡγεῖται. *Lib.* vii. § 20. Besides, these interpretations not only make the two clauses virtually the same in
meaning, but they destroy the parallel between the precept
given, and this example adduced in commendation of it.
The primary object of the apostle is not to tell how great
Christ was by nature, and how low He became, though in his
illustration he has done so ; but to show how He looked to
the things of others, or in what state of mind He descended
to the earth. That purpose is so far missed in the previous
exegesis. We therefore regard the apodosis as commencing
with the clause under review. It begins the tale of His
humiliation by referring to the state of mind which led to it ;
and we look on the clause as having the prime emphasis laid
upon it, as virtually asserting that He did not regard His
own things, and as saying, in connection with the preceding
phrase, what His own things were, and what was His feeling
towards them. Though the form of God was His, He did not
regard it with a selfish and exclusive attachment, but He laid
it aside and became man. So that we agree with those who
give the word that signification in which it is used by Cyril
in the sentence already quoted in reference to Lot. Therefore—

II. Not a few give ἅρπαγμός this meaning—a seizure, or
thing to be snatched at ; or, as Müller renders it—"*non rem
sibi arripiendam et usurpandam indicavit.*" This view is held
by Musculus, Elsner, Bengel, Am Ende, Storr, Keil, Stein,
Schrader, Rilliet, De Wette, Beelen, Bisping, Wiesinger,
Lünemann, Philippi, Müller, Brückner, and others. Though
these writers agree in so understanding the noun, they differ
greatly among themselves as to what is to be understood by
τὸ εἶναι ἴσα Θεῷ, for the views of many of them are modified
by referring the passage simply to Christ as incarnate and on
earth. Some regard it as a possession He had, but did not
use ; others, as something He had not, yet did not aspire to.
We have already said, the phrase means—"the being on a
parity with God," a parity possessed in His pre-incarnate
state. Those who apply the term "form of God" to Jesus
incarnate, consistently regard this phrase as referring to His

abode on earth. While He was among men, lowly and despised, yet He did not aspire to an equality with God, but continued still in the form of a servant. Bengel understands the reference thus—*Esse pariter Deo dicit plenitudinem et altitudinem.* Van Hengel thus takes it—*Hoc vero, vehementer dubito an aliter explicari possit quam æquali modo vivere, quo vivit Deus,* and the meaning is thus given further and fully by him—*Christus hâc in terra, quanquam poterat, gloriosus esse noluit.* Rilliet's notion is somewhat peculiar. He supposes that the element of equality to God is His invisibility, which the apostle signalizes as the distinctive characteristic of the Father—*cette invisibilité Christ y a renoncé au lieu de la vie* ἐνδιάθετος—*immanente, il a accepté l'existence* προφορικός—*manifestée.* His interpretation proceeds upon a wrong idea of μορφή, and does not harmonize with the context. For "form" implies of itself visibility or splendour, and this was parted with. Nay more, the Second Person of the Trinity had, as the Angel of the Covenant, been often patent to the senses prior to the incarnation. Stein and De Wette understand the phrase of the divine honour, a meaning which we reject as limited and insufficient. We do not regard the two phrases, "form of God," and "equal with God," as identical in meaning, for then there needed no such repetition; though we cannot venture to say, with van Hengel, that in such a case a simple τοῦτο would have been sufficient. Meyer pleads for the sameness of the two statements—at least with this distinction, that the first refers to Christ as to His appearance—*Erscheinungs-Form,* and the second as to His essence—*Wesen.* Wiesinger's view is not very different—*forma Dei, conditio divina, quum in forma Dei esset, non arripiendum sibi duxit conditione divina uti.* Our view is somewhat different from any of these, and still, as we think, more in accordance with the spirit of the context. The apostle affirms that Jesus, in His pre-incarnate state, was "in the form of God;" and adds, that He thought it not a seizure, or a thing to be snatched at, to be on a parity with God, but emptied Himself. Now, it seems to us very plain that the parity referred to is not parity in the abstract, or in anything not found in the paragraph, but parity in possession of this form of God. He was in the form of God, and did not think it a thing to be eagerly laid

hold of to be equal with God in having or exhibiting this
form. The apostle adds, ἀλλ᾽ ἑαυτὸν ἐκένωσεν—" but emptied
himself," and the clause is in broad and decided contrast with
ἁρπαγμὸν οὐχ ἡγήσατο τὸ εἶναι ἴσα τῷ Θεῷ. That is to say,
the one clause describes the result of the other. It was because
He did not think it a seizure to be equal with God, that He
emptied Himself. And of what did He empty Himself, but
of this Form ? He was not anxious to be ever on a parity
with God in possessing it, and therefore He divested Himself
of it. He did not look simply to His own things—the glories
of the Godhead ; but He looked to the things of others, and
therefore descended to l. manity and death. His heart was
not so set upon His glory, that He would not appear at any
time without it. There was something which He coveted
more—somewhat which He felt to be truly a ἁρπαγμός, and
that was the redemption of a fallen world by His self-abase-
ment and death. Or, to speak after the manner of men, two
things were present to His mind—either continuance in the
form of God, and being always equal with God, but allowing
humanity to perish in its guilt ; or vailing this form and fore-
going this equality for a season, and delivering, by His condescension and agony, the fallen progeny of Adam. He chose
the latter, or gave it the preference, and therefore " humbled
Himself,and became obedient unto death." From His possession
of this " mind," and in indescribable generosity He looked at
the things of others, and descended with His splendour eclipsed
—appeared not as a God in glory, but clothed in flesh ; not in
royal robes, but in the dress of a village youth ; not as Deity
in fire, but a man in tears ; not in a palace, but in a manger ;
not with the thunderbolt in His hand, but with the hatchet
and hammer of a Gallean mechanic. And in this way He
gave the church an example of that self-abnegation and kindness which the apostle has been inculcating, and which the
Lord's career is adduced to illustrate and confirm.

The view of Meyer, followed so far by Alford, and which
strives to keep that meaning of ἁρπαγμός which its formation
indicates, cannot be borne out. He explains it as—*ein Ver-*
hältniss des Beutemachens—He did not regard equality with
God to be such a relation as is implied in the seizure of a
prey, or of a possession which belonged to others. Meyer

might object to some things in Wiesinger's inferential expansion of his view, but he says, himself, that this clause, corresponding to the previous one—"looking not each at his own
things"—describes what Christ's own things were—His
equality with God.   But whom would Christ have robbed, if,
instead of emptying Himself, He had retained equality with
God ?   Without unduly pressing Wiesinger's question as to
the parties whom such a ἁρπαγμός would have emptied or
robbed, could it have taken place, it may be replied that the
idea is out of unison with the course of thought, and that the
exegesis based upon it omits the turning-point of the illustration—the mind that was in Christ Jesus—and places the
idea of "others" in a totally different relationship from that
expressed in verse 5th.

The exposition of Lünemann and Brückner is also incorrect.
They understand in this clause a reference to that κυριότης
which God possesses, and which, though Christ was in God's
form, He did not wish to possess, save in the way of obedience
and death, while He might have chosen otherwise.   This
notion is founded upon a supposition as inadmissible as that
which Turnbull [1] introduces—"did not meditate a usurpation
to be equal with God;" "that is, did not avail Himself of His
original character, and attempt a sole theocracy for His own
exaltation."   Really such a supposition borders on profanity
—to say of Jesus, that He did not pervert His divinity to
accomplish selfish ends in a spirit of rivalry with God.
Bretschneider, too, *sub voce*, gives this explanation—Christ did
not deem equality with God a thing to be seized on *vi et
astutiâ*, but desired rather to merit the honour by His obedience
unto the death.   But the objections to these views is, that
parity with God is not something to which Christ has been
raised as the reward of His obedience, but something which
He originally possessed as one of His own things, which He
did not so cherish as to exclude all regard to the things of
others.   The error of Arius, so sharply rebuked by Chrysostom,
led him to explain the clause of Christ as Θεὸς ἐλάττων—a
lesser God, who did not aspire to equality with God τῷ
μεγάλῳ—"with God the Great, who was greater than He."
The Greek father asks, in triumph, "is there then a great

[1] Translation of Paul's Epistles, *in loc.*

and a less God? And do ye introduce the doctrines of the
heathens into the church? . . . If He were little, how could
He be God? If man is not greater or less, but his nature is
one, and if that which is not of this one nature is not man,
how can there be a less or a greater God, who is not of that
same nature?"[1] Socinian views are lower still. Thus, in the
notes to the Improved Version, we are told that—"being in
the form of God, means being invested with extraordinary
divine powers;" and of the second clause it is said—"the
meaning is, He did not make an ostentatious display of His
miraculous powers. Or if it should be translated with the
public version, He thought it not robbery to be as God, the
sense would be, He did not regard it as an act of injustice to
exert upon proper occasions His miraculous powers." One
knows not how to characterize the weakness and perversity
of such misinterpretation. Slichting says—*Propterea nec ob
tantam divinitatem ac dignitatem suam superbiit, nec eam longius
ac diutius retinuit quam auctor et dator illius vellet, sed ad ejus
nutum ac voluntatem protinus eâ se abdicavit.* But every good
man is expected to resign a gift, when God pleases; and in
this clause, it is Christ's own generosity, not His submission
to any divine mandate, which the apostle is commending, and
holding up to the imitation of the Philippian church. The
contrast is now brought out—

(Ver. 7.) Ἀλλὰ ἑαυτὸν ἐκένωσε. The pronoun is placed emphatically, but the meaning of this clause is of course shaped or
modified by the view which expositors have taken of the preceding clauses. The verb κενόω is literally to make empty, or bring
about that which κενός represents—*exinanivit,* as in the Vulgate. It does not vaguely mean, as Grotius and others render,
He became poor, or made Himself poor, or He led a poor life—
libenter duxit vitam inopem—for the image is not in harmony
with the preceding clauses. Those who maintain that Christ
is described here only in His historical state, are driven to

---

[1] Οὐ φησὶν ἀλλ' ὅτι Θεὸς ὢν ἐλάττων, οὐχ ἥρπασε τὸ εἶναι ἴσα Θεῷ τῷ μεγάλῳ καὶ μείζονι.
μικρὸς καὶ μέγας Θεὸς ἔνι; καὶ τὰ Ἑλληνικὰ τοῖς τῆς ἐκκλησίας δόγμασιν ἐπεισάγετε;
μέγας γὰρ καὶ μικρὸς παρ' αὐτοῖς Θεός· εἰ δὲ καὶ παρ' ὑμῖν, οὐκ οἶδα· παρὰ μὲν γὰρ ταῖς
γραφαῖς, οὐδαμοῦ εὑρήσεις· ἀλλὰ μέγαν μὲν πανταχοῦ, μικρὸν δὲ οὐδαμοῦ· εἰ γὰρ καὶ
μικρὸς, πῶς Θεός; εἰ μικρὸς οὐκ ἔστιν ἄνθρωπος, καὶ μέγας· ἀλλὰ μία φύσις· καὶ εἴ τι
οὐκ ἔστι τῆς φύσεως ταύτης τῆς μίας οὐκ ἄνθρωπος· πῶς ἂν εἴη μικρὸς Θεὸς καὶ μέγας;
εἰ τοίνυν ὁ Πατὴρ μέγας, καὶ Θεός· ὁ μὴ ὢν ἐκείνης τῆς φύσεως, οὐ Θεός.

such an interpretation. Thus, Tittmann and Keil, followed by van Hengel, give it generally—*sed semet ipse depressit*—a meaning which the word does not bear, and which anticipates the subsequent ἐταπείνωσεν. De Wette refers the phrase not to the first, but the second preceding clause, and understands it as denoting something He might have had, but did not actually possess. But we must not forget, that in his opinion the reference is to the earthly existence of Christ, and that equality with God means divine honour. Müller holds a similar view. When he puts the question, " of what did Jesus despoil Himself ? " he replies, " not of the form of God, for He neither did nor could lay aside the divine nature ; but He laid aside equality with God." Now this confusion proceeds from a previous error—a mistaken idea of the meaning of μορφή—for we have shown that this noun does not signify nature, but external and distinctive aspect, or that by which nature displays itself. The same confusion of thought mars the exegesis of Ellicott, and for the same reason, that he blends the idea of the form of God too much with that of the nature of God, which it implies, but from which it is quite distinct. When we put the question, " of what did He empty Himself ? " our reply at once is, " of the form of God ; " and if it be asked why He did so? the apostle also answers, because He thought it no object of desire, in comparison with man's salvation, to be equal with God, or to be in the possession of this form. When He came to earth, He divested Himself of His glory. There was an occasional gleam, as one may still recognize the sun even when obscured by a cloud. If we go back to the Old Testament, and contemplate the " form of God " as there portrayed, then, keeping still to the sacred imagery employed, we might in all reverence add the following sentences :—Christ came not in that Majesty which He possessed, and by which the old world had been dazzled. No troops of angels girt Him about ; nature did not do Him homage as God ; the voice of the seven thunders was silent ; the " wings of the wind " were collapsed and motionless ; and the " coals of fire " were quenched. Darkness was not His pavilion ; Lebanon did not tremble, nor was Jordan driven back. The lamps of the sky were not trimmed to honour the night in which this " man-child was born into the world."

It was not Jehovah, "as He bowed the heavens and came down," but Jesus made of a woman, and cradled in a manger. It was in short a birth, not a theophany. But Jesus was originally in the form of God, and might have appeared in the world with the appalling majesty of Sinai; or as when the psalmist described Him robed in cloud, storm, and fire-mist, and guarded by a thick spray of burning coals; or as when Habakkuk sublimely sings of Him heralded by the pestilence, the everlasting mountains scattered, and the perpetual hills bowing before Him; or as when He appeared transfigured, His face as the sun, and His raiment as the light. Still further, the apostle says of Him—

μορφὴν δούλου λαβών — "having taken the form of a servant." The participle points out the mode in which this self-emptying was accomplished, and the mode indicates also the means. Kühner, § 668. The act expressed by the aorist participle seems coincident in time with that denoted by the verb. Bernhardy, p. 383; Stallbaum, Phædo, 62, d. When the process of assuming a servant's form was completed, that of self-divestment was completed too. He exchanged the form of God for the form of a servant. The two phrases, μορφὴ Θεοῦ and μορφὴ δούλου, are therefore in pointed contrast. If the "form of God" signify the external aspect or distinctive characteristics of God, "the form of a servant" will signify the external aspect or distinctive characteristics of a servant.

The phrase is not to be taken as expressing either the humility or sorrow of Christ's life, as Piscator, Heinrichs, and Hoelemann emphasize it. The general meaning is—He bore about Him the marks of servitude. The service referred to is service to God; His uniform declaration being —that He came to do His Father's will. But service which was primarily offered to God, was also in itself of benefit to man, intended for him and done for him. Isa. lii. 13, 15; Matt. xx. 28; Luke xxii. 27; Rom. xv. 8. The servant of the Father condescended to minister to man; and Jesus, girt with a towel, and laving the water on Peter's feet, is seen truly in "the form of a servant." Some, however, lay too much stress on His service, as being almost wholly done to men, while Meyer, Wiesinger, van Hengel, Müller, and Baum-

garten-Crusius hold to the idea of exclusive divine service.
But in obeying God, He laboured for men. He who might
have been served upon the throne, stood before it serving.
Such is the striking contrast which the apostle brings out.
Chrysostom remarks on the use of the two participles—περὶ
τῆς θεότητος, ὑπῆρχε, περὶ δὲ τῆς ἀνθρωπότητος, ἔλαβεν—

ἐν ὁμοιώματι ἀνθρώπων γενόμενος—" being made in the likeness of men." Meyer prefers, "having made His appearance"
—referring for examples to Mark i. 4, and *Memorab.* iii. 3, 6.
This clause points out how the form of a servant was assumed,
though there be no connecting particle. Kühner, § 676 ; Stuart,
§ 188. Christ became a servant in becoming man. It is
pressing the participle too much to give it, with Rilliet, the
strict sense of being born—γίνεσθαι, a *le sens de naître ;* nor
does it serve any purpose, with the same author and Rheinwald, to resolve the phrase into—ὅμοιος ἀνθρώποις—though
abstract nouns with a preposition are frequent in Hellenistic
Greek. Meyer would take ἐν in the sense of *Angethanseins*—
that is, to be in, as one is in his clothes, to be clothed in ; a
mere refinement. Ἀνθρώπων is plural, "approaching," as
Robinson says, "to the nature of an adjective," and signifying men generally. Jesus had the likeness of men, or
appeared as men usually appear, was in no way as a man
distinguished from men. But the use of such a noun as
ὁμοίωμα may imply, as has been often said, that still He was
different from other men. He was not identical in all respects
with other men. As Meyer says, He was not *purus putus
homo ;* or, as Theophylact said before him, He was not ψιλὸς
ἄνθρωπος. He was Divinity incarnate—the Word made
flesh. The superhuman was personally allied to the human
—the higher nature was united to His manhood. Whether
the adjuncts of humanity are referred to in the ὁμοίωμα, may
be a question. It is probable that all the ills that characterize
humanity generally may be included ; for that Christ markedly
wanted any of its common characteristics, His likeness to man
would have been lessened in proportion. His sinlessness,
indeed, did not seem to impress his contemporaries, for they
called Him wine-bibber, sabbath-breaker, blasphemer, demo-
niac, and rebel. But he shared in the common lot of men,
and never wrought a miracle to exempt Himself from it.

When hungry, He would not change the stones into bread; when wearied, He lay down on the well of Jacob; when faint on the cross, He exclaimed, "I thirst." But the mere phrase will not of itself express that scorn, contempt, ignominy, and sorrow which threw their shadow over the Saviour's historical career. There is, however, something more in the words than van Hengel deduces—*Christum quamquam Dei imaginem referret, Deique filius esset, se hominum tamen instar mandatis ejus subjecisse.*

The apostle pauses, as if for a moment, in his rapid accumulation. He had described Christ as being in the form of God, as not regarding equality with God as a seizure, and therefore as emptying Himself, having taken upon Him the form of a servant, and being made in the likeness of men. This is, however, only the first portion of the representation —Christ's assumption of a serving humanity, but the picture is not complete. From heaven to earth He descended by emptying Himself; but after being on earth, He humbled Himself by His obedience to the death. Or He laid aside the form of God, and took that of a servant; but in that servant's form He still abased Himself even to the cross. The transition from the one depth to the yet lower depth is marked by καὶ εὑρεθείς— the subject is taken up at this point—such a resumption imparting freshness and emphasis. To make the next clause the concluding one of the description, while the finishing account would then begin abruptly by the verb ἐταπείνωσεν, is bald and disjointed.

(Ver. 8.) **Καὶ σχήματι εὑρεθεὶς ὡς ἄνθρωπος** — "And having been found in fashion as a man." Winer, § 31, 6. The noun σχῆμα, from σχεῖν—ἔχειν, denotes the way in which one holds himself. It sometimes signifies dress—so important in one's *tout-ensemble*—but here it comprehends more, namely, that complex variety of things which, taken together, make up a man's aspect and bearing. The Syriac translator had no equivalent term, and therefore he has introduced the Greek word into his version. It carries neither the notion of dignity nor of its opposite. Nor is it in any case redundant, as some have conjectured. Examples of its use are given by Raphelius and Elsner. Passow, *sub voce*. But it is not synonymous with the previous μορφή and ὁμοίωμα. Perhaps,

as to use, the distinction is, that the first is the more comprehensive; the second is modal; while the third still further
illustrates and confirms. The "form of a servant" does not
of itself imply humanity, while the "likeness of men" is only
fully evinced by the outer manifestations of this σχῆμα. If
He have the σχῆμα, you infer the ὁμοίωμα, and both explain
the μορφὴ δούλου. Or μορφὴ δούλου is in direct contrast
with μορφὴ Θεοῦ; ὁμοίωμα ἀνθρώπων has in it an oblique
reference to ἴσα Θεῷ, while the clause ἐν σχήματι ὡς ἄνθρωπος
depicts the Saviour as He was seen to be, when the form of
a servant and the likeness of men could be predicated of Him
with equal truth. There is no need whatever to take the
particle ὡς as representing the Hebrew *Caph veritatis*, though
some of the older commentators do so. It is simply the adverb of manner. The participle εὑρεθείς is not identical with
ὤν, as Elsner, Keil, and Rheinwald regard it, for it preserves
its own signification. Herodian ii. 12; Luke xvii. 18; Rom.
vii. 10; Gal. ii. 17; Phil. iii. 9; 1 Pet. ii. 22. This verb,
and the verb of simple existence, differ as fully as the English
phrases—to be, and to be found to be. Nor is there any
warrant for giving to ἄνθρωπος other than its usual and
natural signification. The phrase is neither נֶאְדָּם, "as the
first man," with Grotius; nor as a man vile and despised,
according to others. Christ was fully ascertained to be a
man. All about Him, His form and fashion, proclaimed it.
He was seen to possess a man's shape and symmetry, to be
endowed with a man's organs, senses, and instincts, to use a
man's food and apparel, and to speak, think, act, and walk,
like the other partakers of flesh and blood around him. He
showed Himself possessed of a true body and a rational soul
—that body no phantom or disguise, but an organism like
that of all men born of woman, and within it a soul which
grew in wisdom as His body grew in stature, being subject
to human emotions, and possessed of the usual powers of
thought and will. He was "found in fashion as a man" by
those who lived with Him, who saw Him in all aspects, and
in every variety of attitude and circumstance;—His mother
and kinsmen; His fellow-villagers and friends; His disciples
and followers; His enemies and executioners.

Another verb is now used by the apostle, which is not to

be confounded in meaning or application with the preceding ἐκένωσεν—

ἐταπείνωσεν ἑαυτόν—" He humbled Himself." The position of the verb shows that the emphasis is laid upon the action it represents. In the phrase ἑαυτὸν ἐκένωσε, the weight, as Meyer remarks, is laid on the reflexive reference of the act, but here on the reflexive act itself. That is to say, in the first case, when the self-emptying is described, the idea of " Self " predominates, for that " Self " possessed God's form and was on a parity with Him ; whereas in the latter case, His glory being vailed in human nature, it is the act of humiliation which arrests the attention : His person underwent no further change, but He stooped to extreme obedience and death. We cannot agree in the opinion of Meyer, that the two verbs stand in a climactic relation, nor can we say with Keil that they are synonymous, and surely the paraphrase of van Hengel comes short of the full import—*et cum habitu suo deprehenderetur, ut homo quilibet, Dei minister esse, submisse se gessit.* Nor can we say, with Wiesinger, that ἐταπείνωσεν denotes the humiliation which ἐκένωσεν already presupposes. We rather regard the words as quite distinct in reference. By the first verb, ἐκένωσεν, is described the process by which He became man, or laid aside God's form and took upon Him a servant's—in other words, the process by which Divinity became incarnate ; but in the second, ἐταπείνωσεν, is described a further act, after the incarnation and dwelling on our world had taken place—something which He did after being in man's nature. Κένωσις is predicated of Him as being in the form of God, but ταπείνωσις of Him in the likeness and fashion of man. " He emptied Himself " in becoming man, but as man " He humbled Himself." The reference in this verb is therefore to something posterior to the action implied in ἐκένωσεν. Nor is there a climax in this interpretation, for the descent from the throne to the manger is infinitely greater than the step from the manger to the cross. The self-emptying might have existed without this humiliation, for there might have been life, humanity, and service without it.

We do not separate γενόμενος ὑπήκοος from the verb ἐταπείνωσεν, the participle expressing the mode in which this self-humiliation was exemplified; but we connect them with the words μέχρι θανάτου, and do not with Bengel and van Hengel join these last terms to the verb ἐταπείνωσεν. The meaning is not, He humbled Himself unto death, but "He humbled Himself having become, or in that He became, obedient unto death." The preposition μέχρι we regard as one of degree and not of time. 2 Tim. ii. 9; Heb. xii. 4. That death is further and sharply pointed out as indeed the death of the cross—

μέχρι θανάτου, θανάτου δὲ σταυροῦ—"unto death, the death, ay, of the cross." The particle δέ, from such a position and use, with a repeated word, makes its clause intensive. Winer, § 53, 7, b; Hartung, i. 168–169. His obedience reached to the point of death, and not only so, but to show its depth and submissiveness, it reached to the most painful and shameful of deaths—the death of the cross. Verily, in doing so, He humbled Himself.

In the term ὑπήκοος is implied some one to whom obedience is rendered, and the obvious meaning is, that such obedience is offered to God, for on this account God highly exalted Him. Grotius, however, represents it thus—*non opposuit vim illam divinam his capientibus se, damnantibus, interficientibus.* Rosenmüller and Krause agree with him, but the exegesis is wholly unwarranted by the context. Obedience unto death is thus predicated of Christ in His incarnate state—obedience not merely in action, but in suffering. He obeyed as far as it is possible for man to obey—obeyed to the surrender of His life. Death in its most awful form was calmly encountered and willingly endured. And there was no force compelling Him: it was no dark fate or inscrutable destiny which, turn as He might, He could not shun. Nor was it, on the other hand, the sudden outbreak of a wild enthusiasm, or of an irrepressible gallantry, which would not reflect and could not be guided. With all its heroism in meeting the degradation and shock of a public execution, it was yet a calm and collected obedience to a Higher will, under which He had spontaneously placed Himself.

And this death, the death of the cross, was one of special torture and disgrace. Under Roman law, it was inflicted only on slaves and the vilest class of malefactors, and when carried into any of the provinces, its stigma still followed it. *Juvenal*, vi. 184. A death of glory may excite ardour, but death on a gibbet is revolting. Some forms of violent death are sudden and almost painless, but the cross was the means of intense and protracted torture—a thousand deaths in one ; and then, to be treated as a felon, to be hanged on a tree by heathen hands and under a sentence of public law,—the shame was worse than the agony. The sun would not gaze upon the scene, and the sky covered itself in sackcloth. Aaron ascended to the summit of Mount Hor, and calmly expired at God's bidding. Moses climbed the hills of Moab, and, descending into some lonely inner valley, put off in the Divine presence his earthly tabernacle. But so far did God's own Son carry His obedience, that He shrank not from scorn and anguish, for He was reviled as a blasphemer and taunted as an impostor and traitor during the trial that led Him to death ; ay, and that death was the doom of a felon, and He was stripped and nailed in nakedness to the cross, amidst hooting and execrations, gibes and merriment, as if He had been the veriest wretch and criminal in all Judæa. And this victim of sorrow and persecution, of the fury and sport of men, seized and killed so wantonly and cruelly by them, nay, killed by the cross, as if any other form of death would have been insufficient to mark their sense of His baseness—this man, so hanged upon a tree, was originally in the form of God, and thought it no robbery to be equal with God.

In this paragraph there are many deep things, and many questions are suggested which we cannot answer. The incarnation is, indeed, a mystery—especially the existence of the two natures in Christ, and their mutual relations and influences. Speculation has always existed on this subject, and the names of Nestorius, Eutyches, Sabellius, Arius, and others, are mingled up from an early period in the controversies. But this passage was especially the theme of keen discussion in Germany in the beginning of the seventeenth century, between the divines of Giessen and Tübingen. The former party, such as Menzer in his *Defensio* (1621), and Feuerborn in his *Sciagraphia* (1621), and his Κενωσιγραφία (1627), held that Jesus, during His abode on earth, renounced the possession of the divine attributes ; while the latter party, such as Nicolai, and Thummius in his Ταπεινωσιγραφία (1627), maintained, more in accordance with sound exegesis, that Jesus kept the possession of the divine attributes, but without their use—a κτῆσις without a χρῆσις—and that there was only a κρύψις, or concealment of them. The contest involved not a few dialectical subtleties (on the *unio hypostatica,* and the *communicatio idiomatum,* etc.), as, for example, with regard to Christ's omnipresence—His *immensitas in seipso,* and His *adessentia,* or *omnipræsentia operativa.* It needs no great dexterity on this mysterious subject, to suggest and press difficulties which seem to imply contradiction, to raise arguments on detached phraseology, and to put questions, the attempt to answer which proves our ignorance of such first principles as are necessary to a full solution. Divinity, in all we are told of it, is so unlike humanity in all we feel of it, that we cannot wonder that the union of these two natures in Christ should present apparent contradictions in development and result. Mystery envelopes us as soon as we think of a human consciousness in personal oneness with a divine essence, for we know not how they coalesce, what reciprocal connection they sustain, or what is the boundary between them. It is easy, and also correct, to employ the ordinary commonplaces, that there is a personal union without mixture or confusion,[1] that the divine is not transmuted into the human, nor the human lifted or expanded into the divine. But the New Testament does not indulge in those distinctions, and He who had these natures premises no such distinction Himself, when in one place He disclaims omniscience, and confesses that He does not know the period of the judgment, and in another gives a promise which implies the possession of omnipresence —"Lo, I am with you alway." So that, on the points involved in this discussion, such acute men as Chemnitz, Hollaz, Gerhard, and Quenstedt, could with no great trouble invest an inimical theory with difficulties beyond solution, thrust an opponent into a dilemma, or put the case against him, so as to fasten the charge of inconsistency upon his argument, and heresy upon his conclusions. Recent reviews of this controversy will be found in Thomasius, *Christi Person*

---

[1] Or, as in the language of the Council of Chalcedon, the union of the two natures is—ἀσυγχύτως, ἀτρίπτως, ἀδιαιρέτως, ἀχωρίστως.

und Werk, vol. ii., Erlangen, 1857 ; in the second volume of
the *Entwickelungs-geschichte* of Dorner, who does not agree on
many points with Thomasius ; in Hoffmann's *Schriftbeweis*,
etc. ; in the *Christologie* of Gess and Liebner ; in Lechler's
das Apostol. und nachapostol. Zeitalter, 1857 ; in Schmid's
Dogmatik der Evangelisch-Lutherischen Kirche, 3rd edit.,
1853 ; in Sartorius ; and in Baur's *die Christliche Lehre
von der Dreieinigkeit und Menschwerdung Gottes*, vol. iii. p.
415, etc.

So vivid is the apostle's picture of the mind which was in
Christ. So intently did He look at the things of others, so
little was He bound up in His own, that He threw a vail of
flesh over His glory and descended to earth ; and not only so,
but when on earth He humbled Himself to yet a lower degree,
and suffered the ignominy and death of a public execution.
But such self-denial and generosity, involving κένωσις of
infinite extent, a subsequent ταπείνωσις of unfathomed depth,
with a parallel δουλεία of more than human compass, are not
to pass unrewarded. The exaltation is in proportion to the
depth of the earlier self-devotion.

(Ver. 9.) *Διὸ καὶ ὁ Θεὸς αὐτὸν ὑπερύψωσεν*—" Wherefore,
too, God highly exalted Him." The διό refers to the previous
statement—not the obedience in itself, but to that obedience
with the previous self-emptying and self-humiliation. On its
account, and as a recompense, did God exalt Him. The καί
strengthens the inference—connecting it more closely, and
by way of contrast, with the premises, while ὁ Θεός occupies
an emphatic position. This is the natural connection, and
it is not to be explained away as by Calvin, Crocius, Wolf,
and others, who render *quo facto*, or *ex quo*, as if the formula
only indicated the order of events, and not their close and
causal connection. It is the doctrine of Scripture that Christ
in dying for men, and because He did die for them, has
won for Himself eternal renown. Luke xxiv. 26 ; John x.
17 ; Heb. ii. 9, xii. 2, etc. Verbs compounded with ὑπέρ
are favourites with the apostle,[1] and this compound term
represents the immeasurable height of His exaltation. We
cannot say, with Ellicott, that the meaning of ὑπέρ is purely
ethical, for the ethical is figured by a local elevation, which

---

[1] A list will be found in Fritzsche on Rom. vol. i. p. 351.

also gives imagery to the following clauses. Ps. xcvii. 9, xxxvi. 35, xcvi. 10; Dan. iv. 34. The phrase is general, though it contains a reference to the previous verbs, ἐκένωσεν and ἐταπείνωσεν. He divested Himself of the Divine form, and came down; but lower and lower still did He descend, till He was put to death along with vulgar criminals, and therefore the exaltation rises in proportion to the previous depth—from the cross up to the crown. It was no common obedience, and therefore it is no common reward. Nothing could be lower than the degradation of the cross, nothing higher than the mediatorial crown. Infinite condescension surely merits highest glory. The compound verb ὑπερύψωσεν compacts into itself the three several terms used in Isa. lii. 13.

The apostle speaks of the God-man, but of Him especially in that nature in which he obeyed to the death. This supreme exaltation implies His resurrection, as proof of the acceptance of His obedience, and His ascension to heaven. The character of His elevation is now stated—

καὶ ἐχαρίσατο αὐτῷ τὸ ὄνομα τὸ ὑπὲρ πᾶν ὄνομα—" and has given Him the name which is above every name." We prefer τό before ὄνομα on the good authority of A, B, C, 17. Winer, § 20, 4—note. The article specifies the name as something known and honoured. Whether ὄνομα should mean dignity, or have its literal signification, has been disputed. Many assign it the former sense—that of dignity and majesty,—giving emphasis to the word, as when we say in English, He has made himself a name. So the Reformers, Luther, Calvin, and Beza, and among the moderns, Storr, Heinrichs, Hoelemann, Am Ende, Matthies, and Rheinwald. It is, however, more than doubtful whether ὄνομα by itself can bear such a meaning. Such may at times be its sense, but not its undoubted signification. The name itself is still thought of as the centre of the celebrity which it bears.[1] Mark vi. 14; John xii. 28; Acts iii. 16; Rom. i. 5. (See van Hengel in loc.) In fact, the word in classic Greek has two opposite senses, evinced by the context. It has on the one hand the accessory idea of renown or honour, and on the

---

[1] See Gesenius, sub voce שֵׁם, Num. xvi. 2; 1 Chron. xii. 30; Neh. ix. 10.

other that of pretext and deceit—a name and nothing else. See under Eph. i. 21.

That name is above every name, and in this lies its glory. There are many high names, but it is higher than all of them. No name is equal to it, all are beneath it, and without exception. What then is this name of lustre ? Not the title, Son of God—υἱὸς Θεοῦ—as Theophylact and Pelagius thought ; nor as De Wette takes it—Κύριος ; or as van Hengel gives it —nomen domini regni divini ; nor is it Θεός, as Aquinas, Estius, Philippi, and Beelen argue; nor yet Χριστός, as Müller contends for. But the context shows that the person who bears this name is Jesus, who for His high function is termed Κύριος. The name referred to, therefore, is Jesus, and the appellation Κύριος, with which every tongue is to greet Him, characterizes that universal presidence with which He is now entrusted. Jesus is Lord. Acts ii. 36 ; Heb. i. 4. The meaning is, that through His exaltation, He who wears the common name of Jesus, has in it the loftiest of all appellations. Acts ix. 5. It commands unlimited homage, and it does so because of the suffering He has endured, and the reward conferred upon Him by the Father, in consequence of His condescension and death. In the verb ἐχαρίσατο is implied the notion of a gift—without denying that it is compensative in nature. Christ won it, and the Father therefore bestowed it—

(Ver. 10.) Ἵνα ἐν τῷ ὀνόματι Ἰησοῦ πᾶν γόνυ κάμψῃ ἐπουρανίων καὶ ἐπιγείων καὶ καταχθονίων—"That in the name of Jesus every knee should bow, both of beings heavenly, and earthly, and under the earth." It is foreign to the entire spirit of the passage to render ἐν τῷ ὀνόματι "in the name," if it be supposed, with van Hengel and De Wette, that the reference is to mediate homage presented in Christ's name to God. Nor yet does the formula stand for εἰς τὸ ὄνομα, as Storr, Heinrichs, and Keil suppose, and thus mean "in honour of." The phrase points out the foundation or sphere of the homage, as Meyer remarks. 1 Cor. vi. 11 ; Eph. v. 20 ; Col. iii. 17 ; Jas. v. 14 ; 1 Pet. iv. 14. See under Eph. v. 20 ; Col. iii. 17. In such passages, at least in the majority of them, the same idea is apparent, modified more or less by the context. " In the name of Jesus " is in recognition of it, or of the authority and majesty of Him who bears it. The dative is usually placed after κάμπτειν, to express the object worshipped, but here no object is expressed, as in 2 Chron. xxix. 29, and the inference is, that the object is not Θεῷ, as van Hengel supplies. If beings bow in recognition of the name of Jesus, it is to Jesus Himself as bearing such a name, that they offer homage. Acts vii. 59, ix. 14, xxii. 16; Rom. x. 13; 1 Cor. i. 2. According to Pliny's testimony, the early Christians sang hymns *Christo quasi Deo*.[1] It has been remarked, too, that the angels "in heaven" do not need to bow the knee through a mediator, but they bow to Him as Lord. The church adores Him as its Saviour, and the universe adores Him for having saved His Church. Rev. v. 8–13. The phrase expresses homage to Jesus, universal and direct—

πᾶν γόνυ κάμψῃ — "every knee should bow." This posture is one of homage. Ps. xcv. 6; Isa. xlv. 23; Acts xxi. 5; Rom. xiv. 11; Eph. iii. 14. And this profound adoration is not limited in its sphere; it is the homage—

ἐπουρανίων καὶ ἐπιγείων καὶ καταχθονίων—"of beings in heaven, and on earth, and under the earth." These words are evidently to be taken not in the neuter, but in the masculine. The first term designates the inhabitants of heaven; but why should Meyer, Ellicott, and Alford confine it to angels, when the New Testament declares that saints are in glory too? The second epithet describes the inhabitants of earth. But who are meant by the καταχθόνιοι, a word which occurs only here? A large number suppose it to mean the dead, as Alford and Ellicott, or the inhabitants of Hades, as Theodoret, Grotius, Meyer, De Wette, Rilliet, Rheinwald, etc. Many, on the other hand, understand the phrase of demons, such as Chrysostom, Theophylact, Œcumenius, with not a few of the scholastic interpreters, and also Wiesinger. The καταχθόνιοι may be taken as the population of Hades, or the Underworld, in which Hades is pictured as being—and that population is twofold, devils and lost souls. That both are there, is the doctrine of Scripture. As to the last, see Deut. xxxii. 22; Ps. ix. 17; Prov. xxiii. 14; Matt. xi. 23; Luke xvi. 23: and as to the former, Luke viii. 31; Rev. xx. 3; Matt. xxv. 41. There is no doubt, however, that Hades is

---

[1] *Epistolarum*, Lib. x. p. 457, ed. 1650.

sometimes a general term for the spirit-world of the departed, without reference to character. As the result of death, it is personified. 1 Cor. xv. 55; Rev. xx. 13, 14. At the same time, it is the doctrine of the apostle and of the New Testament, that the souls of the blessed are with Christ in heaven. Perhaps, however, the three terms are not to be too strongly pressed. The apostle, by the use of them, seems to designate all ranks of beings in the universe—that is, every form of rational existence in it. For the apostle dwells on the idea of universality—a name above *every* name—*every* knee shall bow—*every* tongue confess. Isa. xlv. 23. The name above every name demands universal submission. No sphere is exempted, no rank of creatures is beyond its jurisdiction, all shall bend the knee; angels, and happy human spirits; all who have lived, or shall live upon earth; the souls of even the finally impenitent; nay, Satan and all his fiends. Jas. ii. 19. It is scarcely worth while to refer to some other interpretations, such as the fancy of Lakemacher, who supposes the heathen gods, heavenly, earthly, and subterranean, to be represented by the three terms. That idea is far from the apostle's thoughts. As grotesque is the folly of Stolz, that the term denotes the dead, the living, and the unborn, there being supposed an allusion in the last term to Ps. cxxxix. 15; or that of those who suppose that the apostle so designates Christians, Jews, and Gentiles; or that of Teller, who takes the triple classification to be one of rank—*homines sortis nobilioris, mediæ, et infimæ.* Estius and Bisping suppose the allusion to be to purgatory. *Pudet has nugas.*

(Ver. 11.) Καὶ πᾶσα γλῶσσα ἐξομολογήσεται ὅτι κύριος Ἰησοῦς Χριστὸς εἰς δόξαν Θεοῦ πατρός. The future form of the verb is read in A, C, D, G, H, J, and K, but the common form—ἐξομολογήσηται—is found in B, and is retained by Lachmann, a reading probably from Rom. xiv. 11. The noun —γλῶσσα—is not used in the figurative sense of nation or people—πάντα τὰ ἔθνα—as Theodoret paraphrases it. "Every tongue" corresponds to "every knee;" or, as Wiesinger says, "the tongue confesses that at which the knee bows." The compound verb adds strength to the idea, for though the Hellenistic usage delights in such verbs, still here the apostle certainly wished to express a plenary confession. See Fritzsche on Matt. iii. 6. The meaning of the verb is not to praise, as Rheinwald and van Hengel understand it, adopting a peculiar view of the connection. The confession made is, "that Jesus Christ is Lord"—that He who vailed His glory, assumed human nature, and in it humbled Himself to death, yea, the death of the cross, that He who stooped to the lowest point of ignominy and agony, has been raised to the highest glory, and now is Universal Governor. For meaning and use of κύριος, see under Eph. i. 2. Compare Eph. iv. 10 ; 1 Cor. xv. 27, etc. The worship of Jesus is absolute, not relative, as some authors quoted by Ellicott seem to hold. They who believe with Bull,[1] Pearson, Cudworth, and others, that the Son in some sense has His origin from the Father, and yet hold Him to be divine, co-eternal—συναΐδιος—and yet derived, not co-ordinate, but subordinate, may suppose that the worship of the Son is reflected upon the Father. See under Eph. i. 17. We cannot, however, regard the statement as sound or scriptural — ex Deo Patre (Filius) traxit originem. But the honour paid to Christ as Mediator redounds to the Father's glory, for the Father set Him apart for the mediatorial work, sustained Him under it, and rewarded Him for it.

What now is the connection of εἰς δόξαν Θεοῦ πατρός, "to the glory of God the Father"? Εἰς cannot signify ἐν, as it is rendered by Pelagius and Bengel, who follow the Vulgate rendering, Quia Dominus Jesus Christus in gloria est Dei Patris. Their idea is, that the Lord Jesus Christ possesses the glory of the Father, which is not the statement of the apostle. Calvin regards the clause as connected more with ὅτι than introduced by it,—that Jesus Christ is Lord, or that as the glory of God was manifested by Christ to men, so it is reflected in Christ, and the Father is glorified in the Son. The most natural connection is with the verb ἐξομολογήσεται, and the previous clauses also. The acknowledgment of Christ's exaltation tends to or issues in the glory of God the Father. The economical subordination of the Son to the

---

[1] Naturam perfectionesque divinas Patri Filioque competere non collateraliter, aut co-ordinate, sed subordinate, hoc est, Filium eandam quidem naturam divinam cum Patre communem habere, sed a Patre communicatam. Thesis Prima. Works, vol. v. p. 14, Oxford, 1827. Pearson on the Creed, vol. i. pp. 170-181, Oxford, 1847.

Father is implied, both in the obedience and in the reception of the reward.

The teaching of the apostle on the exaltation of the Saviour is:—

1. That it is the reward of His self-denial and death. "Wherefore—διό—God hath highly exalted Him." He had come down on an errand of love ; the execution of it involved the indescribable suffering and ignominy of the cross ; and the Father, when He had served in this awful enterprise, promoted Him to the highest honour as He returned in triumph. Heb. ii. 6, 9. This honour, therefore, He has earned for Himself, through the divine appreciation of His career. But might not the results of the service in themselves have been sufficient reward ? It may be replied, that there are certain functions which Christ's exaltation enabled Him to discharge. The government or headship of the Church is committed to Him, and He is to be final Judge. But apart from these public reasons, which are not prominently before the apostle's mind, Christ's exaltation proved God's hearty concurrence in the self-abnegation and death of His Son. It exhibits in bright relief those elements of character which God delights to honour. It teaches the universe the majesty of grace, and excites the earth to imitate its Lord's magnanimous example,—"for he that humbleth himself shall be exalted."

2. That His reward is exaltation to universal government. It is the name above every name—every knee bowing to it, and every tongue confessing that He who bears it is Lord or Governor. No name is surrounded with such splendour, or commands such veneration. He has no superior and no rival. No sphere, however high or distant, is exempted from his control : no creature, however mighty and godlike, has a co-ordinate jurisdiction. Verily, it is the name above every name ! If honour consist in elevation, what station can be higher than the throne of the universe ? If it consist in adoration, what homage can be nobler than that of cherub and seraph, and every order of holy intelligence throughout His vast domains ?

3. That such honour is bestowed especially on His humanity. This exaltation of Jesus is no argument, as some would allege, against our exegesis, that the phrase "form of God"

refers to Christ's pre-existent state. It has been objected,
that this gift on the part of the Father is a gift of something
Christ did not possess before, and which He must have
possessed, if the "form of God" describes a pre-incarnate
condition. The inference does not hold, for it is not of
Christ simply as Divine the apostle speaks, but of the God-
man, and Him especially as possessing the form of a servant,
and assuming the likeness of men. Nor is it a relative
exaltation in reference to us, but a positive advancement to
honour and glory. This glory and government He who was
in the form of God must have possessed, for by the "Word"
all things were made, "and by Him all things consist," but
He did not possess them as God-man or the Son of man, in
this complex person, till the Father bestowed them. Theodoret
says similarly—οὐ τοίνυν ἔλαβεν ἃ μὴ πρότερον εἶχεν ὡς θεὸς,
ἀλλ' ἔλαβεν ὡς ἄνθρωπος ἅπερ εἶχεν ὡς θεός. It has again
been asked—if Jesus in His pre-incarnate state be thus
described, how can additional honour be conferred on God ?
The course of the apostle's thought is,—that this form of God
was laid aside in the days of His humiliation and obedience,
and that in His exaltation He has not simply reassumed it,
but a higher glory has now been conferred on Him. Not that
the infinite lustre of the Godhead can in itself be increased,
but a new element is introduced—the human nature of
Christ. The nature in which He vailed His glory and stooped
to death, ay, such a death, has been elevated; or, in other
words, He has added a new glory to His original splendour,
the glory acquired as Redeemer in our nature to that
originally possessed "with the Father ere the world was."
This is "His own glory"—what He fondly calls "my glory."
John xvii. 24. There is special reference to the element of
humanity, and probably this is suggested by the striking
phrase "at the name of JESUS;" Jesus being His human
name, the name which He bore as a man ; and which, though
it had a special significance, as indicated by the angel, yet
passed among men as the familiar appellation of the Son of
Mary. He that was known as Jesus among men, specifically
as Jesus of Nazareth, He it is who in this very nature commands the homage of the universe. The tablet above Him
in his agony indicated this as the name of the sufferer. But

the brow once crowned with thorns now wears upon it the diadem of universal sovereignty; and that hand once nailed to the cross now holds in it the sceptre of unlimited dominion. The man Jesus is Lord of all—our nature in His person occupies the loftiest position in God's empire.

4. The result is—the divine glory—"to the glory of God the Father." Meyer speaks of a strong monotheism being manifest in this passage—"Absolute Godhead can be ascribed only to the Father—only the Father is ὁ ὢν ἐπὶ πάντων Θεός." Still economic subordination, as of the Son to the Father, and the Holy Spirit to both, is very different from essential or absolute inferiority. If the Son be not God in the highest sense, would not this universal worship be universal idolatry? and might not the same charge be brought against the homage and minstrelsy described as being offered to the Lamb throughout the Apocalypse? Christ as God has the right to the adoration of the universe, but as God-man He has for His special service received a special investiture. He could not be worshipped at all, if He were not God, and He is now worshipped on this peculiar ground, because He has done and suffered as the apostle tells us. But the prime place is occupied by God the Father, to whom service was rendered by Christ, while the success of such service and its consequent reward by Him are a source of glory to Him. In the honour paid to His exalted Son, His own character is more fully seen and admired.—See under Eph. i. 14.

Were we to be guided simply by what appears to be the train of thought and counsel, we should say that the apostle now proceeds to apply the lesson. He had begun with the charge—"Look not every man on his own things, but every man also on the things of others;" and in order to confirm the admonition, he has adduced the wondrous example of Jesus, showing how He minded not His own things, but laid aside His glory, and submitted to death, in pursuance of the welfare of others; and how the Father, for this unparalleled generosity, raised Him to the throne of the universe. And now we naturally expect him to bring home the great practical truth to be gathered from such an inspiring statement.

(Ver. 12.) Ὥστε, ἀγαπητοί μου. The particle ὥστε introduces an inferential lesson. 1 Cor. iii. 21, iv. 5, x. 12;

1 Thess. iv. 18, etc. Followed thus by the imperative, this particle which is so often followed by the infinitive, has the sense of *itaque*—ὡσ-τε. Tittmann, ii. 6 ; Winer, § 41, 5, 1 ; Klotz, Devarius, ii. p. 776. It does not reach back in its sweep to all the preceding statements. We cannot, with Wiesinger, give this as its ground—" Christ has attained to His glory only by the path of self-denial,—Wherefore." We take in the whole picture from the 6th to the 11th verse—" wherefore," or since such were Christ's spirit and career, such His self-denial and reward, since such an example is set before you, you are bound by your very profession to " work out." If He has set it, shall you hesitate to follow it ? Will it not endear itself to your imitation as you look upon it—ἀφορῶντες τὸ παράδειγμα ? The heart of the apostle warms towards them, his soul is bound up in them, and he calls them " my beloved," adding a prefatory note—

καθὼς πάντοτε ὑπηκούσατε, μὴ ὡς ἐν τῇ παρουσίᾳ μου μόνον, ἀλλὰ νῦν πολλῷ μᾶλλον ἐν τῇ ἀπουσίᾳ μου—κατεργάζεσθε. The apostle appeals to their uniform obedience rendered in one sense to himself, but primarily to God, having the same object as ὑπήκοος applied to Christ in verse 8. There should be a comma after ὑπηκούσατε, for the next words belong to the concluding clauses, as the use of μή—νῦν seems to indicate. The construction of the verse is peculiar from its very compactness. Two comparisons are inwoven—my presence, my absence—or " not in my presence only, but much more in my absence ; " and " as ye have *always* obeyed," " so *now* carry out your salvation." The fervid heart of the apostle was not fettered by the minutiæ of formal rhetoric ; parallel thoughts are intertwined, and ideas that should follow in succession are blended in the familiar haste of epistolary composition. Παρουσία, in contrast with ἀπουσία, is not a future presence, as Wiesinger renders it. 2 Cor. x. 10. It is, indeed, applied especially to a future advent of Christ, a presence not now, but afterwards, to be enjoyed. The apostle uses in this epistle the words παρουσία πάλιν, i. 26. The adverb ὡς does not simply denote comparison, but it indicates a supposed or imagined quality which the apostle, indeed, warns against, and will not believe to exist. Rom. ix. 32 ; 2 Cor. ii. 17 ; Gal. iii. 16. The claim of the injunction did not cease with his presence. His absence did not make the obligation less imperative, but it demanded more earnestness and vigilance from them in the discharge of the duty. His voice and person were a guide and stimulant, his addresses and conversations reproved their languor, and excited them to assiduous labour, so that His presence among them wrought like a charm. And now that he was not with them, and they were left to themselves, they were so much the more to double their diligence, and work out salvation. This was to be done μετὰ φόβου καὶ τρόμου—" with fear and trembling."— See under Eph. vi. 5, where the phrase has been explained. 1 Cor. ii. 3 ; 2 Cor. vii. 15 ; Ps. ii. 11. The phrase means something more than Jerome's *non cum negligentia*. It restricts the feeling described too much to one aspect of it, to suppose it to be awe before an omnipresent God, as do the Greek expositors ; or a sense of dependence on God, as does De Wette ; or the apprehension that the work is not performed sufficiently, as do Meyer and Wiesinger. In fact, the phrase describes that state of mind which ought ever to characterize believers—distrust of themselves—earnest solicitude in every duty—humble reliance on divine aid, with the abiding consciousness that after all they do come far short of meeting obligation. There does not seem to be any reference, as some suppose, to the spirit of Christ's δουλεία, but there may be a warning against that pride and vainglory already reprobated by the apostle. In this spirit they are enjoined—

τὴν ἑαυτῶν σωτηρίαν κατεργάζεσθε—" carry out your own salvation." The compound verb here expresses the idea of carrying out, or making perfect. Fritzsche on Rom. ii. 9 ; also Raphelius, vol. ii. p. 495. This sounder philology opposes the explanation of Chrysostom—οὐκ εἶπεν ἐργάζεσθε, ἀλλὰ κατεργάζεσθε, τουτέστι μετὰ πολλῆς τῆς σπουδῆς, μετὰ πολλῆς τῆς ἐπιμελείας. The verb describes not the spirit in which the work is done, but the aim and issue—" carry through ; " while the idea of the Greek Father is only inferential. In the translation—" work out one another's salvation "—which is that of Pierce, Michaelis, Storr, Flatt, and Matthies, we should at once concur, but for a reason to be immediately stated. The reciprocal meaning given to ἑαυτῶν may be found in Eph. iv. 32 ; Col. iii. 16 ; 1 Pet. iv. 8, 10. The context, as van Hengel admits, is in favour of the latter translation which we have given.   De Wette contends that the reference in the verse is quite general—an idea which the inferential particle ὥστε does not sanction ; and he carries the reference back to i. 27, without any warrant whatever.   Rheinwald, Rilliet, and others, uphold the idea that the verse is an inference from the preceding exhibition of Christ's example.   We think that this cannot be doubted, so close and inseparable is the connection. But what is that example intended to illustrate ?   Might we not say the injunction—"Look not every man on his own things, but every man also on the things of others."   If the career of our Lord be introduced to show us what mind was in Him, surely the lesson deduced will be in unison.   If he bid them have the mind of Christ, and then go on to show what it is, surely his inference must be that they should, in their own sphere, exhibit the same mind.   Now the great truth which the exhibition of Christ's example illustrates is self-denying generosity—the very charge He has already given them, and the inference is expected to be in harmony with the starting lesson.   The command—τὴν ἑαυτῶν σωτηρίαν κατεργάζεσθε—will therefore be synonymous in spirit with the previous one in verses 4, 5.   In this way the ὥστε would connect homogeneous ideas.   If the words be rendered, "work out your own salvation," we do not see how it can with the same force be derived as a lesson.   The connection brought out by Alford is—"considering the immense sacrifice which Christ has made for you, and the lofty eminence to which God has now raised Him, be ye more than ever earnest, that you miss not your own share in such salvation."   But there is no hint of this connection in the preceding verses : for, in referring to Christ, the apostle does not speak of Him as a Saviour, nor yet of the salvation which He has secured.   He does not say He died for sin, or died for us.   His reference is to the spirit of His death, and not to its character and results.   It is true that His exaltation proved His mission divine, and His mediation effectual.   But the apostle does not allude to this, nor does he in this paragraph in any way connect the glory of Jesus with a completed redemption.   If he had said—He has died and risen again to save you, the connection could easily be—therefore salvation is perfect, and you are summoned either to receive it, or more fully to realize it. But it is simply of the fact that Christ denied Himself to benefit others that the apostle writes, and the Philippians are to do service to others, and thus evince that the same mind is truly in them which was also in Christ Jesus. Nay more, the connection usually brought out seems also to have this peculiarity, that it seems to make the apostle begin the paragraph with one injunction, and end it by enforcing its opposite. He commences formally—" Look not every man on his own things ; " and he ends by saying virtually—" Look every man on his own things—work out your own salvation." Is he to be understood as either modifying or withdrawing his first injunction, an injunction commended by the example of Christ Jesus.

The only difficulty in the way of this view is philological. The pronoun ἑαυτῶν is used in verse 4th, to signify one's own things ; and in verse 21st it is used with the same meaning, and how should the same word in the intervening verse 12th be used with precisely an opposite signification ? We feel the difficulty to be insuperable, while the leading of the context is so decided. And perhaps this may be the idea— carry forward your own salvation with fear and trembling, for with such a work in progress, and such emotions within you, you will possess the mind of Christ ; for he who thus carries out his own salvation will sympathize with the toils and labours of others, and look not alone at his own things. Their own salvation being secured and carried out, they would not be so selfish as to be wholly occupied with it, so unlike Him who made Himself of no reputation, as to creep up to heaven in selfish solitude. For the law of the kingdom is, that he who stoops the lowest shall rise the highest— Christ the first, and each after Him in order. This loving and lowly spirit God rejoices in—it is the heart of His Son, and the genius of His gospel. How this duty is to be discharged, the apostle does not say, but he adverts to its spirit —" in fear and trembling."

(Ver. 13.) Ὁ Θεὸς γάρ ἐστιν ὁ ἐνεργῶν ἐν ὑμῖν καὶ τὸ θέλειν καὶ τὸ ἐνεργεῖν, ὑπὲρ τῆς εὐδοκίας—"For God it is who worketh in you both to will and to work, in consequence of His own good pleasure." The article of the Received Text before Θεός is omitted in A, B, C, D[1], F, G, and K. Its

absence fixes attention upon Divinity, as in contrast to that
humanity in which He wills and works. The γάρ indicates
the connection, not by assigning a reason in the strict sense
of the term, but by introducing an explanatory statement :—
Engage in this duty; the inducement and the ability to
engage in it are inducement and ability alike from God. It
is too much to infer that the Philippians were despondent,
and that this verse is to be regarded as an encouragement.
But that they needed excitement to duty is plain, however,
from the statement—"and how much more in my absence"
—though certainly Bengel's filling up is far-fetched—*Deus
præsens vobis, etiam absente me.* It is as if he had said—
"Work out with fear and trembling, for God it is that worketh
in you. Engage in the duty, for God prompts and enables
you; engage in it with fear and trembling—emotions which
the nature of the work and such a consciousness of the Divine
presence and co-operation ought always to produce." If the
impulse sprang from themselves, and drew around it the
ability to obey, there might be "strife and vainglory;" but
surely if the motive and the strength came alike from God,
then only in reliance on Him, and with special humility and
self-subduing timidity, could they proceed, in reference to
their own salvation, or in offering one another spiritual
service.

The position of Θεός shows the emphasis placed upon it by
the apostle. God it is who worketh in you—alluding to the
inner operation of Divine grace—for ἐν ὑμῖν is not among
you. There is special force in the form ἐστιν ὁ ἐνεργῶν.
Winer, § 45, 5, note; Fritzsche, *ad Roman.* vol. ii. p. 212.
And the result is twofold—

καὶ τὸ θέλειν καὶ τὸ ἐνεργεῖν—"both to will and to work,"
first and naturally volition, and then action. Rom. vii. 18.
The double καί is emphatic. Winer, § 53, 4. The apostle
uses ἐνεργεῖν both of cause and effect—ἐνεργῶν—ἐνεργεῖν—
whereas the verb denoting the ultimate form of action was
κατεργάζεσθε. The difference is very apparent. The latter
term, the one employed by the apostle in the exhortation of
verse 12th, represents the full and final bringing of an enterprise to a successful issue; whereas ἐνεργεῖν describes action
rather in reference to vital power or ability, than form or

result. The will and the work are alike from God, or from
the operation of His grace and Spirit; not the work without
the will—an effect without its cause; not the will without
the work—an idle and effortless volition.

The concluding words—ὑπὲρ τῆς εὐδοκίας—have given
rise to a good deal of discussion. The phrase has no pronoun,
and what then is its reference? The Syriac renders
ܨܒ̇ܐ ܐܢܬܘܢ — that which you wish. And so Ambrosiaster, followed partly by Erasmus, Grotius, and Michaelis.
But εὐδοκία, as is indicated by the article, belongs here to
the subject of the verb. The preposition ὑπέρ is not
"according to," as it is rendered by Luther and Cameron,
nor *pro*, as Beza and Bengel write it. It signifies "on
account of." John xi. 4; Acts v. 41; Rom. xv. 8; Winer,
§ 47, 1, (3). It is not very different in result from δι᾽
εὐδοκίαν—i. 15—though the mode of representation somewhat varies—the ὑπέρ giving a reason, not in a logical, but
rather in an ethical aspect. See under Eph. i. 5. The noun
itself is defined by Suidas—τὸ ἀγαθὸν θέλημα τοῦ Θεοῦ.
Suicer, i. 1241. Œcumenius gives the true meaning in his
paraphrase—ὑπὲρ τοῦ πληρωθῆναι εἰς ὑμᾶς τὴν εὐδοκίαν καὶ
τὴν βουλὴν αὐτοῦ. It is in consequence of, or to follow out
His own good pleasure, that He works in believers both to
will and to work. He is not an absolute or necessary, but
a voluntary or spontaneous cause. He does it because He
freely wills it, or because it seems good to Him. His
efficacious grace is at His own sovereign disposal. Conybeare
joins ὑπὲρ τῆς εὐδοκίας to the following verse, but the connection is neither natural nor warranted.

The sentiments of the preceding verses have been adduced
as objections both to Pelagianism and Calvinism. Augustine
made good use of them in his day, in defence of the doctrine
of divine grace, and in overthrow of that meagre system which
is based at once on shallow conceptions of man's nature, and
superficial expositions of Scripture, and which, in denuding the
gospel of its mysteries, robs it of its reality and profound
adaptations. In later times, commentators on this passage
have attacked with it what is usually called Calvinism.
"The Calvinistic writers," says Bloomfield in his Recensio

Synoptica, " are exceedingly embarrassed with it ; " and after
reprehending Doddridge for a paraphrase of the verses, not a
whit worse or weaker than his ordinary dilutions, he adds,
" When we see so sensible a writer, and so good a man,
acting so disingenuous a part, we cannot but perceive the weakness of the system of doctrines he adopts, which drives him
to such unwarrantable measures." Now, if we understand
Calvinism at all, these two verses express very definitely its
spirit, belief, and practice. Divested of technical points, it is
this—profound and unquestioning trust in God, united to the
utmost spiritual activity and necessarily leading to it—acting
because acted upon, as the apostle here describes. The terms
employed by him exclude a vast amount of questions often
raised upon the verses—as the injunction is addressed, not to
the unbelieving and unregenerate, but " to saints in Christ
Jesus," to those who not only believed in Christ, but had
suffered for Him. The allusion is not to man's laying hold of
salvation, or to his first reception of it, and the necessity of
gratia præveniens, and therefore queries as to free-will and
grace—their existence or antagonism—are away from the
point. The apostle writes to persons who have received salvation, and he bids them carry it out. And who doubts that
man's highest energies are called out in the work—that every
faculty and feeling is thrown into earnest operation ? What
self-denial and vigilance—what wrestling with the Angel of
the Covenant—what study of the Lord's example—what busy
and humble obedience—what struggles with temptation—
what putting forth of all that is within us—what fervent
improvement of all the means of grace—industry as eager
and resolute as if no grace had been promised, but as if all
depended on itself ! The believer's own conscious and continuous effort in the work of his sanctification, is a very
prominent doctrine of Scripture, and the apostle often
describes his own unrelaxing diligence. On the other hand,
the doctrine of divine influence is caricatured by any such
hypothesis as is implied in the phrase—*homo convertitur
nolens*—or, when even under its " Dordracene " representation, it is styled, as by Ellicott, " all but compelling grace."
For in no sense can faith be forced ; and the freest act of the
human spirit is the surrender of itself under God's grace to

Himself. The rational nature is not violated, the mental mechanism is never shattered or dislocated, and the freedom essential to responsibility is not for a moment disturbed or suppressed. Though God work and work effectually in us "to will," our will is not passively bent and broken, but it wills as God wills it ; and though God work and work effectually in us "to do," our doing is not a course of action to which we are helplessly driven ; but we do, because we have resolved so to do, and because both resolve and action are prompted and shaped by His power that worketh in us—*agimur ut agamus.* This carrying out of our salvation is a willing action; but the will and the acts, though both of man and by him as agent, are not in their origin from him—the *vis* from which they spring being *non nativa sed dativa.* Lazarus came forth from the tomb by his own act, but his life had been already restored by Him in whom is life. The Hebrews walked every weary foot of the distance between Egypt and Canaan, yet to God is justly ascribed their exodus from the one country and their possession of the other. As man's activities are prompted and developed by Him who works in us both to will and to do, so is it that so many calls and commands are issued, urging him to be laborious and indefatigable ; for still he is dealt with as a creature that acts from motive, is deterred by warning, swayed by argument, and bound to obey divine precept. And what an inducement to work out our salvation—God Himself working in us—volition and action prompted and sustained by Him who "knoweth our frame." It is wrong to say with Chrysostom —" If thou wilt, in that case, He will work in thee to will." For the existence of such a previous will would imply that God had wrought already. The exposition of Pelagius was, that as there are three things in man, *posse, velle, agere,* and that as the first is from God, and the other two from ourselves, so the apostle here puts the effect for the cause—*Deus operatur velle, id est, posse, quia dat mihi potentiam ut possim velle. Lex et doctrina* are with him equivalent to, or are the explanation of, *gratia divina.* But law and revelation only tell what is to be done, and as Augustine says, *qua gratia agitur, non solum ut facienda noverimus, verum etiam ut cognita faciamus.—Opera,* vol. x. p. 538, ed. Paris, 1838.

The command, "work out your own salvation," is certainly
not in itself opposed to what Ellicott calls the "Dordracene
doctrine of irrevocable election;" for the divine purpose does
not reduce man to a machine, but works itself out by means
in perfect harmony with the freedom and responsibility of his
moral nature; so that every action has a motive and character.
Were this the place, one might raise other inferential questions— whether this divine operation in the saints can be
finally resisted, and whether it may be finally withdrawn?
or, in another aspect, whether a man whom God has justified
can be at last condemned? or whether the divine life
implanted by the Spirit of God may or can die out? But
the discussion of such questions belongs not to our province,
nor would the mere language of these verses warrant its
introduction.

(Ver. 14.) Πάντα ποιεῖτε χωρὶς γογγυσμῶν καὶ διαλογισ-
μῶν—"do all things without murmurings and doubts." This
counsel is still in unison with the preceding injunctions,
and is not to be taken, with Rheinwald, as an isolated or
independent statement. The duties inculcated might be
discharged in form, yet not in the right spirit. The term
πάντα is restricted in its reference by the context. The noun
γογγυσμός, which Paul uses only here, and which is an imita-
tive Ionic sound like the English murmur, denotes the expression of dissatisfaction with what is said, done, or ordered, Acts
vi. 1, Ex. xvi. 7, 8; or in the use of the verb, 1 Cor. x. 10;
Sept. Num. xi. 1, etc. The other noun διαλογισμός passed
from its original meaning to signify reasoning or thought, and
then descended to denote disputation. Luke ix. 46; 1 Tim.
ii. 8. In Luke xxiv. 38, the reference is to secret doubts;
but our Lord read the heart, and but for His presence, the heart
would soon have prompted the lips to speak out. The Vulgate translator has rendered the term by *hæsitationibus*. The
two nouns are closely connected, and express the same general
idea of dissatisfaction and doubt—opposed to the cheerful
and prompt discharge of present duty. That the last term
refers to such disputes as endanger the peace and unity of the
church, is the idea of Chrysostom, but it is not supported by
the immediate context, though it might be a result of the
conduct condemned; but the notion of Grotius, that the

apostle refers to debates with philosophers, is vain. Nor can
we agree with Theodoret, that there is reference to persecutions—τοὺς ὑπὲρ τοῦ εὐαγγελίου κινδύνους; for such adverse
dispensations are not glanced at. The apostle is not speaking of murmuring under trial, but in discharge of duty.
Meyer contends for Tittmann's distinction between ἄνευ and
χωρίς, that the former depicts the absence of the object from
the subject; and the latter, the separation of the subject
from the object. Tittmann, *Syn.* p. 94. See under Eph. ii.
12. The apostle Paul never uses ἄνευ, but always χωρίς,
while 1 Peter—iv. 9—has ἄνευ γογγυσμῶν. The distinction
is therefore more of an ideal or etymological nature, than
one carried out in use and practice. It seems to us too
restricted on the part of Meyer and De Wette, to take God as
the Being murmured against; or, with Estius and Hoelemann, to make the objects of this murmuring the office-
bearers in the church; or, with Calvin and Wiesinger, the
members of the church. Alford regards both words as having
a human reference, but without satisfactory proof. The feeling of dissatisfaction and hesitation is expressed generally,
and its particular causes and objects are not assigned. No
matter what may tend to excite it, it must not be indulged ;
whether the temptation to it be the divine command, the
nature of the duty, the self-denial which it involves, or the
opposition occasionally encountered. There was neither
grudge nor reluctance with Him whose example is described
in the preceding verses—no murmur at the depth of His
condescension, or doubt as to the amount or severity of the
sufferings which for others He so willingly endured. The
purpose of the injunction is then stated—

(Ver. 15.) "Ἵνα γένησθε ἄμεμπτοι καὶ ἀκέραιοι—" That ye
may be blameless and pure." This reading of the verb has
considerable authority, but so has ἦτε, which is adopted by
Lachmann. The ordinary reading may, perhaps, be preferred. The two adjectives express the same idea in different aspects, the first meaning that to which no blame is
attached, and the latter that of which moral simplicity can be
asserted. There is, therefore, a climax in the statement—not
simply blameless, or escaping censure, but possessing that
spiritual integrity which secures blamelessness. Matt. x. 16 ;

Rom. xvi. 19. Or, as Meyer suggests, the two adjectives correspond to the two previous nouns. If they did all things without murmurings, they should " be blameless; " if without doubts, they should be " sincere." None should censure them, if they were cheerful in duty ; and none could censure them, if this inner integrity characterized them. The conjunction ἵνα brings out this clause as the end or object. If they did all these things without murmurings and doubts, what surer proof of having reached the possession of the same mind which was also in Christ Jesus ? Nay, more, they should be—

τέκνα Θεοῦ ἀμώμητα—"children of God, blameless." For ἀμώμητα, which has good authority, A, B, C read ἄμωμα, the more common form in the New Testament, the previous word occurring only twice. They were already the children of God, but they were to be blameless children of God. How far ἄμεμπτοι, in the previous clause, differs from ἀμώμητα in the present clause, it is difficult to say. Perhaps the last is really a stronger term than the first. If the first mean unblamed, or without moral defect, the second may rise to the higher meaning of without cause of blame, without ground of moral challenge—children breathing the spirit, possessing the image, and exhibiting the purity of their Father-God. And the blamelessness of their character would be the more apparent from the contrast—

μέσον γενεᾶς σκολιᾶς καὶ διεστραμμένης—"in the midst of a crooked and perverse generation." The adverbial form μέσον has preponderant authority over the common reading ἐν μέσῳ—the former having in its favour A, B, C, D¹, F, G. The term is used adverbially. Winer, § 54, 6, note; Num. xxxv. 5. The clause is virtually quoted from Deut. xxxii. 5 —τέκνα μωμητὰ, γενεὰ σκολιὰ καὶ διεστραμμένη.

The noun γενεά is generation—the men living at that period. Matt. xi. 16, xvii. 17 ; Acts ii. 40. The first epithet, σκολιά, meaning bent or crooked, has a similar tropical signification, Acts ii. 40 ; 1 Pet. ii. 18 ; and the second term, διεστραμμένη, signifies physically and ethically what is twisted or distorted. Matt. xvii. 17 ; Luke ix. 41 ; Acts xx. 30. The two adjectives have the same general meaning, the one referring to the inner disposition, and the other to its outer manifestation; and both pointing out, not so much the dulness of disobedience, as its caprices; not so much its fatal stupidity, as its wayward and eccentric courses. What the apostle describes is not spiritual torpor, but spiritual obliquity; his mental reference being to those examples of periodical insanity for which Israel of old was proverbial, and by which Moses had been so surprised and grieved. Sin brought chastening, and though penitence followed punishment, it was soon succeeded by another wanton outbreak. It was sunshine to-day, but shadow to-morrow—a song on the bank of the Red Sea—and then, after a few weeks' advance, the blasphemous howl—"Would to God we had died by the hand of the Lord in the land of Egypt." They were always overmastered by the idea of the moment, the passion of the hour —sinning and suffering, fretting and praying, mere children without firmness of temper or stability of resolve. Their character was uniform only in its variableness and perversity —tears for their chains the one month; tears for the fleshpots the next. A character not identical certainly, but similar in some respects, the apostle ascribes to the Philippian population of that day, not as sunk into sullen unbelief, but moved by tortuous impulses to reject what they could not disprove, and persecute what they could not but admit was innocent in its civil aspect, and pure and benignant in its spiritual results. Nothing would please them; give them one argument, and they cry for another. Tell them of the simplicity of the gospel, and they pray you to dilate on its mysteries; speak of its power, and they bid you dwell on its charity. Both Jew and Pagan at Philippi may have shown such a spirit to the church. The impeachment is not only open wickedness, as Grotius gives it, but also a want of candour and sincerity; public avowals at variance with secret convictions; objections made on mere pretence, the ostensible motive not the true one; one purpose secretly crossed or overlaid by another; their conduct a riddle, and their life a lie. Our Lord depicted a similar feature of his own age. Matt. xi. 16, etc. In the midst of such society, the Philippian believers were to do all things with cheerfulness and promptitude, so as to approve themselves the sons of God by their spiritual integrity and purity, for it was true of them—

ἐν οἷς φαίνεσθε ὡς φωστῆρες ἐν κόσμῳ—"among whom ye
appear as luminaries in the world." The verb is taken as an
imperative by not a few, such as Cyprian, who renders
lucete, and by Theophylact, Erasmus, Calvin, Storr, Rheinwald, and Baumgarten-Crusius. The indicative is preferable,
as the clause describes an existing or actual condition, and so
it is understood by most modern expositors. The plural οἷς
represents the individuals comprised in the γενεά, a frequent
form of construction according to the sense. Matt. xiii. 54;
Luke x. 7; Acts viii. 5; 2 Cor. ii. 13; Winer, 58, § 4, (b).
Wiesinger and Meyer remark that the verb φαίνεσθε is
improperly rendered "ye shine," though the lexicographers
appear to give it that signification. It has this meaning in
the active, and is so employed. John i. 5, v. 35; 2 Pet. i.
19; but in the passive it signifies "to appear." Still, when
coupled with such a word as φωστῆρες, it may be rendered
shine, without any impropriety—for to appear as luminaries,
is simply to shine. In the term φωστῆρες the allusion is to
the heavenly bodies; not to light-houses certainly, as Barnes
supposes; nor yet to torches, as is imagined by Beza and
Cornelius a-Lapide. The concluding words ἐν κόσμῳ do not
belong to the verb, which has already ἐν οἷς before it, but to
φωστῆρες. Κόσμος wants the article (Winer, § 19), and it
serves no purpose in figures of this popular nature to assign
this noun an ethical sense, as Ellicott does. It is strange that
Rheinwald, preceded by Drusius, should take κόσμος to mean
the firmament. Hoelemann, Rilliet, and van Hengel supply
a verb φαίνονται—among whom "as stars shine in the world
ye shine"—but this is not necessary. The figure is, simply,
that the sons of God are in the world what the heavenly
luminaries are to it. The world is the sphere in which they
revolve and shine. The point of comparison is obvious. It
is not first nor simply eminence in virtue, nor conspicuous
position, nor elevation above worldly pursuits and likings,[1]
but the diffusion of light. Matt. v. 14, 15, 16. They did
not only enjoy the light, but they reflected it. They appeared
as luminaries in the world, and its only spiritual light came
from them. There was deep gloom around them, but they
tended to disperse it. What in fact has not the world learned

[1] *Non amant terrena.* Anselm.

from the church ?   The apostle now describes the mode of illumination—

(Ver. 16.) Λόγον ζωῆς ἐπέχοντες —" Holding forth the word of life."   We look on this clause as descriptive or illustrative of the one before it.   Robinson and Baumgarten-Crusius connect it with the epithets ἄμεμπτοι καὶ ἀκέραιοι, a hypothesis which sadly dislocates the paragraph, and is not in harmony with the figure.   By λόγον ζωῆς we understand the gospel ; or, as Theodoret explains it—τὸ κήρυγμα ἐπειδὴ τὴν αἰώνιον προξενεῖ ζωήν.   It is the " word of life "—life being the grand blessing which it reveals—while it proclaims its origin, how it has been secured, and by what means it is applied, what is its present nature, and what shall be its ultimate and glorious destiny.   Rom. i. 16 ; John vi. 63 ; Acts v. 20.   To understand Christ Himself by the phrase, as did some of the older expositors, is unwarranted.   Nor can we, with others, such as Am Ende, give the genitive a subjective sense, and render the " living word ;" or, with Beza and others, the vivifying word—vivificum ab effectu.

The participle ἐπέχοντες has been variously understood. 1. The Syriac translator interprets, but does not render, when he gives the clause — ܠܝܢ ܐܬܪ̈ܐ ܕܗܘܢ ܕܐܝܬܝܟܘܢ, "to be to them for a place of salvation."   He is followed by Michaelis, Zachariae, Flatt, and Storr, who gives it—et vitæ loco esse. The view, however, cannot be maintained by any strong arguments.

2. The literal meaning of the verb is " to have on ; " and so Meyer takes it in the simple sense of " possessing," a meaning it has in the classical writers.   Yet in the passages adduced by him from Herodotus and Thucydides, the word signifies to occupy or govern a district.   Meyer's idea is, however, good in itself, for had they not possessed the word of life, the essence of which is light, they should be as dark as the world round about them.

3. Others give the participle the sense of " holding fast "— the word of life.   Hesychius defines it by κρατοῦντες, and Suidas by φυλάσσοντες.   This view is held by Luther, Bengel, Hoelemann, Heinrichs, De Wette, Robinson, Bretschneider, and Wahl.   The verb does not seem to have such a meaning

anywhere in the New Testament, certainly not in Acts xix. 22. This idea is illustrated by Chrysostom—"What means," he asks, "holding fast—ἐπέχοντες—the word of life? Being destined to live, being of the saved." And he asks again —"What means the word of life? Having the seed of life —that is, having pledges of life, holding fast—κατέχοντες— life itself."

4. We agree with those who understand the word as meaning "holding up or forth." Of this opinion, generally, are van Hengel, Erasmus, Grotius, Rheinwald, and Matthies. Meyer allows that such a meaning does belong to the verb, but objects that it does not harmonize with the figure which represents the subjects themselves as luminaries. Now it may be replied, that this clause describes the mode in which believers are luminaries. They appear as lights in the world —as, or when, or because they are holding forth the word of life. Possessing the word of life they shine, says Meyer; holding up the word of life they are luminaries, is our idea of the image. The possession of the gospel is in itself a source of individual enlightenment, but the exhibition of that gospel throws its light on others.

There is abundant evidence that this is a common meaning of the verb, and such a meaning harmonizes with the context. Numerous examples are given by Passow and the other lexi- cographers—*Iliad* ix. 485, etc., *Od.* xvi. 444—where the verb occurs with οἶνον, as in other places with μαζόν, etc. The gospel or word of life was held forth, and its holders were light-givers in the world. As they made known its doctrines, and impressed men with a sense of its importance, as their actions, in their purity and harmony, exhibited its life and power, did they hold it forth. From them the world learned its true interest and destiny, its connection with God and eternity; they were its only instructors in the highest of the sciences. As Balduin quaintly but truly remarks, Christ is φῶς, and they are φωστῆρες.

Thrice out of the five times in which ἐπέχειν occurs in the New Testament, it signifies to "mark, or give or take heed to." Theodoret gives it the same meaning here, though the construction would require a dative—τῷ λόγῳ προσέ- χοντες τῆς ζωῆς—

εἰς καύχημα ἐμοὶ εἰς ἡμέραν Χριστοῦ—" for rejoicing to me against the day of Christ." Καύχημα is matter of rejoicing. See under c. i. 26. The first preposition denotes result, 2 Cor. i. 14; and the second points to the period for which this result is, as it were, laid up. For the meaning of ἡμέρα X. see under i. 6. The apostle indicates the joy which obedience to his counsels would finally create—a proof, too, that his labours had not been ineffectual—

ὅτι οὐκ εἰς κενὸν ἔδραμον οὐδὲ εἰς κενὸν ἐκοπίασα—" that I did not run in vain, nor labour in vain." The expression is somewhat proverbial—to run in vain was to lose the prize. Compare 1 Cor. ix. 26; Gal. ii. 2, iv. 11; 1 Thess. iii. 5; 2 Tim. iv. 7; Josephus, *Antiq.* xix. 1, 4. The aorists are used to mark the time, as from the standpoint of the day of Christ. The double form of expression—the one a pointed trope, the other more general—and the repetition of εἰς κενόν, mark the intensity of the sentiment. The phrase εἰς κενόν (Diodorus Sic. xix. 9), equivalent in result to μάτην and εἰκῆ and corresponding to the Hebrew לָרִיק, resembles similar expressions, as εἰς καλόν. Krüger, § 68, 21, 11; 2 Cor. vi. 1; Gal. ii. 2; 1 Thess. iii. 5. The second verb is as expressive as the first. If the image of the race-course suggest previous training (1 Cor. ix. 25, 27) and violent exertion, the putting forth of the utmost power in direction of the goal and the garland —the second verb has in it the broader notion of continuous and earnest effort; for the apostle was ἐν κόποις, 2 Cor. vi. 5 —nay, ἐν κόποις περισσοτέρως, 2 Cor. xi. 23. It is very tame, on the part of Wetstein, to explain the figure of running by this matter of fact—*longum iter Hierosolymis per totam Macedoniam.*

The apostle looks forward to the period when all secrets shall be unfolded, when the results of pastoral labour shall be fully disclosed, and he anticipates that when, in the light of eternity, he should behold the result of his apostolic efforts, his bosom should be filled with joy. What purer joy can be imagined than this—what joy nearer in fulness and loftiness to His, who, on the same day, " shall see of the travail of His soul and shall be satisfied " ? And what, in a word, does the apostle regard as the consummation of his labours, or when, in the history of a church, does he reckon that his ministerial

services have fully succeeded ? The preceding verses afford
an answer; for it is only when a church feels and acts as the
apostle has counselled, that he sees in its experience and
destiny the crown and reward of his sufferings and toils. Its
prosperity is neither in its number nor its wealth, but in its
spiritual progress—in its purity and enlightening power—in
short, in its possession and exhibition of the "mind which
was also in Christ Jesus."

(Ver. 17.) Ἀλλ' εἰ καὶ σπένδομαι ἐπὶ τῇ θυσίᾳ καὶ λειτουρ-
γίᾳ τῆς πίστεως ὑμῶν—"But if even I am being poured out
on the sacrifice and service of your faith." Ἀλλά is not *quin*,
as Beza translates it, and he is generally followed by Am
Ende and others, who find no contrast. De Wette connects
it with i. 25, which is too remote for such a purpose, as is also
i. 21, the reference of Storr. Hoelemann supposes the contrast to be with εἰς καύχημα—*Quid, O Paule, recordaris* τοῦ
καυχήματος, *quum undique stipent et urgeant, quæ tristissima
præsagiant?* But such an association had no place in the
fearless and elevated heart of the apostle. Rilliet supposes
the reference to be to an unexpressed thought—"I have not
laboured in vain"—"*non," pense-t-il en lui-même je n'ai pas
travaillé en vain, mais au contraire*. The antithesis in ἀλλά
is to the general thought implied in the previous verse. Not
that, as Alford, following Schrader and van Hengel, says, he
tacitly assumes he should live till the day of Christ. He would
have cause of joy laid up for the day of Christ, if he saw the
Philippians acting as he had enjoined them; on the other
hand, should he be cut off, that joy would not be frustrated.

The phrase εἰ καί—"if even," supposes a case which has
some probability of occurrence, not a case put for argument or
illustration—a form indicated by the reverse position of the
particles καὶ εἰ. Klotz, Devarius, ii. p. 519. If even I am
being poured out, as I feel that I am—εἰ καί—; and if I am
poured out, should it really come to this, as it may—καὶ εἰ.

The next clause is a vivid sacerdotal image. The reference
in σπένδομαι is to the libation poured upon the sacrifice, or at
least round the altar, and is to be understood of his own death,
Numbers xv. 5 ; xxviii. 7. Hesychius and Suidas explain it
by θύομαι—an explanation right as to general sense, but not
correct as to special meaning or form of representation. The

preponderant use of θυσία in the New Testament, is the thing sacrificed, but it is not, as Ellicott affirms, its uniform meaning. It denotes the sacrifice, not simply the process as a rite, but the victim óffered in the performance of that rite—a devoted thing or animal in its ritual presentation to God.   The noun λειτουργία is the priestly ministration, as in Luke i. 23 ; Heb. viii. 6, ix. 21—ministration which the apostle supposes himself to conduct, and not their ministration in promoting Christianity, as Wahl makes it. (*Sub voce* θυσία.) The genitive πίστεως is that of object, and is related to both the nouns with a common article.   Their faith was the matter of the sacrifice, that which the priestly ministration handled.   The apostle's image is that of an altar, on which their faith is laid by him as priest, while his own blood is being poured out as the usual drink-offering or libation.   It is an error, both in philology and imagery, on the part of Rilliet, to render—*Je suis aspergè, ou j'ai reçu l'aspersion*, as if the allusion were to a victim on which a libation had been poured so as to consecrate it for the altar—κατασπένδω being in that case the appropriate term, and it is the term occurring in the majority of the quotations in Wetstein, who adopts the same view.   It is no less wrong to suppose the Philippians to be as priests offering their own faith to God—connecting ὑμῶν exclusively with λειτουργία, than to regard the Philippians themselves as constituting the θυσία, for the image is different here from Rom. xv. 16.   We need scarcely mention the opinion that the money gift of the Philippians is referred to, or quote the view of Rettig, that Christ is the θυσία, thus separating it from πίστεως, and the λειτουργία this pecuniary present.   We take ἐπί in its ordinary acceptation, " upon," not as meaning *während*—" during," with Meyer, nor with Ellicott as signifying " in addition to," or " in," denoting merely a concomitant act.[1]   Ellicott's objection to the rendering " upon," is, that the libation among the Jews was poured not on the altar, but around it.   But it is needless to suppose, that in using such a figure the apostle was bound to keep by the strict letter of the Hebrew rubric, for the very supposition of a drink-offering of human blood was of all things most opposed to it; and he here speaks of

---

[1] For illustrations of the pagan form of the ceremonial, see Raphelius *in loco*. See also Suicer *sub voce*.

his own violent death, or, as Theophylact strips the figure—
εἰ καὶ τελευτῶ. As their faith is laid by himself upon the
altar, and he engaged in the act of presenting it, his own blood
is poured out upon it, and serves as a libation to it,—the
blood of the officiating priest, suddenly slain, would naturally
be sprinkled *over* the sacrifice which he was offering to God.
The apostle's death, as a martyr, was felt by him to be a
very likely event; and while that death would be a judicial
murder, it would yet be an offering poured out on the faith of
his Philippian converts. But the prospect of such a death
lid not fill him with gloomy associations, for he adds in a
very different spirit—

χαίρω καὶ συγχαίρω πᾶσιν ὑμῖν—"I rejoice and give joy
to you all." That the compound verb may bear this sense in
the active voice, is plain from many examples. Passow *sub
voce*. The Vulgate has *congratulor*. In the New Testament,
when persons are the objects, it seems to bear the same mean-
ng. Luke i. 58—Elizabeth's neighbours and relatives heard
of the birth of her son—καὶ συνέχαιρον αὐτῇ—and they
rejoiced with her, or gave her their congratulations. Luke
xv. 6, 9—on the part of the shepherd who has found his
wandered sheep, and on the part of the housewife who has
recovered her lost piece of silver, the cordial call to friends
and kinsfolk is—συγχάρητέ μοι—rejoice with me, that is,
be partakers of my joy, or wish me joy. See also Sept., Gen.
xxi. 6; 3 Macc. i. 8. The ground of this joy and congratula-
tion is not, however, marked by the previous ἐπί. Such
appears to be the view of Chrysostom; but ἐπί is especially
connected with σπένδομαι, and in Paul's style usually follows
χαίρω when connected with it. 1 Cor. xiii. 6; xvi. 17.
The cause of the joy is what is told in the entire verse. His
martyrdom, viewed in the light in which he presents it, was
anticipated with joy and congratulations. The reference in
. 20 is explanatory to some extent, but cannot be taken,
with De Wette, as either a full or an apposite illustration.
The apostle is not content with what he has said, but he
invites a perfect reciprocity of feeling :—

(Ver. 18.) Τὸ δ' αὐτὸ καὶ ὑμεῖς χαίρετε, καὶ συγχαίρετέ
ιοι—"Yea, for the very same reason, do ye also joy and offer
oy to me." The pronominal formula or accusative of refer-

ence—τὸ δ' αὐτό—is governed by χαίρετε. Matt. xxvii. 44 ;
Winer, § 32, 4 ; Kühner, § 553, Anmerk 1. The alternative of his martyrdom was not to dispirit them ; they were
to rejoice and to congratulate him—so nearly were they concerned in it ; their faith being the sacrifice in the offering of
which the apostle is engaged, when his blood, like a drink-
offering, is poured out as an accompaniment.

(Ver. 19.) Ἐλπίζω δὲ ἐν Κυρίῳ Ἰησοῦ, Τιμόθεον ταχέως
πέμψαι ὑμῖν—" But I hope in the Lord Jesus, shortly, to
send Timothy to you." Though the apostle has expressed
himself with this ardour, still he feels that the prospect of
martyrdom is not sure beyond doubt. It was a possibility, a
probability even, but his mind at once turns from it to immediate business—the mission of Timothy, and his own projected
journey to Philippi. The particle δέ indicates transition to
an opposite train of thought ; and the phrase ἐν Κυρίῳ Ἰησοῦ
gives the sphere of his hope, while ἐπί with the dative
would have marked its foundation. He expected to send
Timothy, and that expectation was based upon Christ ; that
He would prepare the way, and so order events that Timothy's
mission might come to pass. Only if Christ so willed it
could it happen, and he felt and hoped that his intention to
send Timothy, after a brief interval, was in accordance with
the mind of Christ. A fuller form of expression occurs in
1 Cor. xvi. 7—" I hope to tarry awhile with you "—ἐὰν ὁ
Κύριος ἐπιτρέπῃ, " if the Lord permit." The dative ὑμῖν
is not the same in reference as πρὸς ὑμᾶς in v. 25, as if
intimating the direction or end of his journey, but it rather
points out the persons with whom he should find himself,
or who should receive him as the apostle's representative.
John xv. 26; 1 Cor. iv. 17 ; Kühner, § 571. And the
purpose of the mission is thus briefly expressed—

ἵνα κἀγὼ εὐψυχῶ, γνοὺς τὰ περὶ ὑμῶν—" that I also may
be of good spirit, when I have known your affairs." The
καί means—" I, as well as you "—you will be of good heart
when you know my affairs, and I, too, shall be of good heart
when I know yours—τὰ περὶ ὑμῶν. Eph. vi. 22. The verb
εὐψυχέω is found only here in the New Testament; but
εὐψυχία, εὐψυχής, εὔψυχος, and εὐψύχως are used by the
classics in both prose and poetry. 2 Macc. xiv. 18 ; Prov.

xxx. 31; 1 Macc. ix. 14; Josephus, *Antiq.* ii. 6. The imperative of the verb is found also on monuments, recording the *farewell* of survivors. (Passow *sub voce.*) The expression implies that the apostle was solicitous about them, as various hints and counsels in this epistle already intimate; but he hoped to receive such accounts through Timothy as should dispel all his anxieties and apprehensions. And he assigns, for his choice of Timothy as his messenger, a reason which could not but commend him to the Philippian church as he discharged his embassy among them.

(Ver. 20.) Οὐδένα γὰρ ἔχω ἰσόψυχον, ὅστις γνησίως τὰ περὶ ὑμῶν μεριμνήσει—"For I have no one like-minded, who will really care for your affairs." The adjective ἰσόψυχον, which occurs nowhere else in the New Testament, though found in the Septuagint (Ps. liv. 13), states a resemblance, not between Timothy and others, as Beza, Calvin, and Rilliet suppose, but between Timothy and the apostle himself as the subject of the sentence. The use of ὅστις is somewhat different from its meaning in some previous verses, and signifies—"as being of a class." Krüger, § 51, 8. The adverb γνησίως qualifies the verb, or describes the genuineness of that solicitude which Timothy would feel for the Philippian converts. The verb, as usual with Paul, governs the accusative, though it has the dative—Matt. vi. 25—and is also followed by περί—"to care about," and ὑπέρ—"to care for." Timothy is of such a nature, has a soul so like my own, that when he comes among you, he will manifest—μεριμνήσει—a true regard for your best interests. What higher eulogy could the apostle have pronounced upon him? And he was shut up to the selection of Timothy—

(Ver. 21.) Οἱ πάντες γὰρ τὰ ἑαυτῶν ζητοῦσιν, οὐ τὰ Ἰησοῦ Χριστοῦ—"For the whole seek their own things, not the things of Jesus Christ." The οἱ πάντες, specifying the entire number, corresponds to the οὐδένα of the previous verse. (For similar use of the article and pronoun, compare Acts xix. 7, xxvii. 37; 1 Cor. ix. 22; Bernhardy, p. 320; Middleton on *Greek Article*, p. 104, note by the Editor.) All, with the exception of Timothy, seek their own things. This is a sweeping censure, and therefore many, such as Hammond, Estius, Rheinwald, and Flatt, seek to modify it in number, by

rendering οἱ πάντες, "the majority;" while others, as Erasmus, Calvin, and Hoelemann, seek to modify it in severity,
by inserting a comparison—all seek their own *more* than the
things of Jesus Christ. But while these modifications are
inadmissible, it must at the same time be borne in mind, that
the apostle's words should be limited to such persons as were
with him, and, farther, to those who might be supposed to be
eligible for such an enterprise; so that probably the brethren
mentioned in i. 15 are to be excluded from the estimate.
It is impossible for us now to ascertain on whom the apostle's
censures light, though Demas may be a representative of the
class. 2 Tim. iv. 10. In the last chapter of the Epistle to the
Colossians, some persons are noticed, but Wiesinger remarks,
after stating that Luke was probably not at Rome, "the
apostle's words do not apply to any of those of his fellow-
labourers, in reference to whom they would have excited our
surprise." Ewald is inclined to regard them as persons from
Philippi, or well acquainted with its affairs, but hostile to the
apostle. The persons so referred to had not that like-souled-
ness with the apostle which he ascribes to Timothy; did not
love Christ's cause above everything; were not so absorbed
in it as to allow nothing, neither ease nor safety, home nor
kindred, to bar them from advancing it. On the other hand,
the eulogy pronounced on Timothy is based upon acknowledged
evidence—

(Ver. 22.) *Τὴν δὲ δοκιμὴν αὐτοῦ γινώσκετε*—"But ye know
his tried character." *Δέ* introduces the contrast between him
and those just referred to. The noun δοκιμή signifies trial—
experimentum—and then the thing tried. Rom. v. 4; 2 Cor.
ii. 9, ix. 13. The process of proof they had possessed already
—Acts xvi.—and therefore γινώσκετε is indicative, not imperative. They were no strangers to his excellence—it had
been tested during previous visits. And the apostle briefly
and tenderly sketches it—

ὅτι, ὡς πατρὶ τέκνον, σὺν ἐμοὶ ἐδούλευσεν εἰς τὸ εὐαγγέλιον
—"that as a child a father, he served with me for the gospel."
Some supply σύν before πατρί, and render with our version—
"as a son with a father." But this supplement mars the
beauty of the eulogy; nor is it in strict accordance with
grammatical usage. A preposition, inserted in the first of a

N

series of clauses, may be omitted in the subsequent ones ; but
the reverse rarely, if ever, happens. Bernhardy, p. 204 ;
Kühner, § 625. And the apostle designedly varies the aspect
of the relation. The expected construction would be—" as a
child serves a father, so he served me for the gospel ; " but
it is changed into—" served with me." Winer, § 63, II. 1.
As a child serves a father is an expressive image, denoting
loving, devoted, and confidential service. But the apostle felt
that in missionary labour it was not he who directly received
the service from Timothy, and he therefore changed the relation into σὺν ἐμοί—still bringing out the idea that Timothy's
service, though directed to a common object with his own,
was yet subordinate to his, was filial, ardent, and unwearied.
Timothy is thus represented not as serving Paul, though Paul
seems to have prescribed his labours and travels, but as
serving with him—both being common servants of the same
Master. But in this service Timothy was directed and governed by his spiritual father, with whom he was so like-
minded. The phrase εἰς τὸ εὐαγγέλιον is " for the gospel,"
as in i. 5, not " in it."

(Ver. 23.) Τοῦτον μὲν οὖν ἐλπίζω πέμψαι—" Him, then, I
hope to send immediately "—ἐξαυτῆς. Τοῦτον is placed emphatically—μέν corresponding to δέ of the following verse,
and οὖν taking up again and repeating, after the break, what
has been said in verse 19. Ἐξαυτῆς, Mark vi. 25; Acts x. 33.

ὡς ἂν ἀφίδω τὰ περὶ ἐμέ—" whenever I shall have seen
how it will go with me." The form ἀφίδω is supposed
to have arisen from the pronunciation of the word with the
digamma (Winer, § 5, 1), and is found in A, B¹, D¹, F, G ;
Jonah iv. 5. The ἀπό seems to be local, as in many other
verbs compounded with it—*prospicere.* The verb, used only
here, is followed by the simple accusative, but sometimes by
εἰς and πρός. Herod. iv. 22; Joseph. *Antiq.* ii. 6, 1 ; 4 Macc.
xvii. 23. See under i. 20. The phrase τὰ περὶ ἐμέ—" the
things about me "—may have in it the idea of development.
The idiom ὡς ἄν marks the writer's uncertainty as to the
time when the events which are the subject of ἀφίδω shall
take place. Chrysostom's paraphrase is ὅταν ἴδω ἐν τίνι
ἕστηκα καὶ ποῖον ἕξει τέλος τὰ κατ' ἐμέ. The apostle, as long as
his fate was undetermined, wished to keep Timothy with him.

When there might be a decision he could not tell, only he
hoped it would be soon ; and as soon as he could ascertain the
issue, he would at once despatch Timothy to Philippi. But
he has, at the same time, a persuasion that he will speedily
visit them himself.

(Ver. 24.) Πέποιθα δὲ ἐν Κυρίῳ, ὅτι καὶ αὐτὸς ταχέως
ἐλεύσομαι—" But I trust in the Lord, that I myself also shall
shortly come." The δέ corresponds to the μέν of the previous
verse, and ἐν Κυρίῳ marks the sphere or nature of his trust,
ver. 19. Not only did he hope to send Timothy soon, but
he cherishes the prospect of a speedy visit in person also—
καὶ αὐτός. The relative period of his own visit is specified by
ταχέως, as that of Timothy's mission has been by ἐξαυτῆς.
Meyer and Ellicott suppose that ταχέως refers to a later
period than ἐξαυτῆς—that Paul hoped to send Timothy soon,
and come himself shortly after ; but both expressions date
from the writing of the epistle, and they are to be taken in a
popular sense. A and C, with some versions and Fathers, add
πρὸς ὑμᾶς. The expression πέποιθα is stronger than the previous ἐλπίζω. See under i. 25.

(Ver. 25.) Ἀναγκαῖον δὲ ἡγησάμην, Ἐπαφρόδιτον—πέμψαι
πρὸς ὑμᾶς—" Yet I judged it necessary to send Epaphroditus
to you." The δέ is so far in contrast with the preceding statement, that he hoped to send Timothy, and trusted also to come
himself ; but in the meantime he judged it necessary to send
Epaphroditus. The necessity, however, did not arise out of the
mere probability or the possible delay of his own and Timothy's
visit, but it is stated at length in the subsequent verses. The
prospect of a speedy visit from himself and Timothy did not
supersede the mission of Epaphroditus, for there were other
reasons for it. He might have gone in Paul's company, but
he is to precede him. The verb ἡγησάμην is in what is called
the epistolary aorist, the time being taken from the ideal period
of the reception of the letter, so that ἡγέομαι to the writer passes
into ἡγησάμην to the readers. Winer, 40, 5, b 2. Of Epaphroditus nothing farther is known. Everything is against
the supposition of Grotius and Schrader that he is the same
as the Epaphras mentioned in the Epistle to the Colossians,
i. 7, iv. 12 ; and in Philemon 23. The name was a common
one. Wetstein has given several examples of it from Sueto-

nius, Josephus, and Arrian. Epaphras might be a contracted
form of Epaphroditus, and Epaphras was also about this time
in Rome. But who could suppose that the Asiatic Epaphras,
a pastor at Colosse and a native of it, could be Epaphroditus,
a messenger delegated to Paul, with a special gift from the
distant European church of Philippi, and by him sent back to
it with this lofty eulogy, and as having a special interest in
its affairs and members ? Other traditions are still more baseless,—that he had been one of the seventy disciples, a bishop,
or one of those commissioned to ordain bishops or proselytes,
—the freedman or secretary of Nero,[1] to whom Josephus dedi-
cated his two books against Apion. Epaphroditus is then
heartily commended, and the apostle first characterizes him
through his relation to himself,—

τὸν ἀδελφὸν καὶ συνεργὸν καὶ συστρατιώτην μου—" my
brother, and fellow-labourer, and fellow-soldier." The epithets rise in intensity,—first a Christian brother—then a
colleague in toil—and then a companion in scenes of danger
and conflict. Philemon 2 ; 2 Tim. ii. 3. Not simply a brother, but an industrious one—not industrious only in times
of peace, but one who had met the adversary in defence of the
gospel. And this was not all, he sustained at the same time
a peculiar relation to the Philippian church,—

ὑμῶν δὲ ἀπόστολον καὶ λειτουργὸν τῆς χρείας μου—" but
your deputy and minister to my need." In the collocation—
μου, ὑμῶν δέ—there is a marked antithetical connection—the
pronoun ὑμῶν defining both the nouns after it which want the
article. Ἀπόστολος is used in its original, and not in its
ecclesiastical sense as a delegate or one who did Paul's work
among them, 2 Cor. viii. 23—far less in its emphatic sense
of apostle, or special founder of a church, or bishop of this
church, as Beelen and Whitby assume. He had been sent
by the Philippian church with a gift to Paul, so that he
became the minister of his need—ὡς τὰ παρ' ὑμῶν ἀποστα-
λέντα κομίσαντα χρήματα, as it is explained by Theodoret.
The noun λειτουργός has the general sense of minister, in connection with the discharge of a religious duty. The apostle's

---

[1] Of Nero Suetonius says (49), *ferrum jugulo adegit, juvante Epaphrodito a
libellis ;* and of this secretary the same author tells again (Domitian, 14), *Epa-
phroditum a libellis capitali pœna condemnavit.*

"need" was simply his want of such things as their gift could supply. The apostle says merely "send," not send back; perhaps, as Bengel conjectures, *nam ideo ad Paulum venerat, ut cum eo maneret.* One special reason why the apostle wished to send Epaphroditus is next given:—

(Ver. 26.) Ἐπειδὴ ἐπιποθῶν ἦν πάντας ὑμᾶς—" Forasmuch as he was longing after you all." The conjunction ἐπειδή— " since now "—assigns the reason why the apostle thought it necessary to send back Epaphroditus. Klotz, Devarius, ii. p. 548. Not only is the epistolary imperfect ἦν employed, but it is here used with the present participle, to denote the continuance of the longing. Winer, § 45, 5. Epaphroditus had not forgotten them, his longing was great towards them —ἐπί. See under i. 8, page 17.

καὶ ἀδημονῶν, διότι ἠκούσατε ὅτι ἠσθένησε—" and was in heaviness, because ye heard that he was sick." The infinitive ἀδημονεῖν describes our Lord's agony in Matt. xxvi. 37; Mark xiv. 33. Its derivation is uncertain. How did the intelligence conveyed to them that he was sick cause Epaphroditus to long for them? Was it to remove their anxiety and sorrow, or did he apprehend some disastrous consequences as the result of the rumour? Or would some parties between whom he had mediated in the church take advantage of it, and fall again into animosity?

(Ver. 27.) Καὶ γὰρ ἠσθένησε παραπλήσιον θανάτῳ—" For he really was sick, nigh unto death." It was a true report about his sickness which they had heard, and the apostle earnestly corroborates it—καὶ γάρ is a strong affirmation. Hartung, i. 132, 138. And his sickness had been all but mortal—παραπλήσιον is, as Ellicott says, " the adverbial neuter followed by the dative of similarity." Bernhardy, p. 96; Krüger, § 48, 13, 8. Many examples might be cited. The idiom is no technical figure of speech, nor do we need to supply ἀφίκετο. As little ground is there for Bengel's saying that the apostle did not wish to alarm them about Epaphroditus. His malady had indeed brought him to the gates of death, but he had been mercifully spared—

ἀλλ᾽ ὁ Θεὸς αὐτὸν ἠλέησεν· οὐκ αὐτὸν δὲ μόνον, ἀλλὰ καὶ ἐμέ, ἵνα μὴ λύπην ἐπὶ λύπην σχῶ—" but God had mercy on him, and not on him alone, but on me also, that I should not have sorrow upon sorrow." The apostle refers his recovery to God's great mercy, which does not seem, however, to have wrought by miracle, but, as one may naturally imagine, in answer to the apostle's fervent intercession. The reading ἐπὶ λύπην, in preference to the more common and classical construction with the dative,[1] is well sustained. "The subjunctive σχῶ," as Ellicott says, "is used after the preterite, to mark the abiding character his sorrow would have assumed." Winer, § 41, 1, a, (β). The apostle felt one sorrow, but the death of Epaphroditus would have been an additional sorrow. The sorrow which he already possessed, and of such an addition to which he was afraid, was not, as Chrysostom and others assumed, the sickness of Epaphroditus; for, even after his convalescence, he speaks of himself as only lightened in sorrow, but not entirely freed from it. A sorrow would still remain after Epaphroditus had departed, as is intimated in the next verse, the sorrow produced by his present situation—his captivity and all its embarrassments. This statement is in no way inconsistent with what he had written i. 20, etc., for his condition is there looked at from a very different point of view.

(Ver. 28.) Σπουδαιοτέρως οὖν ἔπεμψα αὐτόν—"The more speedily therefore have I sent him," or in English idiom, as he carried the letter, "I send." The force of the comparative σπουδαιοτέρως is obvious. Winer, § 35, 4. He would have detained him longer, if they had not received that intelligence of his sickness which greatly grieved Epaphroditus. It is not as Bengel put it—*citius quam Timotheum*—

ἵνα ἰδόντες αὐτὸν πάλιν χαρῆτε κἀγὼ ἀλυπότερος ὦ— "in order that having seen him ye may again rejoice, and I too be less sorrowful." Beza, Grotius, De Wette, with Knapp and other editors, join πάλιν to ἰδόντες—a connection which at first sight seems very natural. The Philippians would rejoice when they saw again their Epaphroditus. But the usage of the apostle is against this exposition, for he commonly places πάλιν before the verb with which it is connected. Examples of this usage are numerous. Rom. xi. 23, xv. 10, 12 ; 1 Cor. vii. 5 ; 2 Cor. i. 16, ii. 1, v. 12, xi. 16, xii.

[1] See examples in Wetstein and Kypke ; also Polybius, i. 57 ; Jer. iv. 20 ; Ezek. vii. 26.

19, 21; Gal. i. 9, 17, ii. 1, 18, iv. 19, v. 1; Phil. iv. 4;
Heb. i. 6, iv. 7, v. 12, vi. 1, 6.   There are, however, some
exceptions, such as 2 Cor. x. 7, where the emphatic position
of τοῦτο throws πάλιν behind the verb; Gal. iv. 9, where the
form of the question produces the same result; and Gal. v. 3,
where the first reason may be again assigned.   See Gersdorf's
Beiträge, p. 490.   The meaning will be—that as they had
been depressed when they heard of the alarming illness of
Epaphroditus, so when they should see him they should
rejoice "again," or as heretofore, in his presence and labours;
and while they rejoiced, he himself should be less sorrowful
—ἀλυπότερος (a word used only here); not without sorrow
absolutely, for he had it through his imprisonment, but a
weight would be taken off his mind, and in proportion as they
rejoiced would his grief be lessened through his oneness of
heart with them.   The sorrow which should thus be mitigated
is not *cogitatio anxietatis vestræ,* as van Hengel misunderstands
it, for the apostle ascribes this feeling to Epaphroditus, not to
himself.

(Ver. 29.) Προσδέχεσθε οὖν αὐτὸν ἐν Κυρίῳ μετὰ πάσης
χαρᾶς—" Receive him, therefore, in the Lord with all joy."
The οὖν refers to the statement of the apostle's purpose in the
previous verse.   Such a reception has its element ἐν Κυρίῳ
—a reception, therefore, Christian in its fervour and object.
It was no cold welcome the apostle enjoined or anticipated,
but one μετὰ πάσης χαρᾶς—" with all joy," and no wonder
that it should be so—

καὶ τοὺς τοιούτους ἐντίμους ἔχετε—" and hold such in
honour," that is, such as Epaphroditus.   The more usual
classic form of expression is, ἐντίμας ἔχειν.   Ast, *Lexicon
Platon. sub voce.*   The class of men οἱ τοιοῦτοι, of whom
Epaphroditus is a noted example, deserve the esteem and
gratitude of the church for their self-denying and disinterested
labours.   And the apostle assigns a special reason in his
case—

(Ver. 30.) Ὅτι διὰ τὸ ἔργον τοῦ Χριστοῦ μέχρι θανάτου
ἤγγισε—" Because that for the work of Christ he came near
even to death."   On the solitary authority of C, Tischendorf
omits τοῦ Χ., while B, F, G omit the article, and A has
Κυρίου.   The peculiar phrase—μέχρι θανάτου ἤγγισε—repeats

more graphically what he had already said in verse 27. Μέχρι is not unlike ἕως[1] in Ps. cvii. 18—ἤγγισαν ἕως τῶν πυλῶν τοῦ θανάτου. Similar idioms are found in the Septuagint, though not so distinctive as the one before us. The verb is sometimes followed by the simple dative, as Ps. lxxxviii. 3 —ἡ ζωή μου τῷ ᾅδῃ ἤγγισε—and sometimes by εἰς with the accusative, as Job xxxiii. 22—ἤγγισε δὲ εἰς θάνατον ἡ ψυχὴ αὐτοῦ. May there not be a tacit reference in μέχρι θανάτου here to the same expression in verse 8 ? as if to show that the mind which was in Christ was in Epaphroditus, and was shown in his self-denial and suffering "for the work of Christ"—

διὰ τὸ ἔργον τοῦ Χριστοῦ. The cause is placed emphatically. The work of Christ, as is explained in the next clause, is not preaching, as Storr, van Hengel, Matthies, and Rilliet contend for. It is service done to the apostle, and through him to Christ. So much was he identified with Christ, that service rendered to him, being directly instrumental in promoting Christ's cause, might be styled the work of Christ. How he came so nigh to death, the apostle describes by the striking words—

παραβολευσάμενος τῇ ψυχῇ—" having hazarded his life." The reading is disputed; many preferring παραβουλευσάμενος, which signifies, as in our version—" not regarding his life." This last reading is retained by Tischendorf in his second edition, being found in C, J, K, and in the Greek Fathers. The majority of editors and more modern expositors prefer the first form, which has the authority of A, B, D, E, F, G. Both words occur nowhere else in classic Greek authors, though the second be often used by the Greek commentators. The Versions are undecided. The *Vetus Itala* has *parabolatus est de anima sua;* the Vulgate, *tradens animam suam;* the Syriac version renders by ܣܠܐ — *spernens;* and the Gothic has *ufarmunnonds saivalai*[2] *seinai,* " forgetting his own life." The verb is formed from παράβολος—" risking, venturesome "—and like many verbs in ενω, which combine the force of the adjective and auxiliary verb, is equivalent in meaning to παράβολον εἶναι, just as ἐπισκοπεύειν is ἐπίσκοπον εἶναι. Winer, § 16, 1, note. Examples will be found as in

---

[1] Found here in Codices D, F, G.

[2] *Saivalai = ꝟeele, soul.*

Lobeck on *Phrynichus*, p. 67, and in the third of his *Parerga* p. 591. Wilke, *Lexicon Append.* p. 552. In result, the word is not different from the better known παραβάλλεσθαι, as in Diodorus Siculus, iii. 36—ἔκριναν παραβάλλεσθαι ταῖς ψυχαῖς; or in Polybius, i. 37, or iii. 90—μήτε παραβάλλεσθαι μήτε διακινδυνεύειν. The example adduced by Phrynichus is— παραβάλλομαι τῇ ἐμαυτοῦ κεφαλῇ — "I risk my head." [1] The verb is here used with the dative of reference, as is also παραβάλλεσθαι, in the example cited from Diodorus Siculus. Polybius, ii. 26. The apostle testifies of Epaphroditus, that he risked or ventured his life; the participle thus giving the reason why he was nigh unto death—ἐπέρριψεν ἑαυτὸν τῷ θανάτῳ, as Theophylact renders it. And the reason why he had so exposed himself was—

ἵνα ἀναπληρώσῃ τὸ ὑμῶν ὑστέρημα τῆς πρός με λειτουργίας —"that he might supply your deficiency in your service to me." The conjunction indicates purpose, and the compound verb —ἀναπληρώσῃ—is to fill up; the ἀνα having the notion of "up to" an ideal measure. 1 Cor. xvi. 17. Or, as Erasmus explains it — *accessione implere, quod plenitudini perfectœ deerat.* The noun ὑστέρημα has two genitives; that of subject—ὑμῶν, as in 2 Cor. viii. 14, ix. 12, xi. 9; and that of reference—λειτουργίας; the first genitive pointing out those of whom the want is predicated; and the second showing in what the want consisted. Kühner, § 542, 3; Winer § 30, 3, Anmerk 3. The ὑμῶν is not to be joined with λειτουργίας, as is done by Beza and van Hengel, who renders—*ut suppleret defectum ministerii a vobis mihi facti.* The noun λειτουργία is used not in the general sense of service, but signifies the special religious services in the money-gift which Epaphroditus had brought from them. He has called him that brought it λειτουργός, v. 25, and he calls itself "an odour of a sweet smell, a sacrifice acceptable," iv. 8. They did this service for the apostle—πρός με; but there was a lack on their part

---

[1] The desperate persons who exposed themselves to combat with wild beasts —*bestiarii*—were called παράβολοι. The self-denying Christians who undertook the hazardous office of nursing the sick, especially during the outbreak of some terrible epidemic, were named Parabolani. The Theodosian code makes special mention of them at Alexandria, where they were numerous; and where, being "men of a bold and daring spirit," they were occasionally turbulent, and were put under strict discipline. Bingham's *Antiquities*, vol. i. p. 391. London, 1843.

which Epaphroditus supplied. The lack was not in the gift itself, but in the ministration of it. They were absent, and could not minister to the apostle; but Epaphroditus, by his kind and assiduous attentions, fully made up what was necessarily wanting on their part. The meaning, therefore, is not that assigned by Hoelemann—*defectus cui subvenistis rerum necessariarum ;* nor is it with Chrysostom, "He alone did, what you all were bound to do." Homberg's view is as unfounded—*ut impleret defectum in ministerio meo.* The λειτουργία did not lack anything in itself, but the Philippians lacked something on their part in connection with it—they did not personally tender it. How Epaphroditus had endangered his life by a sickness nigh unto death, on account of the work of Christ, we know not. There is no proof that he was exposed to persecution, as Chrysostom, Theodoret, and a-Lapide suppose. Nor is there any proof that his evangelical labours had exhausted his physical strength. The probability is, either that his attendance on the apostle in Rome had exposed him in some way or other to a dangerous malady, or that, in his extreme haste to convey the Philippian gift and tender personal service to the prisoner, he had brought on an alarming sickness during his journey. This concluding statement is a pathetic and powerful appeal, and enforces the injunction—"Receive him therefore in the Lord with all gladness." There is no reproof in the words, as Chrysostom wrongly supposes, nor any censure on them, as if they had left one to do the work which was obligatory on them all. The tendency and purpose are the very opposite. It is— Epaphroditus has not only discharged his trust, and is deserving of thanks, but he has also ministered unto me, and done what you could not, though you would; nay, in this personal service he risked his very life, and therefore he is entitled to a joyous welcome, and a high place in your affectionate esteem.

CHAPTER III.

(VER. 1.) *Tὸ λοιπόν*—" Finally." The reader is furnished in the Introduction with some notice of the disputes about the connection of these two following chapters with the previous two; disputes originating in the use of τὸ λοιπόν, when so much literary matter comes after it—indeed, about one half of the epistle. Suffice it now to say, that the use of the phrase implies that the primary object of the writer has been gained; that what especially prompted him to compose the epistle has already found a place in it, and that what follows is more or less supplementary in its nature. 2 Cor. xiii. 11; Eph. vi. 10; 1 Thess. iv. 1; 2 Thess. iii. 1. The phrase marks transition, but toward that which is to form the conclusion. It is therefore wrong on the part of Elsner and others to regard it as a formula of mere transition; nor does it, as Schinz would suppose, simply indicate the turning from the special to the general. Van Hengel, following the interpretation of τὸ λοιπόν given by Elsner, Matthies, and Bertholdt —which assigns it the meaning of " in addition to," or simply " in continuation"[1]—agrees also with Schinz,[2] that the apostle could not here contemplate a conclusion, because he has not as yet expressed his thanks to the Philippian church. But might not the apostle intend to place this thanksgiving in this very conclusion? And who will say that a mere expression of thanks was so important as to be set in the principal portion of the letter? It is argued, too, that the use of τὸ λοιπόν shows that the apostle intended to conclude here, though he was unconsciously carried farther; but surely the writer knew well what were still to be the contents of his letter, though he regarded them in such a light, or in such a supplementary connection with the preceding portion, that he designedly prefaced them by τὸ λοιπόν.

[1] *Talis est ut ad utrumque caput conglutinandum inserviat.* Van Hengel.
[2] *Die Christl. Gemeinde zu Philippi*, p. 88, Zürich, 1833.

As to the connection, Chrysostom, with Œcumenius, Theophylact, Michaelis, Estius, and a-Lapide, deduce it from the previous paragraph. Sources of sorrow are mentioned there, but in God's good providence they have ceased to exist. Chrysostom paraphrases—"You no longer have cause for despondency—you have Epaphroditus, for whose sake you were sorry—you have Timothy, and myself am coming to you —the gospel is gaining ground. What henceforth is wanting to you? rejoice!"[1] But such a connection is not apparent, and, indeed, τὸ λοιπόν breaks up the immediate connection, and the apostle at once passes away from the subject which he had just handled—from the personalities which he had just been detailing. Besides, the addition of ἐν Κυρίῳ shows that the joy is not of such a nature as to be simply prompted by the circumstances to which the writer had been adverting in the conclusion of the second chapter. But while we object to such a connection as that proposed by Chrysostom, we do not think that there is any break produced by some interruption, or indicating any lapse of time, as not a few are inclined to suppose. Nor can the notion of Heinrichs be adopted, that χαίρετε signifies *leben wohl*—farewell.

The apostle addresses the Philippian converts, "as my brethren"—ἀδελφοί μου. See our comment on Col. i. 1. There was no official hauteur with him, no such assumption of superiority as would place him in a higher or more select brotherhood than that which belonged to all the churches.

The injunction is, "rejoice in the Lord"—χαίρετε ἐν Κυρίῳ. The modifying phrase ἐν Κυρίῳ does not mean, "on account of Christ," or as becomes Christians, but it defines the sphere and character of the joy. Rom. xiv. 17; 1 Thess. i. 6; Gal. v. 22; Col. i. 11. The Christian religion is no morose system, stifling every spring of cheerfulness in the heart, or converting its waters into those of Marah. It lifts the spirit out of the thrall and misery of sin, and elevates it to the enjoyment of the divine favour, and the possession of the divine image; nay, there is a luxury in that sorrow which weeps tears of genuine contrition. Therefore, to mope and mourn, to put on sackcloth and cleave to the dust, is not the part of

---

[1] Οὐκ ἔχετε λοιπὸν ἀθυμίας ὑπόθεσιν, ἔχετε ᾽Επαφρόδιτον δι᾽ ὃν ἠλγεῖτε, ἔχετε Τιμόθεον, ἔρχομαι κἀγὼ—τὸ εὐαγγέλιον ἐπιδίδωσι. Τί ὑμῖν λείπει λοιπόν; χαίρετε.

those who are in the Lord, the exalted Saviour, who guarantees them "pleasures for evermore." Such joy is not more remote from a gloomy and morbid melancholy, on the one hand, than it is, on the other hand, from the delirious ecstasies of fanaticism, or the inner trances and raptures of mystic Quietism. Chrysostom remarks that this joy is not κατὰ τὸν κόσμον—" according to the world," and his idea, according to his view of the connection, is, that these tribulations or sorrows referred to, being according to Christ, bring joy. This last opinion, however, is not from the context, though certainly the first remark is correct, for the joy of the world is often as transient as the crackling of thorns under a pot; and it often resembles the cup which, as it sparkles, tempts to the final exhaustion of its bitter dregs. The express definition or limitation in ἐν Κυρίῳ may be meant to show, that beyond the Lord this joy is weakened, or has no place; and that, if the Lord alone is to be rejoiced in, the Lord alone must be trusted in. The sentiment thus warned and fortified them against the Judaizers, whose opinions, in proportion as they tended to lead away from the Lord, must have retarded all joy in Him; while, if the Philippian believers continued to rejoice in the Lord, that emotion, from its source and nature, guarded them against such delusions. The next clause has seemed to many to be an abrupt transition—

τὰ αὐτὰ γράφειν ὑμῖν, ἐμοὶ μὲν οὐκ ὀκνηρὸν, ὑμῖν δὲ ἀσφαλές —" to write to you the same things, to me indeed is not grievous, but for you it is safe." The theories to which the phrase τὰ αὐτὰ γράφειν have given rise, have been examined in the Introduction. It is difficult to arrive at a satisfactory conclusion. To suppose the meaning to be—" to write the same things which I have already spoken to you," is a gratuitous conjecture, and places an unwarranted emphasis on γράφειν; but it is the view of Erasmus, Pelagius, Calvin, Beza, Estius, Rheinwald, and Schrader. Nor can we, with Heinrichs and Wieseler,[1] frame the contrast thus—" to write the same things as I have previously given in charge to Epaphroditus," or say with Macknight—" to write the same things to you as to other churches." Or is the meaning this—" the same things which I have already mentioned in this epistle," or "the same

[1] *Chronologie des Apostol. Zeitalters. etc.. p. 459.*

things which I have written in a previous letter"? The
former view is held by Bengel, Michaelis, Matthiae, van
Hengel, Rilliet, and Wiesinger; and the latter by Hunnius,
Flatt, Meyer, and others. See Introduction. The reference
in the first hypothesis is supposed to be to the expression of
joy in the first or second chapter, repeated in the commencing
clause of the verse before us. Some, as van Hengel and
Wiesinger, refer to ii. 18; but it is a serious objection that
the rejoicing enjoined in ii. 18 is not specially rejoicing in the
Lord, but rejoicing with the apostle in the idea of his martyrdom. Wiesinger contends that the joy in both places is the
same. But the joy in every previous reference is special and
limited. The "joy of faith" referred to is somewhat similar;
but it is not writing "the same things" to them to bid them
"rejoice in the Lord." Some refer "the same things" to the
caution given in the following verse, as if it were repeated
from i. 27, 28; but we cannot perceive the resemblance. As
De Wette remarks, the occurrence of the word ἀσφαλές leads
to the conclusion that what the apostle repeats has reference
to dangers threatening the Philippian church—such dangers,
in all likelihood, as are presupposed in the following admoni-
tions. This statement is fatal to the notion of Alford,
espoused also by Ellicott, and already glanced at, that the reference in τὰ αὐτά is to χαίρετε. The use of the plural pronoun
in reference to a single injunction would indeed be no objection
against their view. Jelf, § 383. We admit, too, that spiritual
joy would be a main safeguard against Judaistic error. But
the abruptness of the sentiment, the precise epithets—" irksome " to him, " safe " to them—and the passing on, without
further remark or connecting link, to forms of dangerous
teaching, lead us to suppose that more is meant by the apostle
than the mere repetition of sentiments previously and vaguely
expressed. The passages quoted by Ellicott as implied in
τὰ αὐτά, such as i. 4, 18, iv. 10, are of a different nature altogether, for they speak of the apostle's own joy, and it would
be no repetition of a phraseology descriptive of his personal
feeling to call on them to rejoice. We are therefore brought
to the conclusion, that the apostle refers to some previous
letter to the Philippians. They had sent once and again to
him, and he may have written once and again to them, and

given them such counsels and warnings as he here proceeds to repeat. See Introduction. And this is the view of Meyer, Beelen, and Bisping.

The adjective ὀκνηρός signifies " tedious." To repeat the same truth is to me no task of irksome monotony. Yet Baur finds in this incidental expression a proof of the writer's poverty of mind and ideas. The apostle only repeats what was profitable to them, for the purpose of more deeply impressing it, and the epithet implies that, in other circumstances, such a repetition might have been a weary and ungrateful task.

The adjective ἀσφαλές signifies safe—safe in consequence of being confirmed. Josephus, *Antiq.* iii. 2, 1 ; Prov. iii. 18. Luther renders *und macht euch desto gewisser,* much as the Syriac renders ܡܠܬ݂ܐ ;ܝܚܕܐ ܡܠܘܢ. Hilary has *necessarium,* but it is wrong from this to conjecture the reading to have been ἀναγκές, or paraphrase, with Erasmus *quod, non vitari potest.*

(Ver. 2.) Βλέπετε τοὺς κύνας—" Look to the dogs," so as to be warned against them. The article points them out as a well-known class. The verb is here followed by a simple accusative, and not by ἀπό with the genitive, and has therefore its original signification only rendered more emphatic. Observe them so as to understand them, the inference being that when they are understood, they will be shunned. Winer, § 32, 1, *b,* (γ). So the Vulgate has *observate.* This hard expression, κύνας, must be judged of by Eastern usage and associations. In very early times the name was applied as an epithet of reproach. In Homer the term is not of so deep a stain, especially as given to women ; yet it resembled, in fact, the coarse appellative employed among the outcasts of society. Iris calls Athena, and Hera calls Artemis, by the term κύων ; nay, Helen names herself one. *Il.* viii. 423, xxi. 481. In the Odyssey, too, the female servants of Ulysses receive the same epithet. *Odyss.* xviii. 338, xix. 91, 154. In countries to the east of Greece, the term was one of extreme contempt, and that seemingly from the earliest times. The dogs there were wild and masterless animals, prowling in the evening, feeding on garbage, and devouring unburied corpses.

as savage generally as they were greedy.　Isaiah lvi. 11.　The
fidelity of the dog is recognised in the Odyssey, xvii. 291, and
by Æschylus, *Agam.* 607.　But rapacity and filth (2 Pet.
ii. 22) are the scriptural associations.　Ps. lix. 6, 14 ; 1 Kings
xiv. 11, xvi. 4, xxi. 19—compared with 1 Sam. xvii. 43 ;
2 Kings viii. 13.　In Hebrew כֶּלֶב was the epithet of the vilest
and foulest sinners.　Deut. xxiii. 19 (18); Rev. xxii. 15.
The term was therefore a strong expression of contempt, and
was given by the Jews to the heathen, Matt. xv. 26, as it is
by Mohammedans to a Christian at the present day, when,
without often meaning a serious insult, they are in the habit
of calling him Giaour.　We must suppose the apostle to use
the word in its general acceptation, and as indicative of
impurity and profanity.　To indicate more minute points of
comparison, such as those of shamelessness, selfishness, savage-
ness, or malevolence, is merely fanciful.　The view of van
Hengel is peculiarly far-fetched—apostates from Christianity
to Judaism—the dog returning to his vomit.　2 Pet. ii. 22.

Who then are the persons on whom the apostle casts this
opprobrious epithet ?　The general and correct opinion is that
they were Judaizers, or, as Chrysostom styles them, " base
and contemptible Jews, greedy of filthy lucre and fond of
power, who, desiring to draw away numbers of believers,
preached at the same time both Christianity and Judaism,
corrupting the gospel—ἐκήρυττον καὶ τὸν Χριστιανισμὸν καὶ
τὸν Ἰουδαϊσμὸν, παραφθείροντες τὸ εὐαγγέλιον."　One is apt
to infer that the apostle here gives them the name which they
themselves flung about so mercilessly against the heathen.　As
in the last clause he nicknames their boasted circumcision, so
here he calls them by a designation which in their contemptuous pride they were wont to lavish on others.　They were
dogs in relation to the purity and privileges of the Church,
" without " which they were.

βλέπετε τοὺς κακοὺς ἐργάτας—" look to the evil-workers."
The verb is repeated for the sake of emphasis, and not because
a second class of persons is pointed out to their wary inspection.　The substantive, applied literally in many places
of the New Testament to labourers in the fields and vine-
yards, is transferred to workers in the church, or with a
general signification.　Luke xiii. 27 ; 2 Tim. ii. 15 ; 2 Cor.

xi. 13, where it has the epithet δόλιοι attached to it. The adjective κακούς describes their character as base and malicious. If they were "dogs," they must work according to their nature. They were not, as Baldwin weakens the force of the epithet, *simpliciter errantes*, but they were set on evil ; theirs was no inoperative speculation ; they were not mere opinionists, but restless agitators ; they were not dreamy theorists, but busy workers—earnest and indefatigable in the support and propagation of their errors.

βλέπετε τὴν κατατομήν—"look to the concision." In the contemptuous and alliterative term, the abstract is used for the concrete, as is the case with περιτομή in the following verse. The term occurs only here, and the apostle, in his indignation, characterizes the class of Judaizers by it. Not that he could speak so satirically of circumcision as a divine institute, but of it only when, as a mere manual mutilation, apart from its spiritual significance, it was insisted on as the only means of admission to the church—as a rite never to be discontinued, but one that was obligatory as well on the Gentile races as on the descendants of Abraham. The term justly designates the men whose creed was, "Except ye be circumcised and keep the whole law of Moses, ye cannot be saved." Viewed in this light, and as enforced for this end, it was only a cutting, and so the apostle calls those who made so much of it "the slashers." Chrysostom well says of them, that so far from performing a religious rite, οὐδὲν ἄλλο ποιοῦσιν ἢ τὴν σάρκα κατατέμνουσιν—"they merely cut their flesh." See our comment on Col. ii. 11, where the apostle says that Christians have a spiritual circumcision—"the offputting not of the foreskin, but of the body of the flesh." Such seems to be the natural meaning of the phrase, as understood in the light of the succeeding context. This play upon words is frequent with the apostle, Winer, § 68, 2 ; though some instances of so-called paronomasia cannot be at all sustained.

Other ideas have, however, been found in the apostle's expression. Theodoret originated one of these theories, when he says of the Judaists—τὴν γὰρ περιτομὴν κηρύττοντες, καὶ τέμνειν πειρῶντες τῆς ἐκκλησίας τὸ σῶμα, and he is virtually followed by Calvin and Beza, Grotius and Hammond, Elsner and Zachariae, and in the English versions of Tyndale and

O

Cranmer. A similar idea was entertained by Luther, as if the sense or implication were the excision of the heart from faith or from the church. Such a thought does not seem to be in the apostle's mind, that it is not in contrast with περιτομή, which besides has a passive, and not an active signification. Beza, again, seems to find an allusion to Lev. xix. 28, xxi. 5, to the Hebrew term שֶׂרֶט, referring to marks or cuttings made in honour of idol-gods. 1 Kings xviii. 28. Storr and Flatt follow this view, as if the apostle meant to say, that such a circumcision as they insisted on and gloried in was on a level with an idolatrous incision. The theory has scarcely the credit of ingenuity. A more extraordinary view still is broached in one of the Ignatian epistles—*partum virginis circumcidentes—hominem a Deo dividentes.* Heumann supposes the reference to be to the speedy abscission or destruction of Judea.

The repetition of the verb proves the anxiety and stern ardour of the apostle. Winer, § 65, 5. "For you it is safe," and their safety lay to some extent in being formally and emphatically warned. Like three peals of a trumpet giving a certain blast, do the three clauses sound with the thrice-repeated verb—βλέπετε. That the same classes of persons are referred to, we have no doubt. Van Hengel supposes that three distinct kinds of errorists are pointed out ;—first, apostates who have relapsed to Judaism ; secondly, actual corrupters of the gospel ; and thirdly, men so reliant on circumcision as to despise Christ. This interpretation is more than the words will bear, and there is no conjunction or particle employed so as to indicate different parties. The same men are described in each clause—as impure and profane, as working spiritual mischief, and as taken up with a puerile faith in flesh-cutting. In the first clause you have their character, in the second their conduct, and in the third their destructive creed. The absurd stress they placed on a mere mutilation warranted the satirical epithet of the concision ; but their convictions on this point drove them into a course of mischievous agitations, and they became the evil-workers ; then from their belief, character, and actings, they stood out as impure and shameless—as dogs. Men who insisted on circumcision as essential to salvation made the rite ridiculous—Judaized ere they Christianized.

To circumcise a Gentile was not only to subject him to a rite
which God never intended for him, but it was to invest him
with a false character.   Circumcision to him was a forgery, and
he carried a lie in his person.   Not a Jew, and yet marked as
one—having the token without the lineage—the seal of descent
and not a drop of Abraham's blood in his veins.   To hinge
salvation, especially in the case of a Gentile, on circumcision,
was such a spurious proselytism—such a total misappreciation
of the Jewish covenant—such a miserable subversion of the
liberty of the gospel—such a perverse and superstitious reliance
on a manual rite, that its advocates might be well caricatured
and branded as the concision.   The rite, so misplaced, was both
a fiction and an anachronism ; for the benefits of circumcision
were to be enjoyed in Palestine, and not in Europe, and
enjoyed up to the period " of the abolition of the law of
commandments contained in ordinances."   What these persons
were may be seen in the Introduction.   They might not have
done damage as yet in Philippi, but there was a danger of
their doing so.   Such a warning, repeated, would put the
Philippians on their guard and contribute to their safety.

(Ver. 3.) Ἡμεῖς γάρ ἐσμεν ἡ περιτομή—" For we are the
circumcision."   The γάρ gives a reason.   Those Judaists are
but the concision, for we are the circumcision—the abstract
again used for the concrete; and by the term is to be understood Paul and the members of the Philippian church, whether
they were Jews or Gentiles.   There were Jews in that church,
and forming the original nucleus of it; though, perhaps, the
greater part might be of Gentile extraction.

The members of the Christian church are now the circumcision.   Theirs is a spiritual seal.   Whatever the old circumcision
typified, they enjoy.   They are really Abraham's children—
blessed with believing Abraham.   Gal. iii. 9, 14 ; Rom. ii. 29 ;
1 Cor. vii. 19 ; Gal. v. 2, 6.   The Jewish circumcision was a
mark of Abrahamic descent.   " And God said unto Abraham,
Thou shalt keep my covenant therefore, thou, and thy seed
after thee, in their generations.   This is my covenant, which
ye shall keep, between me and you, and thy seed after thee ;
Every man-child among you shall be circumcised.   And ye
shall circumcise the flesh of your foreskin ; and it shall be a
token of the covenant betwixt me and you." Gen. xvii. 9, 10,

11.   As the circumcised descendants of the father of the faithful, the Jews enjoyed certain privileges.   They were God's
people, His by His choice, and shown to be His by His
tender protection.   They had access to Him in worship, and
enjoyed His ordinances.   They dwelt in a country which He
had selected for them, and which they held by a divine charter.
The true circumcision enjoys correspondent benefits, especially
do they possess the promised Spirit.   The spiritual offspring
of Abraham have nobler gifts by far than his natural seed—
blessing not wrapped up in civil franchise, or dependent upon
time, or restricted to territory.   So Justin says in the dialogue
with Trypho,—καὶ ἡμεῖς οἱ διὰ τούτου προσχωρήσαντες τῷ
Θεῷ, οὐ ταύτην τὴν κατὰ σάρκα παρελάβομεν περιτομὴν ἀλλὰ
πνευματικήν.   See our comment on Ephesians ii. 11, and
Colossians ii. 11—

οἱ πνεύματι Θεοῦ λατρεύοντες—" who by the Spirit of God
are serving."   The reading Θεοῦ, adopted by Lachmann and
Tischendorf, has decided authority over the common reading
Θεῷ.   The dative form may have sprung from the idea of its
connection with the participle.   The differences of reading
are of an early date.   Augustine, Pelagius, and Ambrose refer
to them—*qui Spiritu Dei serviunt, vel qui Spiritu Deo serviunt.*
Bishop Middleton defends Θεῷ, misled by his own theory of
the Article.   See under Eph. i. 17.   At the same time, the
language is peculiar.   The verb λατρεύω, specially applied in
the New Testament to religious service, is here used absolutely, as in Luke ii. 37; Acts xxvi. 7; Heb. ix. 9.   The
phrase πνεύματι Θεοῦ refers to divine influence put forth
upon the heart by the Spirit of God.   The words do not
point out the norm—*spiritualiter,* as van Hengel supposes, nor
yet the object—*Spiritum Dei colimus,* but the agency or influence which prompts and accompanies the service.   The Spirit
of God is He who dwells in the hearts of believers, sent by
God for this purpose.   It follows, indeed, as a natural inference, that if the Spirit prompt and guide the worship, it will
be spiritual in its nature.   There is thus a quiet but telling
allusion to the external formalities of the Jewish service, to
which the dogmatists were so inordinately attached.   The
Mosaic worship, properly so called, could be celebrated only
on one spot, and according to a certain ritual.   Though of

divine institution, and adapted to express in a powerful form
the religious emotions of the people, it often degenerated into
mere parade. It became a pantomime. Jehovah represents
Himself as being satiated with sacrifices, and wearied out by
the heartless routine. Only on one altar could the victim be
laid, and only one family was privileged to present it. But
the Christian worship may be presented anywhere and at
any time, in the hut and in the cathedral. The Being we
worship is not confined to temples made with hands, nor yet
is He restricted to any periods for the celebration of His worship. Whenever and wherever the Spirit of God moves the
heart to grateful sensation, there is praise; or touches it with
a profound sense of its spiritual wants, there is prayer and
service. How superior this self-expansive power of Christianity to the rigid and cumbrous ceremonial of Israel after
the flesh, and especially to the stiff and narrow bigotry of the
concision!—

καὶ καυχώμενοι ἐν Χριστῷ Ἰησοῦ—"and are making our
boast in Christ Jesus." The meaning of καυχώμενοι, emphatic
from its position, is different from χαίρω used in the first
verse. It is better rendered in Rom. ii. 23 than here—"thou
that makest thy boast in the law." They gloried not in
themselves, or in anything about themselves—not in circumcision or Abrahamic descent, but in Christ Jesus, and in Him
alone—not in Him and Moses—not in Son and servant alike;
gloried in Him; in His great condescension; His birth and
its wonders; His life and its blessings; His death and its
benefits; His ascension and its pledges; His return, and its
stupendous and permanent results. The spiritual circumcision
boasted themselves in Christ Jesus; the implication being,
that the concision boasted themselves in Moses and external
privilege—

καὶ οὐκ ἐν σαρκὶ πεποιθότες—"and have no trust in the
flesh." The adverb οὐ with a participle as a predicate, is an
unqualified negative. Winer, § 55, 5 (ƒ), (β). This clause is
in contrast with the preceding clauses. What the apostle
understands by σάρξ, he proceeds at once to define. It is not
circumcision simply, though the word occurs markedly in Gen.
xvii. 11, 13; Lev. xii. 3; Rom. ii. 28. The "flesh" is another
name for external privilege, such as descent, and points to

such merit as pride thinks due to formal obedience. It is a ground of confidence opposed to the righteousness of Christ —verse 9. Such then, as contrasted with the concision, is the circumcision; the children of believing Abraham, and blessed with him; serving God by His Spirit in a higher and more elastic worship; glorying in Him who has won such privileges and blessings for them, and having no trust in any externals or formalities on which the Judaizer laid so much stress as securing salvation, or as bringing it within an available reach.

(Ver. 4.) Καίπερ ἐγὼ ἔχων πεποίθησιν καὶ ἐν σαρκί— "Though I am in the possession of confidence too in the flesh." The apostle has just classed himself with those who had no trust in the flesh, and now he affirms that he too has trust in the flesh. It seems, but only seems to be a paradox. The conjunction καίπερ, used only here by Paul, qualifies the previous assertion. Devarius, Klotz, ii. 723. Instead of using the simple participle πεποιθώς, he says—ἔχων πεποίθησιν. Had he used the simple participle, there might have been a direct contradiction. He could not have it, and yet not have it at the same time. But he says—ἔχων πεποίθησιν —he *has* it in possession, but not in use; as one may have a staff, though he does not lean upon it; may have money, though he does not spend it. Such is the plain meaning of the words, and thus literally understood, they present no difficulty.

Various attempts have been made to get rid of the supposed difficulty. Our translators have a rendering which the words do not justify—"though I might also have confidence in the flesh"—a translation similar to that of Storr, Rilliet, Matthies, Schinz, and virtually Rheinwald, who resolve it by ἔχειν δύναμενος. Neither is there any reason, with Beza, Calvin, Am Ende, and Hoelemann, to take πεποίθησις by any metonymy for ground or reason of confidence; nor yet, with van Hengel, to refer the language to the past periods of Paul's unconverted life. The apostle had declared of himself, that he belonged to those who have no confidence in the flesh; and lest his opponents should imagine that his want of confidence in the flesh was simply the absence of all foundation for it, and that he was making a virtue of necessity, he adds, that he had all the warrant any man ever had—nay, more warrant,

than most men ever had—to trust in the flesh. And therefore he subjoins—

εἴ τις δοκεῖ ἄλλος πεποιθέναι ἐν σαρκὶ, ἐγὼ μᾶλλον—"if
any other man thinketh that he has confidence in the flesh,
I more." Our translators again follow such as make the verb
fiduciæ materiam habere—"that he hath whereof he might
trust in the flesh." The verb δοκεῖ may denote either to think
or to seem,—if any man thinketh in himself, or if any man
appear to others, etc. Both meanings are found in the New
Testament, and Meyer need scarcely have appealed to Ast's
Lexicon Platonicum in favour of the latter signification. With
Wiesinger and De Wette we prefer the first meaning given—
1 Cor. iii. 18, viii. 2—as being apt and natural, for the apostle
refers to such actual possession as he is about to describe.

As his manner is, the apostle "goes off" in an allusion to
his own history and experience. As he proceeds, the emotion
deepens into vehemence, and while he muses for a moment
on his own inner life, the thoughts welling "out of the abundance" of his heart arrange themselves into a lyrical modu-
lation. He boasts of being a true son of Israel, not sprung
from one of the tribes which had so early apostatized, but
from the honoured tribe of Benjamin. He was also of
untainted descent—an adherent of the "most straitest sect"
—ardent in his profession, as evinced by his persecution of
the church—performing with scrupulous exactness every rite
of fasting, tithing, or sacrifice, so that had salvation been
awarded to the fervent and punctual devotions of the chamber
or the sanctuary, he might have died in confidence and peace.
Therefore he now proceeds to enumerate the advantages which
he possessed, in which he might have trusted, and in some
of which he did once trust. The Judaizing fanatics could
not say, that he made light of these privileges because he
had none of them; for he had more than most of them,
and yet he felt their utter insignificance. The persons whom
the apostle had in his eye were in some respects behind him :
at least he says—"I more." Some of them might be proselytes circumcised in manhood; others might be of mixed
blood; others may have been originally of Sadducean creed :
while few of them had manifested that uniform obedience to
the law which had distinguished him, and that downright

devotedness to Judaism which had led him to seek the extirpation of its young and vigorous rival by violence and blood.

(Ver. 5.) Περιτομῇ ὀκταήμερος—"As to circumcision, an eighth-day one," literally,—"circumcised on the eighth day." The reading of the first noun in the nominative by Erasmus, Bengel, and others, is inadmissible. It is the dative of reference. Winer, § 31, 6. The adjective is used, like similar nouns of number, as τεταρταῖος, John xi. 39—τριήμερος, Greg. Naz. *Orat.* 25 ; Marc. Anton. 3,—δωδεκαταῖος, Theoc. ii. 157. Circumcision on the eighth day was according to divine enactment. Gen. xvii. 12 ; Lev. xii. 3. The apostle was a born Jew, and on the appointed day had received the seal of the Abrahamic covenant. The rite was for no reason deferred, and if any merit accrued from strict compliance with the law, he had it. The apostle makes good his declaration not only of ἐγὼ ἔχων, but of ἐγὼ μᾶλλον. The proselytes and Idumeans could not say so, for only in riper years could they be circumcised. Paul, therefore, left all such boasters behind him—

ἐκ γένους Ἰσραήλ—"of the race of Israel." See under Eph. ii. 12. He had been circumcised on the eighth day ; and not only was he not a proselyte, but he was not the son of proselytes, who might want for their child what they had not in childhood received themselves. No : he was a member of the chosen race, and not of Ishmael or Esau, or any other Abrahamic clan than that of Jacob. The term Ἰσραήλ, too, expresses spiritual nobility, and carries a higher honour than either the epithet Hebrew or Jew. Rom. ix. 4 ; 2 Cor. xi. 22—

φυλῆς Βενιαμίν—"of the tribe of Benjamin." The apostle means to derive some honour from his tribal lineage. It could scarcely be from this, that the first king of Israel belonged to this tribe, or that the apostle bore the royal name. Benjamin was a favourite son by a favourite wife, and the tribe is styled by Moses the "beloved of the Lord." Deut. xxxiii. 12. That tribe also had the capital and temple in its canton, was long identified with the great tribe of Judah, and had returned with it to Palestine, while the more northern tribes had almost ceased to exist as distinct branches of the house of Israel. He could give his genealogy. Rom. xi. 1—

'Εβραῖος ἐξ 'Εβραίων—" a Hebrew of the Hebrews." [1] The phrase is often used in reference to speech, and in contras' with Hellenist. Acts vi. 1. It does not seem to be employe in such a sense here, though Œcumenius affirms it, and he is followed by Witsius, Crellius, and Michaelis. Nor can it refer to place of birth, for Paul was born at Tarsus in Cilicia, Acts xxii. 3—a statement in opposition to the tradition mentioned by Jerome that he was born at Gischala in Galilee, and that on the capture of the place by the Romans, his parents and he emigrated to Tarsus. Nor has it, as Carpzov and Noesselt think, any religious reference, for it was the political name of the nation—that by which they were known among foreigners. The phrase denotes purity of lineal extraction—not simply that he was sprung of an old Hebrew family, as Jaspis and Rheinwald suppose—but that none of his ancestors had been other than a Jew. Meyer's view is, that both his parents were Hebrews, especially his mother. But the force of the phrase goes beyond immediate parentage. He was aware of no hybrid Gentile admixture, though his ancestors may have lived in Gentile countries. He was sprung of pure Hebrew blood, there having been no cross marriage to taint the descent. Thus does the apostle characterize his lineage :— circumcised on the eighth day, and therefore no foreign convert admitted in mature life, but having parents who coveted and transmitted the Abrahamic rite for their family ;—of the stock of Israel, and he 'ng a hereditary right to the seal of the national covenant ith all its blessings ;—of the tribe of Benjamin, able to ascertain and prove his descent, and not of one of any of the tribes g graphically lost or individually absorbed by the rest ;—a Hebrew of the Hebrews, descended from a long line of pure ancestry, without any accidental infusion on either side of foreign blood. There is a species of climax. A proselyte might circumcise his child on the eighth day; another might be of the stock of Israel and yet his mother might not be a Jewess, as was the case with Obed and Timothy ; for such a one might be of the tribe of Benjamin and yet not a Hebrew of the Hebrews. Extraction of undoubted purity distinguished him, while some of his opponents, with all their

---

[1] Examples of similar phraseology are given by Wetstein and Kypke, such as —ἐκ βασιλέων βασιλεῦσιν—δούλους ἐκ δούλων, etc.

Judaizing zeal, could make no such assertion—ἐγὼ μᾶλλον. 2 Cor. xi. 22.

Having enumerated his privileges as a member of Abraham's race, the apostle proceeds to show how he improved them. What he had enjoyed as a child was not lost upon him as a man. He was not contented with being one of the Jewish mass, but he sought in riper years to realize the advantages of his birth. Not satisfied with a passive possession of blood and birth, he laboured to appropriate all its blessings. He was a religious man—sincerely and intelligently attached to the law and all the venerated traditions of the fathers, and not simply a born Jew, proud of his ancestry, but indifferent to their faith—venerating the name of Moses, but careless of his law, save in so far as national customs had habituated him to its observance. Could the same be said of all his adversaries who now made such an outcry about the Abrahamic rite?

κατὰ νόμον Φαρισαῖος—"touching the law a Pharisee." It is wrong to give νόμος the meaning of αἵρεσις, as do Heinrichs, Am Ende, and Rheinwald, nor can it be rendered by *secta* or *disciplina*. Nor need it be understood, with van Hengel, as meaning—" with regard to the interpretation of the law "— *quod legis attinet interpretationem*. In his relation to the law he was a Pharisee. Acts xxvi. 5. The Pharisee was noted for his strong attachment to the law [1]—for his observance of all its ceremonial minutiæ—and his determination, at all hazards, to uphold its validity. Winer; *Real-Wörterbuch, sub voce*. Nay, Paul was not only a Pharisee, but "the son of a Pharisee" —brought up at the feet of Gamaliel, a famous teacher of the sect. His mind had never been tainted by Sadducean unbelief, nor had he been fascinated by the ascetic theosophy of the Essene. If the apostle would not bind the law on the Gentile churches, it was not because he had not studied it or had not understood it, nor yet because he had either lived in indifference to its claims or been trained in prejudice against its venerable authority.

(Ver. 6.) Κατὰ ζῆλος διώκων τὴν ἐκκλησίαν—" As to zeal

---

[1] Josephus says of them—περὶ τὰ πάτρια νόμιμα δοκοῦσιν τῶν ἄλλων ἀκριβείᾳ διαφέρειν, *Vita*, 38; also *Bell. Jud.* ii. 8, 14. Nay, the apostle himself says that he lived a Pharisee—κατὰ τὴν ἀκριβεστάτην αἵρεσιν τῆς ἡμετέρας θρησκείας. Acts xxvi. 5.

persecuting the church." The neuter form ζῆλος has in its favour, A, B, D, F, G. Some MSS., of no high authority, add τοῦ Θεοῦ after ἐκκλησίαν, but the noun often stands by itself. The present participle tells precisely what the apostle means to say, and it would be wrong to follow Grotius, Heinrichs, Am Ende, and Jaspis, and give it the meaning of διώξας. Nor is it necessary to make it a species of substantive with Alford, or of adjective with Ellicott, for it marks his conduct at the same point of time as when he had trust in the flesh, and thought himself blameless. The apostle gives his unconverted state an ideal present time. Compare Acts xxi. 20; Rom. x. 2; Gal. i. 13; 1 Tim. i. 13. The apostle had been no passive supporter of the law. While he upheld it, he upheld it with his might. And when the supremacy of that law seemed to be endangered by the growth of Christianity, with characteristic ardour and impetuosity he flung himself into the contest. He could not be a supine and listless spectator. The question was to him one of conscience and submission to divine authority, and therefore he deemed it his duty to imprison, torture, and kill the abettors of the infant faith, whose most malignant feature, as he thought, was its antagonism to Moses. Others might stand aloof, fold their hands in indifference, and yield a facile acquiescence in events as they occurred. But the disciple of Gamaliel was in terrible earnest. Believing that in speaking "words against Moses" there was open blasphemy, and that the glory of God and the spiritual interests of his country were in imminent hazard, he felt himself doing God service when he resolved to hunt down and extirpate the rising heresy, and "breathed out threatenings and slaughter against the disciples of the Lord." Foremost among the zealots stood Saul of Tarsus. Had his adversaries ever shown a similar fervour—had they so openly committed themselves? His zeal for the law outstripped theirs—ἐγὼ μᾶλλον. If he did not now enforce the Mosaic ceremonial, it was not because he had never loved it, or had been quite careless when it was assaulted. Not one had laboured for it so prodigiously, or fought for it so ferociously —"the witnesses laid their clothes at a young man's feet, whose name was Saul." Higher still—

κατὰ δικαιοσύνην τὴν ἐν νόμῳ γενόμενος ἄμεμπτος—"as

regards righteousness which is in the law being blameless."
The noun δικαιοσύνη, when so used, departs from its ordinary
classic sense, and represents one special meaning of the
Hebrew צֶדֶק. It does not signify either equity or fair dealing
between man and man, but depicts that aspect of state or
relation to the Divine law, which secures, or is believed to
secure, acceptance with God. It is here characterized as
τὴν ἐν νόμῳ—as being found in the law, or having its
source in obedience to the law. With respect to such righteousness, he was 'perfect—γενόμενος ἄμεμπτος. ii. 15. He
thought himself, and others thought him, without a flaw. He
did whatever the law had enjoined; abstained from whatever
the law had forbidden; omitted no duty, and committed no
violation of legal precept. In form at least, and in external
compliance, his obedience was exemplary, without occasional
lapse or visible inconsistency. It is altogether too restricted to
understand the "law" of Pharisaic enactment, or simply of the
ceremonial law, and worse still to adopt the idea of Grotius
and Am Ende, that Paul speaks but of the civil law, as if the
miserable meaning were—*nihil se fecisse quod morte aut ver-
beribus castigandum esset*. It was indeed and in itself what
Matthies styles it—*eine scheinheilige Werkgerechtigkeit;* but
the apostle speaks from the standpoint of his earlier days.
Matt. xix. 20. Such, then, is the record of the apostle's
grounds of confidence in the flesh, and who of those opposed
to him could boast of more of them? He had no confidence
in the flesh, or mere externalism; and yet, if any man was
ever warranted to have such confidence, it was he who had
more of it than most, but who now with changed views so
vehemently decried it, as opposed to the spirituality of the
gospel and fatal to salvation. For he adds with power—

(Ver. 7.) Ἀλλ' ἅτινα ἦν μοι κέρδη, ταῦτα ἥγημαι διὰ τὸν
Χριστὸν ζημίαν—" But whatever things were gains to me,
these I have reckoned loss for Christ." The conjunction ἀλλά
introduces a striking and earnest contrast. In the use of
ἅτινα, which is placed emphatically, the apostle refers to these
previous things enumerated as a class—that class of things
which were objects of gain; the plural κέρδη intimating their
quantity and variety, and not simply corresponding in number
with the plural ἅτινα. Krüger, § 44, 3, Anmerk 5. The

dative μοι is that of "profit," and not that of opinion, as is
supposed by Erasmus, Beza, Rheinwald, De Wette, and
Hoelemann. The apostle still speaks from his old standpoint
—they were objects of gain, inasmuch as and so long as they
were believed to secure acceptance with God. The ζημία is
opposed to κέρδη, and is used in its literal sense in Acts xxvii.
10, 21. The ταῦτα is emphatic—these, yes these, I have
reckoned loss ; and the κέρδη is not, as van Hengel makes it
—non vera lucra, sed opinata. The perfect tense may bear
the meaning of the present—Buttmann, § 113, 7—yet the
use of the present immediately after confines us to the past
signification. These things I have set down as loss, and do
so still. He had come to form a very opposite opinion of
them. It is needless to take ζημία in the sense of mulcta, or
στέρησις. It stands simply in unity, opposed to κέρδη in
plurality—many gains as one loss—denoting the total revolution in the apostle's mind and opinions. Theophylact adds
ἀπεβαλόμην—" and have cast them away," but not correctly,
or in strict unison with the previous declaration, for the
apostle still had them, and says that he still had them—ἔχων
πεποίθησιν. Nor is there more propriety in Calvin's figure,
virtually adopted and deteriorated by Macknight, taken from
navigation, when men make loss of the cargo to lighten the
ship, and save themselves. The apostle now states the grand
reason for his change of estimate—

διὰ τὸν Χριστόν—" on account of Christ." Not " in respect
of Christ," as Heinrichs ; nor specially to enjoy fellowship
with Him, as van Hengel. " On account of Christ "—that is
to say, what was once gain was now reckoned loss, either
because it did not commend him to Christ, or what was held
as something won was regarded now as loss, for it did not
enable to win Christ, nay, kept him from winning Christ.
When he won, he was losing ; nay, the more he won, the
more he must lose. All his advantages in birth, privilege,
sect, earnestness, and obedience, were not only profitless, but
productive of positive loss, as they prevented the gaining of
Christ, and of justification through the faith of Christ.

(Ver. 8.) Ἀλλὰ μὲν οὖν καὶ ἡγοῦμαι πάντα ζημίαν εἶναι—
" But indeed, therefore, I also count or continue to count them
all to be loss." Winer, § 53, 7 (a), says that ἀλλὰ μὲν οὖν

may be rendered *at sane quidem*. Klotz, Devarius, 663,
etc. The ἀλλά puts the two tenses, past and present, into
contrast; while the καί qualifies ἡγοῦμαι, and gives it special
significance, and does not, as Rilliet supposes, connect itself
with πάντα, as if there were a climax—"what things were
gain, these I counted loss; yea, doubtless, I count even all
things loss." This exegesis would require, as Meyer says, the
verbal order to be καὶ πάντα ἡγοῦμαι. Nor can πάντα mean
all things absolutely. It has not the article, indeed, but the
meaning is limited by the context—all things of the class and
character described—the things of which he says immediately
that he had suffered the loss. The estimate was not a hasty
conclusion from fallacious premises, nor the sudden leap of an
enthusiasm which had for a moment urged him. It was his
calm and deliberate judgment still. And again he adduces a
reason—

διὰ τὸ ὑπερέχον τῆς γνώσεως Χριστοῦ Ἰησοῦ τοῦ Κυρίου
μου—"on account of the excellency of the knowledge of Christ
Jesus my Lord." The participle ὑπερέχον is used as a substantive. Bernhardy, p. 156; Matthiae, § 570. There is no
occasion to supply any noun. "Thucydides," says Jelf,
"abounds in neuter participles thus used." § 436, γ.
Besides this way of expressing abstract notions, there
are several other points of resemblance between the style of
the Greek historian and that of the apostle. There is a
comparison implied in the epithet. It transcends all the
things to which the apostle has referred. Still, there is no
occasion, with Am Ende and Rheinwald, to resolve the phrase
into διὰ τὴν ὑπερέχουσαν γνῶσιν. The apostle does not refer
to the knowledge simply, but to one feature of it, its superior
excellence, in comparison with which all things are accounted
loss. That knowledge has for its object Christ Jesus, whom
the apostle names in a burst of veneration and attachment—
"my Lord." Let the elements of loss be calculated. The
"gains" were:—circumcision performed without any deviation
from legal time or method—membership in the house of Israel,
and connection with one of its most honoured tribes—descent
from a long line of pure-blooded ancestry—adherence to a
sect, whose prominent distinction was the observance of the
old statutes—earnest and uncompromising hostility to a

community accused of undermining the authority of the Mosaic code, and a merit based on blameless obedience to the law. These, once gloried and confided in, were counted as a loss, for the sake of a superior gain in the excellency of the knowledge of Christ Jesus. Chrysostom has a long and not very satisfactory argument to show, that the heretics who abused the law could not plead, for their vilification of it, the apostle's language in this place. " He does not say the law *is* loss, but I *count* it loss." The true reply is, that it is not to the law in itself, but to his misconception of its position and of his own relation to it, that the apostle refers. Jerome on Habakkuk, referring to the same abuse of the apostle's words, says he does not refer to the law as such, but has in view *doctrinæ Pharisæorum et precepta hominum, et* δευτερώσεις *Judæorum.* Augustine, also, has more than once written in a similar strain.

The apostle was surely justified in making such a comparison. He was no loser by the loss he had willingly made, for the object of knowledge was the Divine Saviour. To understand His person and character, with His work and its relations, and so to understand them through a living interest in them, is surely knowledge of superior excellence. Is it not super-eminent knowledge to know Him as the " Christ," not simply because He has been anointed " with the oil of gladness," but because we too " have an unction from the Holy One,"—to know Him as " Jesus," not simply because He wears our nature, but because we feel His human heart throbbing in unison with ours under trial and sorrow,—to know Him as Prophet, not simply because He is Light, but because we are light in Him,—to know Him as Priest, not simply because He has laid Himself on the altar, but because the blood of sprinkling is manifest upon our conscience,—to know Him as " Lord," not simply because He wears a crown and wields a sceptre, but because we bow to His loving rule and gather the spoils of the victory which He has won and secured? The apostle made a just calculation ; for neither ritualism, nor Israelitism, nor Pharisaism, nor zealotism, nor legalism could bring him those blessings with which the knowledge of Christ was connected ; nay, until they were held as loss, this gain of gains could not be acquired. The apostle repeats—

δι' ὃν τὰ πάντα ἐζημιώθην—" for whom I have suffered the
loss of them all." It serves no purpose, with van Hengel and
Baumgarten-Crusius, to make this clause a parenthesis, for it
is closely connected with the succeeding one. " On account
of whom," that is to say—Christ Jesus, my Lord. The πάντα
as qualified by the article, refers to the things already specified
—all these things. It is wrong in Chrysostom, then, to describe
them as καὶ τὰ πάλαι καὶ τὰ παρόντα, and in a-Lapide to
write thus—*non tantum bona Judaismi, sed omnia quæ mundus
hic amat et miratur*. The one accusative is still retained with
the passive, as in Matt. xvi. 26. Winer, § 32, 5. Van
Hengel and others needlessly differ from Wiesinger, Meyer,
and De Wette, in giving the passive form a middle
signification.

καὶ ἡγοῦμαι σκύβαλα εἶναι—" and do count them to be
refuse." The infinitive εἶναι is omitted by Lachmann, as not
being found in B, D³, F, G, nor is the correspondent Latin term
in the Vulgate and in many of the Latin Fathers. But it
occurs in A, D¹, E, I, K, in almost all the versions, and Greek
Fathers. One can more easily account for its omission than
for its insertion. The contemptuous term σκύβαλον is usually
derived from ἐς κύνας βαλεῖν (Suidas, *sub voce*), much in the
same way as Stamboul, the name of the Byzantine capital, is
compounded of ἐς τὰν πόλιν. It signifies refuse, sweepings,
manure, κόπρος, *stercora*. Sirach xxvii. 4. The Greek Fathers
understand it to mean husks, chaff, ἄχυρον, and they contrast
it with σῖτος. It expresses not only the utter insignificance
which the apostle now attached to the grounds of his former
trust, but the aversion with which he regarded them, especially
when placed in comparison with Christ. For the end was—

ἵνα Χριστὸν κερδήσω—" that I may gain Christ.". The
verb κερδήσω is used in correspondence with κέρδη in verse 7,
and in contrast with ζημία and ἐζημιώθην. The clause with ἵνα
expresses the great purpose of the apostle, in order to attain
which he had made the previous estimate and suffered the
previous loss. The phrase is somewhat peculiar. One is apt
to smile at the gambling figure of Heumann—*obolum perdidi,
amicum accepi*. Nor is the meaning merely, to gain the favour
of Christ, as Grotius, Am Ende, and Wilke suppose ; nor yet
is it simply to be a Christian, as Krause weakens it. Robin-

son virtually agrees with Grotius, and many others are somewhat vague in their explanations. To win Him is to have
Him—the idea of gain being suggested by the previous
mention of loss. Nor can we say that the verb is explained
by the following clauses, or by any one of them in particular.
They are elements indeed of this gain; but the term " Christ"
seems to denote Him in every aspect, and to win Him is to
enjoy Him in every aspect. It is to have Him as mine, and
to feel that in comparison with such a possession all else may
be regarded as truly loss. To the apostle Christ was so
identified with the truth, that when he gained Him he gained
the highest knowledge ; so identified with life, that when he
gained Him he was endowed with the noblest form of it ; and
so identified with spiritual influence, that when he gained Him
his whole nature was filled with power and gladness. The
name of Christ, so used, covers His entire work and relations,
and, as Wiesinger says—" Christ comes as gain in the place
of the loss he has suffered." And the possession of Christ
is real gain compared with Hebrew lineage, the seal of
Abrahamic descent, or devotedness to the Mosaic ritual and
law.

(Ver. 9.) *Καὶ εὑρεθῶ ἐν αὐτῷ*—" And be found in Him."
The verb is not to be taken with an active sense, as it is taken
by Calvin—*et inveniam in ipso*—thus explained, *Paulum re-
nunciasse omnibus quæ habebat, ut recuperaret in Christo.* Nor
has *εὑρεθῆναι* the same meaning with the simple *εἶναι*, as is
affirmed by Grotius, Am Ende, and Henrichs. It has the
additional idea of being discovered to be, or proved to be.
Rom. vii. 10 ; Gal. ii. 17. See under ii. 8. It does not simply
assert a condition, but it looks at ascertained result. When
we see how the apostle connects with this animated expression
of his feelings " the resurrection of the dead," we would not be
so decided as are Meyer and De Wette, in denying Beza's
supposition of a tacit relation to the day of judgment. The
apostle, however, desires above all things to be found in Him,
now and ever. We would not say, with Meyer, that the previous clause, " that I may win Christ," is subjective, and that
this clause corresponds objectively to it. The former clause
we regard as a general and comprehensive declaration, and
this one as a more special result. To gain Him comprises

P

every blessing, and underlies every aspect of His work—to be found in Him is a special and personal relation to Him. The first effect of gaining Christ is union to Him, and the apostle counts all but loss that this union may not only exist, but may maintain and exhibit its reality—so as that, at the final inquisition, he may be found in Christ and enjoy the resurrection of the dead. The phrase " in Him " signifies no form of external fellowship, nor is it to be explained away as denoting mere discipleship. It is a union as close, tender, vital, and constant, as between the members and the head—a union effected and perpetuated by the Spirit of God,—the same Spirit dwelling in Christ and in all who are His. Participation in blessing depends upon it, as the living and identifying bond which secures communion in all He is and has. Yet more—

μὴ ἔχων ἐμὴν δικαιοσύνην τὴν ἐκ νόμου—" not having mine own righteousness, which is of the law." We would not connect this clause so closely with the preceding one as, like Tischendorf and Lachmann, not to place a comma between them. The meaning brought out in this way by van Hengel is—*et deprehendar in communione ejus non meam qualemcunque habere probitatem*—" and be found in Him not to have mine own righteousness." This idea is not in harmony with the course of thought, which in form is simple and consecutive. Besides, in such a case, as Meyer remarks, ἐν αὐτῷ would be superfluous. We take it and what follows it as descriptive of the results of gaining Christ and of being found in Him. The syntax connects it most closely with εὑρεθῶ. It gives an objective view of the apostle's condition. The subjective particle μή is used, because the absence of his own righteousness is a mental conception, is expressed as purpose, and not as an actual fact. Winer, § 55, 1. The participle is simply " having," as Meyer and De Wette maintain against those who would give it a more pregnant sense of " holding fast." The meaning of δικαιοσύνη we have already referred to. The apostle characterizes it as his own —ἐμήν—as wrought out and secured by himself. Rom. x. 3. And he points out its source by calling it τὴν ἐκ νόμου— " which is out of the law," the law being regarded as its origin, and " works " as its means. The apostle had felt how

vain such a righteousness was, as he has shown in Rom. iii.
19, 20; Gal. ii. 16, 21; and he regarded his being found in
Christ as utterly imcompatible with such a personal and legal
righteousness. The preposition ἐκ is often similarly employed
as in the two places last quoted. In contrast he now adds—
ἀλλὰ τὴν διὰ πίστεως Χριστοῦ—" but that which is through
the faith of Christ." The apostle changes the preposition,
for he intends to express a very different relation. His own
righteousness was out *of* the law, or originated by the law,
and it was *through* his own effort that he obtained it, for the
pronoun ἐμή has in itself the notion of διά. But this other
righteousness is of God, as he says in the next clause, and its
instrument is faith—διὰ πίστεως Χριστοῦ. Χριστοῦ is not
the genitive of source, as Am Ende and Jaspis regard it, but
that of object. Through faith in Christ, as the subjective
medium, is this righteousness enjoyed or received by all who
are found in Him. Having referred to the means of this
righteousness, he must also characterize its source—
τὴν ἐκ Θεοῦ δικαιοσύνην ἐπὶ τῇ πίστει—to wit, " the righteousness which is of God on faith." His own righteousness
was ἐκ νόμου, but this is ἐκ Θεοῦ—having God for its origin,
and it rests—ἐπὶ τῇ πίστει—upon faith. The phrase does not
signify in faith or *in fide*, as the Vulgate renders it; nor *per
fidem*, as Beza supposes it; nor on account of faith, as De Wette
explains it; nor yet exactly on the condition of faith, as is
the view of Matthies, Rilliet, and van Hengel—a view which
is rather secondary and inferential, than primary and exegetical. Meyer regards those words as depending on an understood ἔχων, repeated after ἀλλά. The view does not appear
tenable. " In this case," as Wiesinger asks, " would not
ἔχων have been repeated?" Meyer objects that the connection of this righteousness with faith has been already described
by διὰ πίστεως X., and that it would be mere repetition to
join ἐπὶ τῇ πίστει to δικαιοσύνην. To this objection we
demur. For, first, the use of various prepositions to express
the different relations of an object, is precisely one of the
apostle's peculiarities of style. And, secondly, the difference
of relation expressed by the different prepositions, prevents
tautology. In the first case, when he uses διά, he has a
special contrast in view, which he sharply brings out. He

tells the origin of his own righteousness, and then he contrasts it with evangelical righteousness, not in its origin, but in its means—διὰ πίστεως. Then he reverts to its origin emphatically—ἐκ Θεοῦ—and he connects that origin with its basis in one general expression. If you ask what is the instrument of this righteousness, it is by faith—διὰ πίστεως —as opposed to personal effort or merit—ἐμή. If you inquire for its source, it is ἐκ Θεοῦ, opposed to ἐκ νόμου. And if you seek for its nature and adaptation, it rests ἐπὶ τῇ πίστει—on faith. So that δικαιοσύνην ἐπὶ τῇ πίστει forms really one complex idea, and the non-repetition of the article before ἐπί is no valid objection. Winer, § 20, 2. Wiesinger understands the first clause—διὰ πίστεως X.—as describing faith objectively, and the second—ἐπὶ τῇ πίστει—as pointing out the individual or subjective foundation. Alford renders " on my faith," but the phrase seems to be a portion of a general definition. At all events, while the apostle does not bring out the points of a contrast with the finical order of a rhetorician, he holds up two different aspects of faith—faith as the means, and faith as the foundation. The reason of the διά is to be found in the ἐπί. It is because this righteousness has faith for its ground, that faith becomes its instrument. Such is its peculiar nature, that its effect is made to depend upon faith ; therefore by faith is it realized and appropriated. Physical life is dependent on respiration; therefore by respiration is it sustained.

This righteousness—δικαιοσύνη—which the apostle aspired to possess, is the only ground of acceptance with God. In itself it is not ἐμή, but of God—ἐκ Θεοῦ—as in His grace He has provided it, so that it is said of us—δικαιούμενοι δωρεὰν τῇ αὐτοῦ χάριτι. Rom. iii. 24. It is wrought out by Christ, and in His blood—ἐν τῷ αἵματι αὐτοῦ—Rom. v. 9 ; or it is διὰ τῆς ἀπολυτρώσεως τῆς ἐν Χριστῷ Ἰησοῦ. Rom. iii. 24. It becomes ours through faith, being in one aspect ἐπὶ τῇ πίστει, in another διὰ πίστεως, and in another still, ἐκ πίστεως. Rom. v. 1. And this connection of faith is further described thus—λογίζεται ἡ πίστις εἰς δικαιοσύνην; or, subjectively, καρδίᾳ πιστεύεται εἰς δικαιοσύνην. Rom. x. 10. Of the possessor of such righteousness it may be said—δικαιοῦται παρὰ τῷ Θεῷ. Gal. iii. 11. Christ obeyed the law for us, and

for us suffered its penalty, and the merit of this obedience
unto the death becomes ours, as soon as we can say of ourselves,
καὶ ἡμεῖς εἰς Χριστὸν Ἰησοῦν ἐπιστεύσαμεν. Gal. ii. 16. He
who was ἄδικος becomes δίκαιος, and escapes that κατάκριμα
which sin merits, Rom. viii. 1, the ὀργὴ Θεοῦ—Rom. i. 18 ;
nay, enjoys the benefit of redemption—τὴν ἄφεσιν τῶν παρα-
πτωμάτων. Eph. i. 7. When ἔργα τοῦ νόμου—works of law,
are disclaimed, and faith is simply reposed on God—ἐπὶ τὸν
δικαιοῦντα τὸν ἀσεβῆ—guilt is cancelled, acceptance is enjoyed,
and such a change of state entails a change of character: those
in whom the righteousness of the law is fulfilled, " walk not
after the flesh, but after the spirit." Rom. viii. 4. The sinner
is not indeed held by any legal fiction to be innocent. The
entire process implies his guilt, but he is no longer exposed to
the penalty; he is held, or dealt with, as a righteous person,
" the external justice of Christ Jesus being imputed to him." [1]
And the result is—οὓς δὲ ἐδικαίωσε, τούτους καὶ ἐδόξασεν.
Rom. viii. 30. This righteousness, divine in its origin, awful
in its medium, and fraught with such results, was the
essential element of Paul's religion, and the distinctive tenet
of Paul's theology. His purpose was—

(Ver. 10.) Τοῦ γνῶναι αὐτόν—" So that I may know Him."
The construction beginning with ἵνα is here changed into the
infinitive—no uncommon change in the style of the apostle.
Rom. vi. 6 ; Col. i. 9, 10. Bernhardy (p. 357) shows that
the proper meaning of the genitive is preserved in such a
construction. But what is the connection ?

1. Some take the phrase as parallel with ἵνα κερδήσω καὶ
εὑρεθῶ, and as if it simply stood for ἵνα γνῶ. Such is the
view of Estius, Storr, Flatt, Rheinwald, Rilliet, van Hengel,
De Wette, and Hoelemann. But the very change of construction argues a peculiarity, and seems to connect the sense,
not as a thought parallel with the previous ἵνα, but rather as
the result of an intermediate statement.

2. The Greek Fathers connect it with ἐπὶ τῇ πίστει, and
so do Calvin, Grotius, and Bengel. It is thus supposed to
describe the source or the nature of faith—faith in order to

---

[1] Hooker, *Works*, vol. ii. p. 621, ed. Oxford, 1841. See also Usteri, *Entwick.
des Paulin. Lehrb.* p. 86; Lechler, *die Apostol. und Nachapost. Zeitalter*, p.
112, Stuttgart, 1857.

know Him. But the syntax does not seem to warrant such a narrow connection.

3. Rosenmüller, followed to some extent by Matthies and Peile, joins it to δικαιοσύνην, as if the meaning were—*felicitatem, inquam, cognoscendi eum.* This exegesis is wrong, both in its syntax and in the meaning assigned to δικαιοσύνη.

4. Meyer connects it with the clause μὴ ἔχων, and Wiesinger inclines to join it to εὑρεθῶ. We prefer connecting it with both, that is, with εὑρεθῶ primarily, but as modified and explained by the clause μὴ ἔχων. The apostle reckons all but loss to gain Christ, and be found in Him—found in Him possessed of a peculiar qualification, divine righteousness, and all this "so as to know Him and the power of His resurrection." His object was not simply to be found in Christ so as to know Him, but to be found in Him, divinely justified by faith in Him, so as to know Him. The "excellency of the knowledge of Christ Jesus" is still before his mind, and he does not revert formally to what he had stated as to the superior excellence of this knowledge, for the idea has never left him; and now he avows the design of being in Christ, and of being justified by faith in Him, and that is, to know Him. Not that to this knowledge two prerequisites are asserted to be equally necessary—union to Christ, and the possession of the righteousness of faith. No: union with Christ is the great qualification, that union giving righteousness, and both leading to the knowledge of Christ. The realization of this union to Christ, and the possession of this righteousness, bring one to the inner knowledge of Him in whom we are, and by faith in whom this righteousness is received.

From this statement, and from the following clauses, it is plain that this knowledge is that of a deep and deepening experience. It is not historical insight, nor general and theoretic information. The apostle aimed to know Him as being in Him. Such knowledge is inspired by the consciousness—not elaborated by the intellect. It rises up from within —is not gathered from without. It does not accumulate evidence to test the truth—it "has the witness" in itself. It needs not to repair to the cistern and draw—it has in itself "a well of water springing up unto everlasting life." It knows, because it feels; it ascertains, not because it studies, but because it enjoys union, and possesses the righteousness of God through faith. She that touched the tassel of His robe had a knowledge of Christ deeper and truer by far than the crowds that thronged about Him; for "virtue" had come out of Him, and she felt it in herself. Only this kind of know ledge possesses "the excellency," for it is connected with justification, as was intimated by Isaiah; and it is "eternal life," as declared by Jesus. Isa. liii. 11; John xvii. 3. The apostle could not set so high a value on a mere external knowledge, or a mere acquaintanceship with the facts and dates of Christ's career. For it is quite possible for a man to want the element of living experience, and yet to be able to argue himself into a belief of the Messiahship of the Son of Mary; quite possible for him, without a saving interest in the themes of his study, to stand at the manger and prove the babe's true humanity; to gaze on His miracles, and deduce from them a divine commission, without bowing to its authority; ay, and to linger by the cross, and see in it a mysterious and complete expiation, without accepting the pardon and peace which the blood of atonement secures. Still further—

καὶ τὴν δύναμιν τῆς ἀναστάσεως αὐτοῦ—" and the power of His resurrection." It is an odd notion of Bengel that ἀνάστασις is not resurrection, but *exortus sive adventus Messiæ*. The power of His resurrection is not, as Grotius and Matthies say, the power which caused His resurrection, or which was put forth upon Him, or was experienced by Him when He rose again. It is the power which belongs to His resurrection; that is, the power which His resurrection has or puts forth on those who are in Him, and who are justified by faith in Him. But what is its sphere of operation? Meyer confines it to justification, and the evidence which it affords of it, as in Rom. iv. 25; 1 Cor. xv. 17; Acts xiii. 37, 38. Storr, De Wette, and Schinz restrict it especially to triumph over death—2 Cor. iv. 10; while Wiesinger takes it to be that power which the apostle aims at experiencing in himself, by the renunciation of all that belongs to the old man and the flesh, so as to attain to the object indicated in verse 11. Lastly; others, as van Hengel, identify it with the spiritual power of regeneration.

If the phrase be connected closely with the previous context, then each of these views is more restricted than that context warrants. The knowledge which the apostle coveted is allied to his previous purpose to gain Christ, and to be found in Him, possessed of a righteousness accepted by faith. The power of Christ's resurrection will therefore have respect to those prior points of character or state. The apostle counted all things but vile refuse, that he might gain Christ —Christ in contrast with elements of proud and self-righteous Jewish confidence. May it not be inferred, that the apostle refers to the power of His resurrection in vindication of His Christship? It proved Him to be the promised Messiah. He also coveted to be found in Him—in union with Him; and His resurrection may be viewed in its vivifying power. At least the resurrection of the Lord is viewed in that aspect in the two epistles written about the same period— that to the Ephesians, i. 19, 20, and that to the Colossians, ii. 11, 12. To be in Christ is to enjoy newness of life; and to know the power of His resurrection may be to feel more vividly the pulsations of this existence, or, as Wiesinger says, " this manifestation of the life of Jesus." Then there is no doubt that the apostle refers to the power of His resurrection as giving a warrant for our justification; for it not only proved his mission to be divine, but it proclaimed the success of His mediatorial work.

But perhaps the phrase is in closer connection with what succeeds — fellowship with his sufferings, and conformity to His death. The idea of suffering and death naturally precedes that of resurrection. Christ suffered and died and rose again, and the apostle covets to know the participation of his sufferings, being conformed to His death. In referring to his own experience, he reverses the order of the historical facts—points to the result so dear to him, before he alludes to the previous stages—

καὶ τὴν κοινωνίαν τῶν παθημάτων αὐτοῦ—" and the fellowship of His sufferings," that is, " and to know " the fellowship of His sufferings. It is plain that fellowship does not mean fruition, as it would if the idea of Calovius were sustained, that the fellowship of His sufferings is the appropriation of their atoning merits. Nor is it a spiritual participation, as

Bengel and Zanchius suppose, and take from Gal. ii. 20. Nor
is it, as Matthies and van Hengel assume, suffering endured
for Christ's sake—*cruciatibus Christi causa subeundis.* Nor
is there any necessity, on the part of Hoelemann and others,
to throw in any expression corresponding to δύναμιν in the
preceding clause—neither *vim et pondus,* nor *dulcedinem ac
sanctitatem,* nor *honorem,* as is done by Am Ende and Jaspis;
nor yet, as Bengel puts it—*und einsehen dass Ich wie Christus
Leiden erdulden muss*—the perception that I, like Christ, must
endure suffering.

The general idea is much the same as that which occurs in
Col. i. 24. A share in Christ's actual sufferings was impossible to him. But the sufferings of Christ were not ended
—they are prolonged in his body, and of those the apostle
desired to know the fellowship. He longed so to suffer, for
such fellowship gave him assimilation to his Lord, as he
drank of His cup, and was baptized with His baptism. It
brought him into communion with Christ, purer, closer, and
tenderer than simple service for Him could have achieved.
It gave Him such solace as Christ Himself enjoyed. To
suffer together creates a dearer fellow-feeling than to labour
together. Companionship in sorrow forms the most enduring
of ties,—afflicted hearts cling to each other, grow into each
other. The apostle yearned for this likeness to his Lord,
assured that to suffer with Him was to be glorified with Him,
and that the depth of His sympathies could be fully known
only to such as " through much tribulation " must enter the
kingdom. Christ indeed cannot be known, unless there be
this fellowship in His sufferings.

συμμορφιζόμενος τῷ θανάτῳ αὐτοῦ. This form of the participle has higher authority (such as A, B, D[1]) than συμμορ-
φούμενος, or than the συνφορτίζομενος of F and G. The
participle is connected with γνῶναι, and not with εὑρεθῶ.
The present participle, dependent on γνῶναι, carries the idea
—" while I am being made conformable to His death." The
use of the nominative makes an anacolouthon, and this form
of syntax is frequent with the apostle. Winer, § 63, I. 2, a.
Wiesinger virtually denies that there is any reference to the
apostle's martyrdom; at least he thinks that the phrase can
be explained without any such allusion. Others, with van

Hengel and Rilliet, take it in a spiritual sense, the last saying — *en subissant dans sa propre vie le changement qui doit
résulter pour le chrétien l'appropriation qu'il se fait a lui-même
de la mort de son Maître.*   But perhaps what he has already
said in the previous chapter may bring us to an opposite
conclusion.   Nor can the phrase be explained simply by the
language in Matt. x. 38, xvi. 24, where our Lord uses a
striking figure ; nor by the diction of the apostle in Rom. vi.
3, 5.   The clause has a closer connection with the declaration
made by the apostle in 2 Cor. iv. 10, 11.   This conformity
to His death accompanies the power of His resurrection and
the fellowship of His sufferings.   The death of Jesus was ever
before the apostle's mind, and he died daily.   The process of
conformity was advancing ;—like Him in suffering, like Him
in death—a violent and bloody death as a servant of God.
It mattered not what its external form was—whether by the
sword or the cross, at the stake or on the arena; whether it
was the fate of Stephen or the end of James, the similarity
desired was one of spirit and state.   In all things Paul
coveted conformity to His Lord—even in suffering and death.
Assured that Christ's career was the noblest which humanity
had ever witnessed, or had ever passed through, he felt a
strong desire to resemble Him—as well when He suffered as
when He laboured— as well in His death as in His life.
Christ's death was a sacrifice, and his own was contemplated
in the same light—" I am now ready to be offered."   Christ's
decease at Jerusalem was characterized by unfaltering
submission to the will of God, complete devotion to the
welfare of humanity, and generous forgiveness of His
murderers ; so, no doubt, the apostle gained his wish, and the
martyrdom at Rome was signalized by a similar calmness and
faith—met with a serenity which the apparatus of death
could not disturb, and accompanied with such intercession
for his executioners as Jesus had offered, and the first martyr
had imitated.

(Ver. 11.) *Εἴπως καταντήσω εἰς τὴν ἐξανάστασιν τὴν ἐκ
νεκρῶν*—" If anyhow I may attain to the resurrection from
the dead."   This form of the Greek reading has the highest
authority, having in its favour A, B, D, E.   The conjunction *εἴπως* does not imply doubt, as is supposed by Grotius

and van Hengel, nor yet does it formally denote final purpose,
as Theodoret supposes.   Winer, § 41, 4, b.[1]   It is sometimes
followed by the optative—Acts xxvii. 12—but here, not, as
some suppose, by the future indicative, but by the aorist
subjunctive.   The verb, in its literal sense, " to come down or
opposite to," is followed by the simple accusative in Acts xx.
15, but more usually by εἰς, both in its literal and tropical
signification   It denotes, to reach to the possession of, here,
to obtain as an earnestly desired result.   Eph. iv. 13.   The
object to be obtained is ἐξανάστασις — a compound term
only used here, and giving greater vividness to the image.[2]
The verb occurs in a different sense, signifying to raise up
into existence, as in Mark xii. 19 ; Luke xx. 28.   Why the
apostle should use a different word from that of the preceding
verse, it is difficult to say.   Some, without any authority, as
Grotius and Rosenmüller, give the word the meaning of
resurrectio plena ; others, as Bengel, distinguish it from the
simple term, thus—*Christo* ἀνάστασις, *Christiano* ἐξανάστασις.
Theophylact presents the notion ἐξ—εἰς τὸν ἀέρα. The later
Greek was fond of compound terms.   It is as if he fancied
himself laid in a tomb, and resurrection to him suggested the
image of being brought up and out of that tomb, an image
made more prominent by the words τὴν ἐκ νεκρῶν.   The
context with such phraseology as " the power of His resurrection," " being made conformable to His death," forbids us to
adopt the notion of Balduin, Cocceius, van Hengel, Baumgarten-Crusius, and others, that the noun refers to spiritual
or ethical resurrection.   The last verse of the chapter brings
out more fully the idea which the apostle seems to have had
in his mind.   The exegesis of van Hengel is, *si forte perveniam
ad tempus reditus mortuorum in vitam*—" if perchance I may
come to the time of the return of the dead to life," that is,
the time when Jesus shall return for this purpose.   He is
therefore compelled to take the previous clause in a spiritual
sense—as if the meaning were, that he wished to die to the
world—so that, escaping danger, he might live on to the
second advent.   The hypothesis does not hang well together,

---

[1] Moulton, p. 374, note 1.

[2] The noun is used in the sense of complete expulsion, Polybius, ii. 21, or
ii. 35—οὔτε τὴν τελευταίαν ἐξανάστασιν.

nor can the language at all justify it.   In the use of the verb
time is implied, but time not as the object to be reached.   In
Eph. iv. 13, quoted by van Hengel, the idea is not, till we
arrive at the time when—but till we arrive at the consummation itself—that consummation being imaged as future.
Time is the implied or subordinate idea in the clause.   Acts
xxvi. 7.   The reference is to the resurrection of the Just—
Luke xx. 35—that resurrection described also in 1 Thess. iv.
16, etc.   The resurrection of the dead was an article of his
former creed, which the apostle did not need to change on
his conversion.   Acts xxiii. 6.   But it was the resurrection
to eternal life secured by Christ, that the apostle aspired to
reach.   A glorious privilege—to rise out of the ashes of the
tomb, and meet the descending Lord, to assume a body which
is a fitting home for the pure and perfect soul, to pass into
heaven arrayed in an entire humanity, and to feel in the
resurrection that augmented happiness which is the crown of
redemption !   This blessed consummation the apostle aspired
to reach.   Nothing if possible should keep him from reaching
it.   And the aspiration is closely connected with the preceding
verse. 2 Tim. ii. 12.   Such participation in Christ's sufferings
so identifies the sufferer with Him, that the power of His
resurrection is necessarily experienced.   Such conformity to
His death secures conformity to His resurrection—

> "This I will find, we two are so joined,
> He'll not be in glory, and leave me behind."

Now this burst of individual rapture must not be taken as
the index of overweening and self-deluded confidence.   Every
one was not precisely in his circumstances, or endowed with
his temperament ; though certainly his train of emotions has
presented in outline the grand features of the Christian life.
But though the change on him had been so decided, and had
brought with it such a complete revolution of opinion that
what had been gain was now reckoned loss, nay, held to be as
refuse ; though the present Paul was so wholly another man
from the former Saul ; and though his aspirations for universal likeness to his Lord were so vehement and continuous,
yet did he not complacently regard himself as having reached
perfection.   He felt that, deep though his convictions were,
they might be deepened ; that eager though his longings were,

they might still be intensified. His aim was to be found in Christ, justified by a Divine righteousness; but he was only reaching a full realization of this union, and had not gathered all its blessed fruits. His experience was ample, but it admitted still of amplification; his sufferings had been many and various, but they had not reached their climax in a death like his Lord's; his happiness was great, but its measure was not filled up, nor could it reach its consummation till the resurrection of the just—ἡ ἀνάστασις ἡ πρώτη. So that, lest he should be misunderstood, he adds in explanation—

(Ver. 12.) Οὐχ ὅτι ἤδη ἔλαβον, ἢ ἤδη τετελείωμαι—" Not that I already have attained, either already have been perfected." The phrase οὐχ ὅτι warns against misconception. John vii. 22; 2 Cor. i. 24; Phil. iv. 17. It is almost equivalent to οὐκ ἐρῶ—οὐ λέγω. Bernhardy, p. 352; Winer, § 64, 6;[1] Hermann, ad Viger. p. 804. In the verb ἔλαβον there is the idea of laying hold of something before him which he had not yet reached—" Nor have I been perfected." He had not yet realized the Divine ideal. The verb ἔλαβον has no formal accusative, and its object is left in vagueness. To what then does the apostle refer? The reference is supposed by De Wette, Robinson, and van Hengel, to be to the "excellent knowledge"—a reference not only too remote, but severed by many intermediate objects of aspiration. Nor can we refer the verb to Χριστόν, with Theodoret; nor with Rheinwald to the resurrection; nor with Matthies to the attainment of it, for in that case the expression would be a truism; nor yet with Grotius to the jus resurrectionis, for it would imply too low an estimate of the apostle's faith and privilege. Nor, with Hoelemann, can we take it to be simply moral perfection. More readily would we, with Calvin and Alford, refer it to the previous general statement, for the paragraph itself seems to contain the reference. The figure of the race and its prize rose up directly to the apostle's mind, and as he is about to give it shape, other ideas intrude themselves and claim a prior expression; that is to say, what the apostle had not yet attained to is what he has been describing in the previous verses, but that now especially imaged to his mind as the prize given to one who is victor in the race-

[1] See Moulton, p. 746, note 4

course. In the first clause of the 13th verse the apostle resumes the figure, and in a few vivid touches completes it. We agree, then, with Bengel, Am Ende, Rilliet, and Meyer, that βραβεῖον is really the object, as would seem also to be indicated by the use of διώκω more generally in this verse, and more pointedly in the 14th verse. In the repetition of ἤδη the apostle emphasizes the notion—that *at the present moment* he did not regard himself as perfected. The first verb is an aorist, and keeps its proper past signification, while the second, in the perfect tense, takes up the same thought, and brings it down to the present time. At no past period could I say that "I attained;" nay, "up to the present moment, I have not been perfected." Winer, § 40, 5, *a, β.*[1] It serves no purpose, with Hammond,[2] Rilliet, and others, to give τετελείωμαι a technical reference to the stadium. It is better explained by the various but unwarranted reading—ἢ ἤδη δεδικαίωμαι. But defect begets effort—

διώκω δὲ, εἰ καὶ καταλάβω, ἐφ' ᾧ καὶ κατελήφθην ὑπὸ Χριστοῦ — "but I press on, if indeed I may seize that, for which also I was seized by Christ." Δέ here connects two thoughts—the latter no negation of the former, but still of an opposite nature. Klotz, Devarius, ii. 360. The verb διώκω is employed to express the intense action of the runner in the stadium, and may be either taken absolutely or with an ideal βραβεῖον. Kypke *in loc.*; Lucian, *Hermot.* 77; Loesner *in loc.*[3] For the phrase εἰ καί see under ii. 17. The double use of the verb is Pauline (1 Cor. xiii. 12); the compound verb (κατα) deepens the sense, while the καί seems to bring out this idea—"If over and above this pressing on I may *also* seize the prize;" or, as De Wette says, it may correspond to the καί of the following clause. Some difficulty lies in the formula ἐφ' ᾧ, and various meanings have been assigned to it. The meaning of "because that"—*propterea quod*—has been preferred by Chrysostom, Theodoret, Am Ende, Meyer, and Bisping; others, as Œcumenius and Rheinwald, give it the

---

[1] Moulton, p. 345, note 1.

[2] Hammond *in loc.*; Stuart *on Hebrews* xii. 2; Loesner, p. 354. Among some of the Fathers, τελειοῦσθαι is to suffer martyrdom. Euseb. *Hist. Eccles.* iii. 15.

[3] Thus Theophylact—ἔτι, φησὶν, ἐναγώνιός εἰμι, ἔτι διώκω. Chrysostom too—καὶ ὑκ εἶπε, τρέχω, ἀλλὰ διώκω· εἰκότως. ὁ γὰρ διώκων ἴστε μεθ' ὅσου τόνου διώκει.

sense "whereto," or "in order to which"—*quo consilio;* while Calvin is followed by van Hengel in affixing the more general sense of *quemadmodum.* The two former meanings may both be justified by abundant usage. Examples of the first may be found in Rom. v. 12 ; 2 Cor. v. 4 ; Matt. xix. 9 ; Acts iv. 21 ;—and of the second, Gal. v. 13 ; Phil. iv. 10, etc.   Winer, § 48, c, *d* ; Krüger, § 68, 41.   If we adopt the first interpretation, then the verb is supposed to be used somewhat absolutely—"If indeed I may seize, because indeed I was seized by Christ." In the other case an object or antecedent is supposed—"If indeed I may also seize that, in order to which I was also seized myself by Christ." The Syriac has ܣܝ݇ܠܐ ܡܛܠ ܗܘ —"that for the sake of which." The second signification, adopted by Rilliet, Ellicott, and Alford, is preferable—"I press on to seize the prize, to attain which Christ seized me." This gives a closer connection than the other method. This second *καί*, as Ellicott suggests, is not connected with a supposed *ἐγώ*, nor yet with the verb, but with the preceding relative—"for which, too, for which very salvation I was apprehended."[1]   He means to say, not merely that he pursues a certain course of action because he has been converted, but because this course of action is in unison with the purpose of his conversion. Christ seized him, that he might seize the prize. The apostle's conversion is no less graphically than truly represented as a seizure. The Lord laid hold on him with a sharp and sudden grasp, and ever afterwards wielded him at His pleasure. He was overtaken in the vicinity of Damascus—the vision of Jesus produced instantaneous conviction, and with a force which convulsed him as he fell to the earth. It was not a slow and calm process of judgment, a prolonged and delicate balancing of arguments, or a daily ripening of views and opinions as the mists gradually cleared away, but the shock of a moment, which so changed his entire nature as to make him an utter contrast to his previous self. And Jesus grasped him, that he might grasp the prize. His aim was in unison

[1] In connection with the relative, Klotz remarks—*per particulam καί significamus nos de alia quoque re cogitare aut persona præter eam, de qua hoc prædicatur.* Klotz, Devarius, ii. 636.

with his destiny, that aim being to seize the prize as completely
as the Master had seized him, while to this very destiny had
he been converted and set apart.   Some of the Greek Fathers
introduce the idea, that Paul was fleeing from Christ when he
was arrested.   Thus Chrysostom—καὶ γὰρ αὐτὸς ἡμᾶς ἐδίωκε
φεύγοντας αὐτόν ; but there is no ground for such a supplementary image.   Not content with what he has uttered, he
still proceeds in the same spirit—

    (Ver. 13.) Ἀδελφοὶ, ἐγὼ ἐμαυτὸν οὐ λογίζομαι κατειληφέναι
—" Brethren, I do not reckon myself to have attained," or " to
have laid hold."   The apostle writes ἀδελφοί in his affectionate
confidence, as if he had felt that in the experiences of the
Christian life official rank did not raise him above them.   He
clasps them to him, as he unfolds the earnest struggles and
ambition of his soul, and repeats the previous sentiment.   The
phrase ἐγὼ ἐμαυτόν is emphatic in its form and position.
Winer, § 44, 3 ; John v. 30, vii. 17.   It is the apostle's deliberate opinion of himself—the result of a formal judgment
about himself.   One is almost tempted to adopt the idea of
Zanchius—*audio inter vos nonnullos esse qui fastidientes
doctrinam evangelii jactant sese jam satis novisse Christum*—I,
for my part, make no such boast.   The form οὔπω for οὐ
appears to be an exegetical alteration.   Self-complacency was
no feature of the apostle's character.   He was not injured by
undue elation, either from his labours or his honours—his
sufferings or his successes—his history or his prospects—the
grace he enjoyed or the spiritual gifts he had conveyed.   The
reason is, he looked not to the past, but to the future ; not at
what had been, but what was still to be.   He viewed not so
much the progress made as the progress still to be made—
surveyed rather the distance yet before him—between him and
the goal, than the space that now lay behind him—between
him and the starting-point.   Truly a correct and salutary
mode of measurement—*nil actum reputans, dum quid superesset
agendum.*   Satisfaction is fatal to progress.   But the apostle,
in looking forward to the " mark," and conscious, too, that he
was yet at some distance from it, did not dream away his
energies, or content himself with wondering either why he
was not nearer the prize, or when he should reach it.   But
he adds the following sentiment with a noble ardour, kindled

by the image he employed, and throwing its glow over the
words he writes. The picture is that of a racer in his agony of
struggle and hope ! You see him !—every muscle strained, and
every vein starting—the quick and short heaving of his chest—
the big drops gathered on his brow—his body bending forward,
as if with frantic gesture he already clutched the goal—his
eye, now glancing aside with a momentary sparkle at objects
so rapidly disappearing behind him, and then fixing itself on
the garland in eager anticipation. The apostle is not leaving
"the things behind," but he is "forgetting" them : he is not
merely looking to "the things which are before," but he is
"reaching forth" unto them ; not only does he run, but he
"presses toward the mark ; " nor was he occupied, weakened,
or delayed, by a variety of pursuits—"this one thing I do."
Quicquid voluit, valde voluit.

(Ver. 14.) Ἐν δέ—"But one thing I do." Such, with so
many expositors, we regard as the proper supplement ; not
ἐστί, with Beza ; nor λογίζομαι, with Heinrichs ; nor the
following verb διώκω, with Pierce and van Hengel. Van
Hengel insists that διώκω must have an expressed accusative ;
and not being used absolutely, it must govern ἔν. On the
other hand, see Buttmann's *Lexilogus*, p. 232.[1] Nor with
Matthies and Hoelemann can we take it absolutely—*Eins
aber, unum contra*—nor find with Rheinwald an instance of
aposiopesis. Winer, § 66, 1, b. There was unity of action,
and therefore assurance of success ; his energies were not
dissipated ; his eye was single, and therefore his progress in
the race was visible—

τὰ μὲν ὀπίσω ἐπιλανθανόμενος—"forgetting the things
behind." The use of the compound middle verb is Pauline,
the preposition giving the image of "over and beyond," and
so intensifying the idea of the simple verb. It here governs
the accusative, though the simple form takes the genitive.
Bernhardy, p. 181. By the phrase τὰ ὀπίσω are not to be
understood the things which in verses 5, 6, and 7 the apostle
has already condemned : for these things—that is, trust in
lineage, blood, sect, zeal, and law—belonged to an antecedent
period altogether. The apostle had not then entered on the
course. The "things behind" are in the Christian race,

---

[1] Fishlake's Translation, London, 1840.

Q

and are the earlier and past attainments of his Christian
life—things left behind since he had listened to the high
summons, and commenced to run. His conversion was the
point at which he started, and he describes by "things
behind," his attainments and progress from that moment up
to the present epoch of his life. "Behind" measures the
distance from the period at which he writes, back to the day
when he heard the words—"I am Jesus whom thou perse-
cutest." These past attainments were forgotten; that is, the
apostle did not rest and luxuriate in them—Upward and onward
was his motto. The term "forgetting" is used with special
reference to the figure here employed, for the apostle cherished
the memory of former manifestations, and thanked God for the
least of them. But in his Christian course he did not repose
on memories. What had been gained was only an excitement
to farther progress. While he did not despise "the day of small
things," he laboured to hasten on to the day of large things,—
τοῖς δὲ ἔμπροσθεν ἐπεκτεινόμενος—"but stretching forth to
the things before." The participle ἐπεκτεινόμενος, followed by
the dative of direction, carries in it a vivid image—the keen
attitude of the racer stretching his body out—ἐκ—and toward
—ἐπί—the goal. The things that are in front are not the
prize, as some suppose, but the things that lie between him
and the prize, along the distance which is still to be gone
over ere he reach the goal. The apostle did not detain himself with things behind, nor did he linger among things round
about him, but he stretched forward to things which he had
not yet reached. Progress was made by him, and that progress is still the law of the Christian life. Never satisfied,
still a sense of want; never saying, Enough, but still crying
More; forward and yet forward, and nearer and yet nearer
the mark. This being his ruling passion—
κατὰ σκοπὸν διώκω ἐπὶ τὸ βραβεῖον τῆς ἄνω κλήσεως τοῦ
Θεοῦ ἐν Χριστῷ Ἰησοῦ—"Toward the mark I press on, for
the prize of the high calling of God in Christ Jesus." Σκοπός
is found only in this place. Κατὰ σκοπόν is "in the direction
of the mark," and is not to be rendered "according to my
aim," with Pierce, following Augustine's secundum inten-
tionem; or "in a prescribed course," with Peile; or "along
the mark," that is, within the marked line, with Macknight.

Bisping distorts the figure when he makes the σκοπός Christ Himself: it is the *calx* or τέρμα. The noun σκοπός is used in the Septuagint for the Hebrew מַטָּרָה, to denote the point which an archer aims at. Job xvi. 12, 13 ; Lam. iii. 12.[1] The prize is to be found only at the goal, and to that goal the racer ever strives. If he move away from the course prescribed, he misses the mark, and loses the garland : for racing is not recreation, where one may turn aside as fancy leads him ; the path is chalked out, the law of the course must be observed, and the aim and effort must always be κατὰ σκοπόν. While this phrase marks the aim of the race, the words ἐπὶ τὸ βραβεῖον[2] express the final object, the coveted crown. "Now they do it to obtain a corruptible crown." The prize is certainly eternal perfection and blessedness— "an incorruptible crown." It is to be enjoyed only at the termination of the course. And surely it is sufficient to stimulate ardour, and sustain energy, since it is the realization of man's highest destiny—the woe and sin of the fall not merely neutralized, but a higher glory conferred than the first man of our race originally enjoyed ; not the first Adam, but the second Adam being the type as well as the author of the new life with its glory. For the prize is that of the high calling of God *in Christ Jesus*—

τῆς ἄνω κλήσεως τοῦ Θεοῦ ἐν Χριστῷ Ἰησοῦ—" of the high calling of God in Christ Jesus." The prize, as the genitive indicates, is connected with the Divine calling. Meyer calls it the genitive of subject. According to De Wette, κλῆσις is not the act of calling, but that to which one is called. But the place adduced in proof by him and others, 2 Thess. i. 11, is no proof, for the word there, as elsewhere, is the act of calling. Eph. i. 18, iv. 1. The adverb ἄνω characterizes the call, and the phrase is parallel to Heb. iii. 1. Grotius, Rheinwald, and van Hengel take ἄνω as ἄνωθεν—"from above," but without ground. We cannot agree with Meyer in regarding the adverb as pointing out the specialty of the apostle's own call and conversion ; for though he details his

---

[1] Thus also Pindar, *Olymp. Carmen* ii. 160—ἔσιχε νῦν σκοπῷ τόξον.

[2] It is difficult to say whether the reading should be εἰς or ἐπί—the last being found in D, E, F, G, J, K, in Chrysostom and Theodoret, and the first in A, B, Clement, and others, and it is preferred by Tischendorf, Lachmann, Meyer, and Alford.

own experience, he summons the church to imitate him, and virtually admits in the injunction of the next verse, that they too were to run the race, so as to obtain the prize of their high calling. The call is "above"—ἄνω—and stands in contrast to what is below. Sin is degradation, for what is ignorance but lowness of mind; or sensuality but lowness of heart; or misery but lowness of spirit? But this calling exists in a sphere of moral elevation, high or heavenly in its connection with the most High God, by whom it is issued to men. Col. iii. 1, 2. Nor can we acquiesce in the view of Chrysostom, followed by Meyer, that ἐν Χριστῷ Ἰησοῦ is to be connected with διώκω. The Greek Father remarks—ἐν Χριστῷ Ἰησοῦ τοῦτο ποιῶ, φησιν. But the words are far separated, and the natural union is with κλῆσις—ἐν marking its medium or sphere of operation. Such a construction does not need the repetition of the article, of which usage Winer has given many examples. § 20, 2. Nor is this further definition of the calling superfluous, as Meyer argues. The call is described in an ideally local aspect as high, then it is asserted to be the call of God. But it is not a call of naked Godhead, of bare Divine authority; it approaches us in Christ Jesus. It is from God—a Divine summons that pierces the spirit and ensures compliance, but it is in Christ, for it is a call which the blood of Christ consecrates, and to which His grace gives effect. 1 Cor. vii. 22; 1 Pet. v. 10. It is hard to say whether the apostle carries the figure so fully out as Grotius, Hoelemann, Am Ende, and others suppose, to wit, that he represents God as βραβευτής, summoning by heralds the runners into the course. Only Meyer's argument against it cannot hold, for he objects, that in such a case the calling would be common to all Christians, a conclusion which we believe. Nor is De Wette's objections of higher moment, when he says that such a view would necessitate the taking of κλῆσις as the act of calling, for this is the translation which we hold as the correct one.

(Ver. 15.) Ὅσοι οὖν τέλειοι, τοῦτο φρονῶμεν—"Let as many of us therefore as are perfect think this." Οὖν introduces the inference based on a retrospect. The use of τέλειος is striking, especially in contrast with τετελείωμαι in the 12th verse. There, he says—"Not as if I had taken the prize, or were already perfected;" and now he says—"Let as many as are perfect," not "as many as would, or wish to be perfect," as Peile and Macknight translate. The adjective has plainly a somewhat different sense from the verb. The adjective refers to relative, but the verb to absolute perfection. The one is predicated of him who is in the race and has made some progress; and the other of him who has reached the goal and taken the prize. *Perfecti viatores,* says Augustine, *nondum perfecti possessores.* The apostle's use of the term sanctions this idea. He elsewhere speaks of two classes in the church —"babes and perfect men." 1 Cor. ii. 6; Eph. iv. 12, 13; Heb. v. 13, 14. The terms νήπιος and τέλειος are in contrast. See also 1 Cor. xiv. 20. In the first passage referred to, the allusion is to respective degrees or attainments in knowledge. It is too restricted a view, on the part of Heinrichs, Rheinwald, and Conybeare, to adopt such an illusion here, as it is not of knowledge solely, but also of Christian experience generally, that the apostle has been speaking. Chrysostom well says, οὐ περὶ δογμάτων ἀλλὰ περὶ βίου τελειότητος. The phrase ὅσοι—τέλειοι does not mean we who are perfect, but "as many of us as are perfect," leaving it to each of themselves to determine whether the epithet be applicable to him or not. The perfect ones, among whom by the idiom he employs he places himself, are those who have burst the fetters of intellectual and spiritual bondage; who have made some advancement in the divine life; who are acquainted with the higher forms of truth, and are no strangers to the impulses and powers of divine grace; who are the circumcision; who, by the Spirit, worship God; who are conscious of union with Christ, of possessing righteousness through faith in Him, and some measure of conformity to Him, and who cherish through Him the hope of a happy resurrection. And perhaps, if we take in the previous context, the imperfect are those whose minds had not been able so fully to rise above all confidence in the flesh; who still thought circumcision might not be wholly without value; who would scruple to count all such things dead and positive loss, but hankered after some of them; and who, in formally renouncing them, secretly or unawares clung to them, and might not distinctly comprehend the freeness, adaptation, and

perfection of that righteousness which is through the faith of
Christ. They could not be perfect runners in that course
which the apostle has traced, for they had not laid aside
"every weight." They were entangled at every step, and
progress was impeded. Wiesinger's view is different. He
supposes that a believer is called τέλειος, not in a comparative
sense, but solely on account of that moral nature which he has
received through fellowship with Christ, and that his being
τέλειος is the strongest call to strive after the τελειοῦσθαι.
The general truth is correct, but the statement does not invalidate what we have said. The language used by the apostle
—ὅσοι—intimates that all were not τέλειοι in the Philippian
church ; the idea of relative progress is therefore involved.
Nor does it, as Wiesinger objects, in any way give countenance to self-esteem, for he neither names the τέλειοι, nor
points out precisely in what their perfection consists. On the
other hand, he classes himself among the τέλειοι, and yet he
has declared of himself that he was yet not perfected. In
fact, the perfect one was only in the way of being perfected ;
none knew his imperfection so much, or felt it so deeply, and
therefore he strove with quenchless ardour to move fleetly
onward to the end of the race, and obtain the crown. For
one may be perfect in aim, and yet be far from realizing it.
The perfection referred to was such a progress as vividly
showed defect ; such a stage in the race as revealed most
painfully the distance lying still in front ; such light which,
as it grew, served also to enlarge the circle of darkness round
about it. Chrysostom's notion is peculiar—" What means
the word ? (τέλειος). This—that we should forget those
things which are behind. Therefore it belongs to him who
is perfect, not to regard himself as perfect :"—

τοῦτο φρονῶμεν—" let us be of this mind." The reference in
the pronoun is disputed, some making it of wider, and others
of narrower extent. Calvin, Aretius, Zanchius, Hoelemann,
and others down to De Wette, take it from the previous context. Thus Vatablus—*hoc justitiam esse non ex lege, sed ex fide
Christi.* De Wette glances especially at verses 8–11, while
van Hengel restricts τοῦτο to βραβεῖον, and gives φρονῶμεν the
unwarranted sense of *expetamus.* With Meyer we regard the
special reference to be that which had just been said, beginning

with verse 12. Let this be our thought, not to sit down satisfied with past progress, but heedless of it, and feeling as if nothing were done till all were done, to speed uniformly onward to higher attainment. And yet there is no question that all the previous verses of the chapter are closely connected ; and it is implied that, in order so to feel, and so to act, so to think of the past, and so to throw himself into the future, one must be found in Christ, and be filled with ardent desire to know Him and the power of His resurrection. If he be a Jew, he must abandon trust in external privilege, and cling unreservedly to Jesus. When he loses, then shall he gain, and having won Christ, he is to go " from strength to strength," until, having attained to the resurrection from the dead, his whole nature is crowned with perfection. As these various attainments floated before the apostle's mind, the pursuit of them gradually assumed a pointed form, and took the image of a race—a race which demands vigilant perseverance from all who have entered upon it ; and *this*, the untiring energy of acquisition or progress, was to be a deep and permanent thought within every one of them.

καὶ εἴ τι ἑτέρως φρονεῖτε—" and if in any respect ye think otherwise." The conjunction εἰ is followed by the indicative implying condition, simply and purely, " if, as may be the case." Winer, § 41, 2 ; Klotz, Devarius, ii. 455. Τι is the accusative of reference, and that reference is certainly not to any essential points of doctrine, but to aspects of truth or elements of spiritual experience, which the apostle has been presenting. They might not see those relations of truth so clearly as the apostle, and their convictions might not be so profound, or their progress so rapid and uniform. The adverb ἑτέρως is only used here in the New Testament. This meaning has been assigned to the phrase by Hunnius and others— *si qui vestrum a falsis doctoribus vobis aliter persuaderi passi estis.* The person of the verb is changed, but there is no reason to suppose, with Bengel, Hoelemann, and Rilliet, that the same class of persons is not addressed, and that the νήπιοι are now appealed to. The apostle excludes himself, and so could not use the first person plural. Van Hengel, following out the meaning he assigns to the verb, renders in bald Latin —*si quid boni per aliam viam expetitis.* To disprove this position, there is no occasion with Meyer to introduce one use of ἑτέρως as meaning *adversus.* He might also have adduced its occasional employment as a euphemism for κακός. Passow, *sub voce.* For the true idea is brought out simply by the implied contrast. This difference must be wrong, so far as it does not correspond with the apostle's mind, and the amount of error is just in proportion to the amount of difference; and that it is wrong, is also shown from the apostle's expectation, that God would set them right. The revelation which the apostle promises they should enjoy, had for its purpose to remove such disagreement, and bring them to his mind. Chrysostom's explanation is—τουτέστιν εἰ δέ τις νομίζει τὸ πᾶν κατωρθωκέναι. But this is by far too limited a notion, for it is not so much the spirit in which perfection is to be sought that the apostle refers to, as the way in which to reach it by a knowledge of its constituent element. The apostle thus takes for granted that there might be a difference, and it must have been one not wholly of minor moment, or one which their own judgment, or sense of duty or propriety might rectify. For he predicts—

καὶ τοῦτο ὁ Θεὸς ὑμῖν ἀποκαλύψει—" yea, this shall God reveal to you." Meyer quotes Hartung, i. p. 135, for rendering καί *auch noch;* as if the idea were—as God had already revealed other things, so will He also reveal this. Such is also the view of Alford, and Ellicott in his commentary, though not in his translation. We prefer the rendering " even this " —this matter of difference in which they were wrong,—yea, this God would reveal to them. But what is the reference in τοῦτο—what is it that God would reveal ? Is it the fact that they were otherwise minded, as Œcumenius and Fritzsche [1] suppose, or is it the measure of difference, that God should reveal ? The reference is to τι. When they read the vivid record of the apostle's experience, they might at once, and of themselves, discover what want of harmony was between them and him. But the meaning of the apostle is, that God, by revealing the difference and showing the fault of it, would remove it. The verb ἀποκαλύψει is future, and has not the optative sense which some would give it. It predicts or promises divine illumination. Winer, § 40, 6 ; Eph. i. 17. Such

[1] Dissert. ii. in 2 Cor., p. 92.

spiritual enlightenment was frequent in those times, when the
written oracles of the New Testament were not in circulation,
and indeed is needed at all times, to give the mind a just and
abiding perception of the truth. Ps. xxv. 9; 1 John ii. 20.
It is plain, therefore, that the difference of view was not some
wilful and wicked misconception, or some wretched prejudice,
adhered to with inveterate or malignant obstinacy. It was
rather some truth not fully seen in all its bearings—some
principle not so perceived as to be carried out in all its details
and consequences—some department of duty which they might
apprehend rather than appreciate — or some state of mind
which they might admire in the apostle, but did not really
covet for themselves. The apostle throws his own teaching
into the shade, and ascribes the coming enlightenment to God.
He might have taught them the necessary lesson, or it might
be found in the previous details of the chapter, or Epaphroditus on returning might be commissioned to explain and
enforce it; yet all might be insufficient, and therefore the work
is taken out of man's hand, and the needed insight is declared
to be the gift of the Father of Lights. Chrysostom puts the
distinction well—ὁ Θεὸς ὑμᾶς πείσει οὐχὶ διδάξει ἁπλῶς·
ἐδίδασκε μὲν γὰρ ὁ Παῦλος, ἀλλ᾽ ὁ Θεὸς ἐνῆγε.

(Ver. 16.) Πλὴν εἰς ὃ ἐφθάσαμεν, τῷ αὐτῷ στοιχεῖν—" Howbeit, whereto we have attained, by the same do ye walk." The
Received Text adds κανόνι, τὸ αὐτὸ φρονεῖν. The words are
omitted in A and B, in the Coptic and Æthiopic versions, and
by Hilary and Augustine. There are other forms of various
reading;—D, E, F, G omit κανόνι, and there are several
transpositions. These incidents serve to prove an interpola-
tion, taken probaby from Gal. vi. 16 and Phil. ii. 2. The
adverb πλήν is rendered τέως, "meanwhile," by Chrysostom,
and interim by Estius and Beelen, but without sufficient warrant in usage, though it may bear such a sense inferentially.
See under i. 18. " Nevertheless,"—"even though there be those
who are otherwise minded." The infinitive, as in στοιχεῖν,
may be used for the imperative, but that only in the second
person. Krüger, § 55, I. 1, Anm. 5; Kühner, § 644, a. There
is an undertone of desire or wish, and on this such a use of
the infinitive depends. It is needless, on the part of Bengel,
Am Ende, and Rheinwald, to supply δεῖ. The verb φθάνω

has its complement in εἰς—though sometimes with ἐπί in reference to persons. The reference in ἐφθάσαμεν has been variously understood. The apostle has been supposed to refer to revelations of knowledge, or to attainments in the spiritual life. That is to say, the reference may be to the last verse, or, generally, to the preceding context. But ere we look at this question, there are two opposite modes of connection which may be briefly glanced at.

1. As στοιχεῖν is in the infinitive, some would make it dependent on the preceding verb ἀποκαλύψει. Fritzsche contends for this, and thus renders—*praeterea instituet vos, ut, quam ego consecutus sum τῷ βραβείῳ intentam mentem, ejusdem participes fieri ipsi annitamini.* Homberg thus shapes it—*hoc sentiamus, non alio quam eodem canoni incedere et idem sentire.* Photius, too, makes the στοιχεῖν the theme of the revelation. Meyer has remarked that the plural ἐφθάσαμεν is fatal to such an exegesis. Besides, the syntax would certainly be involved and awkward.

2. Michaelis and Rilliet connect it with the next verse. But this connection also has little to recommend it. It is best to take the verse by itself as to its construction. But the question recurs as to what is supposed to be attained:—

1. Chrysostom, Theophylact, and, with some minor variations, Schinz and van Hengel, suppose the apostle to refer to the spiritual life and its progress. The apostle's figure is that of a race representing spiritual advancement, and he is now supposed to say—"Do not deviate from that line, on which up to a certain point you have already made progress; but still persevere in it." This is a great truth, as well as a solemn warning against deviation. To such a view, however, there are several objections. "They could not," as Wiesinger observes, "be all at the same point of attainment;" each had made progress peculiar to himself—one behind and another farther on. But this deeper meaning cannot be deduced from the simple clause, εἰς ὃ ἐφθάσαμεν. The paraphrase, "on the line on which we have advanced to a given point, let us persevere," is the assigning of a meaning rather than the evolution of it. The εἰς ὅ and τῷ αὐτῷ are not so correlated as to warrant such a sense, for εἰς ὅ is "up to the point," and

not along the line, we have attained. The use of στοιχεῖν will not, though Meyer insists on it, bear out this exegesis. Granted that it may be correlative with ἐφθάσαμεν, it does not of itself describe spiritual progress, but signifies simply to walk by step or rule, and is opposed to irregular or random motion. Taking into view the tenor of the apostle's remarks, the record of his own aspirations, and his earnest desire that in all their fervour they should be cherished by the Philippian church; and remembering his conviction that there was difference of opinion between them which prevented the completion of this harmony of view, and also his hope and expectation that the discrepancy would be cleared away by a divine enlightenment;—we imagine that when he speaks in the next breath of attainment, he refers to the point up to which there was oneness of mind among them, and exhorts them to walk according to it—according to the measure of their present knowledge.

2. Thus we agree with many expositors, who connect the verse closely with the one before it—as containing a cautionary counsel after a promise. Such is the view of De Wette, Rheinwald, Matthies, and Hoelemann. Then the two verbs are in contrast—the future in ἀποκαλύψει, and the aorist in ἐφθάσαμεν—that is, the apostle speaks of a future and farther enlightenment in connection with spiritual progress; but meanwhile he speaks of a degree of present light, and the duty consequent on the possession of it. The two verbs will then refer to the same thing. The revelation may contain new information, but it is also additional information. It presupposes a present amount of knowledge, and the apostle insists upon its use even prior to that accession of insight which God's illumination should bring. God shall reveal so as to clear up the difference, but that difference in some things implies a common agreement in other things, and up to this point to which we attained, let us walk.

The spirit of the warning or injunction is, that knowledge already enjoyed and proved in a spiritual race, should not lie dormant because it is defective. It needed not so much to be rectified, as to be supplemented. Therefore, as far as you have its guidance, take it. Walk up to the light you have, and you will get more. Walk with me so far as you discern

the common path, and at the point of divergence God shall
rightly direct you as to the subsequent course. He who
employs what he has, prepares himself for further gifts.
When the morning bursts suddenly on one wakened out
of sleep, it dazzles and pains him; but to him who on his
journey has blessed the dawn, and walked by its glimmer,
the solar radiance brings with it a gradual and cheering
influence. The following remarks of Neander will be read
with interest:—" Paul accordingly points to this truth, that
the Spirit of God, who revealed to them the light of the
Gospel, will perfect this His revelation in them, and conduct
it to that mark of maturity in Christianity,—that He will yet
more and more further them in true Christian knowledge,
and even in that in which they still err and vary in opinion,
will cause them to find the one right thing. We should not,
therefore, precipitately enter into controversy, by which our
distance from each other is so easily widened, and by which,
through obstinate adherence to our once formed views, we so
readily become hardened in opposition; much less should we
condemn each other, but endeavour to preserve that unity of
the Christian spirit, which is raised above all subordinate
differences. To the common Teacher, the Holy Spirit, should
all yield themselves, and all trust that He, who is the best
Teacher, will yet more and more further them and each other.
While all proceeds from the Divine foundation once laid, the
unfolding and progressive purification of the Divine work
should be left to the operation of the Holy Spirit, who first
began it in each. No attempt should be made to do violence
from without to the unfolding of the Divine life in another,
which follows its own law, grounded in the specialities of his
character; or substitute anything imposed from without, in
place of the free development which proceeds from within.
This would be tantamount to seeking to penetrate into the
inmost soul of man by human arts of persuasion, which can
avail nothing, where they find no sympathetic link in the
already existing views of a man, and to bring forth what
alone can be effected by the Holy Spirit, the inner Teacher,
whom, without constraint and with the entire accord of their
freedom, all follow. Everything, alike in each individual,
proceeds only from the leavening process of the same leaven

of Divine truth, which gradually shall pervade the whole spiritual life, expurgating every heterogeneous element. And when Paul here speaks of a revelation by the Holy Spirit, through which the progressive insight of the believer is effected, this has for its basis the truth, presupposed and expressed throughout Holy Scripture, that all Divine things can be known only in the light of the Holy Spirit; as he says elsewhere, 'No man can call Jesus Lord, but by the Holy Ghost.' The notion of revelation, however, before us, by no means excludes the agency of human thought, which developes and works out according to the laws of human reason, that which it has received from the Divine light. But it is assumed that the agency of man's spirit is inspired and guided by the Holy Spirit, who is the soul of his whole spiritual life; hence all is referred to the Holy Spirit as cause, in so far as all originates in His revelation, guidance, and inspiration; all immediate or mediate progressive insight, proceeding from the Holy Spirit, is included in the notion of revelation." *On Philippians*, p. 58; Edinburgh, 1851.

(Ver 17.) Συμμιμηταί μου γίνεσθε, ἀδελφοί—" Be together imitators of me, brethren." 1 Cor. iv. 16, xi. 1; 1 Thess. i. 6, 7; 2 Thess. iii. 9. See also 1 Cor. x. 6, 11; 1 Tim. iv. 12; Tit. ii. 7. Some difficulty lies in the reference contained in σύν. With whom? Not, surely, as Bengel says— " followers with me of Christ," for no such idea is expressed. Nor can we take it, with Meyer and Beelen, preceded by Estius, a-Lapide, and Theophylact, as signifying—" along with others who follow me." There is no allusion, either distinct or remote, to members of other churches. We prefer the view of Calvin, van Hengel, Hoelemann, De Wette, and Alford, that the apostle says—be followers, " one and all," of me, or be unitedly imitators of me. If it be asked—in what? then the previous context may easily determine the question. Nay farther—

καὶ σκοπεῖτε τοὺς οὕτως περιπατοῦντας καθὼς ἔχετε τύπον ἡμᾶς—" and observe those who walk in such a way as ye have us for an example." Wherever they found the life of the apostle imitated or displayed, they were to mark it, and make it their pattern. Any excellence which they thus discovered, they might by God's grace attain to. It was not some distant spectacle which they were to gaze at and admire, but an embodiment of earnest faith, walking on the same platform with them, and speaking, acting, praying, suffering, and weeping among them. What had been possible to others, was surely not impossible to them. Why should they be behind in any gift or attainment, when the same means of acquisition were within their reach ?

Τύπος means exemplar, as in several other places, and is in the singular, to express the unity of the pattern, though exhibited by a plurality of persons. Kühner, § 407, 2; Bernhardy, p. 60. In καθώς is expressed the manner implied in the previous οὕτως, and not, as Meyer says, an argument for the injunction in the first clause. The arguments of Meyer have been well disposed of by Alford. Meyer lays stress on ἔχετε as used instead of ἔχουσι ; but the apostle is writing to the Philippians, and does not merely say—"Mark them that walk after our example," but mark them who walk in such a way as *ye see* us walking; the τύπος, which these persons followed, is set directly before the Philippians as a model which they were to inspect, a standard which themselves are to apply to the conduct and character of others. The meaning then is—mark them which walk so, just as ye have us for an example (for "them" and "us" are evidently not the same class of persons), and not—be joint followers of me, and mark such as walk in unison with me, inasmuch as ye possess us as a pattern. By "us" we understand not the apostle himself, as Jaspis and Ellicott incline to believe—not "him and all who so walked," for this last notion confounds those who set with those who followed the example; but the reference is—the apostle and those whom he was in the habit of identifying so closely with himself. Their example was in harmony with their teaching. They did not simply and timidly say, Walk as we bid you, but they boldly challenged inspection, and said, Walk as we do.

The reason why the apostle proposed his own example, and that of his associates, is now given by him. His life and theirs was in contrast with that of many others. There were men among them, professedly Christian, whose character was shamelessly sensual and secular. Motives of various kinds must have influenced not a few of the early converts, and brought them within the pale of the church. Novelty might have its share in producing a change which could be only superficial. Minds disgusted with gross superstitions and idolatries might relish the pure theism of the gospel, admire its benevolent and comprehensive ethics, and be entranced with its authoritative announcement of immortality. Yet they might not penetrate into its spirit, nor feel its transforming power. Change of opinion is not conversion, nor is the admiration of truth identical with the reception of its influence; while belief in immortality may create a distant cloudland where one may wander in fancy, and yet be far from inducing hearty and prolonged preparation for heaven. It seems, however, to be not speculative error in itself, but practical inconsistency, perhaps connected with or springing out of it, to which the apostle here refers. Already has he demonstrated the folly of trust in the flesh, of confidence in external privilege; and opening his bosom he has shown his own sensations—what he did once rely on, and might have still relied on. But what a revolution had passed over him; how he panted above all things to be found in Christ, to be justified by His righteousness; to know Him, and to be fully conformed to Him in life and death; how he relates that he is conscious of many shortcomings, that he is far from being what he hopes yet to be, but that, in the meanwhile, he spares no pains to realize his ideal, while he hopes that the Philippian church will exhibit the same earnest and unwearying effort! His mind naturally reverts to those who do not manifest this spirit; who live in the present, and for it; who prefer sensual gratification to spiritual enjoyment and prospect; and whose souls, so far from soaring in kindred aspiration with his, are absorbed in earthly things. The apostle felt that their sluggish and worldly life was fatal to them; nay, as his own attachment to the cross was the source of all his energy and eagerness, so he affirms that their low and grovelling state was the proof and the result of their enmity to the cross.

(Ver. 18.) Πολλοὶ γὰρ περιπατοῦσιν, οὓς πολλάκις ἔλεγον ὑμῖν, νῦν δὲ καὶ κλαίων λέγω, τοὺς ἐχθροὺς τοῦ σταυροῦ τοῦ Χριστοῦ—" For many walk, of whom I often told (or used to tell) you, but now tell you even weeping, that they are those who are the enemies of the cross of Christ." There is some

peculiarity of syntax, which has given rise to various methods
of construction. Rilliet, De Wette, Wiesinger, and others,
following Erasmus, suppose a break in the expression, or
rather, such a grammatical change as indicates that the apostle
did not follow out his original intention. They suppose him
to begin a description of a course of conduct, and then to glide
away to a description of the persons. That is, in περιπατοῦσιν
there is a reference to conduct, and some epithets characterizing that conduct might be expected to follow ; but instead of
these a relative sentence intervenes, and not the walk itself,
but the persons who so walk, are then brought into view—
" the enemies of the cross of Christ." It is certainly simpler to
regard τοὺς ἐχθρούς as placed in the accusative by its relation
to ἔλεγον—" I told you often before of them, and now weeping tell you of them, as the enemies of the cross of Christ."
In similar expressions ὅτι frequently intervenes, though the
conceit of van Hengel to change οὕς into ὡς is wholly groundless. The verb περιπατοῦσιν stands emphatically, and without
any added characteristic. It is awkward, on the part of
Calvin, to connect it directly with one of the following clause,
thus—περιπατοῦσιν—οἱ τὰ ἐπίγεια φρονοῦντες—placing the
intermediate words in parenthesis ; and it dilutes the sense to
subjoin κακῶς or ἑτέρως, or any other epithet. The verb is
certainly to be taken in its usual tropical or ethical meaning,
and is not, with Storr and Heinrichs, to be rendered circu-
lantur—" go about." The apostle, in the previous verse, had
referred to his own life and to those who walked like himself
—τοὺς οὕτως περιπατοῦντας, and now he speaks of others
who do not so walk. But he does not formally express the
difference by an adverb—he does it more effectually by an
entire clause. As he refers to them, their personality rises up
vividly before him, and instead of characterizing their conduct,
he pictures themselves. In this view the verb περιπατοῦσιν
is in no way regarded as equivalent to εἰσί, though in using it
the apostle sketches its subjects ere he describes its character.
The introductory γάρ shows the connection, by stating a
reason in the introduction of a contrast,—" Mark them who
walk like me, and there is the more need of this, for many are
walking who must be branded as enemies of the cross of
Christ, and to whom, in this aspect of their conduct, I have

frequently directed your attention." The persons referred to
were not a few, but πολλοί—"many ; " and the apostle's mind
was so oppressed with the idea of their number and criminality
that he had often spoken of them. There were many of them,
and he had many times mentioned them—πολλοί, πολλάκις.
Lobeck, *Paralipomena*, pp. 56, 57. The apostle did not throw
a veil over such enormities, nor did he apologize for them.
The world might laugh at them, but he wept over them. He
had frequently, and in firm tones, stigmatized them—either in
former epistles, or more likely when he visited Philippi. The
class of persons now referred to may not be those mentioned
in the second verse, for these were probably teachers, distinguished by asceticism rather than by sensual indulgences.
As the apostle thought of their flagrant inconsistencies, his eye
filled, and tears fell upon the manuscript which his secretary
was writing. "Wherefore weeping ? " asks Chrysostom, and
he answers—"Because the evil was urgent, because such
deserved tears"—ὅτι ἐπέτεινε τὸ κακόν, ὅτι δακρύων ἄξιοι οἱ
τοιοῦτοι. Therefore the apostle uses no disguise—

νῦν δὲ καὶ κλαίων λέγω—"but now even weeping." More
in grief than indignation did he refer to them. He wept as he
thought of their lamentable end, of their folly and delusion, and
of the miserable misconception they had formed of the nature
and design of the gospel. He grieved that the gospel should,
through them, be exposed to misrepresentation, that the world
should see it associated with an unchanged and licentious life.
The Lord had shed tears over devoted Jerusalem, and His
apostle, in His spirit, wept over these incorrigible reprobates,
who wore the name but were strangers to the spirit and power
of Christianity. And they are, with one bold and startling
touch, signalized as—

τοὺς ἐχθροὺς τοῦ σταυροῦ τοῦ Χριστοῦ—"the enemies of the
cross of Christ." The article gives the noun special prominence,
or points out the class. The verb λεγώ does not, as Grotius
and van Till render, signify to call—"whom now weeping I
call the enemies," etc.—*dolens appello hostes.* Why should the
apostle so characterize them, or why specify the cross as the
prime object of their enmity ? The words are more pointed
and precise than Calvin supposes them to be, when he renders
them simply *evangelii hostes ;* or than Wilke imagines, when he

R

supposes the " enemies " to be pseudo-apostles, who would not place their hopes of salvation in Christ's death, but on the observance of rites *ex Judæorum mente*. Nor can we, with Rilliet and Bretschneider, regard them as non-Christians, for the context plainly supposes that they were within the pale of the church. As far wrong, on the one hand, is it for Heinrichs to consider them as Roman magistrates guilty of persecution, as, on the other hand, it is for a-Lapide to assert that they were members of the church in Corinth. As to the nature and form of this enmity :—

1. Many hold it to be doctrinal—to be a species of polemical antipathy to the cross. Theodoret says they are so named ὡς διδασκόντας ὅτι δίχα τῆς νομικῆς πολιτείας ἀδύνατον τῆς σωτηρίας τυχεῖν. Theodoret has been followed in this opinion by many interpreters, such as Thomas Aquinas, and in later times by Estius, Rheinwald, Matthies, and Schinz. But there is no hint of this nature in the passage. It was not as in Corinth, where to one party requiring a sign the cross was a " stumbling-block," and to another faction seeking after wisdom it was " foolishness ; " the former regarding it as impossible that their Messiah should die in such ignominy, or be executed under a sentence of law like a malefactor ; and the other deeming it wholly preposterous, that a story so simple as that of Jesus crucified should be a record of divine wisdom, or be the vehicle of divine power and intervention. Nor was it as in Galatia, where the law of Moses was assumed to be of perpetual obligation, and the merit of Christ's death was virtually disparaged ; where, under the error of justification by works of law, the sufferings of Jesus were regarded as superfluous, so that in their bosoms there rankled sore and keenly the " offence of the cross." No charge of speculative error is brought against those whom the apostle here describes—as if they regarded the cross simply as the scene of a tragedy, or of a martyrdom ; or as if they thought the atonement unnecessary, or undervalued the agony of Christ as devoid of expiatory merit.

2. Many take another view, as if this enmity to the cross consisted in their reluctance to bear it themselves. Thus Chrysostom exclaims—" Was not thy Master hung upon a tree ?—crucify thyself, though none crucify thee "—σταύρωσον

σεαυτὸν κᾂν μηδεὶς σε σταυρώσῃ. This interpretation, which has various aspects, has many supporters. Such men will not take up their cross—will not submit to self-denial—will neither crucify the flesh nor endure persecution for the cross of Christ. Therefore they will not, as in the opinion of Meyer, suffer with Christ, or seek any fellowship with His sufferings, or any conformity unto His death. This may be true, and may be included in the true interpretation; but it seems to us somewhat subtle and recondite. So that we prefer another opinion.

3. We rather regard the apostle as speaking of the cross in its ultimate purpose, as pointing not so much to its expiatory agony, as to its sanctifying power. Their hostility to the cross lay in their not realizing its great design. For Christ died at once to provide pardon and secure sanctification, and the reception of the first blessing is meant to prepare for the ultimate process. They are therefore the enemies of the cross who see not in it the evil of sin, so as to forsake it, who remain strangers to its attractions, and who will not submit to the authority, or conform themselves to the example, of Him who died upon it. If the following verse describe, as it seems to do, the character and destiny of these enemies of the cross, then it would seem that their antagonism lay in thwarting its influence, and refusing to feel its elevating and spiritualizing virtue. If their supreme pleasure was in the indulgence of animal appetite, and if their soul was immersed in earthly pursuits and gratifications, then, certainly, all that the cross had done for them was of no avail; what it provided, was not received; what it secured, was not realized; its design was contravened, and its lessons were flung aside; the love of the dying victim was not seen in its tenderness and majesty; nor could His anguish be understood in those causes which made it a necessity, or appreciated as to those results which it was designed to produce, and which it alone can produce, in heart and life. Eph. v. 25–27; Tit. ii. 13, 14. Those men who walked in refusal of its claims, in violation of its design, and in defiance of its lessons, were surely the enemies of the cross, whether they were Jews or Gentiles. How they justified their conduct to themselves, or how they attempted to reconcile their lives with a profession of Christianity, we know not. We cannot tell what

theory led to such practice; whether they wilfully turned "the grace of our God into lasciviousness;" or whether, by some strange perversion, they took warrant to "continue in sin, that grace might abound;" or whether, under the intoxication of some antinomian theory, they dreamed that there was "no law," and that there could therefore be "no transgression."

(Ver. 19.) *Ὧν τὸ τέλος ἀπώλεια*—"Of whom the end is destruction," whose special and ultimate fate is destruction. Rom. vi. 21; 2 Cor. xi. 15; Heb. vi. 8, etc. The clause and context will not warrant the notion of Heinrichs, that ἀπώλεια bears an active signification, and that the meaning may be—whose final purpose is the destruction of the church. The term ἀπώλεια is the opposite of σωτηρία, and denotes a terrible issue. Matt. vii. 13, and in many other places; Phil. i. 28; Rom. ix. 22; 2 Thess. ii. 3. They do not realize the end of their being, and fall short of the glory of God. The cross has not sanctified them, and they cannot enter heaven. The purpose of Christ in dying has not been wrought out in them, and such a failure necessitates exclusion from His presence. The Lamb is the theme of high praise before the throne, but their enmity to the cross incapacitates them from joining in such melodies. Nay, as sin has reigned unchecked within them in spite of all that has been done and suffered for them, they carry the elements of hell within them; their nature remaining unsanctified, in scorn of Christ's blood and His apostle's tears. Gross sensualism characterized them—

ὧν ὁ θεὸς ἡ κοιλία —"whose god is their belly." Rom. xvi. 18. Theodoret adds—διαφερόντως γὰρ οἱ Ἰουδαῖοι πολλὴν ποιοῦνται τροφῆς ἐπιμέλειαν καὶ δικαιοσύνης ὅρον νομίζουσι τὴν ἐν σαββάτῳ χλιδήν. But there is no real ground for supposing the persons referred to to be Jews. The expression is a strong one, and the general meaning is, that they found their divinest happiness in the gratification of animal appetite. This god they loved and served. No idolatry is so unworthy of a rational being; no worship so brutal in form, and brutifying in result. Intemperance, for example, ruins fortune and forfeits character, crazes the body and damns the immortal spirit. And if, as in the figure of the apostle, a man's belly be his god, then his hearth is his altar, and his liturgy turns on the questions, "What shall we eat, or what shall we drink ?" or repeats the chant—"Let us eat and drink, for to-morrow we die." Many passages from the classics have been adduced which refer to such sensuality. Such men are named κοιλιοδαίμονες by Athenæus. The Cyclops in *Euripides*, 335, boasts about his beasts—"I sacrifice to no one but myself, not to the gods, but to this my belly, the greatest of the gods"—

Καὶ τῇ μιγίστῃ τῇδὲ δαιμόνων—

"for to eat and drink each day, is the god for wise men"—

Ζεὺς οὗτος ἀνθρώποισι τοῖσι σώφροσιν.

The cross has for its object to lift man above such ignoble pleasures—to spiritualize and refine him—to excite him to cultivate the nobler part of his nature, that he may rise to communion with the Father of all. But men indulging in these low and unworthy pursuits which darken and endanger the soul, persisting in this γαστριμαργία, as Theodoret calls it, are the enemies of the cross of Christ. Still worse—

καὶ ἡ δόξα ἐν τῇ αἰσχύνῃ αὐτῶν—"and whose glory is in their shame." That is, they find their glory in what is really their shame. It is their shame, though they do not reckon it so; as Origen says—ἐφ᾽ οἷς ἔδει αἰσχύνεσθαι, ἐπὶ τούτοις οἴονται δοξάζεσθαι. The context does not warrant any allu-sion to circumcision and the parts affected by it, *in pudendis*, as is held by some of the Latin Fathers, by Bengel, Michaelis, and Storr; nor yet does it specially describe libidinous indul-gence, as Rosenmüller and Am Ende suppose. The simple αἰσχύνη cannot of itself bear either signification. These enemies of the cross were not hypocrites, but open and avowed sensualists, conscious of no inconsistency, but rather justifying their vices, and thus perverting the gospel formally for such detestable conduct. These victims of gross and grovelling appetites disqualifying themselves from fulfilling the end of their being—to glorify God and to enjoy Him—frustrated the purpose of the cross, and therefore were its enemies. Lastly—

οἱ τὰ ἐπίγεια φρονοῦντες—"they are those who mind earthly things." Col. iii. 2. The nominative is now used, or, to give the clause special emphasis, the original construction is resumed. Winer, § 63, I. 2; Kühner, § 677. The phrase "earthly things" cannot, as Pierce supposes, mean any portion or section of Jewish ordinances. Their heart was set on earthly things—such things as are of the earth in origin, and do not rise above it in destiny. The contrast is—heavenly things—to the love and pursuit of which the cross is meant to raise us who died with Christ, and with Him rose again. When men are so absorbed in earthly things, in the lust of power, pleasure, wealth, fame, or accomplishment, as to forget their high calling to glory, honour, and immortality; when they live so much in time and sense as to be oblivious of life eternal, and seek not a title to it, nor cherish the hope of it, nor yet make preparation for it; they surely are the enemies of the cross, and their end is destruction. On the other hand, listen to Augustine—"*O anima mea, suspira ardenter et desidera vehementer, ut possis pervenire ad illam supernam civitatem de qua tam gloriosa dicta sunt.*" Vol. vi. p. 1399, ed. Paris, 1837.

It is matter of surprise, first, that persons of such a character were found in the early church; and, secondly, that they were not shamed out of it by the earnest piety and the spiritual lives of so many in the same community. Perhaps the novelty of the system attracted numbers toward it, and the freshness of its statements induced their adhesion to it, though they felt not its inner power. As we have said on a recent page, polytheism had lost its hold on many thinking heathens, who had been wearied out with scholastic disputations, and were glad to embrace what proposed some certainties, such as a spiritual worship, an authoritative law, and an assured immortality. But their convictions might be purely intellectual, the truths adopted being held only as opinions, and such change of views might happen without change of heart. The power of Christianity was neither relished nor understood. The cross in its agony might thrill them, but the cross in its spiritual penetration was a mystery. It might be taken as the scene and the symbol of sorrow and triumph, of suffering and bliss, but its efficacy to raise and ennoble, while admitted in theory, might be refused in practice. Such persons lived in a new circle of ideas and associations, but their soul was untouched and unquickened, and therefore, under this sad hallucination, they gratified

without stint their animal propensities, and were immersed in
earthly occupations and epicurean delights.   We could not
have believed in the possibility of such delusions, had not
similar forms of misconception and antagonism been frequently
witnessed in the history of the church.   On the other hand,
the apostle affirms—

(Ver. 20.) Ἡμῶν γὰρ τὸ πολίτευμα ἐν οὐρανοῖς ὑπάρχει
—"For our country is (or exists) in heaven."   The noun
πολίτευμα has a variety of meanings, among which we may
choose:—

1. Our English version, following the Vulgate, renders it
—conversation, that is, mode or form of life, vitæ ratio; or, as
van Hengel gives it—vivendi ratio.   His general rendering is
approved by Calvin, Grotius, Matthies, and De Wette.   The
translation is so far favoured by the context—They mind
earthly things, and are totally opposed to us, for our life is
in heaven.   One course of conduct is placed in contrast with
another.   Still the language so interpreted would be peculiar.
The apostle says, in Col. iii. 3, "Our life is hid with Christ
in God," but he refers to the principle of life, and not certainly
to its present manifestations.   It is one thing to say that the
origin of our life is in heaven, but very different to say that
its actual mode, habit, or manner is in heaven.   If you explain
this by saying that its law is in heaven, then you affix a
new meaning to the noun, or blend, like Rheinwald, several
assumed meanings together.   Nor does the word ever seem to
have such a sense in any place where it occurs; the meaning
is alleged from the verb πολιτεύω, which sometimes signifies
"to be or live as a citizen."   See under i. 27.

2. The noun denotes often what is termed policy—that
course of action or those measures by which the adminis-
tration of a state is conducted, as frequently in Plato and
Demosthenes.   From its connection with πολιτεύω we would
infer this to be a frequent sense.   Such measures imply a
certain form or constitution, and then we have such a phrase
as πολίτευμα δημοκρατίας, or, as in Josephus—θεοκρατίαν
ἀπέδειξε τὸ πολίτευμα.   Contra Ap. ii. 6.   The words have, in
this way, been rendered municipatus noster, as by Tertullian.
But—

3. The word passed into another meaning, and that not

very different from πολιτεία—a state or organized commonwealth. Such is a common tropical change—the measures of a government—the nature of such a government—and then the state so constituted and governed.[1] Not exactly, but somewhat similarly, ἱεράτευμα, though from ἱερατεύω, signifies an organized priestly caste, and not sacerdotal routine. Ex. xix. 6. Πολίτευμα may mean, as it does often, "state or country." It has this meaning in Polybius, as applied by him to Rome and Carthage—αὐτά τε τὰ πολιτεύματα, ἀκμὴν ἀκέραια. i. 13. The Hellenistic writers, Philo and Josephus, also use it in this way—the former writing thus, τῷ μεγίστῳ καὶ τελειοτάτῳ πολιτεύματι ἐγγραφέντες. De Op. p. 33 ; and the other has similar phraseology. Contra Ap. ii. 21. In 2 Maccabees xii. 7, we have likewise this phrase—"As if he would come back to extirpate"—τὸ σύμπαν τῶν Ἰοππιτῶν πολίτευμα. Theophylact thus explains—ὥστε τὰ ἄνω δεῖ ἡμᾶς φρονεῖν πρὸς τὴν πατρίδα ἡμῶν σπεύδειν, ἔνθα καὶ πολιτεύεσθαι ἐτάχθημεν. Similarly says Philo of the souls of the wise, De Confus. Ling.—πατρίδα μὲν τὸν οὐράνιον χῶρον, ἐν ᾧ πολιτεύονται, ξένον δὲ τὸν περίγειον ἐν ᾧ παρῴκησαν νομίζουσαι. This citation virtually explains the meaning—not "our citizenship"—Bürgerrecht—but "our city is in heaven." The confederacy to which we belong, or the spiritual state in which we are enrolled as citizens, is in heaven, and is no doubt that "Jerusalem which is above all." Gal. iv. 26. In that beautiful fragment—the letter to Diognetus, it is said of Christians—ἐπὶ γῆς διατρίβουσιν, ἀλλ᾽ ἐν οὐρανῷ πολιτεύονται—"they live on earth, but they are citizens in heaven." The idea was not unknown to the ancient philosophy. Thus Anaxagoras is reported by Diogenes Laertius to have replied to one who charged him with want of love of country—ἐμοὶ γὰρ σφόδρα μέλει τῆς πατρίδος, δείξας τὸν οὐρανόν. Heraclitus, Ad Amphidamanta, says also —πολιτεύσομαι οὐκ ἐν ἀνθρώποις, ἀλλ᾽ ἐν θεοῖς.

And this translation is quite in keeping with the context. The particle γάρ connects it with what precedes, as if the train thought of were—"they mind earthly things, and therefore are enemies of the cross; but, on the other hand, ye have us for an

---

[1] Aristotle, vol. iii. 7, says—πολιτεία μὲν καὶ πολίτευμα σημαίνει ταὐτὸν πολίτευμα δ᾽ ἐστιν τὸ κύριον τῶν πόλεων.

example—for our country is in heaven, and therefore, though earthly things are around us, we do not mind them." The double γάρ interweaves the thoughts. Walk as ye see us walking, for many walk most unworthily ;—walk as ye see us walking, for our country is in heaven. The second γάρ seems to have this force, while it more specially and ˏclosely brings out the contrast between the apostle's life and that of the persons whom he reprobates. He does not use a simple adversative, but γάρ at once assigns a reason by introducing a contrasted statement. The verb ὑπάρχει gives peculiar force to the assertion. See under ii. 6. The plural form of οὐρανοῖς has no specific difference of meaning attached to it.

The apostle then says, "our city is in heaven." This is certainly true of Christians. Their true country is not on earth. Here they are strangers in a strange land—living in temporary exile. On the earth, they are not of it—among earthly things, they are not attracted by them. The census of the nation includes them, but their joy is that " God shall count " them, when " He writeth up the people." They do not abjure citizenship here ; nay, like the apostle, they may sometimes insist on its privileges, yet they are denizens of another commonwealth. Like him, too, they may have a special attachment to their " brethren, their kinsmen according to the flesh ; " but they have ties and relationships of a more sacred and permanent character with their "fellow-citizens," " the living in Jerusalem." The persons reprobated by the apostle minded earthly things, and the surest preservative against such grovelling inconsistency is the consciousness of possessing this city in heaven. For as we cherish our franchise, we shall long to enjoy it, and be so elevated by the prospect as to nauseate sensual pursuits and mere animal gratifications. He who has his home in the future will be only a pilgrim for the present, and cannot stoop to what is low and loathsome, for his heart is set on the inheritance in ⁊ which " nothing can enter that defileth." The apostle turns now to the second advent—

ἐξ οὗ καὶ Σωτῆρα ἀπεκδεχόμεθα, Κύριον Ἰησοῦν Χριστόν— " whence also we await the Saviour, the Lord Jesus Christ." The phrase ἐξ οὗ might agree with πολίτευμα in form, and Bengel and others assume this, but this can scarcely be supposed to be the reference. The abode of Jesus is always spoken of as the heavens—the heavens received Him, and out of the heavens He comes again. Πολίτευμα is a spiritual idea, but οὐρανοί implies a locality, out of which Jesus is expected to descend. The ἐξ οὗ refers to οὐρανοῖς, and forms a species of adverb. Winer, § 21, 3. The καί indicates the harmony of this sentiment with the one expressed in the previous clause, and precedes Σωτῆρα, which has the emphasis—the Lord Jesus Christ as Saviour. The apostle uses the full title. He is in heaven the exalted Governor or "Lord," and cometh in lordly grandeur; but that glory has not deified His humanity—it only envelops it; He is still "Jesus," "the same Jesus taken up from us into heaven;" and as His commission has not ceased, though His abode on earth has terminated, He is "Christ." Nay more, He is expected as Saviour—Σωτῆρα. He has not resigned this function, and He comes to complete it. Salvation has been in process, now it is to be in fulness. The work ascribed to the Lord Jesus in the next verse, is the last and completing act. And therefore it is as Saviour that He comes, to fit man in his entire nature for glory—to accomplish the deliverance of his body from the penalty of death, and assimilate our whole humanity to His own as its blessed prototype. Salvation has this pregnant meaning in Rom. xiii. 11, and Heb. ix. 28. See also under Eph. i. 13, 14. The middle verb denotes earnest or wishful expectation—"we await." 1 Cor. i. 7; Rom. viii. 19. See under i. 20. The advent has been promised, and as it will secure such blessed results we cannot be indifferent to it; nay, though it be one of transcendent awfulness, we are not alarmed at the prospect—"Amen, even so come, Lord Jesus."

Now, we should have expected the verse we have considered to run thus—"Our country is in heaven, in which we hope soon to be," or some such expression. But he says—"from which also, as Saviour, we expect the Lord Jesus Christ." The result, however, is the same, for the Lord Jesus comes to prepare His people through the resurrection for entering "by the gate into the city." But the mode in which the apostle states these ideas serves two purposes. First, he characterizes Jesus as Saviour, or as expected in the character of Saviour, and thus suggests an

awful contrast, in point of destiny, between himself and those
like-minded with him, and the party reprobated by him in
the two preceding verses. Their end is destruction, but ours
is salvation ;—to the one He descnds as Judge, but to us
as Saviour. If there be such visible difference in present
character, there is more awful contrast in ultimate destiny—
ἀπώλεια—σωτηρία—the two poles of humanity—" everlasting
punishment "—" life eternal." Thus, in his own way, the
apostle inserts a quiet antithesis. And then, secondly, he
describes Jesus as giving our body a likeness to His own—
a change which in its nature, necessity, and results, conveyed
a reproof to such as worshipped their animal appetites and
found supreme gratification in such indulgence, and a lesson
to them also, not the less striking, if any of them imagined
that the body was but a temporary possession, whose lowest
instincts might be indulged to satiety, as if the spirit alone
were capable of entering, through its essential immortality,
into the heavenly world. For that body which gives man at
present so many earthly affinities was destined to a heavenly
abode, so that from its connection with Jesus it should be
preserved in purity, while from the process of refinement
to pass over it, it shall be divested of those very qualities
or susceptibilities of abuse for which it was deified by the
enemies of the cross. For the work of Jesus is thus told—

(Ver. 21.) Ὃς μετασχηματίσει τὸ σῶμα τῆς ταπεινώσεως
ἡμῶν σύμμορφον τῷ σώματι τῆς δόξης αὐτοῦ—" Who shall
transform the body of our humiliation, so as to be conformed
to the body of His glory." The phrase εἰς τὸ γενέσθαι αὐτό
of the Received Text is an evident supplement or filling in
of the syntax, and has but the inferior authority of D³, E, J, K,
etc. The language implies that this change of our bodies is
the special function which Christ shall discharge at His
coming. We look for Him to do this—we anticipate it at
His advent. Both genitives are those of possession, and by
τὸ σῶμα τῆς ταπεινώσεως ἡμῶν—" the body of our humiliation," we understand not simply τὸ σῶμα τὸ ταπεινόν, as
Robinson vaguely explains it, but the body which belongs to
and also characterizes our humble state. The nouns ταπείνωσις and δόξα mark two states in contrast, but connected
by their common possession of a σῶμα. " The body of our

humiliation " is the body possessed by us in this state, and
which also marks its humiliation. It connects us with the
soil out of which it was formed, and by the products of
which it is supported ; on which it walks, and into which it
falls at death. It keeps us in constant physical connection
with earth, whatever be the progress of the spirit towards
its high destiny—its commonwealth in heaven. Nay more,
it limits intellectual power and development, impedes spiritual
growth and enjoyment, and is soon fatigued with the soul's
activity. Let one will as he pleases, his body presents a
check on all sides, and at once warns him by the exhaustion
he feels, and the curbs which so suddenly bring him to a
pause. In it, too, are the seeds of disease and pain, from
functional disorder and organic malady. It is an animal
nature which, in spite of a careful and vigilant government, is
prone to rebellious outbreaks. Such has been the general
view. But Meyer objects, and endeavours to give the words a
more specific reference. He supposes that the enemies of the
cross are those who shun the sufferings which arise from
fellowship with Him who died upon it, and that this clause
pictures that state of privation, persecution, and sufferings
which affects the body, and springs from connection with the
cross. Thus Chrysostom—" Our body suffereth many things ;
it is bound with chains, it is scourged, it suffereth innumerable
evils, but the body of Christ suffered the same." [1] These may
be included, but not alone. It is true that ἡμεῖς stands in
contrast with τοὺς ἐχθρούς, and we apprehend that the
apostle refers to the body and its future change principally
because the class condemned by him so notoriously indulged
themselves in animal gratifications, and made a god of their
belly.

The verb μετασχηματίσει expresses change, and the result
is described by the next clause—σύμμορφον τῷ σώματι τῆς
δόξης αὐτοῦ. The curt or proleptic form of construction is
referred to by Winer, § 66, 3 ; and Kühner, § 477, 2. Rom.
viii. 29 ; 1 Thess. iii. 13. The adjective σύμμορφο. expresses
a conformity which is the result of the change, though it
agrees with σῶμα, the object acted on by the Lord Jesus. The
term δόξης characterizes Christ's σῶμα, as containing or possess-

---

[1] Πολλὰ πάσχει νῦν τὸ ὑμέτερον σῶμα, δεσμεῖται, μαστίζεται, μυρία πάσχει δεινά, etc.

ing it. For that body is enshrined in lustre, and occupies the highest position in the universe. We know not all the elements of its glory. But we know somewhat. The scene on the hill of transfiguration was an anticipative glimpse, when the face " marred more than any man's," glowed with deeper than solar splendour, and the robes, soiled and tattered by frequent journeys, shone with a purer lustre than the snow. When He appeared at the arrest of Saul in the neighbourhood of Damascus, His glory dimmed the mid-day sun, and before the symbolical apparition in Patmos, the disciple who had lain in His bosom was so overpowered, that He " fell at his feet as dead." After He rose, and even before He ascended, His body had lost all its previous sense of pain and fatigue, and possessed new and mysterious power of self-conveyance. Now it lives in heaven. Our body is therefore reserved to a high destiny—it shall be like His. The brightness of heaven does not oppress Him, neither shall it dazzle us. Our humanity dies, indeed, and is decomposed; but when He appears, it shall be raised and beautified, and fitted to dwell in a region which " flesh and blood cannot inherit." Man has been made to dwell on earth, and on no other planet. If he is to spend a happy eternity in a distant sphere, his physical frame must be prepared for it. If he is to see God and yet live—to serve Him in a world where there is no night and no sleep—to worship Him in company with angels which have not the clog of an animal frame, and like them to adore with continuous anthem and without exhaustion — then, surely, his body must be changed, for otherwise it would soon be overpowered by such splendours, and would die of ecstasy amidst such enjoyments. The glory of heaven would speedily become a delicious agony. Therefore these bodies shall cease to be animal without ceasing to be human bodies, and they shall become " spiritual " bodies — etherealized vehicles for the pure spirit which shall be lodged within them. " This corruptible must put on incorruption, and this mortal must put on immortality." Theodoret remarks, that the language does not signify change of figure, but deliverance from corruption; and he adds, that this assimilation to the body of Christ's glory shall be enjoyed—*οὐ κατὰ τὴν ποσό-τητα τῆς δόξης, ἀλλὰ κατὰ τὴν ποιότητα.* Still, the body of

Christ's glory is the pattern, and not, as Delitzsch imagines, the body of the first man in its original state, and prior to the extraction of Eve.[1]

Why then should the body be now degraded and besotted? Is it not an essential portion of humanity, specially cared for, and to be permanently glorified by the Lord Jesus? If such is to be its end, what should be its present honour? Should it not be preserved in purity, for the sake of Him who made it, and in fealty to Him who is to assimilate it to His own glorious body? Such a prospect would be a perfect safeguard against those vicious and grovelling indulgences which the apostle denounces in the previous verses.

As in the second chapter, the apostle does not formally teach the divinity of Christ, though he introduces it as giving effect and example to the lesson which he inculcates; so here it is also to be noted, that the apostle is not teaching the doctrine either of a resurrection of the dead, or a change of the living at the second advent. He is conducting no argument or exposition of this nature. On the other hand, he is inculcating a pure and spiritual life, contrasting his own demeanour with that of other parties who were sunk in sensual pursuits. The reference to the change and glorification of the body is introduced, as well to show why the apostle so acted, as to point out the inconsistency of those sensualists and worldlings. It may be that they either denied or misunderstood the doctrine of the resurrection. At least, in the other European churches of the East, as at Corinth and Thessalonica, similar errors prevailed. Not that there was among them any direct Gnostic dogma of the inherent sinfulness of matter, but the creed had become a common one, that the grave should never open, nor the urn yield up its ashes; and that, though the spirit should be immortal, the material frame might never be summoned out of its resting-place. So that there was a strong temptation to the sins reprobated by the apostle. Some of the Philippian converts might deem bliss of soul enough, and reckon, as at least a harmless thing,

---

[1] Sie werden sein wie der Leib des ersten Adam vor der geschlechtlichen Differenzirung, aber herrlicher, als dieser, weil sie die Herrlichkeit erlangt haben werden, welche der psychische Leib des ersten Adam erlangen sollte und durch den Fall verwirkte. Delitzsch, *Bibl. Psychologie*, p. 401.

the undue gratification of animal appetite, for the body with
all belonging to it was soon to pass into eternal oblivion.
Contented with the idea of the spirit's immortality, as revealed
in the gospel, they might feel it no disgrace to eat and drink
to licentious satiety, since the instrument of such indulgence
had no share in their hopes, and no connection with their
future personality, but was speedily to sink into darkness and
dust, and cease for ever to be a part of them. Therefore the
apostle refers so pointedly to the future existence of the body;
and not only so, but describes its high destiny. It is to exist
for ever, though in a changed and nobler form. It will still
be the soul's minister and tabernacle. The saved spirit is to
be hereafter embodied, but in no newly created mansion.
Therefore the body must now be esteemed as sacred, and
kept free from contamination. It is not to be enslaved as
subordinate, or despised as temporary. It is an essential and
eternal constituent of man's nature—a recipient, according to
its capabilities and functions, of the redeeming work of Christ.
Must it not then be treated as reason dictates, and the gospel
warrants? The apostle does not speak of the resurrection,
but of its results. He passes over the intermediate stages,
and simply describes the ultimate condition or quality of the
body. (On the question whether the apostle's language
warrants the notion that he hoped to survive till the second
advent, see under i. 26.) And Christ's ability to effect this
change cannot be doubted, for this is His range of prerogative—

κατὰ τὴν ἐνέργειαν τοῦ δύνασθαι αὐτὸν καὶ ὑποτάξαι αὐτῷ
τὰ πάντα—" according to the inworking of his ability, even
to subdue to Himself all things." The form αὐτῷ in preference to ἑαυτῷ has the authority of A, B¹, D¹, F, G. On the
relations of ἐνέργεια and δύναμις, see Eph. i. 19. Κατά has
its usual ethical force, and which, as it really points out the
norm or measure, inferentially advances an argument for the
previous statement. The two infinitives are not simply
connected by καί, as Rheinwald and Hoelemann construe,
but the one governs the other—the first being governed
itself by the substantive, and virtually taking the place
of a genitive, but expressing more than the noun would
—the permanence and sweep of His power. Winer, § 44, 4 ;
1 Cor. ix. 6 ; 1 Pet. iv. 17, etc. We take τὰ πάντα without

limitation, while καί is emphatic and ascensive. He is able to change the body, and not only so, but also to subdue all things. If He can subject everything to Himself or His own purposes, He can surely so change our body as to give it a full and final conformity to His own. Thus Chrysostom —ἔδειξε μείζονα ἔργα τῆς δυνάμεως αὐτοῦ, ἵνα καὶ τούτοις πιστεύσῃς. That all things are under Christ's control is the apostle's doctrine, and his virtual inference in this verse from the greater to the less cannot be disputed. Mind and matter are alike subservient—" all power is given to Me in heaven and in earth." The apostle, in 1 Cor. xv. 35, etc., shows some of the manifestations of this all-subduing power—the harvest springing from the seed which had died under the clod, and according to the species sown ; the various forms of existence in the universe, both in animal constitutions on earth and in the orbs or the angels of heaven—proofs that matter can assume vast differences of shapes, and be endowed with an exhaustless number of qualities—and that therefore such a change as is here predicted is neither beyond possibility nor without parallel. The apostle does not say, as Ellicott argues, that Christ will subject all things. He speaks only of His ability, though the inference may be that He will put it forth. While omniscience is the actual possession or exercise of all knowledge, omnipotence is universal ability, which may or may not yet have put forth all its energies, for what is possible to it may not have been effected by it. But Christ shall put forth His power, as we know from other sources, and death itself shall be swallowed up in victory— that which has swallowed up all humanity shall be surrounded by a wider vortex and be itself engulphed.

How the change of σχῆμα in reference to the body shall be effected we know not. It is a process far beyond our conception, and outside the limits of our experience, but not above the all-subduing power of the Redeemer. The statement is, that the body, this body of our humiliation, shall feel the wondrous transforming energy. The apostle speaks of the body, σῶμα, and not of the flesh, σάρξ. Resurrection is not formally predicated of the flesh in the New Testament, but only of the man, or of the dead—" I will raise him up." The kind of distinction we refer to is seen in the double question—

" How are the dead raised, and with what body do they come?"
Change implies difference, in this case an inconceivable
difference, but the identity of the body is not in every sense
destroyed by the change. That identity cannot certainly
consist of mere physical material, nor does Scripture ever say
so. The reader may remember how that subject is discussed
in Locke's " Second Reply" to the Bishop of Worcester.[1] The
changes of which matter is susceptible are indeed beyond conception, and if, as is alleged by some profound investigators,
the ultimate elements of matter are indivisible points, without
extension and surrounded by spheres of forces ; then such
spheres of attraction being changed, new bodies would be
exhibited without any alteration in their so-called chemical
constitution. Such hypotheses point to the possibility of
infinite changes—all within the reach of Him " who is able
to subdue all things unto Himself." According to the
apostle's illustration, the glorious body bears such a relation
to the earthly one, as the grain on the stalk in autumn bears
to the seed cast into the furrow in spring, and dying and
being decomposed under the clod. The body is therefore the
same in relationship, but different in material and structure
—once organized for a ψυχή, or animal life ; now prepared to
suit a πνεῦμα, or the higher spiritual life. 1 Cor. xv. 36–50.

The soul out of the body is said to be " naked." It has been
a common opinion, current among the Rabbins and vaguely
seen in the Fathers, that this epithet is only relative, and that
the soul has, as Müller says, " some organ of self-revelation
even in death," [2] or possesses what Delitzsch calls " an
immaterial corporeity "—immaterielle Leiblichkeit.[3] Lange,
Kern, Goeschel, Schubert, and Rudloff,[4] might be quoted to the
same effect. These speculations bring us near the " vehicular
state " which that curious thinker, Abraham Tucker, has
described, in the twenty-first chapter of his Light of Nature
Pursued. The arguments for the theory are specious, but of

[1] Works, vol. iv.; London, 1823.
[2] Die Christliche Lehre von der Sünde, vol. ii. p. 415.
[3] Diese immaterielle Leiblichkeit ist, verglichen mit der materiellen, einerseits
nur ein Schemen dieser, andererseits aber, so zu sagen, ihre Essenz oder ihr
Extract. Psychologie, p. 370.
[4] Die Lehre vom Menschen nach Geist, Seele und Leib, etc., p. 54, etc.
Leipzig, 1858.

S

little weight. It is no proof in favour of it, from physiology,
that a man feels, or seems to feel, pains located for a long
period in an organ or limb which has been amputated, as such
nervous sensations may be otherwise accounted for. Nor is
there any force in Delitzsch's argument, drawn from the appearance of Samuel to the witch of Endor, or that of Moses and
Elias on the hill of transfiguration, or from the pictures of the
population of Hades or Heaven in Scripture—as in the parable
of the rich man and Lazarus, and in the Apocalypse. The
language in such cases is plainly that of popular delineation ;
for metaphysical exactness would be unintelligible. Spirits are
not spoken of as essences, but are pictured as persons, feeling,
speaking, and being clothed, in such a way that their human
identity may be at once recognized. The present life throws
such a reflection upon the future life, as enables us to comprehend it and feel its oneness with ourselves. For the spirit-
world revealed in Scripture is no dreamy or shadowy sphere,
where personality is either obscured or is blended with the
great source of existence. The individual life is still single
and separate as on earth, yet not inert, but endowed with its
own consciousness, and possessed of its own memories and
hopes. So that it is naturally represented as having its prior
face, form, and garb. Not for identical, but for analogous
reasons, similar language is employed to set out the personality
of God—the Great Spirit. He covers Himself " with light as
with a garment "—He speaks " face to face "—He opens " His
hand," and makes bare " His holy arm "—" His eyes run to
and fro "—the waters feel " the blast of the breath of His
nostrils "—" His lips are full of indignation "—" the voice of
the Lord is powerful "—and " the clouds are the dust of His
feet."

Nor does Scripture furnish any definite proof. 2 Cor. v.
1, 3, does not speak of a *Zwischenleiblichkeit*, an interim
corporeity ; or, as Reiche[1] calls it—*mortui organum quasi
provisorium*, and as Schott, Lange, Nitzsch, and Martensen
suppose. The third verse has been variously understood, but
its meaning as a confirmative explanation of the previous
verse, is opposed to the theory to which we are referring. It
may either be ;—" seeing that when we are also clothed, we

[1] *Commentarius Criticus*, p. 353.

shall not be found naked;" or rather, " seeing in fact that we shall really be found clothed, not naked." The apostle had no desire to be unclothed, but divestment was a necessary stage in the process of glorification. The unclothing is unnatural, but it prepares for the assumption of the final raiment, when mortality shall be swallowed up in life. See under i. 23–26.

And this *Nerven-geist*—what, and whence is it? Is it an inner envelope which the soul already possesses, intermediate between its own subtleness and the grossness of its outer covering, something that aids its power of sensation, perception, and thought? No such inner film is necessary, as the mind at once receives impressions, and needs no re-presentative medium, but is directly conscious of what is beyond it, without the intervention of what were once called ideas or phantasms. Or if it do not exist now, is it created for the spirit when it leaves the body ; or does the spirit evolve it out of those finer particles of its corporeity, and clothe itself with it? Would consciousness be extinguished without it? or without it would the faculty of communication with the world of spirit or matter around it cease? The sphere of sensation and perception is indeed enveloped in mystery, for it is that bourne where self and not-self come into contact, and where the spiritual subject seems to blend with the material object. But there needs no subjective re-presentation of objective realities—the connection involved in sensation is immediate, and the conviction produced rests upon a primitive and irresistible belief—the " common sense " of mankind.

Nor can such a psychological theory help us either to a better proof or a clearer conception of corporeal identity. Nitzsch indeed says—"Whoever supposes that the departed are without a body prior to the resurrection will scarcely find, in the mere ashes of the mouldered body, a connecting point for the identity of the past and future corporeity. The medium of identity must be sought rather in that corporeity in which the departed soul remains." [1] And this is changed or developed so as to enable it to reach its final state. Such a notion seems to deny a resurrection in the ordinary sense of the term, and is no way parallel to or typified by the great

[1] *System der Christlichen Lehre,* § 217.

historical fact of Christ's resurrection. It is not the so-called
Nerve-spirit that the Saviour is to develop, and brighten into
the likeness of His own body; but it is "the body of our
humiliation" which He is to change and conform to the
body of His glory. Each body fits in to the spirit which
inhabits it, imparts a character to it, and derives a character
from it—possesses, in short, such an individuality as may
give us some proof of a resurrection, but it unfolds nothing
of its mystery. This "body of our humiliation" has
therefore some surviving element, or some indissoluble link,
which warrants the notion and shall secure the consciousness of identity, in whatever that identity may consist; for
it is indispensable to that judgment where each shall
receive according to deeds done in the body—τὰ διὰ τοῦ
σώματος—that is, "deeds done by the body" as an organ, as
the instrument of responsible action. We need again and
again on this subject to be reminded of the Lord's rebuke to
the Sadducees—"Ye do err, not knowing the Scriptures, nor
the power of God."

CHAPTER IV.

Now follows a pointed and brief application, which should have been joined to the preceding chapter. Matthies and van Hengel connect it unnaturally with the following counsels. The particle ὥστε carries us back to the preceding statements, and marks a deduction from them.

(Ver. 1.) Ὥστε, ἀδελφοί μου ἀγαπητοὶ καὶ ἐπιπόθητοι, χαρὰ καὶ στέφανός μου, οὕτως, στήκετε ἐν Κυρίῳ, ἀγαπητοί— "Wherefore, my brethren, loved and longed for, my joy and crown, so stand in the Lord, beloved." The apostle's mind turns away from the enemies of the cross to the genuine believers; and his heart opens itself to them, and opens all the more unreservedly from the contrast. He weeps over the one party, as he thinks of their awful destiny; but his soul is filled with holy rapture when he turns to the other party, and as he contemplates their coming glory. The epithets are the coinage of a jubilant spirit. The accumulation of them proceeds from his conscious inability to express all his ardour. Indeed, the language of endearment is fond of such repetitions.

Meyer says that we need not carry the reference in ὥστε farther than the 17th verse, where the address in the second person commences,—"Be followers of me." This idea is so far correct; yet, though the counsel in the last section rises to a climax, the entire chapter is closely compacted, and in the very first verse there is a direct personal appeal. One might say, too, that the injunction, "stand fast in the Lord," naturally results from such warnings as are found as far back as the second verse. At all events, the narrow view of Grotius cannot be sustained—*quum tanta nobis præposita sunt præmia;* and the opposite view of De Wette and Wiesinger is at the same time too vague. We might conclude that ὥστε is generally and in spirit an inference from the entire chapter, and in form and more especially from its last paragraph, which describes such power as believers hope to be realized at the second advent. (On the meaning of ὥστε with the imperative, see under ii. 12.) The apostle terms them "brethren beloved"—children of one spiritual Parent—forming one happy family—and rejoicing to meet at length in the Father's house of "many mansions." They were spiritually dear to him; his heart clasped them with special fondness—ἐπιπόθητοι. See i. 8; ii. 26. The word occurs only here in the New Testament. The apostle's heart yearned toward them, and there was reason for this indescribable longing,—they were his "joy and crown"—χαρὰ καὶ στέφανός μου. 1 Thess. ii. 19. There is no reason for Calvin's taking the first term as referring to the present, and the second to the future, or for Alford referring both to the future. The words are both the expression of present emotion. They were a source of gladness to him, in their rescue from sin and danger, in their spiritual change, and in its visible development. Nay, as he had been so instrumental in their conversion, they were to him even now a wreath of honour. The term στέφανος is often used in a similar sense. Sophocles, *Ajax*, 465—

ὧν αὐτὸς ἔσχε στέφανον εὐκλείας μέγαν,

where, however, the noun is explained by the genitive which it governs; or *Philoct.* 841—

τοῦδε γάρ ὁ στέφανος,

where, however, the image is different. See also Prov. iv. 9, xii. 4, xiv. 24, xvi. 31, xvii. 6; Isa. xxviii. 5. The expression was a common one. The scene of the first introduction of the gospel to Philippi recurred for a moment to his memory—the preaching of the truth, the impression made, the anxious inquiries put, the decided change produced, the organization of the church, and its growth and prosperity, as the result of his labours, prayers, and sufferings. His success he wore as a garland of imperishable verdure. If he who saved in battle the life of a Roman citizen received from his grateful countrymen an oaken garland, *ob civem servatum*, how much more might their apostle call them saved and blessed by his ministry, "my crown"! He was not insensible

tò the high honour of being the founder and guardian of such
a community. That this joy might not fail, and that this
crown might not wither, he adds in earnest and loving tone—
οὕτως στήκετε ἐν Κυρίῳ—" so stand in the Lord." 1 Thess.
iii. 8. The preposition ἐν points out the sphere or element.
To stand, or stand fast, in the Lord, is neither to wander out
of Him, nor even to waver in connection with Him, but to
remain immoveable in fellowship with Him,—to live in Him
without pause—to walk in Him without digression—to love
Him without rival—and serve Him without compromise. It
is here to be untouched by the ceremonial pride of the concision, and especially to be proof against the sensualism of the
enemies of the cross. But what is implied in οὕτως—" thus " ?
Is it, " stand so as you are doing," or, " so as I have prescribed " ? The former view, which is that of the Greek
Fathers, Calvin, Bengel, and Am Ende, is not so utterly
untenable as Meyer represents it; for the apostle has already
praised them for consistency and perseverance (i. 6), and the
verb might bear such a pregnant meaning. Yet, as Meyer,
De Wette, and others argue, there may be a reference to
iii. 17—" Be ye unitedly followers of me," and οὕτως here
may correspond to οὕτως there. Van Hengel is self-consistent
in bringing out this idea—ut rivendi ratio quam sequamini in
cœlis sit. To give it the turn which Elsner proposes in his
translation—ita dilecti—is out of the question, nor is Drusius
waranted so to Hebraize as to bring out this sense—state recte.
We therefore take the reference as being especially to the two
preceding verses, and as being in virtual contrast with the
description of verses 18, 19. In opposition to those who
were sunk in sensuality and earthliness, and on whom the
cross of Christ exercised no spiritualizing power, they were to
live as the citizens of a better country, their mind lifted above
the world by such an ennobling connection, and thrilled at
the same time with the prospect of the Saviour's advent, to
transform and prepare their physical nature for that realm in
which they should have an ultimate and a permanent residence. And he concludes with a second ἀγαπητοί,—so great
is the reaction from καὶ κλαίων, and so great his attachment
to his Philippian converts; or, as Theodoret describes it, μετ᾽
εὐφημίας πολλῆς ἡ παραίνεσις.

The remaining statements and counsels are somewhat detached in their nature — are the ethical miscellany with
which the apostle often concludes an epistle. They are
personal, too, in character, and presuppose a confidential
intimacy.

(Ver. 2.) Εὐοδίαν παρακαλῶ, καὶ Συντύχην παρακαλῶ, τὸ
αὐτὸ φρονεῖν ἐν Κυρίῳ—"Euodia I exhort and Syntyche I
exhort to be of one mind in the Lord." That these are the
Greek names of women is plain from the feminine pronouns
of the following verse, to which they are the antecedents.
The words ἐν Κυρίῳ point out the sphere of this concord, and
belong not to the verb παρακαλῶ, as Beza and Storr suppose,
nor yet can we sustain the rendering of Grotius—*propter
Dominum*. Who these women were, what was their position
in the church, and about what they had disagreed, we know
not. Not a few suppose them to have been deaconesses—
πρεσβύτιδες. At all events, they had laboured in the gospel
with earnestness and success. The apostle does not say on
whose side the fault lay, but he repeats the παρακαλῶ, not
simply, as Alford limits it, to "hint at their present separation," but to show that he placed the like obligation on each
of them. He does not exhort the one to be reconciled to the
other, for they might have doubted who should take the
initiative, and they might wonder, from the position of their
names and construction of the sentence, to which of them the
apostle attached the more blame. But he exhorts them both,
the one and the other, to think the same thing—not only to
come to a mutual understanding, but to preserve it. See under
ii. 2. Van Hengel needlessly supposes that they had laboured
with the apostle at Rome, and were now about to proceed
to Philippi with Epaphroditus—this counsel to them being,
that in all things they did for the gospel they should act in
concert. But the previous intimations in the epistle prove
that there had been tendencies to disunion in the church, and
the second verse of the second chapter these women might
read with a special and personal concern. The cause of quarrel
might be some unworthy question about priority or privilege
even in the prosecution of the good work—vainglory leading
to strife, as already hinted by the apostle toward the commencement of the second chapter. It does not seem to have

been any difference in creed or practice, and wholly groundless
is the hypothesis of Baur and Schwegler, that the names
represent two parties in the church at Philippi—Euodia the
Jewish, and Syntyche the heathen party.

(Ver. 3.) Ναὶ ἐρωτῶ καί σε, γνήσιε σύνζυγε—"Yea, I ask
thee too, true yoke-fellow." A third party is appealed to, to
interpose his good offices—a proof that the apostle reckoned
the harmony of these two women a matter of no small importance. The ναί is preferred to καί on preponderant authority,
and is confirmatory in its nature. The verb ἐρωτάω, as
different from αἰτέω, carries in it the idea of authority.
Trench, *Synon.* p. 164. What this third person was to do is
thus stated—

συλλαμβάνου αὐταῖς, αἵτινες ἐν τῷ εὐαγγελίῳ συνήθλησάν
μοι—"help these women, as being persons who (or because
they) have striven along with me in the gospel." The first
middle verb signifies to assist—"Take them up together."
Luke v. 7. It was not to help them pecuniarily, as Justinian
absurdly imagines, but he, whoever he was, was to be a
mediator, and to use all his influence with them, so that they
should make advances to each other. And there was the
more reason for his benign interference, for these women
had been specially useful. They had (αἵτινες—*quippe quæ*)
striven side by side with Paul in the gospel. The verb
contains an idea more intense than that represented by
"laboured," as also in i. 27. In the place now referred to, the
object for which agonistic exertion is made is placed in the
simple dative—here the sphere of the striving is represented
by the preposition ἐν. They strove together in the gospel,
and for its furtherance. They had rendered the apostle
essential assistance in his evangelical efforts and toils, and if
they were so labouring still in their own spheres, they must be
reconciled. From their past efforts, their misunderstanding
was the more unseemly, and the more necessary it was to heal
the breach. Spheres of labour for females were specially
open in such cities as Philippi, and among their own sex, to
whom they might have access (for the γυναικωνῖτις was kept
in jealous seclusion), and whose delicacies and difficulties they
could instinctively comprehend or remove. Rom. xvi. 3–12.
Women were the first who received the gospel at Philippi.

Acts xvi. 13.   These women were not the apostle's only
fellow-workers, for he adds, that they laboured—
μετὰ καὶ Κλήμεντος καὶ τῶν λοιπῶν συνεργῶν μου—" along
with Clement, too, and my fellow-labourers." The insertion
of καί between the preposition and its noun is not common,
though other particles are placed in this way.   Hartung, i. p.
143.   By the use of καί . . . καί, things or persons are
simultaneously thought of or represented.   Winer, § 53, 4.
It is out of the question to join this clause with ἐρωτῶ, as if
the request were his and Clement's.   Clement is mentioned
nowhere else.   There is no solid ground for supposing that
he was the well-known Clemens Romanus, as ecclesiastical
tradition, Jerome, van Hengel, and Baur for his own purpose,
suppose.[1]   All we know of him is, that in fellowship with
those women he had laboured along with the apostle at
Philippi, in diffusing the gospel and building up the church.
Euodia, Syntyche, and Clement must have been hearty and
prominent in their co-operation ; and Clement is mentioned
as if the apostle had such a cordial recollection of him, that he
could not but mention him.   Others are also referred to, but
not named.   Some, as Storr, Flatt, and Cocceius, would join
the clause to συλλαμβάνου αὐταῖς ; but, as Meyer suggests,
not μετά, but the simple dative would in that case be
appropriate—καὶ τῷ Κλήμεντι.   Of Clement's colleagues
the apostle adds—
ὧν τὰ ὀνόματα ἐν βίβλῳ ζωῆς—"whose names are in the
book of life."   The book of life is a figure, sometimes having
reference to present life, as in Athens, where the catalogue
of living citizens was scrupulously kept.   Ps. lxix. 28 ; Ezek.
xiii. 9.   See also Ex. xxxii. 32 ; Isa. iv. 3.   Then it came
to be used in reference to life beyond the grave.   Dan. xii.
1–8 ; Rev. iii. 5, xiii. 8, xx. 15, xxi. 27 ; and somewhat
differently, Luke x. 50 ; Heb. xii. 23.   This inscription of
their names shows the certainty of their future happiness, for
those names will not be erased.   The image of such a register
presents to us the minuteness and infallibility of the divine
omniscience, and the assured glory of Christ's followers and
servants.   The relative has τῶν λοιπῶν for its antecedent, and

---

[1] Ὁ Κλήμης . . . Παύλου συνεργός.   Euseb. Hist. Eccl. iii. 4 ; Winer, Real-
Wort. sub voce.

probably the phraseology was suggested by the fact that their names are unnoticed in the epistle. The apostle does not name them, they are summed up in a brief and anonymous τῶν λοιπῶν; but they are not forgotten, for their names are written by no human hand in the register of that blessed assemblage which shall inherit eternal life. A greater honour by far than being mentioned even in the list of an apostle's eulogy.

But who was the third party so earnestly appealed to by the apostle as γνήσιε σύνζυγε? The noun, commonly spelt σύζυγος, occurs only here in the New Testament.

1. It is often used of a wife in classic Greek, and hence some would understand by it the spouse of the apostle. Clement of Alexandria[1] alludes to it, so does Isidore, and the view is held by Erasmus, Flacius, Musculus, Cajetan, Zuingli, Bullinger, and Justinian. Many popish interpreters keenly rebut this opinion, and Bellarmine confronts it with five distinct arguments. The adjective ought, in such a case, to be feminine. Then, too, the notion would seem to contradict what Paul himself has said of his unmarried state in 1 Cor. vii. 7, etc.[2] Theodoret justly remarks, that this view is held by some ἀνοήτως.

2. Dwelling still upon the same usage, some suppose the person referred to to be the husband of one of the women. Chrysostom says—ἢ ἀδελφόν τινα αὐτῶν ἢ καὶ ἄνδρα μιᾶς αὐτῶν οὕτω καλεῖ. But there are no grounds for such an opinion. The yoke is supposed to be borne in company with the apostle, and not with any of these women.

---

[1] Strom. iii. 53—καὶ ὅγε Παῦλος οὐκ ὀκνεῖ ἔν τινι ἐπιστολῇ τὴν αὐτοῦ προσαγορεύειν σύζυγον, ἣν οὐ περιεκόμιζε διὰ τὸ τῆς ὑπηρεσίας εὐσταλές.

[2] Whether Paul had ever been married cannot be determined. Much depends on the precise meaning of the phrase κατήνεγκα ψῆφον—"I gave my vote against them." Acts xxvi. 10. If the words are to be taken in their literal acceptation, and there appears no good reason why they should not, then they imply that Saul was at the period a member of the Sanhedrim; and one necessary qualification for a seat in that high court was to be a husband and a father. But his wife and children had not long survived, for when the apostle wrote to the church in Corinth he was unmarried. One objection to this view is, that chiefly men of years were admitted to the Sanhedrim, and Saul must have been comparatively young at the time. But perhaps his zeal and courage may have opened the path to him, and as for the qualification referred to, we know that it was customary for the Jews to marry at a rather early age.

3. Passing to the plain meaning of the term, many give it the rendering of our version—a colleague in labour, either in actual pastoral office, or at least one who had done good service to the church in Philippi, and was so well known as not to require to be named. This honour is assigned to various persons. Grotius, Cocceius, and Michaelis assign it to Epaphroditus, though he was at this period with the apostle in Rome. Zeltner and Bengel put in a claim for Silas— Estius upholds Timothy—Koehler pleads for Barnabas. Still the great majority regard the words as meaning fellow-labourer—*germane compar*, as in the Vulgate. Should this interpretation be adopted, it would follow, as Bengel remarks, that the term denotes a closer union than συνεργός; and it looks as if the person referred to were he to whom the epistle should be first carried, and by whom it should be first read. It might be Epaphroditus, who, though present with the apostle, was so addressed, for he was to carry the epistle to Philippi, and as the pastor reading it, and being so addressed in it, might thus exhibit his commission as a peacemaker.

4. Another idea, started by Chrysostom and Œcumenius, and strenuously contended for by Meyer, is that σύζυγος is a proper name[1]—"I ask thee, genuine Syzygus;" that is, his name was a symbol of his character and labours. Chrysostom says, as if by the way—τινὲς δέ φασι ὄνομα ἐκεῖνο κύριον εἶναι τὸ Σύζυγε, but adds πλὴν εἴτε τοῦτο, εἴτε ἐκεῖνο, οὐ σφόδρα ἀκριβολογεῖσθαι δεῖ. This hypothesis has the advantage of singling out an individual and addressing him, but the only plausible argument for it is, that as proper names occur in these verses, this in all likelihood is a proper name too. It is a strange conceit of Wieseler (*Chronol.* p. 458), that the "true yoke-fellow" is Christ Himself, and that ναί introduces a prayer to Him. But the question cannot be fully determined.

(Ver. 4.) Χαίρετε ἐν Κυρίῳ πάντοτε· πάλιν ἐρῶ, χαίρετε— "Rejoice in the Lord always; again will I say, rejoice." The apostle reverts to what he had started with in the 1st verse of the third chapter. There is no need to suppose any connection between this and the preceding verse. The adverb

---

[1] Storr and Heinrichs hold it to be a translation of the name Κολληγᾶς found in Josephus, *Bell. Jud.* vii. 3, 4. Primasius and Peter Lombard are inclined to make the epithet a proper name.

πάντοτε, which refers to time and not to place, belongs to the first clause. Κύριος, as usual, designates Christ, while ἐν points to Him as the element or sphere of this joy. The joy was to be continual—not a fitful rapture, but a uniform emotion. And the apostle repeats the injunction, which is very different in meaning from the Latin *valete*, and Cicero's formula—*vale, vale et salve.*[1] The apostle wished them to come to a full appreciation of their position and their connection with Christ. Could they but judge truly their condition and prospects, and contrast them with their past state of gloom and unhappiness—could they but realize the nobleness and power of the truth they had embraced, and the riches and certainty of the hopes they were cherishing—could they estimate the saving change effected in their souls, and picture too that glorification which was to pass over their bodies—then, as they traced all blessing to Christ and to union with Him, they would rejoice in the Lord, not in themselves as recipients, but in Him as Source, not only in the gifts conferred, but in Him especially as the gracious benefactor. To rejoice in Him is to exult in Him, not as a dim abstraction, but as a living person—so near and so loving, so generous and so powerful, that the spirit ever turns to him in admiring grateful homage, covets His presence as its sunshine, and revels in fellowship with Him. Despondency is weakness, but joy is strength. Is it rash to say, in fine, that the churches of Christ are strangers by far too much to this repeated charge of the apostle—that the current ideas of Christ are too historic in their character, and want the freshness of a personal reality—that He is thought of more as a Being in remoteness and glory, far above and beyond the stars, than as a personal and sympathizing Saviour—that salvation is regarded more as a process a man thankfully submits to, than a continuous and happy union with Jesus— and that therefore, though Christians may run and are not weary, and may walk and are not faint, they seldom mount

---

[1] That χαίρειν is often employed in the sense of *valere*, every one knows, as in Xenophon viii. 5, 42—χαίρειν ταύτην τὴν εὐδαιμονίαν κελεύω—"I bid this happiness farewell," or Euripides, *Herc. Fur.* 576—χαιρόντων πόνοι—"farewell toils." The English idiom is similar—farewell, or fare ye well—in itself a wish for happiness, though losing entirely such a sense in its idiomatic use, as in "Farewell, sour annoy,"—"Farewell, world and sin."

up with wings as eagles, and then, if they do, is not their flight brief and exhaustive ? On the reduplication of the precept, Chrysostom briefly says—*καλῶς τὸν λόγον ἐδιπλασίασεν.* The earnest English expositor of this epistle thus writes— " Now see how it pleaseth the Lord, that as the Apostle comes againe and againe unto this holy exhortation, and leaves it not with once or twice, but even the third time also exhorteth them to rejoyce in the Lord ; so I should come unto you againe and againe, even three severall times with the same exhortation to rejoyce in the Lord. *Againe*, saith the Apostle, *I say rejoyce, even in the Lord alwayes*, for that is to be added, and resumed to the former place. From which doubling and redoubling of this exhortation, I observe both how needful and withall how hard a matter it is to perswade this constant rejoycing in the Lord, to rejoyce in the Lord alwayes. For to this end doth the Holy Ghost often in the Scriptures use to double and redouble His speech even to shew both the needfulness of His speech, and the difficultie in respect of man of enforcing His speech. In the Psalme, how often doth the Prophet exhort the faithful unto the praises of the Lord, even before all the people, that they and their posteritie might know them, saying, *O that men would therefore praise the Lord for His goodnesse, and declare the wonders that He doth for the children of men !* Even foure several times in that one Psalme. And wherefore ? but to shew how needfull it was they should do so, and how hardly men are drawne to do so. How often likewise doth our Saviour exhort His disciples unto humilitie and meekness ? sometimes saying unto them, *Learne of Me that I am meeke and lowly in heart ;* sometimes telling them, that whosoever among them would be great, should be servant unto the rest; sometimes washing their feete, etc., thereby to teach them humilitie. And wherefore doth He so often beate upon it, but to shew how needfull it was they should be humble and meeke, and likewise how hard a thing it is to draw men unto humilitie and meeknesse ? How often likewise doth the Holy Ghost exhort to the putting off of the old man, and the putting on of the new man ! No part of Scripture throughout the whole Bible, wherein the Holy Ghost doth not speake much, though not haply in these words, yet to this purpose. And where-

fore else is it, but to imply both how needfull a matter it is to
be perswaded, and how hard a matter it is to perswade the
mortification of the old man, and the quickening of the new
man ?   And to let other instances passe, in the point whereof
we now speake, how oft doth our Saviour exhort to rejoyce
and be glad in persecution, because of the reward laid up for
us by God in heaven ; to rejoyce because our names are
written in heaven by the finger of God's own hand ; to be of
good comfort, because He hath overcome the world, that is,
to rejoyce in the Lord ! And wherefore, but to show how
needfull it is to rejoyce in the Lord, and how hard it is to
perswade this rejoicing ? So that by the usuall course of the
Scripture it appeareth, that our Apostle doubling and redoubling this his exhortation, thereby sheweth both how needfull,
and withall how hard a matter it is to perswade this constant
rejoycing in the Lord, to rejoyce in the Lord alwayes : so
needfull, that it must be perswaded again and again, and
withall so hard to be perswaded, that it cannot be too much
urged and beaten upon.

" But it will not be amisse yet a little more particularly to
looke into the reasons why it is so needfull to rejoyce in the
Lord alwayes, and why we are so hardly perswaded to rejoyce
in the Lord alwayes.   Who seeth not, that considereth anything, what mightie enemies we have alwayes to fight withall,
the flesh within us to snare and deceive us, the world without
us to fight and wage warre against us, and the devil ever
seeking like a roaring lion whom he may devour ? Who
seeth not, what fightings without, what terrors within, what
anguishes in the soul, what griefes in the bodie, what perils
abroade, what practices at home, what troubles we have on
every side ? When then Satan that old dragon casts out many
flouds or persecutions against us ; when wicked men cruelly,
disdainfully, and despitefully speake against us ; when lying,
slandering, and deceitful mouthes are opened upon us ; when
we are mocked and jested at, and had in derision of all them
that are about us ; when we are afflicted, tormented, and made
the world's wonder ; when the sorrowes of death compasse us
and the flouds of wickednesse make us afraid, and the paines
of hell come even unto our soule : what is it that holds up our
heads that we sinke not ? how is it that we stand either not

shaken, or if shaken, yet not cast downe? Is it not by our rejoycing which we have in Christ Jesus?"[1] The next injunction is—

(Ver. 5.) Τὸ ἐπιεικὲς ὑμῶν γνωσθήτω πᾶσιν ἀνθρώποις— "Let your forbearance be known to all men." The phrase τὸ ἐπιεικὲς ὑμῶν has much the force of a substantive with the possessive pronoun. Kühner, § 479, b. See under iii. 8. The adjective bears a variety of meanings. Composed of ἐπί and εἰκός—ἔοικα, it signifies originally what is meet or fitting, or characterizes any object or quality as being what it should be. It also describes what is proper or fair, or what is kind and reasonable, especially in the form of considerateness and as opposed to the harshness of law. That it should at length settle down into the meaning of gentleness, or rather forbearance, was natural; and this is a meaning found in Plato, Polybius, Plutarch, and also in Philo. Hesychius defines the adverb—πάνυ λίαν πράως. Plato's first definition of it is— δικαίων καὶ συμφερόντων ἐλάττωσις; and his second is— μετριότης ἐν συμβολαίοις. Definit. Opera, ed. Bekker, vol. ix. p. 265. Aristotle draws the contrast—ὁ μὴ ἀκριβοδίκαιος ἐπὶ τὸ χεῖρον, ἀλλ' ἐλαττικώτατος καίπερ ἔχων τὸν νόμον βοηθὸν ἐπιεικής ἐστιν, καὶ ἕξις αὕτη ἐπιείκεια. Eth. Nicom. v. 10. The prevailing sense in the New Testament seems to be that of forbearance. Thus, too, in Ps. lxxxvi. 5—ὅτι σὺ Κύριε χρηστὸς καὶ ἐπιεικὴς καὶ πολυέλεος. It is associated in the New Testament with πρᾳότης, 2 Cor. x. 1; with ἄμαχος twice, 1 Tim. iii. 3, Tit. iii. 2; with εὐπειθής, Jas. iii. 17; and with ἀγαθός, 1 Pet. ii. 18. As Trench justly says of it—"clementia sets forth one side; æquitas another; and, perhaps, modestia a third." Theodoret restricts the meaning by far too much, when he paraphrases—μὴ ἀμύνεσθε κακῷ τὸ κακόν. It is not gentleness as an innate feeling, but as the result of self-restraint. It bears no resemblance to the selfish calculation often expressed by those words which have acquired an ethical significance—in medio tutissimus ibis. It does not insist on what is its due; it does not stand on etiquette or right, but it descends and complies. It is opposed

[1] Lectures on the whole Epistle of Paul to the Philippians, by the Reverend and Faithful Servant of Christ, Henry Airay, Doctor in Divinity and late

to that rigour which never bends nor deviates, and which, as it gives the last farthing, uniformly exacts it. It is not facile pliability—a reed in the breeze—but that generous and indulgent feeling that knows what is its right, but recedes from it, is conscious of what is merited, but does not contend for strict proportion. It is, in short, that grace which was defective in one or other, or both of the women, who are charged by the apostle to be of one mind in the Lord. For, slow to take offence, it is swift to forgive it. Let a misunderstanding arise, and no false delicacy will prevent it from taking the first step towards reconciliation or adjustment of opinion. And truly such an element of character well becomes a man who expects a Saviour in whom this feeling was so predominant. This grace was to be notorious among them— γνωσθήτω, "let it be known" to all men—not simply to the enemies of the cross, or of the gospel, or to one another, as many allege, but to all without exception. It was so to characterize them, that if any one should describe their behaviour, he could not overlook it, but must dwell upon it. Our life is seriously defective without it; and let a man be zealous and enterprising, pure and upright, yet what a rebuke to his Christianity, if he is universally declared to be stiff, impracticable, unamiable, and austere in general deportment! If this joy in the Lord were felt in its fulness, the spirit so cheered and exalted would cease to insist on mere personal right, and practise forbearance. It is solemnly added—

ὁ Κύριος ἐγγύς, "the Lord is near." We are inclined to take Κύριος as referring to Jesus—such being its common reference in Pauline usage, though many, including Luther, Calvin, Rheinwald, Rilliet, and Müller, suppose that God is meant. The language—ii. 11, iii. 20—and the reference of the term in the first three verses of the chapter, oblige us to understand Jesus by the epithet. Ἐγγύς may be used either of place or time—"The Lord is at hand," either in position or approach. If the clause be connected with the preceding counsel, the meaning might be—"Let your forbearance be known to all men," and one great motive is, "the Lord is at hand." Storr and De Wette take the view of the Greek Fathers, that God is thought of as judge, and that this idea is an inducement to cherish clemency even toward enemies, for God, the Judge

and Redresser of every injury, is near. Velasquez and Beelen
take it more generally, referring it—*ad auxiliarem opem quam
Deus suis afferre consuevit*. Such an extension of meaning
is not warranted, though certainly one might be invited to
manifest the grace by this consideration, that the Lord
will be Judge in all such cases as call for its exhibition, and by
Himself this virtue has been specially and fully exhibited.

Or the clause may be connected with the following admonition. Meyer adopts this view—that is, the near coming of
Jesus ought to prevent all His people from cherishing an
undue anxiety. " Be careful for nothing," Christ is at hand,
and abundance will be the result of His advent. Or, " be careful
for nothing," He is ever near to supply all your wants. We
prefer to take ἐγγύς in reference to time, and the general
meaning of the formula may be gathered t. ›m Matt. xvi. 28 ;
Luke xxi. 31; 1 Cor. xvi. 22 ; Jas. v. 9 ; 1 Pet. iv. 7 ;
1 John ii. 28. It cannot mean " always present or near," as in
Ps. xxxiv. 18, cxix. 151, cxlv. 18. The notion here is, that
one who has been away is returning, and will soon arrive.
But may not the clause be connected with both verses ? It
has no formal connection with either. And as it stands by
itself, and seems to represent a familiar Christian idea, may it
not be at the same time mentally joined to the charges both
before and after it ? It is introduced after a counsel to exhibit
forbearance, and may be regarded as a motive to it ; but while
the apostle writes it, there starts up in his mind another use
of it, and in consequence of its appropriateness he subjoins—
' be careful for nothing." It thus becomes a link in a train
of thought, suggested by what precedes, and suggesting what
follows it.

(Ver. 6.) Μηδὲν μεριμνᾶτε—" Be careful for nothing." The
accusative μηδέν, emphatic from position, is that of object.
The verb is followed sometimes by the dative, expressing
that on account of which anxiety is felt, though περί and
ὑπέρ are also used, as well as εἰς in Matt. vi. 34. There is no
occasion with Wahl to supply μετά, nor with Hoelemann to
suppose the accusative used adverbially. Chrysostom connects
this with the previous verse,—" If their enemies opposed them,
and they saw the wicked live in luxury, they were not to be distressed." But the apostle has passed away from that previous

thought, and speaks now of another subject. The solicitude guarded against is that state of mind in which one frets himself to know more than he is able, or reach something too far beyond him, or is anxious to make provision for contingencies, to guard against suspected evils, and nerve himself against apprehended failures and disasters. The spirit is thrown into a fever by such troubles, so that joy in the Lord is abridged, and this forbearance would be seriously endangered. Not that the apostle counsels utter indifference, for indifference would preclude prayer; but his meaning is, that no one of them should tease and torment himself about anything, when he may get what he wants by prayer. There is nothing any one would be the better of having, which he may not hopefully ask from God. Why then should he be anxious?— why, especially, should any one prolong such anxiety, or nurse it into a chronic distemper? Matt. vi. 25; 1 Pet. v. 7. The apostle does not counsel an unnatural stoicism. He was a true friend of humanity, and taught it not how to despise, but how to lighten its burdens. If it could not bear them itself, he showed it how to cast them on God. For thus he counsels—

ἀλλ᾽ ἐν παντὶ τῇ προσευχῇ καὶ τῇ δεήσει μετὰ εὐχαριστίας τὰ αἰτήματα ὑμῶν γνωριζέσθω πρὸς τὸν Θεόν—" but in everything by prayer and supplication, along with thanksgiving, let your requests be made known to God." The noun αἴτημα means literally a thing asked. Luke xxiii. 24; 1 John v. 15. By a natural process it also signifies, as here, a thing desired and therefore to be asked. Hence the phrase τὰ αἰτήματα τῆς καρδίας. Ps. xxxvii. 4. Let the things you seek be made known—πρὸς τὸν Θεόν. The construction is peculiar. This preposition is often used after verbs of similar meaning, and seems to signify, as Ast gives it—apud, coram. Lex. Platon., sub voce. It points out destination or direction—" Let your requests be made known toward God "—disclosed before Him, that they may reach him. The simple dative would have merely implied direct information to Him; but πρός points to the hearer of prayer as One in whose august presence petitions are to be made known. Acts viii. 24. See under ii. 19.

The form which the presentation of such requests was to assume was τῇ προσευχῇ καὶ τῇ δεήσει—" by prayer and supplication." The datives express the manner or means, for the one involves the other, by which the action enjoined in γνωριζέσθω was to be performed. Bernhardy, p. 100. The two nouns are not synonymous, and mean something more than Storr's *sociis precibus.* See under Eph. vi. 18 for the peculiar distinction. The repetition of the article gives each of the nouns a special independence. Winer, § 19, 5, (*a*). By the use of the first noun they are bidden tell their wants to God in religious feeling and form ; and by the second they are counselled to make them known in earnest and direct petition, in every case as the circumstances might require. But to this exercise of prayer and supplication is added thanksgiving — μετὰ εὐχαριστίας — "accompanied with thanksgiving." This noun has not the article, and, as Ellicott says, only twice has it the article in the writings of the apostle— 1 Cor. xiv. 16 ; 2 Cor. iv. 15. Alford's idea is, that the article is omitted "because the matters themselves may not be recognized as grounds of εὐχαριστία, but *it* should *accompany* every request." Ellicott thinks that "εὐχαριστία, thanksgiving for past blessings, is in its nature more general and comprehensive." Both notions, though true in themselves, are rather limited in the grounds assigned for them. For not only are there many reasons for thanksgiving to God, who has already conferred on us so much, while we are asking for more, but thankfulness is also due to Him for the very privilege of making known our requests to Him ; for the promises He has given us, and of which we put Him in remembrance when we pray to Him ; for the confidence He has created in us that such solicitations shall not be in vain ; and for the hope that He will do for us "exceeding abundantly above all that we ask or think." That He is on a throne of grace, and is ever accessible—that He is never weary with our asking—and that His gifts are never exhausted and never lose their adaptation, is surely matter of thankfulness to be ever expressed before Him by all suppliants. 1 Thess. v. 18 ; 1 Tim. ii. 1. See under Col. iv. 2.

The apostle advises such a practice universally—

ἐν παντί—"in everything." The Syriac version renders the phrase ܒܟܠܙܒܢ—"in all time," and this rendering is adopted by Grotius and Rheinwald. The phrase however stands in

direct contrast to μηδέν—care for nothing, but in everything
pray. 1 Cor. i. 5 ; 2 Cor. iv. 8, vi. 4, vii. 5, ix. 11 ; 1 Thess.
v. 18. Chrysostom thus explains—ἐν παντὶ, τουτέστι, πράγ-
ματι. Matthies proposes to connect both meanings—that of
time and place, but this would mar the directness of antithesis.
The apostle makes no exception. Nothing should disturb
their equanimity, and whatever threatened to do it should be
made matter of prayer—that God would order it otherwise,
or give grace to bear it ; or deepen reliance on Himself ; or
give them that elevation and quiet which spring from the
assurance that "the Lord is at hand." Such prayer and
supplication with thanksgiving relieves the spirit, evinces its
confidence in God, deepens its earnestness, and prepares it for
the expected answer.

(Ver. 7.) Καὶ ἡ εἰρήνη τοῦ Θεοῦ ἡ ὑπερέχουσα πάντα νοῦν,
φρουρήσει τὰς καρδίας ὑμῶν καὶ τὰ νοήματα ὑμῶν ἐν Χριστῷ
Ἰησοῦ—" And the peace of God which passes all understanding shall guard your hearts and your thoughts in Christ
Jesus." The connection indicated by καί is that of result,
and it might be paraphrased " and then," or " and so." Winer,
§ 53, 3. We find two extremes of misconception as to the
meaning of εἰρήνη τοῦ Θεοῦ—Θεοῦ being the genitive of origin,
and not of object, as Green supposes. *Greek Gram.* p. 262.
The Greek Fathers, followed by Erasmus, Estius, Crocius,
and Matthies, understand the phrase of reconciliation :—
" Peace," said Chrysostom, " that is, the reconciliation, the
love of God "—ἡ ἀγάπη τοῦ Θεοῦ. No doubt this peace is the
result of reconciliation or peace πρὸς τὸν Θεόν. But this peace
flowing from pardon and acceptance was already possessed by
them—they had been reconciled ; and what the apostle refers
to is a state of mind which has this reconciliation for its basis.
The former peace has a special relation to God, the controversy between Him and the soul being terminated—the latter
is more personal and absolute. This peace is but another
name for happiness, for it is beyond the reach of disturbance.
Come what will, it cannot injure—come when it likes, it is
welcome—and come as it may, it is blessing in disguise.
It can neither dissolve union to Christ, nor cloud the sense of
God's forgiving love, nor exclude the prospect of heavenly
glory. It is not indigenous : it is the " peace of God."

Man may train himself to apathy, or nerve himself into hardihood—the one an effort to sink below nature, and the other to rise above it. But this divine gift—the image of God's own tranquillity—is produced by close relationship to Himself, is the realization of that legacy which the Elder Brother has bequeathed. John xiv. 27. To know that it is well with me now, and that it shall be so for ever—to feel that God is my guide and protector, while His Son pleads for me and His Spirit dwells within me as His shrine—to feel that I am moving onward along a path divinely prescribed and guarded, to join the eternal banquet in the company of all I love and all I live for—the emotion produced by such strong conviction is peace, ay, the "peace of God." This view is adopted generally by expositors. See what is said in our comment under Col. iii. 15. Augustine, followed by Anselm and Beelen, explains the phrase—"peace of God"—as *pax, qua ipse Deus pacatus est. De Civ. Dei*, lib. xxii. 29. We may place two English expositors side by side—Macknight, who understands by "peace of God" the hope of eternal life, and Pierce, who takes it to mean, "a sense of the great advantage of having peace with God." In much the same spirit, men of the school of Glassius would take τοῦ Θεοῦ as the so-called Hebrew superlative,—an idiom unknown to the New Testament, and a miserable dilution of the sense.

The notion of Meyer, preceded by Hammond and Michaelis, that this "peace of God" is unity or ecclesiastical concord, cannot be sustained. Εἰρήνη, according to him, has always a relative meaning—*verhältniss zu andern Menschen oder zu Gott ;* but the places quoted by him will not suffice as proof. In the majority of them peace is described as a personal blessing. Rom. xv. 33 ; John xiv. 27. It is true that the apostle in the second and third verses of this chapter counsels the healing of a breach, or the restoration of peace, but he has now passed from these matters to other advices. He has uttered the keynote—"Rejoice in the Lord," and he now speaks in its spirit. There may in the ἐπιεικές be an allusion to the exhortation to Euodia and Syntyche—as Theodoret supposes in his reference, ὡς ὑπαλλήλων ὄντων τῶν διωγμῶν, but the contrast to εἰρήνη lies in μηδὲν μεριμνᾶτε. Now, this "being careful" could scarcely be the ground of disunion among the Philippians, as Meyer s hypothesis would make it; for it seems to have been vainglory and ostentation. The allusion is more general—and if this solicitude be relieved by free and cordial prayerfulness, then unbroken tranquillity should guard the soul. The apostle describes this peace as a gift "passing all knowledge"—ἡ ὑπερέχουσα πάντα νοῦν. See what is said under Eph. iii. 19. The participle here governs the accusative, and not, as is common with verbs of its class, the genitive, Kühner, § 539; or Jelf, § 504, *Obser.* 2. The noun νοῦς is here used of mind in its power of grasp or conception, as in Luke xxiv. 45, where it is said—τότε διήνοιξεν αὐτῶν τὸν νοῦν— "then opened He their mind that they might understand the Scriptures," Rev. xiii. 18. The mind cannot rightly estimate this peace, or rise to an adequate comprehension of it. It is so rich, so pure, so noble, so fraught with bliss, that you cannot imagine its magnitude. It is out of the question to suppose, with De Wette, who forgets the sweep of the epithet πάντα, that νοῦς is a doubting or distracted mind, which can find neither end nor issue, and that therefore this peace passes all understanding, as it rests on faith and feeling. Chrysostom, influenced by the signification he has attached to peace, gives another turn to the meaning, as in this question—τίς γὰρ ἂν προσεδόκησε τίς δὲ ἂν ἤλπισε τοσαῦτα ἔσεσθαι ἀγαθά ; The opinion of Estius is somewhat similar, while Calvin, looking more to the result, says—*quia nihil humano ingenio magis adversum, quam in summa desperatione nihilominus sperare.* The apostle means that even its possessor is not able fully to understand its nature and blessedness. He then says what this peace, which is above all conception, shall effect—

φρουρήσει τὰς καρδίας ὑμῶν καὶ τὰ νοήματα ὑμῶν—" shall guard your hearts and your thoughts." The verb is used of a military guard, like that set over a prisoner. 2 Cor. xi. 32; Gal. iii. 23; Xen. *Cyro.* i. 2, 12; Josephus, *Bell. Jud.* iii. 8, 2; Thucyd. iii. 17. The verb is in the future and is to be so translated and understood, and not, with many, as if it were in the subjunctive and expressed a charge, or as if it were optative and contained a wish. It predicts a sure result of the habit described and enforced in the preceding verse. The last of the two nouns, νοήματα, signifies the results or offspring of the active νοῦς, while καρδία in such a connection may denote the seat or source of feeling and thought. But νοῦς is so allied to the καρδία, the centre of all spiritual life and activity, that these νοήματα are supposed to spring from the latter. Usteri, *Paulin. Lehrb.* p. 411. Both the one and the other shall be guarded—the heart kept from disquietude, and the same unrest warded away from the thoughts and associations. Whatever should enter into the one and beget uneasiness, or suggest such a train of ideas, forebodings, or questions to the other, as should tend to perplexity and alarm, is charmed away by "the peace of God." For while that against which heart and thoughts are guarded is taken absolutely, it may, specially, be the origination of such a state as is implied in the warning—μηδὲν μεριμνᾶτε, and not generally enemies, or Satan, or evil cogitations, or, as Theophylact expounds—ὥστε μηδὲ ἐννοῆσαί τι πονηρόν. The apostle next refers to the sphere in which that safekeeping takes place—

ἐν Χριστῷ Ἰησοῦ—" in Christ Jesus." Ἐν is not synonymous with διά, is neither *per* nor *propter.* This guardianship of heart and thought takes effect only "in Christ Jesus." Nay, the peace itself is based on union with Jesus, and its vigilance and success are derived from a closer enjoyment of the presence and a more vivid appreciation of the promises of Christ. Others take this clause as indicating the result of the verb φρουρήσει—" shall keep your hearts and your thoughts in Christ Jesus," that is, shall preserve your union with Him. De Wette holds this view in imitation of Luther, and it is adopted by Storr, Rheinwald, van Hengel, Rilliet, and Wiesinger. Chrysostom has already stated as the result— ὥστε μένειν καὶ μὴ ἐκπεσεῖν αὐτοῦ τῆς πίστεως. But it is rather union with Christ which secures this peace, and not this peace which cements the union. The more one realizes this union, the more does he possess of such a peace. And as every gift of God is in Christ conferred, and every act of God is done in Him, so in Him too does the peace of God exert its guarding influence. As the result of prayer, of the unbosoming of themselves to God about everything, they should enjoy profound tranquillity. Committing their way unto God, they would feel that " He would make perfect that

which concerned them," and should have within them an
unruffled calm—bliss beyond all conception.

(Ver. 8.) The apostle brings this section to a conclusion by
the common formula—τὸ λοιπόν—"in fine." In a composition like this letter, where compactness is not to be expected,
it would be finical to refer this τὸ λοιπόν to that occurring in
iii. 1. There it introduces, here it terminates a section. The
apostle winds up the sundry counsels contained in the preceding verse. We admit a connection, and therefore deny van
Hengel's notion—*ad rem alius argumenti transgreditur, ut
ostendit formula* τὸ λοιπόν. But we cannot wholly acquiesce
in De Wette's idea, that the connection is of this kind—verse
seventh showing what God does, and verse eighth what remains
for man to do. Perhaps the previous verses suggested this
summing up to the apostle, which is still in the spirit of the
precept, "Rejoice in the Lord," and they intimate that while
there is freedom from solicitude through prayer, there should
be a reaching after perfection ; and that in order to preserve
this peace unbroken within them, they should sedulously
cultivate those elements of Christian morality which are next
enumerated with singular fervour and succinctness.

The syntax is peculiar. Six ethical terms are employed,
and each has ὅσα prefixed, and in token of emphasis the whole
is prefaced by ἀδελφοί. The rhythm and repetition are impressive. We do not think, with Wiesinger, that the apostle
means to designate the entire compass of Christian morality.
We rather think that the virtues referred to are such as not
only specially adorn "the doctrine of God our Saviour," but
also such as may have been needed in Philippi. In each
case, the apostle does not use abstract terms, but says—
"Whatever things," that is, what things come under the cate-
gory of each designation—"these things meditate," the ὅσα
giving to each the notion of universality, and of course that
of conformity to the verb λογίζεσθε. And first—

ὅσα ἐστὶν ἀληθῆ—"whatsoever things are true." It is too
vague, on the part of Œcumenius, to explain ἀληθῆ by τὰ
ἐνάρετα—"the excellent." The adjective does not signify
what is credible in opposition to what is fictitious, or what is
substantial in contrast with what is shadowy. Nor should
we, with Robinson, Meyer, and De Wette, confine the epithet

to the gospel and its truth; nor with Theodoret, Bengel, and Bisping, to language; nor with others, to the absence of dissimulation. We take it to mean generally—"morally truthful," whether specially referred to and illustrated in the gospel or not. For truth exists independently of the gospel, though the gospel has shed special light on its nature and obligation. They are to think on "the true" in everything of which it can be predicated—both in reference to God and man, the church and the world, themselves and others—the true in its spiritual and secular relations, in thought, speech, and position. See under Eph. iv. 25.

ὅσα σεμνά—"whatsoever things are grave," or "decorous." The adjective characterizes persons in 1 Tim. iii. 8, 11, and Tit. ii. 2, in which places it stands opposed to a double tongue, to intemperance and avarice, to slander and unfaithfulness, and may denote becomingness or gravity of conduct. In classic Greek it has the sense of revered or venerated, from its connection with σέβομαι. Benfey, *Wurzellex.* i. p. 407. As applied to things, it may denote what in itself commands respect—what is noble or honourable—*magnifica*, as in Ambrosiaster. The *pudica* of the Vulgate is too limited. Our translators have used the epithet "honest" in its Latin or old English sense, signifying, but in fuller form, what is now termed "honourable." Thus, in the Bible of 1551—"and upon those members of the body which we thynke lest *honest*, put we moste *honestie* on." "Goodness," says Sir William Temple, in his *Essay on Government*, "in our language, goes rather by the name of honesty." Or in Ben Jonson—"You have *honested* my lodgings with your presence." Richardson's *Dictionary, sub voce.* To illustrate this restricted sense of the term, one may recall the lines of Burns about the Scottish Muse—

> "Her eye, even turned on empty space,
> Beamed keen with honour."

But σεμνά has a wider reach of meaning. We find it associated with such epithets as ἅγιον, μέτριον, καλὸν κἀγαθόν, and μεγαλοπρεπές, and it may point out the things which in dignity and honour, in gravity and nobleness, befit the position, character, and destiny of a believer. It is opposed to what is mean, frivolous, indecorous, and unworthy. *Quid*

verum atque decens curo et rogo, et omnis in hoc sum.   Horace,
Ep. lib. i. 1.

ὅσα δίκαια—" whatsoever things are right "—whatsoever
things are in accordance with eternal and unchanging rectitude.   We would not with many restrict it to equity or justice
as springing out of mutual relations.   Thus Calvin—*ne quem
lædamus, ne quem fraudemus*, which is only one province of the
right.   The last epithet appeals more to sentiment, but this
to principle.   The right does not depend on legislation, but is
everlasting and immutable.   It is but a fallacious word-worship
on the part of Horne Tooke to assert that right is simply
what is *ordered, rectum*—(*regitum*), but quite in accordance
with the theory of Hobbes.   Dugald Stewart's *Philosophical
Essays*, Essay v. 2nd ed.; Edin. 1816.

ὅσα ἀγνά—" whatsoever things are pure."   The Vulgate
renders *sancta*, as if the Greek epithet had been ἅγια.   Tittmann's *Syn.* i. p. 22.   This term is used specially of chastity
or modesty— 2 Cor. xi. 2 ; Tit. ii. 5—and several critics,
as Grotius and Estius, take such to be its meaning here.   We
take it in the broader sense in which it is found in 2 Cor.
vi. 6, vii. 11 ; 1 Tim. v. 22 ; Jas. iii. 17.   " Whatever things
are pure "—which are neither tainted nor corrupt—free from
all debasing elements, clear in nature, transparent in purpose,
leaving no blot on the conscience and no stain on the character.
In Pindar it is the epithet of Apollo or the Sun—καὶ ἀγνὸν
Ἀπόλλωνα, *Pyth.* ix. 112.   Chrysostom's distinction between
this and the preceding epithet is, τὸ σεμνὸν τῆς ἔξω ἐστὶ
δυνάμεως, τὸ δὲ ἀγνὸν τῆς ψυχῆς.

ὅσα προσφιλῆ —" whatsoever things are lovely."   This
term occurs only here in the New Testament.   It is, however,
not uncommon with classical writers, and signifies what is
dear to any one, or has in it such a quality as engages affection
—lovely as exciting love.   Sirach iv. 7, xx. 13.   The meaning
is too much diluted by the Greek expositors and others who
follow them in giving the term a relation τοῖς πιστοῖς καὶ
τῷ Θεῷ.   Grotius and Erasmus hold another view, which is not
warranted by the context.   According to them, it may denote
" benignant," or " kindly disposed."   But special virtues, as
Meyer says, are not here enumerated.   " Whatsoever things are
lovely "—whatever modes of action tend to endear him that

does them, to give him with others not simply the approval of their judgment, but to open for him a place in their hearts—whatever things breathe the spirit of that religion which is love, and the doing of which should be homage to Him who is Love—"these things think on."

ὅσα εὔφημα —"whatsoever things are of good report." This word, like the former, is found only here in the New Testament, though the noun occurs in 2 Cor. vi. 8. Its composition tells its force—"what is well spoken of." It had a peculiar meaning in Pagan usage—that which is of good omen, and a similar meaning Meyer would find here —was einen glücklichen Laut hat. But the result is not different in the more ordinary acceptation. Hesychius gives it the meaning of ἐπαινετά. Storr, without ground, prefers another sense, which makes the verb mean bene precari—to express good wishes for others, and he renders the adjective by benedictum. Whatever things on being seen lead all who behold them to exclaim—"Well-done!"—or indicate on the part of the actor such elements of character as are usually admired and well spoken of; deeds that sound well on being named, whether they consist of chivalrous generosity or meek condescension—a great feat or a good one—noble in idea or happy in execution. An action as right is vindicated by the judgment, as good it is approved by the heart, but as indicating generosity or nobleness of soul it is applauded. The apostle subjoins in his earnestness—

εἴ τις ἀρετὴ, καὶ εἴ τις ἔπαινος—"whatever virtue there is, and whatever praise there is." Some MSS., as D¹, E¹, F, G, add ἐπιστήμης; Vulgate, disciplinæ. In the phrase εἴ τις there is no expression of doubt, on the one hand; nor, on the other hand, is the meaning that assigned by De Wette, van Hengel, Rheinwald, and others—if there be any other virtue, or any other object of praise, that is, other than those already mentioned, but not formally expressed. The clause is an emphatic and earnest summation. See under ii. 1. The term ἀρετή is only here used by Paul. In the philosophical writings of Greece it signified all virtue, and not any special form of it, as it does in Homer and others. The apostle nowhere else uses it—it had been too much debased and soiled in some of the schools, and ideas were oftentimes attached to it very different from that moral excellence which with him was virtue. It is therefore here employed in its widest and highest sense of moral excellence—*virtus*, that which becomes a man redeemed by the blood of Christ and tenanted by the Holy Spirit. It is spoken of God in 1 Pet. ii. 9. From its connection with the Sanscrit *vri*—to be strong—Latin, *vir*—*vires*—*virtus*; or with Ἄρης—ἄριστος, it seems to signify what best becomes a man—manhood, strength or valour, in early times. Benfey, *Wurzellex*. i. p. 315. But the signification has been modified by national character and temperament. The warlike Romans placed their virtue in military courage; while their successors, the modern degenerate Italians, often apply it to a knowledge of antiquities or fine arts. The remains of other and nobler times are articles of virtu, and he who has most acquaintance with them is a virtuoso or man of virtue. In our common English, a woman's virtue is simply and alone her chastity, as being first and indispensable; and with our Scottish ancestors virtue was thrift or industry.[1] Amidst such national variations, and the unsettled metaphysical disquisitions as to what forms virtue or what is its basis, it needed that He who created man for Himself should tell him what best became him—what he was made for and what he should aspire to. The noun ἔπαινος is praise in itself, and not *res laudabilis*, a thing to be praised, though many, including the lexicographers Robinson, Wahl, and Bretschneider, take such a view. It is not therefore anything to be praised, but any praise to be bestowed—*laus comes virtutis*, as Erasmus writes; or as Cicero—*consentiens laus bonorum incorrupta vox bene judicantium de excellente virtute*. Meyer gives as an example the thirteenth chapter of 1 Cor. —the praise of charity. And the apostle concludes with the expressive charge—

ταῦτα λογίζεσθε—"these things think upon." They were to ponder on these things, not as matters of mere speculation, but of highest ethical moment, and of immediate practical utility.

The apostle does not mean to exhibit every element of a

---

[1] An old Act commands schools or houses of "vertue," in which might be manufactured "cloth and sergis," to be erected in every shire. Jamieson's *Scottish Dictionary*, Supplement.

perfect character, but only some of its phases. Cicero says,
De Fin. iii. 4, 14—*Quonam modo, inquam, si una virtus,
unum istud, quod honestum appellas, rectum, laudabile, decorum
—erit enim notius quale sit pluribus notatum vocabulis idem
declarantibus.* These ethical terms are closely united, nay,
they blend together; the true, the decorous, the right, and the
pure, are but different aspects or exemplifications of one great
principle, leaves on the same stem. The first four terms
seem to be gathered together into ἀρετή; the two last—
"lovely and of good report"—into ἔπαινος. The true, the
becoming, the right, and the pure are elements of virtue or
moral excellence in themselves; but when exhibited in the
living pursuit and practice of them, they assume the form of
the lovely and well-reported, and then they merit and command praise. In still closer connection, the apostle enjoins—

(Ver. 9.) ᾍ καὶ ἐμάθετε, καὶ παρελάβετε, καὶ ἠκούσατε, καὶ
εἴδετε ἐν ἐμοί, ταῦτα πράσσετε—"which things also ye learned
and received, and heard and saw in me, these things do."
Bengel says, with his usual point—*facit transitionem a gene-
ralibus ad Paulina.* By the pronoun ἅ the apostle refers to
things just enumerated and enforced, and not to other things
yet and now to be spoken of. He does not write ὅσα, but ἅ
—giving precision and definiteness to his counsels. The first
καί, as Meyer remarks, is simply "also," the meaning being
virtually "which things"—those of ver. 8—"ye have also
learned of me." The sentences, at the same time, are so far
distinct as the concluding verbs of each indicate. The four
verbs are simply connected by καί, and the meaning is not—
which ye have as well learned as received, as in the recent
version of Ewald—*was ihr wie lerntet so annahmet wie hörtet so
sahet an mir.* The four verbs are to be distinguished, for
they are neither synonymous nor is the clause tautological.
The first, ἐμάθετε, refers to instruction. Rom. xvi. 17 ; Col.
i. 7. The next term, παρελάβετε, denotes the result of
instruction, the appropriation of the knowledge conveyed, or
the fact that they had assented to it or had embraced it.
1 Cor. xv. 1 ; Gal. i. 12 ; 1 Thess. ii. 13. They had been
instructed, and they had accepted the instruction, and therefore were they bound to abide by it. It is unwarranted in
Grotius to find in ἐμάθετε the sense of *prima institutio*, and in

παρελάβετε that of *exactior doctrina.* Hoelemann as ground-
lessly refers the first verb to the genus, and the others to the
species, though he admits that the structure of the verse does
not favour his view. Rilliet, too, makes this distinction—*son
enseignement direct,* μανθάνω *les instructions qu'il leur a trans-
mises sous une forme quelconque*—παραλαμβάνω. But more
precisely—

καὶ ἠκούσατε καὶ εἴδετε ἐν ἐμοί—"and heard and saw in
me." The phrase ἐν ἐμοί is connected with both verbs. The
apostle has referred to his public instructions, and now he
concludes with his personal example. What they heard in
connection with him is the report about him circulating in the
church—the character which was usually given him. Chap.
iii. 17. Calvin and some others suppose the "hearing" to
refer to Paul's oral instructions in Philippi—*les recits,* as
Rilliet writes; but after the two preceding verbs this would
be a needless repetition. Nor does it vaguely signify *de me
absente,* as Hoelemann gives it. "And saw in me"—what
they had witnessed in his conduct and character. His appeal
is as in 1 Thess. ii. 9–12. The two first verbs seem to refer
to his official conduct, and the two last to his private demeanour. In connecting ἐν ἐμοί with ἠκούσατε as well as εἴδετε,
it is needless to resort to the supposition of a zeugma. Nor
is there any use in supposing, with Rilliet and van Hengel,
that ἐν ἐμοί belongs equally and formally to all the four
verbs. And the charge is—

ταῦτα πράσσετε—"these things practise." It is not simply
now—λογίζεσθε. Chrysostom says—μὴ λέγετε μόνον, ἀλλὰ
καὶ πράττετε, but no contrast of this nature is intended, for
the one term includes the other. Meyer supposes that there
is a kind of formal parallelism—that both verbs really belong
to both verses. Rom. x. 10. Perhaps this is too refined.
The apostle first enumerates the things possessed of certain
specified qualities, and bids his readers think on them, for a
mindless obedience would be accidental, and therefore worthless. But then he connects the previous general statement
with his personal instructions, and their received tuition ; nay,
embodies it in his own character, and therefore he boldly
bids them reproduce his lessons and example in their own
experience and life. The four verbs are a species of climax :

—ἐμάθετε, παρελάβετε, ἠκούσατε, εἴδετε—" ye learned," more general; " ye took up," more pointed; " ye heard," more personal; " ye saw in me," decided and definite. It is not simply Paul the teacher, but Paul the man, how he was reported of, nay, how he demeaned himself. It is not, do as I taught you, but also do as ye heard of me doing and saw me doing, in reference to all the elements of virtue and praise. And then—

καὶ ὁ Θεὸς τῆς εἰρήνης ἔσται μεθ' ὑμῶν—" and then," or " and so the God of peace shall be with you." The meaning of καί is as in the beginning of verse 7. The phrase God of peace is parallel to the preceding one—peace of God. In the former case the peace is described in its connection with God, and now God is pointed out as the inworker of this peace. It characterizes Him, and in this aspect belongs to what Scheuerlein calls die dominirenden Eigenschaften, p. 115. The phrase " God of peace" must not be weakened into Deus benignissimus. The words μεθ' ὑμῶν resemble a common expression in the Old Testament—עִמָּכֶם. To specify any single purpose which the presence of the God of peace with them should accomplish is useless and restricted, for He will work out every purpose—συνεργὸς τῶν ὅλων. The presence and operations of the God of peace are like the peace of God —they pass all understanding. And this sounds like the apostle's farewell—a pledge of peace to those who were aiming at the high Christian excellence described in the two previous verses, in whom the faith of the gospel had wrought a change which might ripen at length into the perfection of ethical symmetry and beauty.

(Ver. 10.) Ἐχάρην δὲ ἐν Κυρίῳ μεγάλως—" But I rejoiced in the Lord greatly." The apostle with the metabatic δέ passes to the business part of the letter—a personal subject which seems to have in part suggested the composition of the epistle. A gift had been brought to him, and he acknowledges it. The style of acknowledgment is quite like himself. In the fulness of his heart he first pours out a variety of suggestive and momentous counsels, and towards the conclusion he adds a passing word on the boon which Epaphroditus had brought him. He rejoiced over the gift in no selfish spirit; his joy was ἐν Κυρίῳ, in the Lord, iii. 1, iv. 1. That is to say, his

was a Christian gladness. The gift was contributed in the
Lord, and in a like spirit he exulted in the reception of it.
It was a proof to him, not simply that personally he was not
forgotten, but also that his converts still realized their special
and tender obligations to him as their spiritual father. And
his joy was rapturous—μεγάλως. 1 Chron. xxix. 9—εὐφράνθη
μεγάλως. Neh. xii. 43—ὁ Θεὸς ηὔφρανεν αὐτοὺς μεγάλως.
In the past tense of the verb, the apostle refers to his emotion
when he first touched the gift, and for the form ἐχάρην see
Buttmann, § 114.

The apostle now uses expressive phraseology; the figure
being suggested not by the season of the year at which the
gift was sent, as Bengel's fancy is, but the thought in its
freshness budded into poetry—

ὅτι ἤδη ποτὲ ἀνεθάλετε τὸ ὑπὲρ ἐμοῦ φρονεῖν—" that now at
length ye have flourished again in mindfulness for me." The
language implies that some time had elapsed since the state
expressed by the first verb had been previously witnessed.
The interval may have exceeded five years, and Chrysostom,
specifying—it as μακρόν, thinks, without foundation, that
the clause implies a rebuke. The ποτέ throws a shade of
indefiniteness over the ἤδη. Devarius, Klotz, vol. ii. p. 607;
Kypke, ad Rom. i. 10. The apostle does not deny the existence of the φρονεῖν at any moment; he simply hints that for
some time it had not been in a fertile or productive state. The
churches of Macedonia are highly praised for their liberality.
2 Cor. viii. 1, 2. We take the infinitive φρονεῖν as simply
dependent upon ἀνεθάλετε used in an intransitive sense, and
τὸ ὑπὲρ ἐμοῦ as its object.

There is indeed no grammatical objection to the transitive
meaning. The word is found only here in the New Testament;
but in the Hellenistic Greek of the Septuagint and Apocrypha
it occurs often with the transitive sense. Ezek. xvii. 24;
Sirach i. 18; xi. 22; l. 10. It is taken in this sense here by
Cocceius, Hoelemann, Rilliet, and De Wette. It is difficult to
render the sentence literally into English. In their care of
the apostle they had put forth new shoots; they had been as
a tree which had been bare and blossomless in winter, but
they had grown green again and had yielded fruit; for this
last idea is implied in the context. The transitive form of

the verb would preserve the notion of activity or conscious effort on their part, as one source of the apostle's joy. On the other hand, many, perhaps the majority, prefer the passive signification, adopted by the Greek expositors and many others. Thus Chrysostom—ἐπὶ δένδρων βλαστησάντων, εἶτα ξηρανθέντων, καὶ πάλιν βλαστησάντων. The word occurs with this signification in Ps. xxviii. 7; Wisd. iv. 4. Thus we may either speak of a tree revived, or a tree putting forth its buds and foliage. Wiesinger objects to the transitive sense, because ἀναθάλλειν is represented as not having been dependent on the will of the Philippians. But this is to press the figure too hardly, and to destroy the merit of the gift. The apostle's idea is—that the season had been inclement, and that during its continuance they could not flourish in their care of him, though they greatly desired it. Their bud had been nipped, but revirescence had begun. Meyer, objecting to the transitive sense, holds that τὸ ὑπὲρ ἐμοῦ φρονεῖν is not the object of ἀνεθάλετε, and that the verb is simply connected with the infinitive φρονεῖν. But in his opinion, they flourished green again, not in their care for the apostle, which had never withered, but in their own temporal circumstances. In this view he had been preceded by Schleusner, Wahl, Matthies, and van Hengel, who says—*ut Philippenses ad priscam prosperitatem rediise significaret.* The idea, however, is not supported by the context—they did care, the apostle affirms, but they wanted opportunity, not ability. He therefore seems to say, that their care of him had been for a time like sap and life in the veins of a tree, but an inclement season had prevented it from forming foliage and blossom.

ἐφ' ᾧ καὶ ἐφρονεῖτε. What is the proper meaning of ἐφ' ᾧ? We cannot, with Calvin, Rilliet, and Bretschneider, make μου the antecedent, or supply to ᾧ the name of the apostle—*erga quem*—the formula being invariably used by the apostle in the neuter gender. Various other renderings have been given. Thus De Wette—*qua de re;* a-Lapide, *in qua re;* while others make it *in quo*, in respect of which. Not a few contend for an adverbial signification, the Vulgate having *sicut*, and van Hengel *quemadmodum*, Luther *wiewohl*, and Winer *weshalb*. To give to ἐφ' ᾧ the entire clause as antecedent would, as Meyer and Wiesinger say, bring out this strange collocation—ἐφρονεῖτε ἐπὶ τῷ τὸ ὑπὲρ ἐμοῦ φρονεῖν; yet Wiesinger inclines to adopt it, and he is followed by Ellicott. Wiesinger gives φρονεῖν a somewhat different sense in the two clauses, and says—"Could not the apostle, while he regarded the first φρονεῖν as a proof of their solicitude for him, say with perfect propriety, such an actual care for me was the object of your care?" that is, you were solicitous to show or prove your solicitude. But this construction does appear clumsy and illogical. The phrase ἐφ' ᾧ might indeed be taken in an adverbial sense, might be rendered "for," or *propterea quod*. Rom. v. 12; 2 Cor. v. 4. Thus Thomas Magister—ἐφ' ᾧ, ἀντὶ διότι. See also Phavorinus—ἐφ' ᾧ, ἀντὶ τοῦ διότι. See under iii. 12, p. 194. See also Meyer, Fritzsche, Philippi, and Olshausen *on Rom.* v. 12. It might then be rendered — "I rejoiced that you have flourished again in your care for me, because indeed ye were caring for me, but ye lacked opportunity." But perhaps the phrase τὸ ὑπὲρ ἐμοῦ φρονεῖν is best resolved, as we have said, by taking τὸ ὑπὲρ ἐμοῦ as the object of the verb, and regarding it as meaning "my interest;" and then τὸ ὑπὲρ ἐμοῦ becomes the antecedent to ἐφ' ᾧ—"for which," that is, for my interest, or as to what specially befits me, ye were also mindful. The cause of his joy was not their care for him in itself—that had never been absent, as he says; but he rejoiced that it had found renewed opportunity of manifestation. Θάλλειν could once be predicated of their solicitude, as when they sent once and again to Thessalonica to his necessities; but the season became unpropitious. What made it so we know not—probably the distance of the apostle from them; or perhaps they thought that other churches should take up on them the obligation. Their solicitude was during all this period still in existence, but θάλλειν could not be predicated of it—they were unproductive. But now they burst into verdure, and the apostle says to them ἀνεθάλετε—ye came into leaf again. They were not to suppose that he censured them for forgetting him; and lest his language should be so misconstrued, he adds—for my interest ye were also mindful. The contrast, then, lies between the simple imperfect ἐφρονεῖτε—the care of him being all the while present—and the ἀνεθάλετε φρονεῖν, a new and flourishing manifestation of

it. The apostle, in a word, does not joy over the existence of
their care, for of its existence he had never doubted, but over
its second spring. Meyer thinks that the omission of μέν
after ἐφρονεῖτε gives emphasis to the contrast. For examples
of the opposite—of μέν without δέ—see Acts i. 1, iv. 16.

ἠκαιρεῖσθε δέ—"but ye lacked opportunity." The verb
belongs to the later Greek. Phryn. Lobeck, p. 125. It occurs
only here in the New Testament; ἀκαίρως is used in 2 Tim.
iv. 2 ; but the opposite compound εὐκαιρεῖν and its substantive
and adjective are found several times. The phrase may mean
more than *opportunitas mittendi*—ye would, but ye could not
find an opportune period or occasion. Circumstances were
unpropitious, but we have no means of discovering the actual
cause. So that the view of Chrysostom cannot be sustained
—οὐκ εἴχετε ἐν χερσίν. He says that this meaning which he
gives the verb was a common one, derived from popular use
—ἀπὸ τῆς κοινῆς συνηθείας. Theodore of Mopsuestia has the
same view. As vain is it, on the part of Storr and Flatt, to
refer the obstacle to Judaizing teachers. It may be remem-
bered that one of the earliest fruits of the apostle's labours at
Philippi was the kindness of hospitality. Lydia said, " Come
into my house and abide there, and she constrained us."
And the jailor even, when his heart had been touched, " took
them the same hour of the night and washed their stripes "—
" brought them into his house and set meat before them."
Acts xvi. 15, 33, 34. If the mindfulness of the Philippian
church resembled these specimens, the apostle could have no
hesitation in saying—" ye were also careful, but ye lacked
opportunity."

The apostle now with a peculiar delicacy guards himself
against misconstruction. He might have referred to the lofty
disinterestedness of his past life ; to the fact that he had
wrought with his own hands to supply his necessities ; that he
had not been ashamed to stoop to the craft he had learned in
youth, and earn by it a scanty subsistence—waiving in some
cases the right which he had firmly vindicated, and based
more on equity than generosity, that "they which preach the
gospel should live of the gospel."

(Ver. 11.) Οὐχ ὅτι καθ᾽ ὑστέρησιν λέγω—"Not that I speak
on account of want." The formula οὐχ ὅτι, introducing an

explanation, occurs in iii. 12, iv. 17 ; 2 Cor. i. 24 ; 2 Thess.
iii. 9. Winer, § 64, 6. See under iii. 12, p. 193. The κατά
has the signification here which it has in various places, and
denotes " occasion." Matt. xix. 3 ; Acts iii. 17 ; Winer,
§ 49, d, b, (b) ; Robinson, *sub voce ;* Raphel. *in loc.* The Syriac
has given it quite correctly—" I have not spoken because
there is need to me," and Wycliffe—" I seie not as for nede."
Van Hengel's care to give κατά its ordinary meaning, " after
the manner of," is superfluous—*ut more receptum est penuriæ.*
Theophylact explains it by διά. The two senses of the preposition are intimately connected, the one suggesting and
warranting the other. It was not the pressure of penury that
prompted the apostle's joy, nor yet the mere value of that sum
sent to secure relief. He was in straits—the Roman law
allowed no luxury to its prisoners ; but he was excited to this
utterance not by a sense of want, but by other motives of a
higher and nobler nature. The gold and silver sent to him
were not valued and made a matter of thanksgiving simply
as the means of rescue from indigence, or as enabling him
either to procure this comfort or to discharge that obligation.
He rose above such a feeling, for to want he was no stranger,
and he had learned contentment under all circumstances. At
the same time, as Wiesinger says, " he does not deny the fact
of his being in want." But he received the gift as the symbol
of spiritual good wrought in Philippi by his preaching, and
the reception of it proving their tender attachment to him still,
was all the more soothing and refreshing amidst the coldness
and hostility which he was encountering at Rome. Chap.
i. 12, etc. He proceeds to give the great reason why it was
that he had so spoken, but not for want's sake—

ἐγὼ γὰρ ἔμαθον, ἐν οἷς εἰμὶ, αὐτάρκης εἶναι—" for I (for my
part) have learned in the circumstances in which I am to be
content." The epithet αὐτάρκης means self-sufficing, having
within one what produces contentment. The special idea of
not being dependent on others is sometimes found in it, as πόλις
αὐτάρκης, a city that does not need to import. Thucyd. i. 37.
Perhaps, however, this idea is not formally connected with
the word when used ethically, though still it may be implied.
Wiesinger objects that this state of self-competence, or of not
requiring the assistance of others, never can be learned. Now,

surely there is no lesson more frequent: for the mind, as it is thrown upon its own resources, learns its strength, and becomes through such discipline its own support. The apostle was content, and that state of contentment was the result of a long and varied experience—ἔμαθον. He does not, by the use of this verb, refer, as Pelagius and Bengel imagine, to divinely-given instruction—" a Christo." Heb. v. 8. In the use and position of the ἐγώ, he gives prominence to his own individual training, and its result—"I for my part." The apostle learned contentment, but he does not say that he had created it within him. He had learned it in whatever way it could be acquired, and he cherished it. It was not self-infused, but experience had brought it to him. This was true philosophy, for discontent could not have removed the evil, and would only have embittered what little good remained. The captive may shake the chain, but as he cannot shake it off, his impatient effort only galls his limbs with aggravated severity.

And that contentment was not an incidental state of mind, nor restricted to his present state, for he says—ἐν οἷς εἰμί, " in the condition in which I am." The relative is neuter, and not masculine, as Luther renders it. Kypke, *Observ.* ii. p. 319. The right translation is not " in whatever state I may be," but " in whatever state I am"—realizing as present, not only each of the various states described in the following verse, but any state in which Providence might place him. The contentment which the apostle universally and uniformly possessed, sprang not from indifference, apathy, or desperation. It was not sullen submission to his fate, not the death of hope within him. He felt what want was, and keenly felt it, and therefore he gladly accepted of relief, and rejoiced in all such manifestations of Christian sympathy. Nor was he self-sufficient in the ordinary or the common sense of the term. It was no egotistic delusion that upheld him, nor did he ever invoke the storm to show that he could brave it. But his mind calmly bowed to the will of God in every condition in which he was placed. For that wondrous equanimity and cheerfulness which far excelled the stolid and stubborn endurance ascribed to heathen stoicism, gave him the mastery over circumstances. He felt the evil, but surmounted it—a purer triumph than with a petrified heart to be unconscious of it. Socrates in

Stobæus, lib. v. § 43, is reported to have said—αὐτάρκεια φύσεώς ἐστι πλοῦτος. See Barrow's five sermons on this text. Jeremy Taylor, *Holy Living*, iv., with his wonted wealth of genius, writes :—" If your estate be lessened, you need the less to care who governs the province, whether he be rude or gentle. I am crossed in my journey, and yet I 'scaped robbers ; and I consider, that if I had been set upon by villains, I would have redeemed that evil by this, which I now suffer, and have counted it a deliverance : or if I did fall into the hands of thieves, yet they did not steal my land. Or I am fallen into the hands of publicans and sequestrators, and they have taken all from me : what now ? let me look about me. They have left me the sun and moon, fire and water, a loving wife, and many friends to pity me, and some to relieve me, and I can still discourse ; and, unless I list, they have not taken away my merry countenance, and my cheerful spirit, and a good conscience : they still have left me the providence of God, and all the promises of the gospel, and my religion, and my hopes of heaven, and my charity to them too ; and still I sleep and digest, I eat and drink, I read and meditate, I can walk in my neighbour's pleasant fields, and see the varieties of natural beauties and delight in all that in which God delights, that is, in virtue and wisdom, in the whole creation, and in God Himself. And he that hath so many causes of joy, and so great, is very much in love with sorrow and peevishness, who loses all these pleasures, and chooses to sit down upon his little handful of thorns. Is that beast better, that hath two or three mountains to graze on, than the little bee that feeds on dew or manna, and lives upon what falls every morning from the storehouses of heaven, clouds and Providence ? Can a man quench his thirst better out of a river than a full urn, or drink better from the fountain, which is finely paved with marble, than when it swells over the green turf ? Pride and artificial gluttonies do but adulterate nature, making our diet healthless, our appetites impatient and unsatisfiable, and the taste mixed, fantastical, and meretricious. But that which we miscall poverty, is indeed nature : and its proportions are the just measures of a man, and the best instruments of content. But when we create needs that God or nature never made, we have erected to

ourselves an infinite stock of trouble, that can have no period.
Sempronius complained of want of clothes, and was much
troubled for a new suit, being ashamed to appear in the
theatre with his gown a little threadbare: but when he got
it, and gave his old clothes to Codrus, the poor man was
ravished with joy, and went and gave God thanks for his new
purchase; and Codrus was made richly fine and cheerfully
warm by that which Sempronius was ashamed to wear ; and
yet their natural needs were both alike."

(Ver. 12.) Οἶδα καὶ ταπεινοῦσθαι, οἶδα καὶ περισσεύειν--" I
know also to be abased, I know also to abound." The καί after
the first οἶδα is accepted on preponderant authority, instead
of the δέ of the common text. In οἶδα the apostle speaks not
of the results, but of the sources of ἔμαθον. And that knowledge
was not one-sided, or an acquaintance with only one aspect
of life—καὶ ταπεινοῦσθαι. The first καί is "also," connecting
special instances with the previous general statement. Winer,
§ 53, 3. The verb here refers to condition, not to mental
state. Lev. xxv. 39 ; Prov. xiii. 7 ; 2 Cor. xi. 7. Its opposite
ὑψοῦσθαι is not employed, but another verb of a more general
nature. For the apostle did not mean to mark such a narrow
contrast as—" I know also to be elevated ; " but he writes
καὶ περισσεύειν. This second καί, not in itself but from the
sense, contrasts as it connects. ⁻The two verbs are not to
be taken in any confined signification, but with a general
sense as indicative of two opposite states; the one marking
depression and want, and the other sufficiency and more.
The repetition of οἶδα exhibits the earnest fulness of his
heart; and the rhetoric is even a proof of his uniform satisfaction and complacency, for he writes as equably of the one
condition as of the other. He does not curse his poverty,
nor sting with satirical epithets, but he verifies the remark
ἐν οἷς εἰμί. Nay, warming with his subject, he adds in higher
emphasis—

ἐν παντὶ καὶ ἐν πᾶσιν μεμύημαι—" in everything and in all
things I have been initiated." It seems a refinement on the
part of many to define the two adjectives separately. Thus
Luther takes the first as neuter, and the second as masculine ;
Conybeare renders, " in all things, and among all men ; " while
Chrysostom refers παντί to time, and Beza and Calvin to place,

following the reading of the Vulgate—*ubique*. To supply either χρόνῳ or τόπῳ is too precise. 2 Cor. ix. 8, xi. 6. The phrase, in its repetition, expresses the unlimited sphere of initiation. We cannot follow Meyer and Alford in connecting the phrase so closely with the two following infinitives. For if the infinitives stand as direct accusatives to μεμύημαι, then we should almost expect the definite article to precede them. Kühner, § 643. It is true that this verb usually governs two accusatives of person and thing, and in the passive has the latter, and that the thing into which one is initiated is put in the accusative, and not in the dative preceded by ἐν. But we do not regard the phrase as pointing out that in which he was instructed, but as an adverbial formula showing the universality of the initiation, and not its objects. Nay, opposites or extremes are chosen to show the warrant he had for the sweeping assertion—ἐν παντὶ καὶ ἐν πᾶσιν. Nor do we, with Meyer, regard it as analogous to ἐν οἷς εἰμί, but simply as qualifying μεμύημαι; while the infinitives are generally illustrative of the entire clause, as well of the objects of initiation as of the universality. The verb is borrowed from the nomenclature of the Grecian mysteries, and signifies the learning of something with preparatory toil and discipline. Hesychius defines μύησις by μάθησις. There is no idea of secret training—*disciplina arcana*, as Bengel puts it. The Greek Fathers explain it by πεῖραν ἔλαβον πάντων; but it is more than this, for it is not simply to have experience, but to have profited, or to have been instructed by that experience. 3 Maccabees ii. 30; Münthe, *Observat.* p. 383. I am instructed—

καὶ χορτάζεσθαι καὶ πεινᾶν, καὶ περισσεύειν καὶ ὑστερεῖσθαι —"both to be filled and to be famished, both to abound and to be in want." Χορτάζω, literally to feed with hay or grass, represents the Hebrew שָׂבַע in the Septuagint, and is a word of the later Greek in its application to persons. Sturz, *De Dialecto Maced.* pp. 200–202. It is used frequently in the Gospels. The peculiar form πεινᾶν for πεινῆν also belongs to the later writers. Phryn. Lobeck, p. 61; A. Buttmann, p. 38;[1] Winer, § 13, 3. Περισσεύειν has its proper antithesis

[1] *Grammatik der Neutest. Sprach. Im Anschlusse an Philip Buttmann's Griech. Grammatik,* von Alex. Buttmann. Erste Abth. Berlin, 1857.

in ὑστερεῖσθαι. The apostle's experience had led him to touch both extremes. It was not uniform penury under which he was content. The scene was checkered—shadow and sunshine—no unmanly depression in the one, no undue elation in the other. Equable, contented, patient, and hopeful was he in every condition. The verbs employed by the apostle are ἔμαθον—οἶδα—μεμνῆμαι, but they do not form a climax, as some suppose. The first is general, and looks to experiential result, or the lesson of contentment. How he came to that lesson he tells us in οἶδα, and how he acquired this knowledge he says in μεμνῆμαι. See Suicer, *sub voce*. There was first the initiation into the various states, then the consequent knowledge of their nature, and lastly, the great practical lesson of contentment which was learned under them. The apostle waxes yet bolder, and exclaims—

(Ver. 13.) Πάντα ἰσχύω ἐν τῷ ἐνδυναμοῦντί με—" I can do all things in Him strengthening me." The Χριστῷ in the Received Text has in its favour D³, E, F, G, J, K, and the Syriac also, while some of the Fathers read Χριστῷ Ἰησοῦ, and other forms occur, as in Origen and others. But the omission of the name has the higher authority of A, B, D¹, with the Vulgate and others. The reference is unmistakeable, and the omission of the name gives a peculiar point to the starting declaration. It is wrong to insert an infinitive between ἰσχύω and πάντα, for πάντα is the accusative of object, as in Gal. v. 6, Jas. v. 16, in which places τι and πολύ are similarly employed with πάντα. Wisd. xvi. 20.[1] Such an accusative expresses measure or extent—*das Mass und die Ausdehnung*. Madvig, § 27. It is to spiritual might that the verb refers, and that might has no limitations. For πάντα (not τὰ πάντα) is not bounded by the preceding references, as van Hengel gives it *in omnia memorata*. Knowledge is power; and the apostle rises from knowledge to power—tells what he knows, and then what he can achieve. It was no idle boast, for he refers at once to the source of this all-daring energy—

ἐν τῷ ἐνδυναμοῦντί με. 2 Cor. xii. 9. The preposition ἐν marks the union through which this moral energy is enjoyed

---

[1] Wahl proposes to insert such an infinitive as the Latin *ferre*, and thereby also narrows unduly the meaning of the verse.

—" in Him strengthening me," that is, in His strength communicated to me.   Acts ix. 22 ; Eph. vi. 10 ; 1 Tim. i. 12 ;
2 Tim. iv. 17 ; Heb. xi. 34.   We have the simple form of the
verb in Col. i. 11.   Had we retained the term " inforce," with
the same meaning as its common compound " re-inforce," we
should have had a good and equivalent translation of the
participle.   Richardson gives an instance from old English
—" clasping their legges together, they inforce themselves
with strength."   The rendering of the Vulgate employs a verb
from the same root—*qui me confortat*.   The apostle boasts
not only of a high courage in reference to such triumphs
as he had achieved, and others of a similar class or nature,
but he claims a moral omnipotence, and allows no limit to its
sweep and energy.   His allusion is probably, however, to a
certain sphere of operation, such as that presented in outline in
the previous verses.   Where unassisted humanity should sink
and be vanquished, he should prove his wondrous superiority.
Privation, suffering, and martyrdom could not subdue him,
and what might seem impracticable should be surmounted by
him in his borrowed might.   He could attempt all which duty
required, and he could succeed in all ; for to him the epithet
impossible, in an ethical aspect, had no existence.   The verse
is virtually climactic.   After saying that he had learned contentment under every condition, and telling that he had known
so many varieties and extremes of condition—it being implied
that he was uninfluenced by any of them—he adds, in earnest
and final summation—Not these alone, but all things I can do
in Him strengthening me.   It is also to be borne in mind
that this ability came not from his commission as an apostle,
but from his faith as a saint.   The endowment was not of
miracle, but of grace.

(Ver. 14.) Πλὴν καλῶς ἐποιήσατε, συγκοινωνήσαντές μου
τῇ θλίψει—" Howbeit ye did well in that ye had fellowship
with my affliction."   By checking himself and writing πλήν,
the apostle guards against a misinterpretation of what he had
just uttered.   See under i. 18, iii. 16.   Though he had learned
contentment in every situation, and his mind could accommo-
date itself to every change of circumstances ; though he had
fresh and inexhaustible sources of consolation within himself,
and had been so disciplined as to acquire the mastery over his

external condition and to achieve anything in Christ, yet he felt thankful for the sympathy of the Philippian church, and praised them for it. His humanity was not absorbed in his apostleship, and his heart, though self-sufficed, was deeply moved by such tokens of affection. Notwithstanding what I feel and have said, and though I am not dependent for happiness on such gifts—"ye did well." For this common use of καλῶς see Mark vii. 9; Acts x. 33. The phrase καλῶς ἐποιήσατε is connected with the participle, and the action in the participle, while it is of the same time as the verb ἐποιήσατε, points out that in which their well-doing was exhibited. They did well, when or in that they did this. Winer, § 45, 6, b. The same form of construction is found in Acts x. 33. Elsner, *in loc.*; Raphelius, *in loc.* The participle presents the ethical view in which the apostle regarded their pecuniary gift, and συγκοινωνεῖν means "to be a partaker with." Eph. v. 11. They had become, through their substantial sympathy, partakers of his affliction, and in so far they had lightened his burden, for θλῖψις depicts not simply his penury, but his entire state. See under i. 7, 17. Though he was contented, he yet felt that there was "affliction" —loss of liberty—jealous surveillance—inability to fulfil the great end of his apostolic vocation. This sympathy on the part of the Philippians with the suffering representative of Christ and His cause, is the very trait of character which the Judge selects for eulogy at last. Matt. xxv. 35, etc. The apostle proceeds to remind them that such intercourse was no novelty on their part. They had distinguished themselves above other churches for it and similar manifestations, and he has already given thanks to God ἐπὶ τῇ κοινωνίᾳ ὑμῶν. See i. 5. How the church at a later period did communicate in temporal and spiritual things with the affliction of sufferers, may be seen in Tertullian's address *ad Martyras.*[1]

(Ver. 15.) Οἴδατε δὲ καὶ ὑμεῖς, Φιλιππήσιοι, ὅτι ἐν ἀρχῇ τοῦ εὐαγγελίου, ὅτε ἐξῆλθον ἀπὸ Μακεδονίας, οὐδεμία μοι ἐκκλησία ἐκοινώνησεν εἰς λόγον δόσεως καὶ λήψεως, εἰ μὴ ὑμεῖς μόνοι—

---

[1] Thus he writes—*Inter carnis alimenta, benedicti martyres designati, quæ vobis et domina mater ecclesia de uberibus suis, et singuli fratres de opibus suis propriis in carcerem subministrant, capite aliquid et a nobis, quod faciat ad spiritum quoque educandum.* Vol. i. p. 3. *Opera,* ed. Oehler, 1853.

" But you, Philippians, are also yourselves aware, that at the introduction of the gospel, when I departed from Macedonia, no church communicated with me to account of gift and receipt, but you alone." Οἴδατε καὶ ὑμεῖς is—" you know as well as I," and by δέ the apostle goes back in contrast to previous gifts and services. The phrase cannot have the meaning which Peile inclines to give it—" of yourselves ye must remember." And in the fulness of his heart he names them. 2 Cor. vi. 11; Gal. iii. 1. The insertion of the name is a peculiar emphasis, but it is not " my Philippians," as a term of endearment. The phrase ἐν ἀρχῇ τοῦ εὐαγγελίου is —" in the beginning or introduction of the gospel "—the period when they received it, as the following clause intimates.

The phrase εἰς λόγον δόσεως καὶ λήψεως has been variously understood. The peculiar use of λόγος in verse 17 points to a similar sense here. There it denotes " to your account," or, to be included in such reckoning as belongs to you. Matt. xviii. 23; Luke xvi. 2. It therefore signifies here more than " in reference to," though Bengel, van Hengel, Lünemann, and Brückner so regard it. ⸀As to the words δόσις καὶ λήψις, the earliest opinion was, that in the first term the apostle alludes to the temporal remuneration which the Philippians *gave* him, and by the second to the spiritual instruction which they in return *received.*⸂ So Chrysostom, Œcumenius, and Theophylact, the first of whom calls this intercommunication εἰς λόγον δόσεως, τῶν σαρκικῶν, καὶ λήψεως, τῶν πνευματικῶν. The same exegesis is adopted by Pelagius and Calvin, Estius and a-Lapide, by Zanchius and Hammond, Wiesinger, Bisping, and Ellicott. It is true that the apostle in other places vindicates this reciprocal communication, affirms that the sowing of spiritual things warrants in equity the reaping of carnal things, and indicates the inferiority of a church that did not discharge this duty to its teachers—*spiritualia dantes, temporalia accipientes.* 1 Cor. ix. 1–15; 2 Cor. xi. 9, xii. 13. But there does not seem to be any such allusion in the verse before us. The apostle is not conducting an argument as to the duty of the church, nor could the simple terms employed bear such a complex meaning. He alludes simply to the fact of communication, and not to its principles or obligation.

Nor does he seem to hint at the spiritual good which he had effected among them.

The same objections apply to a second form of explanation, adopted by Meyer and Alford:—the Philippians kept an account of outlay to Paul and receipt by him; and so, on the other hand, the apostle kept an account of what was given to the Philippians and its receipt by them. But the idea of such reciprocity is not contained in the words ; for the entire context seems to refer simply to what the apostle received from the church. Meyer is obliged to confess, that according to his theory the accounts were curiously kept—that in the Philippian account-book the column of receivings would be empty, and so in that of Paul would be the column of givings —an idea which virtually destroys that of reciprocity. Meyer's explanation is well styled by Brückner, *nimis arti-ficiose.* Nor, thirdly, should we look at the words so literally as to suppose δόσις to refer to the Philippians who gave, and λῆψις to Paul who allowed himself to receive. Rheinwald reverses this order, and thinks while the Philippians gave the money, they also received from him similar gifts in return— gifts collected by the other churches. The Macedonian churches made liberal collections, but we do not read that any were ever made for them. Others, again, have this notion —No church gave me a sum so large as to be worth entering in an account-book, but you. Thus Hoog[1]—*tot tantaque erant, ut digna essent, quare in libro notarentur.* Probably we may regard the phrase as idiomatic, and as expressing generally pecuniary transactions. Thus Sirach xlii. 7—δόσις καὶ λῆψις πάντα ἐν γραφῇ ; or Cicero — *ratio acceptorum et datorum. Lael.* 16. See also Schoettgen, vol. i. p. 804. No church entered into pecuniary reckonings with me, but yourselves. The apostle means of course gifts for himself, and not as when some churches had entrusted him with funds on behalf of the poorer saints. He is anxious still to show that the gift sent to Rome was no novelty, but that such intercourse between him and the Philippian church is of an old date, though it had been suspended for a season. He refers back to the introduction of the gospel among them, and more specifically— ὅτε ἐξῆλθον ἀπὸ Μακεδονίας—" when I departed from

[1] *De Coetus Philip. conditione,* etc., p. 95 ; Lugduni Batavorum, 1825.

Macedonia." Many, like van Hengel, De Wette, and Wie-
singer, are disposed to take the aorist as a pluperfect,—" after
I had taken my departure from Macedonia." The reference
is then supposed to be to the monies received by him at
Corinth, alluded to in 2 Cor. xi. 9. The aorist may have in
some cases a pluperfect meaning. Winer, § 40, 5 ; Jelf, § 404.[1]
But we agree with Meyer that this supposition is needless.
Wiesinger presents the difficulty—" Wherefore does the apostle
mention in the next verse what is earlier in point of time ? "
We believe the apostle to refer to two points of time, close
indeed on one another—the introduction of the gospel, and his
departure from Macedonia. As he was leaving their province
and going away from them, they helped him. It may have been
the remissness of the Thessalonian church which impressed
the benefaction more deeply on his mind, or it may have been
the circumstance that he had got the gift as he was leaving
the province ; or it may be that the period of his departure is
fixed upon, since it was the commencement of a correspondence
with him as a labourer in foreign stations—the first of a
series of contributions sent him on his distant missionary
tours, and when he had no longer a personal claim for
immediate service rendered. So long as he was in their
province he might feel himself to be at home with them.
But to justify the expression the apostle recurs to an earlier
period, even before he had left Macedonia, and says—

(Ver. 16.) Ὅτι καὶ ἐν Θεσσαλονίκῃ καὶ ἅπαξ καὶ δὶς εἰς τὴν
χρείαν μοι ἐπέμψατε—" For even in Thessalonica both once
and a second time ye sent to me for my necessity." Hoelemann,
van Hengel, Rilliet, and others give ὅτι the sense of " that,"
and so connect it with οἴδατε ; but the verse in that case
would want a definite purpose, and the connection would be
awkward and entangled. On the other hand, we take this
verse, with Luther, Meyer, and others, as expressing an
argument. The apostle reverts to a period earlier than his
departure from the province, and says, that even in Thessalonica, and before he had gone from the province of Macedonia
in which Thessalonica was situated, they more than once
communicated with him. When labouring at Thessalonica,

---

[1] It is a strange feat of legerdemain that Pierce performs with this word—
ὅτι ἐξῆλθον is put for ὅτι ἂν ἐξῆλθον, and that for ἂν ἐξέλθοιμι.

the apostle speaks thus of himself—"labouring night and day, because we would not be chargeable unto any of you." 1 Thess. ii. 9. And he says in his second epistle—iii. 8, 9— " Neither did we eat any man's bread for nought, but wrought with labour and travail night and day, that we might not be chargeable to any of you ; not because we have not power, but to make ourselves an ensample unto you to follow us." The sums sent from Philippi did not fully supply the need of the apostle, for he was still obliged to work; but it argued goodwill on the part of the Philippian church, and the apostle refers with gratitude to their liberality. Even in Thessalonica, a neighbouring city, which ought to have supported him, but where for several reasons he did not have support or rather refused to have it, the Philippian brethren had shown a noble spirit and sent to him. Not only when he left the province, but at a prior period they had shown their generous appreciation of his services, and sent what the apostle without any false delicacy names—εἰς τὴν χρείαν μοι —" to my need "—a need they well understood, and sought to relieve. Εἰς marks destination. Winer, § 49, a. This they did ἅπαξ καὶ δίς. The phrase represents in the Septuagint different Hebrew formulas, such as פַּעַם וּשְׁתַּיִם, Neh. xiii. 20, or כְּפַעַם־בְּפַעַם, 1 Sam. iii. 10. The repetition of the conjunction καί—καί gives a conscious force. Mark ix. 22 ; Rom. xiv. 9 ; 1 Thess. ii. 18 ; 1 Macc. iii. 30 ; Hartung, p. 143. The use of both numerical terms is a rhetorical formula, in which the repetition is warmly dwelt on, and so acquires prominence. The similar phrase δὶς καὶ τρίς occurs also in the classics, as in Herodotus ii. 121. But the language does not warrant us to suppose with Michaelis that the Philippians sent to the apostle an " annual bounty." The καί before ἐν Θεσσαλονίκῃ signifies even, etiam. Hartung, i. 135. Chrysostom's explanation of the καί is, that it insinuates the importance of Thessalonica: even in such a great city—ἐν τῇ μητροπόλει—he was supported by the Christians of a smaller one. The verb ἐπέμψατε has no formal accusative—it being supplied by the sense of the clause. Acts xi. 29. The words ἐν Θεσσαλονίκῃ occur by a common idiom. It is somewhat tame to connect them with μοι—" to me being in Thessalonica ye sent." This is indeed the sense, but the apostle more

pregnantly expresses it. His shade of meaning is not merely
that they had sent the gift into Thessalonica, but that
the deputies had travelled into Thessalonica, and in it had
found the apostle, and had put into his hands the liberality of
the Philippian church. 'Ἐν is not used for εἰς. Winer, § 50,
4, a; Thucydides, iv. 14. The various readings of the verse
are εἰς omitted in A, D¹, E², as well as in the Syriac—an
omission probably caused through the similar final letters (ις)
of the preceding word; and μοι is the true reading in opposition to μου, which has only a few inferior authorities. Chrysostom's remark is finical,—the apostle does not say τὰς ἐμάς
—my wants, but speaks absolutely, ἁπλῶς. The apostle is
jealous lest this free-speaking should be misunderstood, lest
he should be supposed to rate the contribution only at its
money value, and perhaps, too, lest his thankfulness for past
benefactions should be construed into a quiet hint that future
and larger favours are expected by him. Such a misinterpretation he at once disclaims—

(Ver. 17.) Οὐχ ὅτι ἐπιζητῶ τὸ δόμα—" Not that I seek for
the gift "—that is, not precisely the gift he had got, but such
a gift as that on which he had been commenting, and for
which he had so earnestly thanked them. The compound
verb denotes desire towards—ἐπί marking direction. See
p. 17. It is useless, on the part of Rosenmüller and ´Am
Ende, to say that δόμα stands for δόσις. The gift in itself
excited no desire. The apostle uses the present tense, as
Meyer says, to denote the usual and characteristic tendency
of his mind, but perhaps also to show that, even at the present
moment, and when a prisoner in need, and debarred also from
the slight remuneration of a manual employment, he does not
set his heart upon the gift for itself. In receiving the gift,
and eulogizing them for it, there is something he intimates
as higher than it—something he desires of nobler interest.
Οὐχ ὅτι is the same as in verse 11. See also iii. 12. The
unselfish soul of the apostle looked not to its "own things;"
it could willingly " endure all things for the elect's sake;"
" not yours, but you," was its motto—

ἀλλ᾿ ἐπιζητῶ τὸν καρπὸν τὸν πλεονάζοντα εἰς λόγον ὑμῶν—
" but I seek for the fruit that does abound to your account."
The repetition of the verb adds a certain emphasis—my heart

x

is not set upon that, but my heart is set upon this. Similar repetition may be found, Eph. ii. 17, 19 ; Rom. viii. 15 ; Heb. xii. 18, 22. The substantive καρπός is not fruit generally, as many understand, or as Rilliet phrases it—"*fruits de vie religieuse.*" It is plainly, fruit as future recompense connected with the δόμα. It is not the gift he covets, but that rich spiritual blessing which the gift secures to its donor. The words εἰς λόγον ὑμῶν may be connected either with ἐπιζητῶ, or the participle πλεονάζοντα. In behalf of the former, it is urged by van Hengel that πλεονάζω is never in Paul's writing followed by εἰς. The statement is scarcely correct. We cannot indeed say, with Meyer, that 2 Thess. i. 3 is an exception to van Hengel's remark, for there we think εἰς ἀλλήλους is evidently connected with ἑνὸς ἑκάστου πάντων —the intensive phrase, "each one of you all," demands the filling up εἰς ἀλλήλους. Similar is 1 Thess. iii. 12. In other instances it is used intransitively, and without any complement, so that the non-occurrence of πλεονάζω with εἰς will not invalidate the proposed connection here—a connection which is at once natural and logical. The very phrase—τὸν καρπὸν τὸν πλεονάζοντα—seems to necessitate such a complement as εἰς λόγον ὑμῶν—an idiom which evidently bases itself on the previous εἰς λόγον δόσεως. This suggests that the first phrase has special reference to the apostle's giving and receiving, reckoned or put down by him to his own account ; but he wishes the fruit that abounds to their account. The καρπός is their fruit springing from the δόμα and put down to the donor's credit. The apostle wished them to reap the growing spiritual interest of their generous expenditure. Not for his own sake but theirs, does he desire the gift. He knew that the state of mind which devised and contributed such a gift, was blessed in itself ; that it must attract divine blessing, for t indicated the depth and amount of spiritual good which the apostle had done to them, and for which they thus expressed heir gratitude ; and it showed their sympathy with the cause of Christ, when they had sought to enable their spiritual Founder in former days to give his whole time, without distraction or physical exhaustion, to the work of his apostleship. This was a spiritual condition which could not but meet with the divine approbation, and secure the divine reward. Having, in the words following οὐχ ὅτι, not only guarded himself against misconstruction, but also given a positive revelation of his feelings, he proceeds again to the course of thought found in verses 14, 15, 16. He thanks them for their gift, assures them that he has not forgotten their previous kindness, in doing which they stood alone among the churches at the time, and which they commenced at an early period. And now, as the result of their last benefaction, he says—

(Ver. 18.) Ἀπέχω δὲ πάντα καὶ περισσεύω—"But I have all things, and I abound." The particle δέ is closely allied to the 17th verse—" not that I desire a gift—but I am so well gifted, that I can say I have all." It may also resume the sentiment of verse 14, and be illustrative of the words καλῶς ἐποιήσατε —" ye did well," for the result is, " I have all." If Meyer's view be adopted, that this verse has a connection only with the preceding one, it would suppose the apostle to give a second and subsidiary reason why he did not desire the gift. Now he has given the real reason in the second clause of the previous verse ; and this clause cannot be an additional reason, unless the meaning of the phrase—" not that I desire the gift "—be, not that I desire any further gift. But such is not its precise meaning, and therefore we understand him to say—ye did well in communicating : well ; but now I have all things, and abound—δέ suggested by the statement in the immediately previous verse. A strange view is entertained of the phrase ἀπέχω δὲ πάντα by Erasmus, Grotius, Beza, a-Lapide, and others, as if it were a form of receipt, acknowledging on his part the possession of the whole gift. The marginal reading of our version is—" I have received all." It is a dull remark of Bloomfield—" ἀπέχω is for ἔχω," corrected in his " Supplemental Volume " thus—" It is rightly rendered by accepi, or acceptum teneo." The groundlessness of this view is shown by the close connection of ἀπέχω with περισσεύω, for the apostle speaks not of the possession as a matter of acknowledgment, but as a matter of conscious enjoyment. The result of their gift was, that he had enough and to spare. The compound verb ἀπέχω is to have in full, or to have all one needs or expects. Winer, § 40, 4 ; Palairet, ad Matt. vi. 5 ; Observat. p. 25. Thus, in the impersonal form ἀπέχει— " it suffices," and Hesychius defines it by ἐξαρκεῖ. But the

apostle had not only enough, he had more than enough—
καὶ περισσεύω, "and I abound." The verb is used absolutely,
without any complement, as in verse 12. The gift more than
sufficed for all the apostle's wants. As he was rich in his own
contentment, he was easily satisfied with pecuniary benefactions, and he does not for a moment balance the amount
of the gift either against his own claims, or against their
ability or resources. He took it cheerfully, and blessed them
for it; for it was to him a relief, nay, a portion of it was a
present superfluity. He says—ἀπέχω, περισσεύω. He adds
in climax—

πεπλήρωμαι — "I have been filled." The verb is used
absolutely, and not the less intensely on that account. How
he had been filled, the apostle next declares—

δεξάμενος παρὰ Ἐπαφροδίτου τὰ παρ' ὑμῶν—"having
received from Epaphroditus the things sent from you." The
words παρὰ Ἐπαφροδίτου are omitted in A; D¹, E¹ read τό,
and insert πεμφθέν; while F and G have πεμφθέντα; the
Vulgate _quæ misistis;_ so the Syriac ܐܪ̈ܒܟ; and Wycliffe
"which ye senten." By the preposition παρά the apostle
characterizes the gift in a double but similar relationship,
"from Epaphroditus"—"from you." The participle, while
it exhibits the ground of the fulness, defines also its time.
But he at once rises above the human aspect of the transaction.
It was a donation made by the Philippians to him, but it had
another and loftier phase. It was, while presented to him,
an offering also to God; while it was hailed by him, it was
acceptable to God. He thanked them for the gift, but God
delighted in the oblation—

ὀσμὴν εὐωδίας—"an odour of a sweet smell." The genitive
is not used for the adjective εὐώδης. Winer, § 34, _b_,[1] note.
The phrase represents the רֵיחַ נִיחוֹחַ of the Levitical statute.
The accusative ὀσμήν is in apposition with the previous
τὰ παρ' ὑμῶν—the same contribution in its two aspects. By
this clause in apposition the apostle expresses an opinion of
the gift. Ellicott objects, that the "apposition is not to the
verbal action contained in the sentence." It may not, nor is
it necessary, for it is the gift as brought from them, to

---

[1] Moulton's Winer, p. 297, note 4.

himself in his need, which the apostle characterizes by
ὀσμὴν εὐωδίας. The apostle does not, and could not say, he
received it as a sacrifice, yet the things received were in his
judgment a sacrifice. It was a gift in which God delighted,
fragrant as the sweet-smelling incense which burned in the
censer. Eph. v. 2. More plainly—

θυσίαν δεκτὴν, εὐάρεστον τῷ Θεῷ—" a sacrifice acceptable,
well-pleasing to God." The dative τῷ Θεῷ belongs to the
two adjectives. In using θυσία the apostle employs a strong
term in a figurative sense. The word originally designated
a victim, an animal slain and offered to God. As to its
secondary sense, see Rom. xii. 1; Heb. xiii. 15, 16; 1 Pet.
ii. 5, and in this epistle, ii. 17. The two adjectives express
generally the same idea. Isa. lvi. 7. Their benefaction is
thus set out by the apostle in the aspect of a sacrifice. The
idea of a spiritual or figurative sacrifice is found in the Old
Testament, and was the result of a natural development of
ideas and associations. The Levitical statute prescribed
certain offerings on the altar, but the primary notion was
always presentation to God. The first-fruits and the victim
were given to God, in token that originally they are His.
The worshipper took them from his fields, and they were his
in a lower sense, but the presentation was an acknowledgment
that they were also his in a higher sense. Consecration to
God of what was theirs through His bounty was apart from
the idea of expiation, the central conception. And that conception naturally extended beyond the legal ceremonial, and
sprang up with peculiar freshness under the New Testament.
It was felt that God is supreme benefactor, and that all pos-
sessions are His gracious gift; that these have an end beyond
the mere personal enjoyment of them; that they may and
ought to be employed in God's service; and that the spirit of
such employment is the entire dedication of them to Him.
Thus the apostle has spoken of the sacrifice of their faith,
ii. 17, and elsewhere of the "sacrifice of praise." Heb. xiii.
15. Beneficence is also a sacrifice. Heb. xiii. 16. The
Gentile believers are an "offering." Rom. xv. 16. Their
"bodies" are a "living sacrifice." Rom. xii. 1. The "holy
priesthood" present "spiritual sacrifices." 1 Pet. ii. 5. There
were, as Hammond remarks, two altars in the Jewish temple,

the altar of incense and the altar of burnt-offering, and " on
these two were offered all things that were offered to God."
A figure uniting both is found here.　In the case before us,
the apostle, by the use of this sacrificial language, teaches
that the Philippians had been discharging a religious duty.
The money, while contributed to him, was offered to God.
It was not simply a token of friendship, an act of common
generosity, or opportune aid to a friendless prisoner ; but the
remittance was an offering to Him " whose is the silver and
whose is the gold," in token of their thankfulness to Him
by whom the apostle's steps had been directed to Philippi,
and by whose blessing his labours and sufferings had been
productive of so many and so permanent benefits.　They
discharged a spiritual function in doing a secular act—" the
altar sanctifieth the gift."　And the acceptance of the sacrifice
would bring down rich compensative blessing, for the apostle
thus promises—

(Ver. 19.) Ὁ δὲ Θεός μου πληρώσει πᾶσαν χρείαν ὑμῶν—
" But my God shall supply all your need."　The reading
πληρώσαι in the aorist optative is not sufficiently supported,
and is evidently an exegetical emendation.　By the particle
δέ the apostle passes not to a different theme, but to a different feature or aspect of it.　The idea of Hoelemann presses
too far — quemadmodum vos.　In the phrase " my God,"
emphatic from its position, the apostle does not merely express
his own relationship to God, as in i. 3, but he means his
readers to infer this idea—this God who accepts your sacrifice
is " my God ; " and " my God," so honoured and so pleased
with your gift to me, will supply all your need.　I who receive
your contribution can only thank you, but my God who
accepts the sacrifice will nobly reward you.　You have supplied
one element of my need—εἰς τὴν χρείαν μοι, but my God will
supply every need of yours—πᾶσαν χρείαν ὑμῶν.　I have been
filled, he says in verse 18—πεπλήρωμαι, and God, my God,
will in turn fill all your need—πληρώσει.　Chrysostom notices,
in his comment, a different reading, χάριν or χαράν, but does
not adopt it.　The apostle uses the simple future, as if he
pledged himself for God ; for he felt most assured, that God
as his God would act as he promised in His name.

It is surely a limited view, on the part of Chrysostom and

many modern commentators, to confine the meaning of the
noun to bodily necessities—" He blesses them that they may
abound to have wherewith to sow. . . . For it is not unseemly
to pray for sufficiency and plenty for those who thus use them."
It would be rash and wrong to exclude this idea, for God has
many ways of temporally rewarding liberality displayed in His
cause, though certainly no one can expect the blessing who
gives with such a selfish calculation and motive, and tries to
traffic with God in the hope of receiving a high interest or
return.   It is as restricted, on the other hand, to refer the
promise solely to spiritual need.   Thus Rilliet bases his argument on the occurrence of the term πλοῦτος, as if it uniformly
referred to spiritual blessings.   But in the citations made by
him πλοῦτος has its meaning modified by a following genitive, or as in Rom. x. 12, where the participle is used, the
context limits and explains the signification.   The usage
therefore forms no argument why χρεία here should apply
exclusively to spiritual necessity, especially when it is uni-
versalized by πᾶσαν.   It is true that χρεία is used of bodily
need in the context, and this is generally its sense in the
classics ; and no wonder, for the heathen could scarcely know
of any other.   But the apostle, as if to show that he meant
more than physical necessity, adds, " according to His riches
in glory "—language, one would think, too noble to be dwarfed
into a description of the source of mere pecuniary compensa-
tion.   While we agree with Meyer in giving this broad sense
to πᾶσαν χρείαν, we cannot accede to his view that such
supply is to be received only in the future kingdom of
Messiah ; for we hold that even now the promise is realized.
The loving-kindness of God surrounds and blesses His people
who are so interested in His cause, implanting every absent
grace, giving health and power to every grace already implanted.   The very appreciation, on the part of the Philippian
church, of the apostle's position, labours, and relations, implied
the existence of a genuine piety among them, which God
would foster by his Spirit, while He blessed them at the same
time " in their basket and store."   Wiesinger well asks—
" If the apostle says of himself πεπλήρωμαι, why should he
in πληρώσει refer his readers to the day of the second coming
for the supply of their every want ?   He does not do this in

2 Cor. ix. 8 ; and the Lord Himself does not refer His people
to a period beyond the present life for the supply of their
every want." Matt. vi. 33. Mark x. 29, 30.

κατὰ τὸ πλοῦτος αὐτοῦ ἐν δόξῃ ἐν Χριστῷ Ἰησοῦ—"according to His riches in glory in Christ Jesus." The neuter
form τὸ πλοῦτος is preferred to the masculine on the authority
of A, B, D¹, F, G, etc. The mode or measure of supply is
indicated by κατὰ τὸ πλοῦτος. According to their "deep"
poverty they might supply his need, but God according to His
riches would supply all their need. The connection of the
next words ἐν δόξῃ is attended with some difficulty. Grotius,
Rheinwald, Heinrichs, Flatt, Storr, and Baumgarten-Crusius
join them to the preceding πλοῦτος, as if they indicated in
what this glory consisted, or as if it were "according to His
riches of glory," or κατὰ τὸ πλοῦτος τῆς δόξης. It is objected
to this that such a construction with ἐν is never employed by
the apostle, but always the genitive of the object. Rom. ii. 4,
ix. 23 ; Eph. i. 7, 18, ii. 7, iii. 16 ; Col. i. 27, ii. 2. If
separated then from τὸ πλοῦτος, the phrase may denote either
that by which the action of the verb is realized, or the manner
in which that action is performed. Meyer takes the former
view, which is quite consistent with his theory, which refers
the supply to the glory to be awarded at the second coming.
The verb in Eph. v. 18 is followed by ἐν, with special reference to the Spirit, and sometimes the simple dative is employed. But believing that χρεία comprehends temporal need,
we cannot see how glory could be used as an adequate term
for its supply. Nor indeed could the term be used in any
sense for supply of want—grace being the word more usually
employed. Glory is not on earth the means of supply—it
results from this supply, but is not its material. Therefore
we take ἐν δόξῃ not as the complement—"with glory," as
Ellicott takes it, but as a modal qualification—"in a glorious
way." Such is the view of van Hengel, Hoelemann, and
Rilliet. He will supply every want in glory—like Himself
—not grudgingly or with a pittance, but with divine generosity. And He would do this as He does all things—

ἐν Χριστῷ Ἰησοῦ—"in Christ Jesus." This designates
the sphere of God's action. In Christ Jesus will He supply
their wants, or from the fulness in Him, His merit and

mediation being the ground of it. What a glorious promise
for the apostle to make on God's behalf to them!—a perfect
supply for every want of body or soul, for time or eternity,
for earth or heaven. If man is but a mass of wants, wants
for this world and wants for the world to come, and if God
alone can supply them, what confidence should not such a
pledge produce ? Is it physical fare ?—He heareth "the
young ravens" when they cry. Is it the forgiveness of sin ?
—He "delighteth in mercy." Is it purification of soul ?—
His Spirit produces His own image. Is it courage ?—He is
"Jehovah-Nissi." Is it enlightenment ?—His words are,
"I will instruct thee." Is it the hope of glory ?—Then it is,
"Christ in you." Is it preparation for heaven ?—He makes
"us meet to be partakers of the inheritance of the saints in
light." Is it contentment in any circumstance ?—All things
may be done in the strength of Christ. Nor was it rash in
Paul to make such a promise, nor did he exceed his commission.
He did not speak without a warrant. He knew the character
of his God, and did not take his name in vain, for his varied
and prolonged experience had fully informed him, and he was
assured that the state of heart in the Philippian church must
attract towards it the blessing. Would God resile from His
servant's pledge, or act as if in thus vouching for Him he
had taken too much upon him ? The idea of his close and
tender relationship to God as his God, and his assurance that
the promise made in His name would be realized ; the thought
of such a promise, so ample in its sweep, and so glorious in
its fulfilment, with the idea that all whether pledged or
enjoyed is of God the Giver, suggest the brief doxology of
the following verse—

(Ver. 20.) Τῷ δὲ Θεῷ καὶ Πατρὶ ἡμῶν ἡ δόξα εἰς τοὺς
αἰῶνας τῶν αἰώνων. Ἀμήν—" Now to God and our Father be
glory for ever and ever. Amen." The apostle does not mean
by this glorification to conclude ; it bursts from the fulness of
his heart, as in Rom. xi. 36 ; Gal. i. 5 ; Eph. iii. 21 ; 1 Tim.
i. 17 ; 2 Tim. iv. 18. Ὁ Θεὸς καὶ ὁ Πατήρ forms one
distinctive and complete title, followed sometimes by a
genitive, as here and in Gal. i. 4. For the meaning of the
last intensive phrase, and generally of the whole verse, see
under Eph. iii. 21. The optative εἴη may be supplied to

δόξα, which has the article specifying it as the glory which especially and characteristically is God's. Rom. xi. 36, xvi. 27; Gal. i. 5; Eph. iii. 21; 2 Tim. iv. 18; Heb. xiii. 21; 2 Pet. iii. 18. The last phrase—"to the ages of the ages"—is an imitation of the Hebrew superlative לְעוֹלָם עוֹלָמִים (Gal. i. 5; 1 Tim. i. 17; 2 Tim. iv. 18), and means a very long and indefinite period—the image taken from the cycles or calendars of time, to represent an immeasurable eternity. God is glorified in the aspect or character of Father, and "our Father," implying that those whose wants are supplied by Him, are His children. Rom. viii. 15. To God, even our Father, the kind and liberal supplier of every want to every child, be eternal glory ascribed. The ascription of praise is the language of spiritual instinct, which cannot be repressed. Let the child realize its relation to the Father who feeds it, clothes it, and keeps it in life, who enlightens and guides it, pardons and purifies it, strengthens and upholds it, and all this in Christ Jesus, and it cannot but in its glowing consciousness cry out—"Now to God and our Father be the glory for ever."[1] The Amen is a fitting conclusion. As the lips shut themselves, the heart surveys again the facts and the grounds of praise, and adds—So be it.

The apostle had praised them for their κοινωνία εἰς τὸ εὐαγγέλιον already, and he bids them give another practical manifestation of it—

(Ver. 21.) Ἀσπάσασθε πάντα ἅγιον ἐν Χριστῷ Ἰησοῦ— "Salute every saint in Christ Jesus." The singular individualizes—singulatim, as Bengel gives it. The words ἐν Χριστῷ Ἰησοῦ may be connected either with ἅγιον, as in i. 1, or with the verb. We prefer the opinion of those who take the latter view, inasmuch as ἅγιος can stand by itself, whereas ἀσπάσασθε would seem to require some qualifying term, in order to define its character. The addition of ἐν Χριστῷ Ἰησοῦ in the address of the epistles, has a specific purpose not needed on the ordinary recurrence of the epithet. Thus ἐν Κυρίῳ in Rom. xvi. 22, and 1 Cor. xvi. 19. Salutation in the Lord is in His name to one of His members.

---

[1] We are tempted to place in contrast the doxology with which Velasquez concludes his Commentary on this Epistle—Omnipotenti Deo, purissimæ Deiparæ, sanctissimis Paulo et Ignatio, honor et gloria. Vol. ii. 552.

And every saint was to be so greeted; the spirit of universal affection was to prevail. The apostle sends one cluster of salutations—

ἀσπάζονται ὑμᾶς οἱ σὺν ἐμοὶ ἀδελφοί—" the brethren with me greet you." And then he adds another—

(Ver. 22.) 'Ασπάζονται ὑμᾶς πάντες οἱ ἅγιοι—" All the saints salute you." Of course the brethren are saints, but all the saints are not brethren in the very same sense. The apostle refers to two circles of Christians about him; those bound by some nearer and more special tie to him, and named "brethren;" and those beyond them having no such familiar relationship with him, "the saints." Who composed this inner circle we know not. He may refer to the brethren spoken of in i. 14, or principally to those mentioned by him in the epistles written at this period to the church in Colosse, and to Philemon. Chrysostom alludes to a difficulty. The apostle has said, in ii. 20, 21, that none with him were like-minded with Timothy, and that all sought their own, and his solution is, that "he did not refuse to call even them brethren." Nor might all these brethren be qualified for such a mission as Timothy's. See p. 149. A special class are subjoined—

μάλιστα δὲ οἱ ἐκ Καίσαρος οἰκίας—" but chiefly they of Cæsar's household." A special prominence is attached to their salutation. The very source of it must have excited wonder and gratitude. Calvin remarks—*ac eo quidem admirabilius, quo rarius est exemplum, sanctitatem in aulis regnare.* They of Cæsar's household must have taken a deep interest in the apostle, and might have been converted by him during his imprisonment. They must also, so far as permitted to them, have ministered to his comfort, and they could not but feel a special sympathy for a church which had sent Epaphroditus to do a similar service. Who they were, has been keenly disputed.

The term οἰκία is not the same with πραιτώριον, but refers to the imperial residence. Matthies indeed says—*so ist dieses am natürlichsten hier zu verstehen, und an solche aus der Kaiserlichen Leibwache zu denken.* But the statement is unsupported. It has been supposed to mean:—

1. The emperor's family or relatives. So van Hengel and many others, including Baur, for a sinister purpose of his

own. The words may bear such a signification—1 Cor. xvi. 15, οἴδατε τὴν οἰκίαν Στεφανᾶ; Luke i. 27, ii. 4, ἐξ οἴκου Δαυίδ. 2. The word is used in an inferior sense to signify domestics generally. So in Josephus, *Antiq.* xvii. 5. 8—τοῦ Καίσαρος τὴν οἰκίαν. Also Philo—τὸν ἐπίτροπον τῆς οἰκίας, and in a yet more honourable sense—εἰ δὲ μὴ βασιλεὺς ἀλλὰ τις τῶν ἐκ τῆς Καίσαρος οἰκίας—" if he had not been king, but only one of Cæsar's household, ought he not to have had some precedence and honour ?" *In Flaccum,* vol. ii. p. 522. Or Tacitus, *Hist.* ii. 92—*quidam in domum Cæsaris transgressi, atque ipsis dominis potentiores.* Nero, as has been often remarked, had but few relations,[1] and the probability is, that domestics, either slaves or freedmen, are here intended. The persons referred to are not named, as Epaphroditus could give the Philippians the requisite information. It is almost needless to allude to any hypothesis on this subject; yet out of this reference arose the fiction of Paul's correspondence with Seneca, Nero's preceptor. Lucan the poet, Seneca's nephew, has also been included.[2] Estius refers to two names, Evellius and Torpetes, as being *Neronis familiares,* and as occupying a place in the Roman martyrology of this period. But this is all uncertainty. Witsius gives Pomponia Græcina, a name occurring in Tacitus. *Meletem. Leid.* p. 212. Some have fixed on Poppæa Sabina, Nero's wife. These domestics were, in all probability, brought into contact with the apostle during his confinement in the prætorium. For the opinions of those who think that this epistle was written at Cæsarea the reader may turn to the Introduction.

(Ver. 23.) Ἡ χάρις τοῦ Κυρίου Ἰησοῦ Χριστοῦ μετὰ τοῦ πνεύματος ὑμῶν—" The grace of the Lord Jesus Christ be with your spirit." The reading ἡμῶν after Κυρίου has very little support. The received reading is μετὰ πάντων ὑμῶν, which Meyer retains. The new reading is supported by A, D, E, F, G, 17, 67², 73-80, by the Vulgate, etc., and is adopted by Lachmann and Tischendorf, etc. The common reading

---

[1] Suetonius—*Galba,* i.—*Progenies Cæsarum in Nerone defecit;* or Eutropius —vii. 9—*in Nerone omnis familia Augusti consumpta est.*

[2] Jerome—*de Viris Illustr.* Winer—*Bibl. Realwört.*—Art. "Paul and Gallio."

is found in B, J, K, the Syriac, and in Chrysostom and
Theodoret. It is difficult to say which reading is preferable,
as the new one may have been formed from Gal. vi. 18 ;
Philem. 25 ; or 2 Tim. iv. 22. The sense in either case is
not materially different. He wished them to enjoy that grace
which Christ bestows. If the critical reading be adopted,
then the apostle wished the favour of Christ to descend upon
their higher nature, or that portion of their nature for which
it was specially fitted, and which indeed could alone enjoy it.
Tischendorf rejects the ᾿Aμήν, and Lachmann puts it within
brackets. The apostle concludes with a benediction or salutation—probably an autograph. Col. iv. 18 ; 2 Thess. iii. 17.
In parting from his readers, he wishes them to possess the
grace of the Lord Jesus; that grace which blesses and cheers,
which strengthens and consoles, and at last ripens into glory.
The unauthorized postscript is variously read, both in the
MSS., Versions, and Fathers ; the received Text being—πρὸς
Φιλιππησίους ἐγράφη ἀπὸ ʻΡώμης δι᾿ ᾿Επαφροδίτου.

INDEX.

—o—

INDEX OF GREEK TERMS MORE PARTICULARLY REFERRED TO.

———o———

124177